MW01077938

The Cheng School Gao Style Baguazhang Manual

Cheng School Gao Style Baguazhang
Lineage Masters

Dong Haichuan

Cheng Tinghua

Gao Yisheng

Liu Fengcai

海福壽山永，強毅定國基

昌明光大陸，道德建無極

As eternal as the blessed ocean and ancient mountains;
Strong and resolute in establishing the foundation of the nation;
Flourishing and bright, shining across this great continent;
The way and its virtue building without limit

The Cheng School Gao Style Baguazhang Manual

Gao Yisheng's *Bagua Twisting-Body Connected Palm*

Written by Gao Yisheng

Chinese Editions Editor-in-Chief: Liu Fengcai

BLUE SNAKE BOOKS
BERKELEY, CALIFORNIA

Copyright © 2013 by Vincent Black. All rights reserved. No portion of this book, except for brief review, may be reproduced, stored in a retrieval system, or transmitted in any form or by any means—electronic, mechanical, photocopying, recording, or otherwise—without written permission of the publisher. For information contact Blue Snake Books ᶜ/o North Atlantic Books.

Published by Blue Snake Books, an imprint of North Atlantic Books
P.O. Box 12327
Berkeley, California 94712

Cover photos courtesy of Liu Shuhang
Cover and book design by Brad Greene
Printed in the United States of America

The Cheng School Gao Style Baguazhang Manual: Gao Yisheng's Bagua Twisting-Body Connected Palm is sponsored by the Society for the Study of Native Arts and Sciences, a nonprofit educational corporation whose goals are to develop an educational and cross-cultural perspective linking various scientific, social, and artistic fields; to nurture a holistic view of arts, sciences, humanities, and healing; and to publish and distribute literature on the relationship of mind, body, and nature.

North Atlantic Books' publications are available through most bookstores. For further information, call 800-733-3000 or visit our websites at www.northatlanticbooks.com and www.bluesnakebooks.com.

PLEASE NOTE: The creators and publishers of this book disclaim any liabilities for loss in connection with following any of the practices, exercises, and advice contained herein. To reduce the chance of injury or any other harm, the reader should consult a professional before undertaking this or any other martial arts, movement, meditative arts, health, or exercise program. The instructions and advice printed in this book are not in any way intended as a substitute for medical, mental, or emotional counseling with a licensed physician or healthcare provider.

Library of Congress Cataloging-in-Publication Data

Yisheng, Gao.
  The Cheng school Gao style baguazhang manual : Gao Yisheng's bagua twisting-body connected palm / written by Gao Yisheng.
      pages cm
  Includes bibliographical references and index.
  Summary: "In its first English-language edition, this highly detailed training manual offers a complete history and theory of Gao-style bagua zhang as well as step-by-step instruction in basic techniques and empty-hand forms"—Provided by publisher.
  ISBN 978-1-58394-607-7 (alk. paper)
1. Hand-to-hand fighting, Oriental. I. Title.
  GV1112.Y62 2013
  796.815—dc23
                                                    2013006286

1 2 3 4 5 6 7 8 9 SHERIDAN 18 17 16 15 14 13
Printed on recycled paper

Chinese Editions Senior Editors
Wang Shusheng, Liu Shuhang

Third Chinese Edition Editors
Liu Shuhang, Gao Jinhua

Third Chinese Edition Associate Editors
Liu Yungang, Liu Lingjie

Contributing Editors

Liu Jitang	Liu Gang	Zhang Yang
Gao Guilin	Liu Anxiang	Liu Jianxin
Gao Jinhua	Ge Shuxian	Liu Lingjie
Liu Shuhang	Liu Guozhu	Wang Xu
Pi Shuqiang	Zhao Li	Gao Haihua
Li Zhongfang	Li Yongfu	Chen Tao
Li Cang	Jiang Xiafang	Wang Bin
Shi Jitao	Du Zhigang	Yao Xiangkui
Xiao Jun	Li Shaolu	Ma Jian
Liu Changzai	Huang Guoqing	Ou Weilin
Gao Guoyou	Zhang Shoukun	Su Mingchao
Chen Demin	Liu Yungang	Qiu Peng

English Edition Editor
Vincent Black

Translated from the third Chinese edition
by John Groschwitz

～

Dedicated to all Baguazhang enthusiasts worldwide
～ 2012 ～

***Cheng School Gao Style Baguazhang
Association, Tianjin, China***

***North American Tang Shou Tao
Association, Tucson, Arizona***

TABLE OF CONTENTS

PREFACE TO THE ENGLISH EDITION

I am humbled and honored to be asked to write a preface to this first English edition of the Cheng School Gao Style Baguazhang Manual, a comprehensive treatment of Master Gao Yisheng's legacy and discussion of the system's components and methods. It is an excellent treatise on one Bagua family's history and evolution going back over three generations to Grand Master Cheng Tinghua. I want to thank Liu Shuhang and the entire Gao Bagua family for their kind considerations and thoughtful inclusion in this undertaking.

I first met Liu Shuhang in the early 1990s while on a six-month sabbatical in China. I was researching Chinese Medicine, interning in the hospitals, and seeking out reliable sources of Baguazhang and Xingyiquan for the North American Tang Shou Tao Association. I had spent time in Shanghai, Xi'an, Taiyuan, Beijing, and finally Tianjin. It was near the end of the trip when I met Mr. Liu and his associates to discuss their Baguazhang. The whole Gao Baguazhang family stood out to me when comparing them with other Baguazhang families that I had interacted with in the previous months in China. While it is only natural for everyone to have at least a portion of their aspirations invested in their own personal interest, this family was the most free from the distrustful cynicism and suspicion that was so palpable with all the other groups I had encountered. It was reassuring to find people to work with who naturally exercised willingness to negotiate and to give the other side an opportunity to show that they also can have integrity and can be trusted.

My previous seventeen years of training and teaching was with and for my Xingyiquan family from Taiwan. That Taiwan lineage springs from Zhang Junfeng, my teacher's grand-teacher, who was a student of Master Gao Yisheng and a classmate of Mr. Liu's grand-uncle Liu Fengcai, a major contributor to this book. I could not help feeling that this coincidence was auspicious.

Subsequently, throughout the following twenty years, the North American Tang Shou Tao Association and the Tianjin Cheng School Gao Style Baguazhang family have been working together prodigiously to transplant this art to America through group excursions of American students going to train in China, group excursions of Gao family disciples coming to America to teach even larger groups directly, and several mutual excursions where the Chinese teachers and American students met in Thailand for some intensive weeks of training. So much shared passion over time establishes true deep feelings and friendships.

In conversation and in writing, Mr. Liu often refers to "martial destiny," and it is clear that he has meditated on this subject considerably. This book is a hub around which all of our collective destinies have revolved; without it, all of us would have perhaps lacked the unifying force with which we have persevered in promoting this art. We now hope that our efforts to provide a comprehensive record of Master Gao's achievements to the English-speaking world will provide a tool with which all lovers of Gao Style Baguazhang can network and share this art together more globally.

Master Dong Haichuan taught his disciples according to their individual martial skills (martial truth), and many of them were already accomplished martial artists with good reputations and some renown; hence there is a wide diversity of styles and expressions within Baguazhang overall. This aspect of Baguazhang's history also allows for unavoidable divergence in accounts of the origin and various related historical events. The editors for this edition, Liu Shuhang, Gao Jinhua, and Liu Yungang, wisely included the latest and most complete and concise accounts of these matters. In clarifying the history of Baguazhang, the Chinese editors included an essay by Kang Gewu, a most distinguished scholar and historian of Chinese martial arts, and Baguazhang in particular. Mr. Kang's contribution is unquestionable.

John Groschwitz is to be commended for his extensive efforts to truly "own" the art by training in it for over fifteen years, then teaching it, and eventually—along with thirteen fellow students—formalizing his relationship with the Gao family through a Bai Shi Ceremony. As a formal family disciple, Mr. Groschwitz has an intimacy with the art and the family and resultingly has produced for the English-speaking world at large an excellent translation of a very important text on the art of Baguazhang. As the reader will see, his personal relationship with Mr. Liu enabled him to catch the subtle nuances of syntax and complex and often profound thought processes within the expressions of Mr. Liu's explanatory comments woven throughout the book.

In closing, I want to reiterate my gratitude and offer congratulations to the entire Gao Style Baguazhang family for this milestone achievement for both the Gao Yisheng legacy and the world at large, who will be the beneficiary of this effort. I also want to thank all the North American Tang Shou Tao Association members whose efforts in support of all the events and excursions over the years have helped bring this book to fruition.

Anyone in the United States desiring to embrace this family's Baguazhang can contact the North American Tang Shou Tao Association to facilitate connecting with family members and working with the material in a most efficient way. The association also has branches in Canada and Europe.

Vincent Black
October 2012

1940. Gao Yisheng's seventy-sixth birthday celebration with twenty-eight students, including Gao Fengming (middle row, fifth from right), Liu Fengcai (middle row, third from left), Gao Wencai (middle row, right), Xu Mingqiao (front row, fourth from left), Qu Kezhang (front row, right), and Li Zijin (back row, second from left). Other students are not identified.

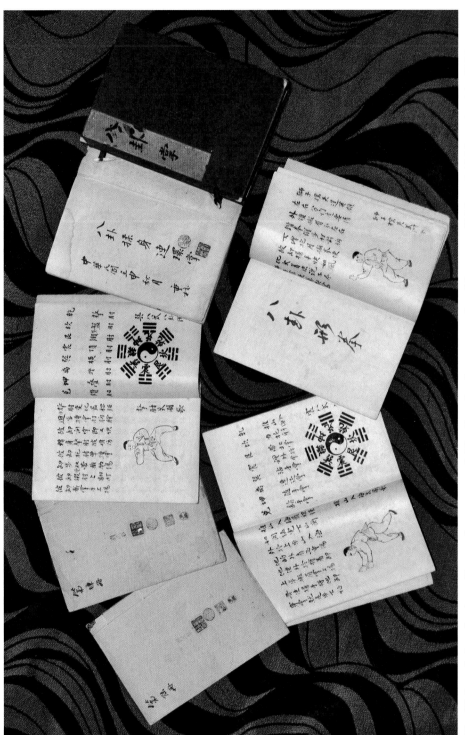

Gao Yisheng's handwritten Baguazhang manual. The first draft was completed between 1909 and 1926; revised in 1932; following Gao's examination and approval transcribed into six volumes in 1936; passed on to Liu Fengcai in approximately 1946; passed on to Liu Shuhang in 1983.

Right: *Commemorative photo of Liu Fengcai's return to his ancestral home in 1983, accompanied by Liu Shuhang (back left) and welcomed by Liu Huicheng (back right).*

Below: *Liu Fengcai (front right) during a return trip to Tianjin in 1985, with Wang Shusheng (front left), Liu Shuhang (back center), Zhu Xiliang (back right), and Ge Guoliang (back left).*

Opposite top: *Liu Shuhang (right) and Li Xueyi (second from left) meeting with He Kecai and his wife (center), along with Wu Weiming (left) in 1992.*

Opposite bottom: *Pan Yue (second from left) and Liu Zhen (second from right) from Taiwan visiting Wang Shusheng (center), Liu Shuhang (left), and Ge Guoliang (right) in Tianjin in 1992.*

Vincent Black visiting Tianjin in 1993. Kneeling (left to right): Li Xueyi, Tian Qingping, Zhao Junde, Liu Shuhang. Standing (left to right): William Tucker, Ge Shuzhen, Ge Guoliang, Ge Shuxian, Wang Shusheng, Dan Miller, Pan Yue, Vincent Black.

NATSTA training, Tianjin, 1994. Left to right: Li Xueyi, Kim Black, Wang Shusheng, Vincent Black, Liu Shuhang, Ge Guoliang.

NATSTA training, Tianjin, 1994. Seated (left to right): Li Xueyi, Liu Shuhang, Wang Shusheng, Ge Guoliang. Standing behind Liu Shuhang: Kim Black, Vincent Black.

Pan Yue (third from left), being accepted as a disciple of Wang Shusheng (seated), with fellow students, 1994.

Grand gravestone-raising ceremony for Liu Fengcai held during the Qingming Festival in Wudi County, Dashan Township, north of Liu Family Yellow Dragon Bay Village, April 5, 1995, attended by national, provincial, county, and township-level officials as well as international and domestic funders, direct descendants, and village neighbors.

Left to right: Liu Zhen, Liu Shuhang, Wang Shusheng, Kang Gewu, Pan Yue, April 5, 1995.

Left to right: Ge Guoliang, Pan Yue, Liu Shuhang, Liu Jinwang, Li Xueyi, Yuan Pengfu, 1996.

Greeting the Japanese Hanshin Bagua Research and Study Group on their tenth visit to China, 2001. Left to right: Tsujimoto Saburomaru, Ms. Teramura, Ge Guoliang, Ikeda Ruriko, Liu Shuhang, Ms. Motokubo, Li Xueyi, Tsujita Noboru, Okuda Ryoichi.

NATSTA training, Tianjin, 2001. Seated (left to right): Li Xueyi, Ge Guoliang, Liu Shuhang. Standing, first row: John Tesi, Harmony Wagner, Neil Clark, Jennifer Minor, Miranda Warburton, Brandy Peterson, Richard Rabb, Jan Vanderlinden, Mike Davidson, Marc Melton. Standing, back row: Ashton Wolfswinkel, Nelson Tai, Jason Redinbo, Gregory Steerman, Ethan Murchie, Travis Joern, Al Joern.

Teaching Baguazhang in Japan, 2002. Seated (left to right): Tsujita Noboru, Li Xueyi, Ge Guoliang, Tsujimoto Saburomaru, Liu Shuhang.

NATSTA Gao Bagua seminar, Tucson, 2003. Seated (left to right): Vincent Black, Liu Shuhang, Ge Guoliang, Li Xueyi, Kim Black.

Presenting a photocopied set of Gao Yisheng's Baguazhang manual to the North American Tang Shou Tao as a gift, 2003. Left to right: Ge Guoliang, Liu Shuhang, Li Xueyi, Vincent Black.

NATSTA Gao Bagua seminar, Tucson, 2005. Seated (left to right): Kim Black, Li Xueyi, Vincent Black, Liu Shuhang, Ge Guoliang, Peter Davis.

NATSTA Gao Bagua seminar, Tucson, 2007. Seated (left to right): Kim Black, John Tesi, Ge Guoliang, Ge Shuxian, Vincent Black, Liu Shuhang, Li Xueyi, Ethan Murchie.

NATSTA First International Teachers Congress on Traditional Gongfu and Medicine, Phit-sanulok, Thailand, 2008. First row (left to right): Sean Orlando, John Tesi, Gao Xiuying, Gao Jiwu, Boon Chartpanic, Li Gaixian, Li Runxi, Vincent Black, Kim Black, Liu Baozhu, Liu Shuhang, Niu Zhongming, Niu Ping, Ethan Murchie, William Fantozzi Jr.

NATSTA Annual Conference, Tucson, 2009. Seated (left to right): Kim Black, Grandmaster Harry Hererra (Kajukenbo KSDI), Niu Zhongming, Vincent Black, Liu Shuhang, Grand-master Dechi Emperado (Kajukenbo KSDI), Ethan Murchie.

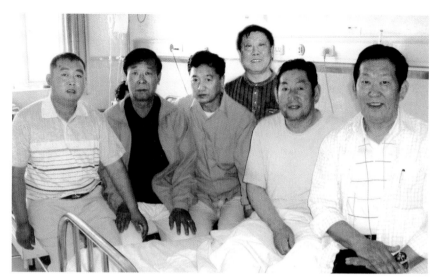

Fellow practitioners from Tianjin, Ji'nan, Binzhou, Yanxin, and elsewhere gather during the Qingming Festival on the fifteenth anniversary of the raising of Liu Fengcai's gravestone to sweep his grave, April 5, 2010. Attending were Gao Jinhua, Li Cang, Pi Shuqiang, Shi Jitao, Liu Gang, Zhang Liqing, Chen Demin, Wang Yun, Mu Qiuwang, Liu Huicheng, Liu Hongjun, Zhao Li, Liu Lingjie, and Wang Xu, among others.

Left to right: Gao Yisheng's great-grandson Gao Haihua, famed Wujiquan practitioner Meng Jinsheng, famed Taijiquan practitioner Niu Zhongming, Gao Jinhua, Gao Yisheng's grandson Gao Guilin, Liu Shuhang, 2010.

Commemorative photo of fellow practitioners in Guangrao County, August 2010. Front row (left to right): Du Zhigang, Bai Nianan, Pi Shuqiang, Li Cang, Liu Shuhang, Gao Jinhua, Li Yongfu, Jiang Xiafang, Shi Jitao, Li Shaolu. Back row (left to right): Zhang Wenjun, Wang Xu, Wang Yun, Ming Qiliang, Liu Zhongqing, Sun Jianmin, Liu Xinyuan, Liu Lingjie.

Honored guests and Liu Shuhang with his new disciples, 2010. Front row (left to right): Ou Weilin, Chen Tao, Li Yan, Liu Xintian, Meng Xiangguo, Guo Jinming, Gao Ming. Second row: Yue Peng, Yao Xiangkui, Lan Guangwei, Ma Jian, Wang Bin, Liu Chunyuan, Wang Gang, Zhang Hualong, Su Mingchao, Wang Qiang. Third row: Yang Xiangquan, Wang Hongsheng, Meng Jinsheng, Niu Zhongming, Gao Jinhua, Liu Jitang, Wang Fuling, Zhang Maoqing, Gao Tiejing, Chen Lianfa. Fourth row: Ge Shuzhen, Wang Yun, Liu Anxiang, Li Cang, De Zhao, Liu Shuhang, De Chao, Pi Shuqiang, Liu Gang, Zhang Liqing, Ge Guoliang. Back row: Wang Xu, Zhang Yang, Liu Lingjie, Liu Jianxin, Liu Yungang, Liu Guozhu, Zhang Shoukun, Ge Shuxian, Li Xueyi, Li Zuxun, Zhou Shiping, Zhao Li, Cui Zhimao.

NATSTA Gao Bagua seminar, Tucson, 2011. Seated (left to right): Neil Clark, Ethan Murchie, Liu Lingjie, Liu Shuhang, Vincent Black, Kim Black, Professor Patrice Lim (Kajukenbo), Grandmaster George Lim (Kajukenbo).

NATSTA Gao Bagua seminar, Tucson, 2012. Seated (left to right): Neil Clark, Ethan Murchie, Liu Shuhang, Gao Jinhua, Vincent Black, Master John Price (first president of the U.S. Shen Lung Tang Shou Tao Association), Liu Lingjie.

Discipleship Ceremony, Tucson, May 5, 2012. Seated (left to right): Kim Black, Liu Shuhang, Vincent Black, Gao Jinhua. Disciples, standing (left to right): Miranda Warburton, David Nicoletti, Neil Clark, Gregory Steerman, Sean Orlando, Naoko Koike, Benjamin Scharfenberger, Ethan Murchie, Sylas Navar, Jennifer Minor, Jarrod Lash, John Groschwitz, Eli Schwartz-Gralla, Liu Lingjie, Harmony Wagner (not pictured).

Gold and silver commemorative coins bearing the logos of the North American Tang Shou Tao and Tianjin Cheng School Gao Style Baguazhang Associations, presented to Masters and disciples at the 2012 Discipleship Ceremony.

Circular Destiny

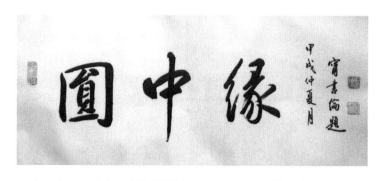

Circular is the movement of walking and turning the circle in Baguazhang; destiny is the movements of heaven and earth that determine the matters and meetings of people. Between heaven and earth, nothing is more precious than humankind. Of all life's treasures, nothing is more precious than health. Gold has a price; health is priceless. Health is even more valuable than gold. Health is the foundation of vitality and an everlasting subject of research for humanity. The body is the vessel of life, and only when healthy can it bear the weight of the ten thousand things. Health has the real number value of one; wealth and possessions that lie outside of the body are all zero. A person has only one life; to lose health is to lose everything. Aside from one's congenital condition, the health of the body and mind are not decreed by heaven but are based on personal effort. Therefore, today, all those in China and elsewhere who are expert in the ways of movement and stillness have healthy bodies and long lives. Baguazhang is a martial art that strengthens the being and builds the body. Increasing martial ability is based on strengthening the being and building the body. This manual is a specialized writing on the martial study of Baguazhang. Understand its principles, practice its exercises, obtain its skills, and become proficient in its methods, and you will receive benefits unto the end of your days. Toward this goal, I offer this manual to all friends who value health-building and whose destiny is tied to Baguazhang. If one seeks circularity in life, one finds that destiny is all around. For those who become connected to Baguazhang, that is the circular nature of destiny.

Martial Destiny

Destiny is determined by heaven; position is fixed through one's conduct. Everywhere in life there is both auspicious and inauspicious destiny. In the absence of destiny, there is no gathering. Following destiny, one is at ease. Martial destiny is the destiny attached to the martial study of Baguazhang. This is an auspicious destiny.

Calligraphy by Liu Shuhang.

PREFACE TO VOLUME 1 OF THE 2010
THIRD CHINESE EDITION

The martial arts are not simply a set of skills but are a type of scholarly inquiry and a type of culture. They are a type of scholarly inquiry that takes humans and human survival as its subjects and that contains profound aspects of Chinese traditional culture. China has already listed martial arts as an item of intangible cultural heritage. Modern experts consider the martial arts to be traditional physical education with Chinese culture as the theoretical foundation; fighting methods as the core content; and forms, combat, and skill training as the primary movement forms. The authors feel that increasing fighting ability while strengthening the being and building the body is the essential nature of martial arts, while the essence of Chinese culture—such as the Eight Trigrams and the changing of yin and yang from *Yijing* theory, the treatise on the substantial and the insubstantial from Sun Tzu's *The Art of War*, the Confucian concepts of centered and harmonious, the Daoist theory of what is natural, and the Buddhist theory of enlightenment—is the soul of the martial arts. Because of this, some humanists place martial arts as one of the four great cultural inventions of China.

As the world watched with interest, martial arts served as an important symbol of Chinese traditional culture during the imposing and majestic opening ceremonies of the 2008 Beijing Olympics. Emerging before the people of the globe, and now imprinted on the hearts of the citizens of every continent, this had far-reaching historical significance in promoting Chinese martial arts more broadly to the entire world. The complete success of the Beijing Olympics not only aroused great feelings of national pride in Chinese youth but also was another step in arousing interest and admiration for Chinese traditional culture in people around the world. As inheritors who carry on the lineage of Chinese martial arts, we feel a deep responsibility to further promote Chinese traditional martial arts culture to enthusiasts both at home and abroad. To this end, we spent nearly two years again revising this manual. To increase its collectability, in this edition we reproduced for all readers Gao Yisheng's original *Bagua Twisting-Body Connected Palm* manual, which exists in one handwritten copy produced in winter 1936.

The first edition of this manual was published in 1991, introducing the theory and life-cultivation aspects of the Gao Style Baguazhang system along with the Pre-Heaven and Post-Heaven forms. This was an important marker in establishing the academic position of Cheng School Gao Style Baguazhang, serving as a bridge to connect fellow practitioners and enthusiasts at home and abroad, enlarging Cheng School Gao Style Baguazhang's impact both in China and elsewhere, and prompting fellow practitioners and enthusiasts from Tianjin, Shandong, Hebei, Hong Kong, Taiwan, Japan, and the United States to mutually establish close and friendly relationships. In 2005, after undergoing revisions and proofreading and adding sections on weapons, animals, and writings by junior practitioners, the second edition of this manual was published in Taiwan, providing a more or less complete picture of the Cheng School Gao Style Baguazhang system, and making the cultural and practical value of the manual even greater. Unfortunately, owing to the rushed nature of proofreading at the time, the text of the second edition was careless and had many mistakes. This edition has undergone corrections, additions, and deletions in over two hundred places, and many new photos have also been added, including a very rare group photo of Gao Yisheng and twenty-eight of his students and disciples in Tianjin in 1940, as well as lineage charts for the Gao and Liu families, revised disciple lineage charts, and a biography of Wang Shusheng. This edition has also replaced all postural diagrams from the manual with photographs, with the results being more lively and realistic. Among these, we have used Liu Fengcai's photographs of the Pre-Heaven Palms where possible, and supplemented the remaining with photos of Liu Shuhang.

Reproducing Gao Yisheng's written manual in this edition was intended not only to increase the collectability of this manual; our aim was also to commemorate the hundredth anniversary of Gao Yisheng's creation and transmission of the Cheng School Gao Style Baguazhang system; to remember the historical achievements of Gao Yisheng and Liu Fengcai and other elder-generation Baguazhang sages in creating, developing, inheriting, and passing on Baguazhang; and to share with fellow practitioners and enthusiasts the research and new creations of the previous generations.

Both Kang Gewu, a noted martial artist, doctoral adviser, and Chinese Wushu Association Secretary, and Yang Xiangquan, a postdoctoral fellow well-known within the Chinese martial arts world and also a professor and graduate adviser at the Tianjin University of Sport, attached extreme importance to the revision and reissue of this manual, and with a high degree of attention provided meticulous guidance, help, and support. One of the giants of the contemporary calligraphy world, Venerable Master De Zhao, provided the cover calligraphy. Gao Yisheng's grandson Gao Guilin and Liu Fengcai's direct disciple Liu Jitang, along with many other Cheng School Gao Style Baguazhang lineage holders, directly participated in the revision of this edition. Upon hearing that the authors were undertaking revision of this manual, Li Zhongfang, living several hundred miles distant from Tianjin in Hubei Province, immediately sent an email offering his opinions on revisions in three main sections with thirty-three subsections. Aside from this, this edition also received the help and support of the Tianjin Metro Harmony, Chengda, and Fudaojia property management companies. To all, as a group, we offer here our heartfelt thanks.

The editorial committee for the revision and reissue of this manual lists thirty-two contributing editors. Aside from father and son Gao Guilin and Gao Haihua, almost all of the other editors were Liu Fengcai's direct disciples and grand-students. Every one has directly participated in revising and proofreading this edition, or provided important materials, photos, and information for the revisions. Through the joint effort of this group and through meticulous editing, we have striven to create a collector's edition. However, it is difficult to make something completely perfect, and very likely there are still many textual shortcomings. We sincerely hope that our readers and experts will provide critiques and corrections to aid the next generation in their further revisions and reissues.

Liu Shuhang and Gao Jinhua, third edition editors
Liu Yungang and Liu Lingjie, third edition associate editors
January 2010

Advancing with the Times; Seeking the Roots to Understand the Truth: Several Points of Insight and Explanation in Reproducing Gao Yisheng's Manuscript

The handwritten *Bagua Twisting-Body Connected Palm* manual photo-reproduced here [in the third Chinese edition] is the only extant copy of Master Gao Yisheng's (hereinafter "Master Gao") old Gao-style manual (hereinafter "the old manual"), the final version of which was approved, copied, and bound in winter 1936. It is a summary of the creation, research, and transmission of Baguazhang theory and techniques by Master Gao and other elder-generation sages. It is the crystallization of his lifelong dedication to promoting Baguazhang martial culture, and his utmost effort, life blood, and intensive labor leaves for later practitioners an extremely valuable representative work of the cultural legacy of traditional Baguazhang.

Even though there are many places in the old manual where the textual content, illustrations, or structure still are perhaps not completely elegant, every word and every sentence of each chapter's brilliant analysis, each section's detailed rendering, and each rhyme-song paragraph's refinement embody the blood, sweat, and wisdom of Master Gao and

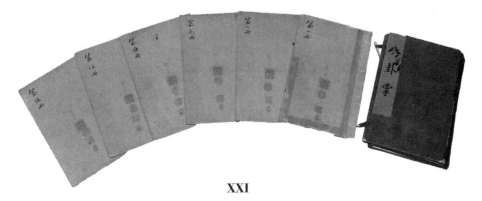

other elder-generation Baguazhang sages. In overall content and form, it can be called an exquisite work of the highest caliber. This old manual was viewed by the former sages as a treasure, and since its copying and binding into manual form, it has never been displayed to others casually, belonging to the category of not-transmitted secret books. In their lifetimes, both Master Gao and Master Liu said, "if not a personally taught inner-chamber disciple, then it's difficult to get a glimpse." Today, we have decided to make public a photo reproduction of Master Gao's old manual alongside the third revision and reissuing of the new *Cheng School Gao Style Baguazhang Manual* (hereinafter "the new manual"), edited by Master Liu Fengcai (hereinafter "Master Liu"), to present to all those readers, colleagues, practitioners, and enthusiasts who love Baguazhang the fruits of creation from Master Gao's lifetime of research, and to share with all the original essence and original flavor of the theory and skills of the Gao Style Baguazhang system. Our aim is to dispel all types of mystical legends and, together with fellow practitioners and enthusiasts, using a scientific concept of development, to continue to advance with the times. Standing at the heights of this new era, we should meticulously read, meticulously contemplate, and meticulously research and compare the old and new manuals and their related material, source drafts, and writings to seek truth from facts. In seeking the root to understand the truth and absorbing the most outstanding, we hope to jointly strive to promote all the Baguazhang that Master Gao taught, so that it may be inherited and passed on for a hundred generations of scientific development. At the time of the reproduction and publishing of this old manual, I record the following three insights and two explanations:

Three Insights

1. Cheng School Gao Style Baguazhang is an important branch of Baguazhang established by Master Gao Yisheng that has become its own training method.

Cheng School Gao Style Baguazhang uses traditional Baguazhang training methods as its foundation, but it also has quite a few original aspects.

It does not lose the common characteristics of Baguazhang movement, yet it also has its own unique movement flavor, creating an art and a system distinct and different from other branches of Baguazhang, becoming its own training method. As clearly and exhaustively described by the noted Chinese martial artist, doctoral adviser, and secretary of the Chinese Martial Arts Association, Kang Gewu, in his 1991 essay "The Formation of Gao Yisheng's Baguazhang Corpus" (see the Preface to the 1991 first Chinese edition), which we completely approve, Cheng School Gao Style Baguazhang was created by Master Gao.

Baguazhang is an important type of Chinese traditional boxing, formed between approximately 1866 and 1894. Its most fundamental special characteristic is walking a circle as its basic movement pattern, and in the course of turning the circle, walking and spinning, changing fighting postures. Master Gao's branch art Baguazhang system was created between 1909 and 1936, with its most evident special characteristic being the use of *Yijing* philosophy as its guide, with the Pre-Heaven and Post-Heaven trained separately. Its Pre-Heaven Palms are inherited from Master Cheng Tinghua, using the traditional Eight Big Turning Palms as the main body, in accordance with the Eight Trigrams. Its Post-Heaven Sixty-Four Palms are all individually practiced movements, in accordance with the sixty-four post-heaven hexagrams. Moreover, each of these can be broken down into six hands, totaling 384 hands, to accord with the 384 lines of the hexagrams.

Regarding the branch art system of Baguazhang created by Master Gao, the old manual was named *Bagua Twisting-Body Connected Palm.* In 1981, after the discussion of Liu Fengcai and his disciples and students, and with the endorsement of experts, in order to differentiate from, yet also exhibit the relationship of inheritance from, Cheng Tinghua to Gao Yisheng, the name of all of the Baguazhang passed on by Master Gao was finally fixed as Cheng School Gao Style Baguazhang.

The new manual, published almost twenty years ago, has established the scholarly standing of Cheng School Gao Style Baguazhang and created a bridge for communication with fellow practitioners and enthusiasts both at home and abroad. The students, disciples, and enthusiasts taught by Master Gao and Master Liu who were spread throughout the motherland have one after another been connected by the thread of the new manual. From Taiwan, Hong Kong, the United States, and Japan, all those Baguazhang practitioners and enthusiasts whose art has origins in Gao Yisheng's teachings have all established connections with Tianjin inheritors, and their interactions and exchanges have been continuous. Today, those who recognize, practice, and admire Cheng School Gao Style Baguazhang are more and more numerous; its transmission at home and abroad is more and more extensive; its name is more and more esteemed; and its influence is greater and greater.

Although now the appreciation of many practitioners and enthusiasts for Cheng School Gao Style Baguazhang has increased, even today differing viewpoints regarding the origin and lineage of the Baguazhang taught by Master Gao still exist. These differing viewpoints all arise from a few legends, and mostly belong to friendly and good-natured investigation, and from one side reflect the attention and importance practitioners and enthusiasts at home and abroad place on the Baguazhang taught by Master Gao. Because the lineages of those who studied were different, the times they lived in were different, their environment was different, their experiences were different, and their values were different, and on top of this the materials they had at hand were different, having these different viewpoints is normal and can be understood. These different viewpoints provide us a larger space for advancing further in investigation and research of Cheng School Gao Style Baguazhang.

In actuality, suffering the limitations of society's historical development, taking any school of boxing and linking it to some famous historical person or monk, or borrowing mystical teaching to increase the social value of an art is seen repeatedly and is not new in the history of the development of Chinese martial arts. Baguazhang is not an exception to this, and its lineage and origins have also been draped in mystical colors for a long time.

For example, Dong Haichuan passed away in the eighth year of the

Guangxu period [1882], and in the ninth year [1883], Yin Fu, Cheng Tinghua, and others raised a tombstone for him, inscribing on it that Master Dong "traveled the four directions" and "when traveling the south, later encountered a yellow cap,[1]" and "was instructed by him, gradually refining boxing bravery." Then in the thirtieth year of Guangxu [1904], when Yin Fu and others again raised a stone in his memory, the inscription records that "Master's miraculous strength was learned from nature, but his art was acquired from an immortal." In the nineteenth year of the republic [1930], Ma Gui, Men Baozhen, and others again raised a stone with an inscription which notes that Master Dong "traveled to Jiuhua Mountain in Jiangnan, and there came to meet an immortal who taught him his art." The same year, fourth-generation inheritor Lu Shukui and others also raised a stone with an inscription that notes that Master Dong's art "was really obtained from an immortal." Only finally in 1981, through repeated investigation by experts did we finally reach a conclusion: Baguazhang was created by Dong Haichuan. In 1982 Master Dong's grave was moved from Beijing's Dongzhimen, he was reburied at Wan'an Cemetery, and Li Ziming and other later practitioners erected a tombstone for him, recording that Master Dong "created Turning Palm," which later gradually evolved into Bagua Turning Palm, or Baguazhang.

Similar to others, Master Gao suffered the influence of every type of legend—such as that Master Dong learning from an immortal—and in the old manual also recorded two stories full of mystical color.

First is in the grave inscription "Record of the Beginning and End of Master Dong's Tutelage," which records that Master Dong was educated from an early age, and as an adult then studied martial arts. Later, traveling for the purpose of visiting friends, he learned his art in a dream at "an old temple on a mountain peak in Jiangnan" called "Snowflake Mountain Buddhist Temple," thus placing Master Dong under the Damo School. The text starts by saying "One day Master Dong arrived in Jiangxi and saw by the side of road in a pine forest two monks sparring, one old and one young," then relates the course of Master Dong's study with Damo. Later it records that the old monk "copied a book and bestowed it to Dong, the monk saying 'I am Damo.' Immediately Master Dong became aware that he was unconscious, as if in a deep sleep; although his ears could hear, his eyes could not see. A short while later, his eyes began to open, and looking around he found himself in the same pine forest, without knowing where the mountain was, or in which direction the temple lay." Finally, it says: "a few days later he returned to look for this master, and the temple had vanished without a trace."

Second is in the foreword to the old manual, where Master Gao again relates a fantastic story. In 1909:

> Through the arrangement of a friend I returned to my hometown of Haifeng, Shandong (really Dashan Township, Wudi County, Shandong Province) to run an herb business. While at leisure researching martial arts with a village friend, someone who looked like a beggar approached and came to call upon me, but when pressed for his name refused to give it, instead breaking into song, saying: "Don't ask of my origin; we are both one family; studying arts is without end; I am Song Yiren, who has studied the complete learning, and now transmits the arts to all worthy gentlemen under Heaven; transmitting without holding anything back; only this can be called pioneering," and thus we called him Song the Exceptional.[2] Later he and I gradually became amiable, and our interaction became quite close. One day by chance I toured Big Mountain and saw this exceptional one living in a cave at the peak... and politely requested instruction, and after several years was suddenly aware and enlightened.

"Exceptional" means not a common person, and can be understood as a Song Dynasty (960–1279) worthy, or a Song Dynasty immortal.

The editor feels that in that era, roughly one hundred years ago, for Master Gao to increase the importance of his art or make it easier to promote the art that he created by borrowing this mystical teaching or attaching it to the tutelage of Song the Exceptional can wholly be understood. However, being a modern person of the twenty-first century, if we only rely on these several tomb inscriptions and a few legends, and do not confirm through research and do not apply analysis, only parroting what we hear and firmly believing it to be completely true, then this certainly is a little of cherishing the outmoded and preserving the outworn, and this ignorance is regrettable.

Although the Snowflake Mountain Buddhist Temple where Master Dong studied his art "vanished without a trace" and cannot be found anywhere, luckily Dashan Township in Wudi County, Shandong Province, does have a mountain. It is outside the editor's hometown of Dahsan Township, and in the last few years its name has been changed to Tablet Stone Mountain. From Tianjin, traveling through the Qikou port and Huanghua port along the Yanhai highway, after about one hundred miles one can see this mountain. The editor once made a special trip home to climb this mountain and conduct research; at the time it had not yet been renamed.

Big Mountain is not big; it is only a small hill, with a height not over about two hundred feet and an area of only ninety-six acres. However, because the surrounding area is a level plain, this protruding solitary hill, although it's not big, is called Big Mountain. It is also called "the first mountain south of the capital." This mountain is the cinder cone formed by a volcanic eruption 730,000 years ago, and the whole mountain is composed of igneous rock—rock as black as dark coke, also called pyroclastic bombs. In the past even grass had difficulty growing here, as it is barren wasteland. The editor climbed this mountain, and not only is there no cave at the ridge, which is really a peak, no caves could be found on the slopes either. Accordingly, the editor feels that the possibility of Song Yiren living "in a cave at the peak" at that time is impossible. Master Gao studying his art on this mountain is then even more impossible.

In the last century, at the beginning of the 1980s, in order to clean up the new manual, the editor visited the elderly in the various villages near our ancestral home, including Dashan Township, to inquire about Song Yiren. These few villages are almost all places where Master Gao taught his art in the early days, and almost every village had an elder who knew this as soon as Master Gao's Baguazhang was mentioned, with a few villages even having people who still practice this art. But when asked about Song Yiren, not one person had heard of anyone who had ever seen him, and in fact not one elder had even heard of this name. Because of this, the editor once asked for guidance from Liu Fengcai. I recall when the editor first saw Master Gao's old manual at the home of Liu Fengcai, in 1981. Before this, I had heard many times the tale of Song Yiren, and after reading the old manual, asked Master Liu, in his view, if there was or wasn't really a Song Yiren.

MASTER LIU. Master Gao said there was, and wrote it in his manual. Can we not believe him?

EDITOR. You started studying Baguazhang in our hometown at age nine with fourth uncle [Liu Lianzhi, one of Master Gao's early disciples]. At that time, did you hear of Song Yiren?

MASTER LIU. I never heard of him. At that time I started learning turning the circle, and a few individual applications. There was already the concept of Pre-Heaven and Post-Heaven Palms, but there was no Form Boxing and no study of weapons.

EDITOR. When you started studying Baguazhang, did you often see Master Gao?

MASTER LIU. Before I studied, for the first few years I often saw Master Gao when he came to our house. I called him "old grand-uncle." Later, when your fourth uncle stared to teach us, I did not see Master Gao, and I heard he'd already returned to Wuqing.

EDITOR. Afterward, in what year did Master Gao again return to his hometown to transmit his art?

MASTER LIU. That year I was nineteen [actually eighteen], and it was my cart that brought him back to the village. That year I formally started studying with Master Gao, and moreover started studying again from the beginning—Pre-Heaven Palms, Post-Heaven Sixty-Four Palms, eight sets of Form Boxing, broadsword, spear, straight sword, heart-height staff. Lastly, I studied double rattan sticks. Altogether it was nine years [1926–1935]. Master Gao came to our house after every fall, and in wheat-harvesting season, he returned to Wuqing. Sometimes in the middle he would return to return to Wuqing to celebrate New Year's.

EDITOR. In these nine years, did you ever hear of Song Yiren?

MASTER LIU. I did not hear of him. At that time I just practiced the art. Whatever Master Gao taught, I studied; other things I seldom asked about. And I never heard Master Gao bring up Song Yiren.

EDITOR. Then when did you finally hear of Song Yiren?

MASTER LIU. That was after I went to Tianjin [1936], but the exact date, I can't remember. But definitely Master Gao first told his other disciples, and later it got spread around, and still later it was written into the manual.

At the same time, Master Liu also told the editor that because Master Gao told his Tianjin disciples that his Pre-Heaven Palm art was obtained through Cheng Tinghua and his school-brother Zhou Yuxiang, while the Post-Heaven Palms were learned under the tutelage of Song Yiren of Shandong, and also because Master Gao taught his art in Shandong before this, many in the Tianjin martial arts world and his disciples in the early years called what Master Gao taught "Shandong Bagua."

Master Gao created his system of Baguazhang techniques through the long and slow process of repeated testing, repeated contemplation, and repeated revision and alteration over the course of several decades. His systematization of these skills was extremely meticulous, especially his core material of Pre-Heaven Palms and Post-Heaven Sixty-Four Palms. From a theoretical standpoint, practical techniques standpoint, and technical requirements standpoint, the system underwent Master Gao's blending and unifying until one cannot see the traces of his original material, and it does not have any parts that are uncoordinated. However, amid meticulousness there are always errors. The reason that Master Gao added a preface to complete the old manuscript was because Du Shaotang, acting without permission, took his draft—which was still in the process of creation—and published it as a reproduction in the spring of 1936. In a fit of anger, Master Gao quickly reedited his compilation in only several months' time, finally approving and copying it into a final edition, adding his own preface. This was a bit rushed, and thus it was difficult to avoid mistakes in his haste. In the old manual, therefore, the five elements and twelve images included in the fifth volume, as well as the eight sets of Form Boxing, all somewhat lack careful scrutiny. For example, Master Gao listed the eight sets of Form Boxing in the manual as being the third subsystem within his Baguazhang, calling it "internal Bagua." Yet almost all start with moving-step Drilling Fist or advancing-step Splitting Fist, and this still allows later practitioners to see easily and quickly the original traces of Xingyiquan within the third subsystem of Baguazhang techniques created by Master Gao.

From everything related above, we can reach the following summary: Firstly, the system of Cheng School Gao Style Baguazhang was created by Gao Yisheng, and it is a system of Baguazhang techniques with unique characteristics and unified training methods that differ from other traditional Baguazhang schools. Secondly, the system of Baguazhang created by Master Gao was formed between 1909 and 1936, more or less passing through the following stages:

- 1909–1916: the initial formation stage. Using the idea that "the Pre-Heaven Palms are the basis for the Post-Heaven Palms; the Post-Heaven Palms are the application of the Pre-Heaven Palms" as a guide, Master Gao completed the concept of his art and first raised the idea of the separation of the Pre-Heaven and Post-Heaven Palms in training. According to the principle of simultaneously "teaching, creating, and perfecting," he began to create a new system of Baguazhang.
- 1916–1926: the original form stage. By 1926 the Baguazhang system created by Master Gao already had the original forms of the Pre-Heaven Palms, Post-Heaven Sixty-Four Palms, and eight sets of Form Boxing, and had begun to be transmitted in Wuqing and Wudi, Shandong Province.
- 1926–1932: the preliminary completion stage. By 1932, when Mas-

ter Gao's son Gao Fengming proofread the draft manual, there was already a structure exhibiting both fundamental technique and theory.

- 1936: Master Gao's approval of the manual manuscript, addition of a preface, and recopying it into a final edition marks the point that his contributions to the creation of a new Baguazhang system were in all aspects complete.

Thirdly, Song Yiren was a fictional person. In creating this fictional character, Master Gao's aim was mainly to add weight to the social value of the Baguazhang system that he created and transmitted, utilizing people's curiosity and sense of mystery, which were prevalent in society at that time, guiding the interest and enthusiasm of numerous practitioners. Master Gao transmitted his art for many years in Shandong and never told people of Song Yiren, and it was only after he arrived in Tianjin that he spoke to his disciples about "Shandong Song Yiren." One can imagine how much thought he gave to this matter.

The editor feels that attaching Song Yiren's teaching to the "way of the Post-Heaven" was done by Master Gao and several of his disciples who helped in editing the original draft material, through clever conception and elaborate design, using the sound of Song Yiren to secretly point to "those who gave the art."[3] If today we again reclaim Song Yiren to be "those who gave the art," its truth reveals exactly Master Gao's intention at the time the original draft was compiled, and his sentiment for and feeling of appreciation toward all the masters of former generations.

2. Regarding the origin of the handwritten old manual by Master Gao.

According to Liu Fengcai, the Baguazhang manual created by Master Gao was edited through at least three editions: the first edition, completed in roughly 1926; the revised edition, or 1932 edition, edited by Gao Fengming; and lastly the 1936 finalized old manual edition. How much material the original drafts contained while in the process of organization cannot be clearly stated.

Around 2002 a friend sent the editor two books published in Taiwan. The first was the beautifully decorated *Universal Fantastic Arts,* with no author listed. The other was *Swimming-Body Linking Baguazhang,* signed as written by Du Shaotang (hereinafter "the Du manual"). From very early on I had heard Master Liu talk of the matter of Du Shaotang printing Master Gao's manual without obtaining permission, but I had never read this book in detail.

Recently, in casually reviewing the outline of the Du manual and comparing it to Master Gao's old manual, I carried out a simple comparison, and then realized that the Du manual simply cannot reflect completely, correctly, and systematically the full aspect of the Gao Style Baguazhang system. I also reviewed *Universal Fantastic Arts* and, in comparing them to Master Gao's old manual, felt that these two books, while having similarities with the old manual, are quite lacking in content. The palm names are different and arranged in a different practice sequence; differences in the songs of the sixty-four dismantling palms are quite marked; and many other technique names are also different. Especially lacking is the Du manual, which even mistakes Master Gao's lineage. It is no wonder Master Gao was angry. Master Gao was Cheng Tinghua's disciple, but the Du manual places him under Yin Fu's school. Generally, anyone with a little Baguazhang knowledge would know that Cheng School Baguazhang uses Dragon Claw Palm, and Yin School Baguazhang uses Ox-Tongue Palm; not only are the two palm shapes different, but the forms are different and the special lineage system characteristics are different—within Cheng School Bagua everyone starts by first learning Turning Palms, while in orthodox Yin School Bagua one must first practice Luohan Boxing. The differences between the two are very large and absolutely cannot be confused. To address the Du manual's confusion of one thing for another, Master Gao explained specifically in his preface that he "placed himself in Master Cheng's school" in order to ensure a correct understanding of the facts.

The editor remembers perfectly clearly that Master Liu talked many times about the origin of Master Gao's old manual. The earliest reason for compiling and recopying the old manual in winter 1936 was because of Du Shaotang's unauthorized publishing of his not-yet-finalized draft. Master Liu said that in about 1935, Master Gao started publicly taking disciples and transmitting his art in Tianjin at the English Soccer Stadium (now the Heping District Xinhua Road Sports Stadium). At the time, Master Gao rented a home in Xiangyang Lane, Huang Family Flower Garden, very near the stadium, only about a ten-minute walk. At the time, Master Gao had a handwritten draft version of the old manual, four volumes altogether. Most likely this was the 1932 revised draft, and many Tianjin disciples and students borrowed and circulated it. In 1936, during the New Year's festival, Master Gao retuned to Wuqing County to visit relatives and celebrate the holiday. His disciple, Du Shaotang, at the time the short-story editor of the New Tianjin Press, without obtaining Master Gao's approval, took this boxing manual draft to the printing division of the New Tianjin Press to be copied and published, signing his own name and fixing the book name as *Swimming-Body Connected Baguazhang.* When Master Gao returned from Wuqing and learned of this incident, he was extremely angry. He said that the manual was still in the process of revision, and there were many places that were not complete, requiring further scrutiny and editing or expansion and completion, so how could it be publicly printed and published? Anger aside, to avoid spreading rumors and errors for later practitioners and to redeem the situation, Master Gao hastily revised and organized his manual. With the help of his son Gao Fengming and others, he carried out substantial revision and correction of the four-volume handwritten draft. After Master Gao's meticulous revision, and with his disciple Liu Boyang writing the preface at the beginning of the first volume on his behalf, "in order to record its origin," the manual was meticulously copied into six volumes and presented to the world in the first month of winter 1936, with the name fixed as *Bagua Twisting-Body Connected Palm.* Master Gao gave this sole handwritten original copy of the manual to Liu Fengcai, and later Liu Fengcai gave it to Liu Shuhang.

From the editor recalling these past events, we can realize at least the following two points: first, several decades passed like a single day in the process of Master Gao creating his Baguazhang system. Through repeated refinement and constant striving to improve, his writing underwent successive revisions and many editions, with rough drafts even more numerous. The editor feels that the legends attached to the Baguazhang that Master Gao taught—including the concept of the Guanghua Mountain Bagua School and the treatise Universal Fantastic Arts—spring from the organization and form of the not-yet-realized source material drafts that were in the process of creation by Master Gao, or possibly belong to the elaborations of Master Gao's students based on these drafts and legends. Owing to different times, different environments and locations, and different lineages and teachers, it is understandable that the manuals that students of Master Gao possessed or copied and then handed down were not entirely the same.

Second, the final approved old manual containing the preface by Master Gao completed in the first month of winter 1936 should be seen as the finalized edition, and it is the sole standard edition for the Baguazhang system Master Gao taught. All other versions, although more or less the same as this finalized edition, should be seen as not-yet-finalized drafts, of course including the Du manual.

The creation of Master Gao's finalized edition signified that all of the Baguazhang system that he taught was fully formed and fixed in design, and laid the foundation for later practitioners to establish the scholarly position of Cheng School Gao Style Baguazhang.

3. The new manual edited by Master Liu and the old manual of Master Gao also have dissimilarities.

The world is material, and the material is moving and changing. Movement and change have regularity, and this regularity can be recognized. People's recognition is always from the outward in, from shallow to deep, or from low to high, gradually reaching a scientific style. The world is not composed of anything that does not change, and Baguazhang is no exception to this. Since founding Master Dong Haichuan first taught Turning Palms, to the formation of the Baguazhang school, and its designation—along with Shaolin, Xingyi, and Taiji—as one of the four big

Chinese boxing styles, Baguazhang has undergone a gradual process of supplementing and perfecting. Dong Haichuan took the original arts studied by his disciples and, according to the rules, special characteristics and requirements of the Turning Palm techniques, selectively incorporated them into the Turning Palms. The Luohan Boxing studied originally by Yin Fu, or the art of Shuaijiao learned originally by Cheng Tinghua, or the twelve roads of Springy Legs trained by Shi Number Six all were separately reorganized and incorporated into the Baguazhang system. Because of this, the second-generation inheritors after Master Dong formed different Baguazhang schools each with different practice styles and special characteristics, such as Yin Style, Cheng Style, Liang Style, and Zhang Zhankui's creation, Xingyi Bagua. The third generation then witnessed Sun Fuquan's creation of Sun Style Boxing and Gao Yisheng's creation of Gao Style Baguazhang.

Master Gao started transmitting his art in Tianjin at age seventy, and most of his disciples came to him with another art, selecting which part of the art they wanted to study. Only Liu Fengcai studied with him for nine years in their hometown, and then came to Tianjin to follow Master Gao to continue advanced studies. Compared to all the other disciples that Master Gao taught in Tianjin, Liu Fengcai began studying with Master Gao the earliest and studied with him for the longest duration, and his inheritance was the most multifaceted, most systematic, and most complete. As a representative inheritor of this art, his Baguazhang skill was the most refined, he taught the most students, his reputation both at home and abroad is the highest, and his influence was the greatest. Therefore there is the saying "Gao-style boxing taught by the Liu family."

There is no doubt that Liu Fengcai was Master Gao's most loyal disciple, but in the process of editing the new manual, his loyalty to Master Gao's teachings does not mean he did not change anything. Because Master Liu began studying his art earlier than the completion of the old manual, what was contained in the old manual and what Master Liu studied had some differences, which were the result of changes by Master Gao advancing in his research. Of course, not only does what Master Liu studied differ from the old manual, but he also had his own understanding, insights, and new developments.

The editor feels that the old manual is the origin of the new manual, but the new manual is definitely not simply a reprint of the old manual. In the process of editing the new manual, Master Liu was loyal to the old manual, absorbing its essence but not rigidly sticking to its form. Upon the foundation of the comprehensive system inherited and passed on by Master Gao, in the new manual Master Liu also added his own insights and understanding from following Master Gao for many years. It should be said that the new manual is an expansion of the old manual. The root and origins of the old and new manuals are the same, but their branches, leaves, and buds are distinct. This is a further refinement, enrichment, and perfection of the old manual carried out by Liu Fengcai and his disciples, as a promotion and development of all of the Baguazhang system that Gao Yisheng taught. Because of this, it is easily understood why there may be differences between the old and new manuals.

Two Points of Explanation
1. An explanation regarding excerpted practice of the thirteen postures.

Master Gao's old manual records the "excerpted practice of the thirteen postures," which is followed immediately by the four-line maxim "Move and walk like a dragon, the palms like the wind / When acting, one cannot retain any kind emotions / If the heart is compassionate and the face soft, in the end there is no victory / Black hands and a ruthless heart makes men fear." Clearly, these individual thirteen postures and their practice are important training methods designed specifically for fighting and practical usage.

Liu Fengcai explained that excerpted practice means important individual training methods extracted from the forms, and that thirteen is the number of the five elements and eight trigrams. The excerpted thirteen postures are those that, at the time, Master Gao thought to be the best and most practical foundational fighting skills, extracted and emphasized through individual training. Liu Fengcai called this "Individual Practice of the Thirteen Postures."

Liu Fengcai often said: "There is no form that cannot be taught; there is no skill that cannot be victorious." To be victorious over others first relies on power and second relies on trained skill. He also said that "Within the ten thousand changes of Baguazhang, there are no movements that are empty; though differing for each person, any movement that is trained skillfully can gain victory over others." Just as Zhou Yuxiang's Opening Palm can be called supreme, Master Gao was exceptional in applying Testing Palm, and Gao Wencai's (Liu Fengcai's cousin) Crashing Palm was very powerful. This is the skill they developed in daily training. Liu Fengcai required the editor to become adept at taking those palm methods that I enjoyed and that were "easy to use and effective in fighting" and memorize them, placing them by my side, wholeheartedly spending time to practice them individually, and in this way, gradually and naturally over time, skill would develop. He also once warned me that after one has achieved a certain skill, one must not incautiously push hands or spar with others and test their skills, "which easily leads both parties to view whoever is injured as not skilled," and not to practice—or especially cross hands—after drinking, so as to avoid making a fool of oneself. One must know self-respect and self-love, and more importantly must understand respecting others. If you're not friends, don't test hands; between school brothers and friends, when testing hands, stop with first contact; if it's not an enemy, don't act, but in protecting oneself and facing an opponent, don't have any kind emotions.

In the process of revising this manual as the primary editors, Gao Jinhua (Gao Wencai's son) and I have together specifically carried out sequential diligent research and repeated experimentation and testing of the excerpted practice of the thirteen postures in Master Gao's writing. Uniting all that Liu Fengcai taught with our own discovery and understanding, we again selected carefully among the best, according to the principles of practicality and ease of practice, and finally we have again selected thirteen foundational skills and fixed these under the name Individual Practice of the Thirteen Postures, as follows:

Single Crashing Palm; Double Crashing Palm; Turning-Body Palm; Tiger Stomping Palm; Testing Palm; Shaving Palm; Pressing Palm; Affixing the Seal Palm; Piercing Palm; Uplifting Palm; Bending Elbow Shoulder Strike; Outward Kicking/Inward Hanging Stomping; Downward Cutting/Straight Crashing/Kicking.

"Knowing a thousand techniques is not as good as doing one technique expertly." Upon the foundation of complete and thorough training of the forms, practitioners may, according to their own interests and preferences, refine three to five selected techniques, repeatedly training them individually. Once acquiring some skill with these, they will all be very effective in testing hands or self-defense. Of course, individual practice must be gradual, using the middle path as a measure and following scientifically, and one must not train recklessly.

2. Master Gao's handwritten old manual is altogether six volumes.

Accompanying this reediting and reissue of the new manual we have only photo-reproduced the first four volumes of the old manual, and the fifth and sixth volumes were not printed. The reasons for this are respectfully explained as follows:

The primary content of the fifth volume is:

- First, the five elements: Drilling Fist, Cross-Step Testing Palm, Crushing Fist, Uplifting Palm, Crossing Fist.
- Second, the twelve images: Wildcat Pounces on the Mouse, Monkey Climbs the Pole, Green Dragon Seizes the Helmet, Malevolent Tiger Pounces on Prey, Yellow Eagle Spreads its Wings, Bear Form Double Yanking, White Snake Spits out Its Tongue, Golden Leopard Leaps the Mountain, Golden Rooster Stands on One Leg, Wild Horse Gallops, Phoenix Spreads Its Wings, Lion Shakes Its Head.
- Third, the Bagua Form Boxing: Lion Waves, Snake Wraps, Tiger Crouches, Dragon Form, Swallow Overturns, Eagle Tears, Bear Yanks, Monkey Image.

We must point out that these five elements are similar to but different from the five elements of Xingyi. The five elements and the twelve images are all individually trained movements, in the same manner as the Sixty-Four Palms. The Bagua Form Boxing is the uniting of Pre-Heaven and Post-Heaven Palms in form. The first four sets maintain walking the circle with both Pre-Heaven and Post-Heaven postures, while the last four sets include the Post-Heaven Palms and all types of kicking techniques.

The content of the sixth volume is Life-Cultivation Arts, and its table of contents is:

- Discussion on the Three Dantians
- Discussion on the Three Passes of the Back
- Preserving *Jing, Qi,* and *Shen*
- Ancient Times Had Perfected Beings, Enlightened Beings, Sages, and Worthies
- Discussion on the Ancient Heavenly Truth
- The Four Seasons Regulating the Spirit
- The Way of the Heart in Curing Illness
- Emptying the Heart and Joining with the Dao
- Studying the Dao Is Never too Late or Early
- The Human Heart and the Heavenly Mechanism
- Transporting Sustenance, Anmo Guided Breathing
- Important Points in Absorbing Food
- Returning Elixir Internal Training Method
- Prohibition in Cultivating One's Nature
- The Accordance of the Four Seasons
- Maxims of Former Worthies
- Essentials of the Body
- Essentials of the Supreme Treasure
- Kidney-Cultivating Method

The reason that the last two volumes were not reprinted is not because the editor is reluctant to print them, but mainly arises from the following considerations:

Firstly, the core of the Baguazhang system that Master Gao created is the Pre-Heaven Palms and Post-Heaven Sixty-Four Palms, which stress "application, response, development, evolution" and emphasize that the Pre-Heaven Palms are the basis for the Post-Heaven Palms; the Post-Heaven Palms are the application of the Pre-Heaven Palms. The first four volumes of his work already completely contain this basic content.

Secondly, the material in the last two volumes was taught to very few people by Masters Gao and Liu. Moreover, because Master Liu trained in the arts before Master Gao completed his manual, the art taught by Master Liu is not completely the same as that recorded by Master Gao in his manual. For example, for the five elements, twelve images, and eight sets of Form Boxing, today those who can perform these sets were all directly taught by Master Liu, such as Gao Jinhua and Liu Shuhang, and today no one trains these exactly according to Master Gao's old manual.

Thirdly, the new manual edited by Liu Fengcai has already incorporated much of the content of the old manual's fifth and sixth volumes, such as the Bagua Form Boxing and Life-Cultivation Arts.

Lastly, publishing this edition with the old and new manuals combined in one set resulted in a very large volume, so the editor was forced to remove the noncore material of the fifth and sixth chapters from the revised edition. If there are enthusiasts who especially require it, the editor can separately and individually photocopy and offer them as a gift.

PREFACE TO THE 2005 SECOND CHINESE EDITION

Baguazhang originated in China, but it belongs to the world. Baguazhang is not simply a traditional physical program that can be used for fighting, health-building, performance, entertainment, and leisure, but it is in fact the outstanding martial culture of the Chinese people that embodies the tolerant spirit that "the gentleman should broaden his virtue to support all things," and the fighting spirit of "the gentleman should be self-improving without cease."[1]

The eight-trigram theory of the *Book of Changes,* or *Yijing,* is one of the important wellsprings of the traditional culture of the Chinese people. Baguazhang uses *Yijing* theory to explain boxing theory and borrows martial techniques to cultivate the body. With the theory of "the mind should be still, the body should move; within movement seek stillness, within stillness seek movement," it takes traditional Chinese culture, the essence of martial skill, and life-cultivation techniques and combines them by walking and turning the circle, "uniting the civil and martial; joining the body and application," forming a shining example of glorious Chinese traditional culture. Its long history, deep cultural connection, enjoyable and pleasant forms, evident health-building results, and miraculous fighting skill, as well as its strong artistic nature, watchability, and uniqueness, can broadly satisfy people's different levels of requirements for survival, safety, social contact, social respect, and expression of self-worth in modern society.

Baguazhang cultivates one's nature and life, and it trains the internal and external together. Cultivating internal power and fighting skill is Baguazhang's basic martial value. Increasing the health of body and mind is Baguazhang's basic physical exercise value. Used as performance, it can express a complete and unified whole-body aesthetic combining strength, health, coordination, and hardness and softness—uniting jing, qi, and shen[2] in one—which causes both the performer and the observer to attain simultaneously a type of enjoyment in the heart; this is Baguazhang's basic artistic value. Because of this, researching and training Baguazhang can not only develop correct qi within the body, increase internal life force, alleviate exhaustion, raise disease-preventing and disease-fighting functions, refine fighting ability, and increase internal martial power while increasing overall constitution, it can also increase virtue cultivation; train a person's disposition, intention, and will; develop self-respect, self-confidence, self-sufficiency, and a spirit of making oneself strong and untiring, and from this increase the ability to respond to the innumerable changes of the social environment, and wholly increase one's life span. Because of this, domestic and overseas experts predict that Baguazhang will certainly gain wide acceptance and development in the twenty-first century, becoming one of humanity's most favored exercise regimens.

Cheng School Gao Style Baguazhang is an important branch of traditional Baguazhang that was first transmitted by third-generation Bagua practitioner Gao Yisheng. Gao Yisheng inherited as a foundation all that was taught by Cheng Tinghua; picked broadly from the best of other sources; refined the essence, adding his new creations and developments; and through combining, organizing, and developing, gradually formed a separate and unique Baguazhang system. Before his death, Liu Fengcai discussed with his many disciples and fixed the name of all of Master Gao's teachings as Cheng School Gao Style Baguazhang. In 1997, after undergoing judgment by an investigative committee and receiving the approval of the national sports committee, this name was recognized by experts, and Cheng School Gao Style Baguazhang was promoted to the world by its inclusion in Volume Two (Martial Arts/Health Preservation) of *Chinese Physical Education Health-Building Methods.*

The Cheng School Gao Style Baguazhang Manual is compiled and edited from Gao Yisheng's handwritten *Bagua Twisting-Body Connected Palm* manual. The Manual systematically introduces the origin and transmission of the Cheng School Gao Style Baguazhang system, its foundational theory, practice sequence, methods, and content, and it combines the experience and understanding of three generations of noted Baguazhang practitioners—Gao Yisheng, Liu Fengcai, and Wang Shusheng. The editing and first publication of this manual by Liu Fengcai was an important marker in establishing the academic position of Cheng School Gao Style Baguazhang, serving as a bridge to connect fellow practitioners and enthusiasts at home and abroad, and also providing basic teaching materials to promote the exchange of Cheng School Gao Style Baguazhang, earning the appreciation of fellow Bagua practitioners and enthusiasts. Until the present day, we have often had people from many countries, including Taiwan, Hong Kong, Japan, and the United States, sending representatives and sending letters seeking this book. Unfortunately, the author no longer has any copies left to give. Because of this, it was decided to revise and republish this work, to thank fellow Baguazhang practitioners for their sincere admiration.

This revised edition of the manual retains completely the form and content of the first edition, adding additional chapters on weapons and animals, among others. The original chapters were proofread, and minor edits or additions were made. After revision and republishing, the Manual contains a more or less complete picture of the Cheng School Gao Style Baguazhang system, its content filled in and completed, the language made simpler and easier to understand, and its literary nature, readability, and practicality improved.

Great assistance in the revision and republishing of this Manual was received from noted Taiwanese Cheng School Gao Style Baguazhang practitioner Pan Yue; noted Beijing Baguazhang practitioner Wang Tong provided the very valuable photo of Cheng Tinghua; Liu Fengcai's inheritors in Tianjin—Wang Fuling, Zhu Xiliang, Han Fengrui, Liu Jianying, Chen Lianfa, Liu Jinwang, Ge Shuzhen, Ge Shuxian, Tian Qingping, Zhao Junde, Zhang Jinhe, Li Xuemin, Yuan Pengfu, Zhang Shoukun, Liu Liangang, and Zhang Xiang—have all proofread the manuscript. Here we express our gratitude to you all.

The aim of this revised edition of the manual is to move one step further in summarizing the combined experiences and knowledge of Gao Yisheng and Liu Fengcai, the noted older-generation practitioners of

Cheng School Gao Style Baguazhang; to encourage junior practitioners in this style and Baguazhang enthusiasts in general; and to promote the broader transmission, dissemination, and development of Cheng School Gao Style Baguazhang. Revisions began in the twentieth century, in the 1990s, continually and gradually gathering the thoughts and suggestions of fellow practitioners. However, because of the limitations of the editors and the difficulty in avoiding careless mistakes or ommissions, we invite experts and readers to offer critiques and corrections.

Liu Shuhang, revised edition editor
Ge Guoliang and Li Xueyi, revised edition associate editors
October 18, 2000

The Formation of Gao Yisheng's Baguazhang Corpus

The Cheng School Gao Style Baguazhang Manual that you, gentle readers, now hold in your hands is a specialized writing that systematically introduces Gao Yisheng's Baguazhang corpus. I have formerly carried out research into the formation of this system, and take everything that I have collected and recount it here, as a gift of congratulations on the publishing of this work and as a dedication to all those who have made contributions to the formation and development of the Cheng School Gao Style Baguazhang system.

In 1980, in order to investigate the origins of Baguazhang, I made a special trip to Tianjin, where I met the chief editor of this book, Liu Fengcai, and his disciples Wang Shusheng and Liu Shuhang. Liu Fengcai was from the same hometown as Gao Yisheng and was a blood relation. From a young age he followed Gao and studied this skill, later again following Gao to Tianjin to establish a place to transmit this art, and he was Master Gao's skilled assistant instructor. Master Liu's body and hands were nimble, and even in later years he could expertly demonstrate the special flavor of Gao-style boxing skill. He also knew a great deal of the details of Master Gao's life, almost to the degree that there was nothing he did not know. My interactions with them allowed me to see a complete picture of the Gao-style boxing art and informed me of materials required to resolve questions about the formation of the Gao Yisheng Baguazhang system.

Regarding the question of when the Gao Yisheng Baguazhang system was formed, Liu Fengcai stated that from 1909 to 1916—when, at the invitation of a friend, Gao Yisheng resided in his hometown of Dashan Township, Wudi County, to teach boxing—Gao taught only the Eight

Big Palms and a few fighting applications. In 1926, when he left Wuqing in the suburbs of Tianjin and again returned to his hometown to establish a school and teach his art, he started to teach the sixty-four palms. Master Liu also provided me with a copy of Gao Yisheng's *Bagua Twisting-Body Connected Palm* manuscript, which lists both Pre-Heaven Palms and Post-Heaven Palms as the main content of the art and uses the explanation of Pre-Heaven and Post-Heaven trigrams as a framework for boxing theory, including it as Gao-style teaching content. On the first page of the manuscript is written "Revised in autumn of the *renshen* year of the Republic of China." The renshen year of the Republic was 1932. At the back of the manuscript there is an undated Preface, and crowning it at its beginning is another Preface, inscribed "First month of winter, twenty-fifth year of the Republic, Gao Yisheng of Shandong, prefaced in Tianjin, respectfully copied by student Liu Boyong." At the end of this preface it says: "This book was completed and finalized after copying, reading, and reviewing; therefore this preface records its genesis." From these circumstances we can see: in 1926 the Gao Style Baguazhang system already exhibited its fledgling shape; in 1932, when the boxing manual was revised, it already possessed an early framework for practice and theory; by 1936 Gao's finalizing of his manuscript signified that the achievements in systematizing the Gao Style Baguazhang system were complete.

The origin of the Gao Style Baguazhang system was formerly clouded by a mystical tone. The reason for this is the Preface added by Master Gao in 1936. In it he states that between 1909 and 1916, when he was teaching boxing in Dashan Township, he "swallowed his pride and sought instruction from . . . one who said his name was Song Yiren [and] had the appearance of a beggar." Furthermore, he solidifies this by saying, "What I first studied with Master Zhou [Yuxiang] was Bagua's Pre-Heaven art, but that which I studied from Song Yiren was the way of Post-Heaven." After this, doubts surrounding Song Yiren began to arise, and false interpretations were offered. However, according to Liu Fengcai, these words come only from the preface by Gao

Yisheng; no one in Dashan Township ever saw Song Yiren, and at the time, Zhou Yuxiang "desired to travel himself to Shandong and visit Song Yiren. However, because Song's tracks were unclear, he was not able to fulfill this desire."

In the course of interaction and discussion with Gao Style inheritors I discovered that if we take the Gao Style Post-Heaven Palms as sixty-four individual movements, then in each posture we can find clear traces of the transmission from teacher to student. Liu Fengcai related that Gao Yisheng once directly stated that when he first met Zhou Yuxiang, he was knocked down with Zhou's use of Carrying Palm. Carrying Palm is the third posture of the fourth set of Post-Heaven Palms. Master Liu also said that Zhou Yuxiang was skilled in applying Opening Palm, and people called this his "Ultimate Palm." Opening Palm is the head of the Sixty-Four Palms, positioned as the first posture of the first set. Master Gao's grand-student Deng Changcheng, who studied under He Kecai, once sent me a comparison chart of the thirty-four postures in Yan Dehua's *Practical Applications of Baguazhang* and Master Gao Yisheng's Pre- and Post-Heaven Palms. The results of comparison show that, of Yan's thirty-four postures, thirty-one are identical with thirty-one of the Gao Style Post-Heaven Palms, and the remaining three postures are the same as postures found within the Gao Style Pre-Heaven Palms. Yan Dehua studied under Zhou Yuxiang, and his writing was published in Tianjin in 1936. Gao Yisheng writes in his 1936 preface, "At the age of thirty I followed Zhou Yuxiang of Wafang Village, Wuqing County, in the study and practice of Baguazhang. Later, taking advantage of Zhou's visiting the capital, and with him as a sponsor, I started to travel there with him and inserted myself into Master Cheng's school." Clearly, the origin of almost half of the Gao Style Post-Heaven Palm postures is the practical applications of Baguazhang taught by Zhou Yuxiang. In the summer of 1983 I traveled to Tianjin to visit friends and had an all-night discussion with Wang Shusheng and Liu Shuhang—associate editor and compiler, respectively, of this book—again involving the topic of the origin of Gao-style skills. From the Big Red Boxing studied by Gao early on, we can separate out the original source material for the eight kicks and eight elbows of the Post-Heaven Palms. Big Red Boxing was the skill gained by Master Gao, who "from his youth loved martial arts and followed the family teachings."

The basic theory of Gao Style Baguazhang also has its clear sources. First, Master Gao emphasized that the "Pre-Heaven Palms are the basis for the Post-Heaven Palms; the Post-Heaven Palms are the application of the Pre-Heaven Palms; without the Pre-Heaven Palms, one's Baguazhang has no root; without Post-Heaven Palms, one's Baguazhang is not complete," using this as a framework to discriminatingly deal with the relationship between the Pre-Heaven Palms and Post-Heaven Palms. This theory was already written down in 1916 by Gao Yisheng's school brother Sun Lutang in his *Study of Baguazhang.* The twentieth chapter of that book says, "The Pre-Heaven is the body of the Post-Heaven; Post-Heaven is the application of the Pre-Heaven. Without the Pre-Heaven, there is no root; without Post-Heaven, the Pre-Heaven is not complete." Moreover, Liu Boyong, the compiler of the draft of the Gao Style *Bagua Twisting-Body Connected Palm* boxing manual, was an academic. Du Shaotang, who—two years before Gao's *Bagua Twisting-Body Connected Palm* was approved and finalized—published *Swimming-Body Connected Baguazhang* to introduce Gao Yisheng's boxing art, was short-story editor at the New Tianjin Press. The special flavor of the songs in the Gao Style boxing manual, and the legendary nature of the origin of these boxing skills, are most likely not without connection to these two individuals.

Relating the above investigation does not help us find Song Yiren, whose "tracks were unclear" but conversely helps us clearly see a group of "those who gave the art." Those individuals who gave the art wove together the basic ingredients of Gao Yisheng's Post-Heaven Palms. If we say that the phrase *those who gave the art* sounds the same as *Song Yiren,* and that the mystical nature of this obscures the art, then let us reclaim those who gave the art over Song Yiren, and let the honesty of this allow people to see the wise men who made contributions to the formation and development of the Gao Style Baguazhang system. At the same time, as we remember these sages, let it also inspire us to seek the inherent patterns in the origin, formation, and development of a boxing art and serve as a reference to foster the ceaseless development of these martial arts exercises.

During the process of the formation of the Gao Style Baguazhang system, the dedication of those who gave the art is an aspect that cannot be overlooked, but it is also not the decisive element. The decisive element was the creative work put forth by Gao Yisheng. In other words, the Gao Style Baguazhang system is not just the sum of boxing skills that Master Gao once studied. Utilizing as a model the Cheng School Baguazhang learned from his teacher Cheng Tinghua and school brother Zhou Yuxiang—which took the Eight Big Palms as its core—he undertook, according to specific principles, the selection and inclusion of other boxing skills. Only through systematizing and organizing according to a specific process, finally unifying the material coherently according to definite rules, did he in the end create the unique characteristics of the Gao Style Baguazhang system.

In the aspect of inclusion, Gao Yisheng followed the principle of "Pre-Heaven as the body; Post-Heaven as the application." Boxing skills that aided in internal training and fostering the root, and that were easy to incorporate into turning the circle, were absorbed into the Pre-Heaven Palms. Those skills that aided in engaging the offensive and defensive usage of all parts of the body, and with which the special characteristics of Baguazhang striking methods were easily merged, were included in the Post-Heaven Palms. For example, Gao Yisheng did not choose those broad and open pouncing, leaping, jumping, and soaring postures showing the special characteristics of Big Red Boxing, but from these he selectively included a few leg techniques and elbow techniques as material for the Post-Heaven Palms. Gao Yisheng studied Xingyiquan and received Li Cunyi's direct instruction but did not borrow the five movements that serve as the basic fists of Xingyiquan, selecting and absorbing instead the training process and force-issuing methods of the five fists as reference for the Post-Heaven Palms. In the aspect of organizing, Gao Yisheng pursued standardization in training the forms and systematization of the fighting methods.

Gao Style Pre-Heaven Palms were created by revising the Eight Big Palms. The Eight Big Palms are also called Old Eight Palms or Eight Mother Palms. Their traditional training method was as eight combined exercise sets of individual but linked moves, each with opening and closing postures. The transmissions from his teacher Cheng Tinghua and Zhou Yuxiang were also like this. In 1916, Cheng Tinghua's disciple Sun Lutang, in his *Study of Baguazhang,* takes the Single Palm Change and double palm change of the Old Eight Palms and explains them as the Two Principles and Four Images, placing them before the eight palms. Gao Yisheng used Sun's framework as a reference, using Single Palm Change as the head of the palms, while creating Black Dragon Whips Its Tail and placing it after the eight palms as an ending. He named this training sequence of Gao Style Eight Big Palms, organized with a head and a tail, Pre-Heaven Palms, which became a subsystem within the Gao Style Baguazhang system. Gao Style's method of training the sixty-four Post-Heaven postures is different than the sixty-four hands created and transmitted in Beijing by Liu Dekuan, and also different from the sixty-four palms created within the Central Martial Arts Academy system by Wu Junshan. Gao Yisheng's method utilizes as its source material all the fighting applications taught by Zhou Yuxiang and his teacher Cheng Tinghua, along with other incorporated boxing postures. Using eight-trigram numerology as palm numerology, while adhering to the special characteristics of Bagua fighting methods as a standard, he carried out categorization and organization, forming eight training sets of exemplary fighting skills, each with eight movements. As a whole, each of the eight sets contains eight types of fighting methods, creating sixty-four postures, coinciding with the number of stacked trigrams, which Master Gao called Post-Heaven Palms and which also serves as another subsystem.

After the Pre-Heaven Palms and Post-Heaven Palms subsystems took shape, Gao Yisheng borrowed the theory that the "Pre-Heaven is the body of the Post-Heaven; the Post-Heaven is the application of the Pre-Heaven; without the Pre-Heaven, the Post-Heaven has no root; without the Post-Heaven, the Pre-Heaven is not complete," synthesizing the Pre- and Post-Heaven Palms and weaving together the basic skills of the Gao Style Baguazhang system.

In terms of synthesizing and unifying, Gao Yisheng carried out unification of the system he created according to rules of consistent form, energy, and movement style. For example, each of the Gao Style Pre-Heaven Palms follows the circle walking and spinning, with power in each posture rounded and supple, everywhere connected and flowing, the entire form created from one energy. One cannot see where Black Dragon Whips Its Tail or the other movements created by Master Gao have even the slightest aspects that are not integrated and, in fact, they give one a feeling of his having added flowers to brocade. Each and every posture of the Gao Style sixty-four Post-Heaven Palms is trained individually, following a straight line back and forth, extending long and striking far. Even the eight elbows and eight legs applications originating in Big Red Boxing carry out training according to this form and energy method, and no longer have the flavor of Red Boxing.

Through Gao Yisheng's efforts in these three areas, the boxing system he created uses traditional Baguazhang training methods as its basis, but also contains rather many new clever aspects. It did not lose similarity to Baguazhang movement, yet also had its own special movement characteristics, creating a system of skills different from other traditional Baguazhang lineages and branches, becoming its own self-contained training method.

Through the dedication of Master Gao and his disciples in transmitting this art, Gao Style Baguazhang, which was passed on only in Tianjin, Wuqing, and Wudi, is now transmitted to the four corners of our motherland as well as to Hong Kong and Taiwan, and has even been transmitted to faraway lands such as Japan, the United States, and other countries. This publication of the *Cheng School Gao Style Baguazhang Manual* will assist even more enthusiasts in understanding and studying Gao Style

Baguazhang, and it will make a new contribution toward the popularization and development of Gao Style Baguazhang.

Kang Gewu
New Year's Day, 1991, Beijing

Note: the author of this preface, Kang Gewu, is a researcher at the Chinese Martial Arts Research Institute and executive director of the International Baguazhang Friendship Association.

INTRODUCTION

Baguazhang is one of the important styles of Chinese traditional martial arts. Together with Taijiquan and Xingyiquan, it is called one of the big three internal arts, and it is a traditional exercise for building health and strengthening the body, familiar to a large number of martial arts enthusiasts.

Since the latter years of the Qing Dynasty (1644–1912), when First Master Dong Haichuan created Baguazhang, it has been transmitted for over one hundred years, changing according to each individual and forming numerous groups with different styles. Gao Yisheng recognized Dong Haichuan as the art's founder, and studied under Cheng Tinghua. This book introduces the Baguazhang taught by Gao Yisheng: Bagua Twisting-Body Connected Palm. Because his method of performance has its own unique points, such as the Pre-Heaven Palms and Post-Heaven Palms practiced separately, it is different than the many styles of Baguazhang currently practiced at home and abroad. Also, because it is developed from the foundations learned from the Cheng Tinghua school of Baguazhang, its name is fixed as Cheng School Gao Style Baguazhang.

Because Cheng School Gao Style Baguazhang's method of performance has its own unique style that has become its own system, emphasizing that the "Pre-Heaven Palms are the basis for the Post-Heaven Palms; the Post-Heaven Palms are the application of the Pre-Heaven Palms," stressing cultivating the body and building the body while also emphasizing fighting interaction, and is a traditional martial arts exercise that closely unites building the body and fighting, it is deeply appreciated by many martial arts enthusiasts. Also, because of the concerted effort of well-known former martial arts instructors to promote and transmit this art, it has been transmitted widely at home and abroad, with throngs of inheritors in mainland China, Hong Kong, Taiwan, and even a certain number in Japan and the United States.

Cheng School Gao Style Baguazhang's curriculum is very rich, incorporating the Pre-Heaven Eight Big Palms and the Post-Heaven Sixty-Four Palms as well as weapons, animals, and Post-Standing. The Pre-Heaven Eight Big Palms use turning the circle as their basic form of exercise along with the twenty-four important points of internal skill to complete their form. Following the traditional performance methods of Cheng School Baguazhang, one changes postures while walking and turning the circle. Using the turning palm as the beginning, and changing palm as the mother, eight sets of body-overturning are created, including Snake-Form Flowing-Posture Palm, Dragon-Form Piercing-Hand Palm, Turning-Body Tiger-Striking Palm, Swallow-Overturning Covering-Hand Palm, Spinning-Body Back-Covering Palm, Twisting-Body Forward-Searching Palm, Overturning-Body Backward-Inserting Palm, Stopping-Body Moving-Hooking Palm, and lastly Black Dragon Whips Its Tail as a closing posture. The aim of the Pre-Heaven Palms is to train the internal base, and they are primarily used in building health and strengthening the body, increasing qi, and extending power.

The Post-Heaven Sixty-Four Palms use sixty-four individually practiced forms as basic exercises along with the Twenty-Four Requirements to complete their form. The Post-Heaven Palms all originate in the Pre-Heaven Palms, each of the Pre-Heaven Eight Big Palms producing eight postures—sixty-four forms altogether, in accordance with the Eight Trigrams. They are:

- the eight Heaven postures: Open, Scoop, Yank, Test, Rise, Uplift, Cover, Wrap
- the eight Water postures: Smash, Hide, Chop, Shave, Two, Tiger, Steal, Link
- the eight Mountain postures: Pierce, Move, Intercept, Arrest, Stop, Overturn, Walk, Spin
- the eight Thunder postures: Push, Uphold, Carry, Lead, Stick, Join, Follow, Adhere
- the eight Wind postures: Slam, Coil, Drop, Gore, Twist, File, Stack, Drill

- the eight Fire postures: Chase, Stomp, Swing, Hang, Kick, Cut, Step, Connect
- the eight Earth postures: Press, Squeeze, Clamp, Seize, Crush, Crash, Hook, Swipe
- the eight Marsh postures: Pass, Pound, Draw, Gather, Wave, Evade, Cross, Leap

The Pre-Heaven Palms are the basis for the Post-Heaven Palms; the Post-Heaven Palms are the application of the Pre-Heaven Palms. All of the Post-Heaven Palms have fighting intention, and this intent is easily understood: the way it is practiced is the way it is used. The Post-Heaven Palms primarily train for fighting and crossing hands, according to the four principles of application, response, development, and evolution. Each posture can be broken down into six hands, 384 hands altogether, corresponding to the 384 lines of change in the Bagua.

The traditional Baguazhang weapon forms taught by Master Gao are of five types, including Bagua Rolling-Hand Broadsword, Bagua Connected Links Straight Sword, Bagua Yin-Yang Mandarin Duck Knives, and Bagua Cane. The first four types were said to have been created by Dong Haichuan, while the Bagua Cane began with the Heart-Height Staff form created by Cheng Tinghua and took shape through Master Gao Yisheng's changing practice, so he revised the name. Additionally, there are three other unique weapon forms that have the favor and esteem of Cheng School Gao Style Bagua practitioners. The first came from the Purple Hammer School—the Double Rattan Sticks form, which has simple, easy-to-use movements and was Master Gao Yisheng's art of personal protection. The second came from the Shaolin School—the two-person Night-Fighting Saber form, with peculiar postures that approximate actual combat and which was Liu Fengcai's ultimate skill for self-protection. The third is the Wudang Straight Sword form, the famous sword from the Wudang School, Zhen Mountain, which was the form that Liu Fengcai taught most frequently to his students.

Cheng School Gao Style Baguazhang also has eight animal forms: Lion Waves, Snake Wraps, Tiger Crouches, Dragon Form, Swallow Overturns, Eagle Tears, Bear Yanks, and Monkey Image. These were created and passed on solely by Gao Yisheng, and they are an important part of the Cheng School Gao Style Baguazhang system. Cheng School Gao Style Baguazhang's Post-Standing includes static posts and moving posts.

This book uses the rich writings of Gao Yisheng as a foundation and, having referenced domestic and foreign specialized publications of the same type, fairly completely synthesizes the practical experience of three generations of practitioners: Gao Yisheng, Liu Fengcai, and Wang Shusheng. Due to the limits of size, this edition focuses on introducing the basic practice methods of the Pre-Heaven Palms and Post-Heaven Palms while providing only a brief introduction to the weapons, animals, fighting, and separating palms.

The work of organizing this edition began in 1980 with Liu Fengcai as chief editor, his inner-chamber disciple Wang Shusheng assisting, and his family-taught disciple Liu Shuhang as compiler. The work spanned ten years, and the manuscript was revised four times. From beginning to end, this project has received the guidance of related experts from the Beijing Baguazhang Research Association and has received great support from organizations such as the Tianjin Nankai District Martial Arts Academy, Tianjin Metro Management Bureau Workers Union, and Tianjin Geology Research Center Press as well as the concerted help of important inheritors of Cheng School Gao Style Baguazhang: Liu Shaochen, An Shubao, Gao Jinhua, Zhu Xiliang, Han Fengrui, Han Timing, Wang Fuling, Li Zongxun, Wang Yuting, Li Tingquan, Ge Shuxian, Ge Shuzhen, Ge Guoliang, Li Xueyi, Zhao Zengmin, Li Cang, and Shi Jitao. Kang Gewu, the vice president of the Beijing Baguazhang Research Association, has provided a preface. Here I express my gratitude to you all.

Given that the editor's abilities are limited, within this book it is hard to avoid instances of error, and I respectfully ask for critiques and corrections from the greater world of martial arts enthusiasts.

Editor
October 31, 1990, Tianjin

GAO YISHENG'S STUDY OF MARTIAL ARTS

Gao Yisheng.

Gao Yisheng (1865–1947), courtesy name Deyuan, from Dazhuangzi Village, Dashan Township, Wudi County, Shandong Province, was my grandmother's younger brother. As a youth, because his family was poor, he moved with his parents to Hebei Province, first to Xiaogao Village in Wuqing County; later they settled in Aipu Village. In his early years he followed the family teachings and practiced Shaolin Big Red Boxing. Later he also studied Xingyiquan, and once received instruction from noted Xingyi practitioner Li Cunyi. He was a top student of Cheng Tinghua, a third-generation Baguazhang inheritor, and the first-generation founder of Gao Style Bagua.

At age twenty-nine, in 1894, he met Zhou Yuxiang of Wafang Village, Wuqing County, who was a top student of noted Baguazhang master Cheng Tinghua. Zhou's achievements in Baguazhang were many, and he was especially skilled in fighting. Very good at striking with his palm, he very seldom lost. Because of this he acquired the nickname "Ultimate Palm." When Gao first met Zhou, they both performed what they practiced and then compared hands. He was beaten by Zhou three times in a row, and immediately wanted to acknowledge Master Zhou as his teacher. As Zhou was only three years older than Gao, "according to the age similarity, he could not record [Gao] on his school wall, but could only look upon him with the etiquette of a brother." Following Gao's entreaties, the two met and traveled together to the capital, and "using Master Zhou as a sponsor," Gao Yisheng bowed to Master Cheng Tinghua in Beijing as his master, "inserting himself in Master Cheng's school." After returning to Wuqing, he received instruction from Master Zhou on behalf of their teacher, and Gao also often went to the capital to seek instruction from Cheng. In three years, Gao's art was complete, having studied the traditional Baguazhang eight big postures, as well as Bagua broadsword, Bagua spear, Bagua straight sword, Bagua knives, and Bagua Heart-Height Staff, as well as a few fighting applications and individual developmental postures. From this time, Gao Yisheng took teaching martial arts as his profession, and began to transmit his art and accept students in and around Wuqing.

When he was forty-four years old, in 1909, he returned to his hometown in Shandong to teach boxing. Shandong was a hotbed of martial practice, and around Dahsan Township in Wudi, almost every village had a boxing hall. Most practiced Shaolin Boxing, and Bagua was not something known by the locals. When Gao first returned to his hometown, according to local custom, those who studied martial arts elsewhere and returned home had to compare their skills with local practitioners. Gao used the Baguazhang that he had learned to first win against the village martial arts instructor Wu Huishan, and later to win against the teacher Ma Yuanbiao, known as "The Tiger of the Dashan Streets," and also to defeat the martial arts instructor Li Xuewu, known as "Iron Palm Li Number Two." Gao's name quickly spread and attracted those practicing martial arts from a dozen villages surrounding Dashan, who, hearing his name, thronged toward Gao and sought to become disciples and seek instruction. Because Gao not only studied martial arts but was also skilled in treating various injuries—his first patient was Wu Huishan—many people raised funds and opened an herb stand for Master Gao outside Dashan Village. From this time on, Gao taught his Baguazhang in and around Dashan and ran his herb stand. Master Gao wrote in his Bagua manual that, during this time in Dashan Township, one day "someone who looked like a beggar came to call on me, and when pressed for his name refused to give it, instead breaking into song, saying: 'Don't ask of my origin; we are both one family; studying arts is without end; I am Song Yiren, who has studied the complete learning, and now transmits the arts to all worthy gentlemen under heaven; transmitting without holding anything back; only this can be called pioneering; therefore just call me exceptional.'" He and Gao "talked excitedly of their arts," and their discussion gradually became harmonious; later their "interaction becoming quite close." According to Yiren, "What you, Gao Yisheng, have learned from Cheng Tinghua and Zhou Yuxiang are the Pre-Heaven aspects of Bagua, and what I, Yiren, have learned includes the Post-Heaven techniques of Bagua." At this, Gao "politely requested instruction," and studied the Post-Heaven Baguazhang from Song Yiren. Later, Gao combined all of the individual movements taught by Cheng Tinghua and Zhou Yuxiang and created the Sixty-Four Post-Heaven Palms.

When Master Gao was roughly fifty-one, in 1916, he left his ancestral home in Shandong and returned to Wuqing, continuing to transmit his Baguazhang around Yang Village. At age sixty-one, in 1926, he returned to his hometown in Shandong on personal matters, and was invited by me, the author, to my home in Dashan Township, Liu Family Yellow Dragon Bay Village. I am a close relative of Master Gao, and at the time I was eighteen years old. Since nine years of age I had continuously studied Baguazhang with my fourth uncle. Gao saw that my physique was good, I was intelligent and liked learning, and I already had a certain foundation, so he subsequently accepted me as an inner-chamber disciple, often residing at my house, and personally taught me wholeheartedly, move by move, for nine years.

At age seventy, in 1935, accepting the invitation of a friend in Tianjin, Master Gao started to teach Baguazhang at Tianjin Stadium (now the Xinhua Road Sports Complex). For some reason he returned to Wuqing in 1946, and in the winter of 1947 he passed away in his Wuqing home at the age of eighty-three.

Through many years of study and practice, Master Gao's boxing-art skills gradually became complete, his achievements exquisite and deep. Especially after creating the Post-Heaven Sixty-Four Palms, his fighting methods exhibited breakthrough advancement. He tested hands with other skilled martial artists in Tianjin, Shandong, Wuqing, and other locales, often using clever changes to snatch victory. At that time, at Tianjin Stadium, there was one who called himself a practitioner of "Spirit Taiji" who was known as "Thunderbolt Fierce Wind." He promoted himself by saying that his Spirit Taiji specifically countered Baguazhang. One day this person arrived at Master Gao's residence and asked him to compare hands, and he was struck to the ground by Gao's use of Testing Palm. Because of this he was unable to recover, and never again showed his face. Other respected martial artists, including Yan Dehua and Wu Xueliang (Wu Mengxia), were all beaten by Master Gao. When Wu Xueliang was knocked down by Gao, he immediately crouched to the ground, kowtowed, and recognized him as master, becoming Master Gao's first kowtow disciple in Tianjin. When Zhou Yuxiang later tested hands with Master Gao, he also had difficulty in snatching victory. Once in Yang Village in Wuqing, Master Zhou wanted to test how much Master Gao's hand methods had advanced; he advanced twice, and both times his attacks were neutralized by Gao. When he advanced a third time, he was knocked away by Gao's reversal of Opening Palm. Because of this, he heaped praise on the Post-Heaven Bagua Sixty-Four Palms that Master Gao had studied, and wanted to travel himself to Shandong to visit Song Yiren. However, because Song's path was unclear, he was not able to fulfill this desire.

Gao Yisheng devoted his life to practicing, researching, and transmitting Baguazhang, and his accomplishments were exquisite and deep. Because of this, those who bowed to him as master and sought instruction to learn this form of boxing were numerous, and most were already learned in other arts. Known examples include Wu Huishan, Wu Hongshan, Wu Xiudong, Guan Yunfa, Gao Fengming, Zhang Yufeng, An Jihai, Li Yunzhang, Zhang Junfeng, Xu Mingqiao, Liu Fengcai, Qu Kezhang, Yan Peilin, Wu Mengxia, Zhao Baichuan, Du Shaotang, He Kecai, Yu Yixian, Liu Boyong, and Li Zhuangfei. These few students all had some achievement in their studies and were important transmitters of Cheng School Gao Style Baguazhang both at home and abroad.

From 1909 until 1926, using his own understanding from many years of Bagua martial studies, Master Gao spent energy on systematically organizing and synthesizing his own experience researching and studying Baguazhang, and during this time completed the first draft of the

Baguazhang Manual. With the help of his son Gao Fengming, he revised it in 1932, and in 1936 approved and finalized it, adding his own introduction; this was copied by his disciple Liu Boyong into six handwritten volumes and passed on with the name fixed as *Bagua Twisting-Body Connected Palm.* In 1946 the original handwritten copy of this Manual was given to the author.

The system of Baguazhang created by Gao Yisheng embodies his superior wisdom and lifetime of dedication. In the manual, he summarizes his several decades of experience training in Baguazhang, and he fairly completely introduces the basic content and requirements for the practice of Baguazhang. Upon the foundation of the traditional training methods that he inherited from Cheng Tinghua, he took all that was taught by Song Yiren, organized it, and incorporated it as the Bagua Post-Heaven Sixty-Four Palms, calling the traditional training methods Pre-Heaven Baguazhang. He specifically stressed that the "Pre-Heaven Palms are the basis for the Post-Heaven Palms; the Post-Heaven Palms are the application of the Pre-Heaven Palms; without the Pre-Heaven Palms, one's Baguazhang has no root; without the Post-Heaven Palms, one's Baguazhang is not complete." He also felt that "The Pre-Heaven Palms are the precious method to cultivate the body, build the body, and strengthen the body, while the Post-Heaven Palms are the ingenious art for self-protection, self-defense, and fighting." Thus the Cheng School Gao Style Baguazhang that he created, and which became its own system, has enriched traditional Baguazhang both theoretically and practically, and it has made an important historical contribution to the continuation and development of Baguazhang.

Liu Fengcai, student
April 1985, Binzhou City, Shandong
Liu Shuhang, grand-student
Revised October 2000
Reedited 2010

LIU FENGCAI'S STUDY OF MARTIAL ARTS

Liu Fengcai.

Liu Fengcai, courtesy name Junchen, of Liu Family Yellow Dragon Bay Village, Dashan Township, Wudi County, Shandong Province, was born the 15th of the first month of the lunar calendar in 1908, and departed the world on February 10, 1987. He was from the same town as Gao Yisheng and was his relative. He became one of the most famous martial artists in China as a fourth-generation Bagua practitioner and second-generation Master of Cheng School Gao Style Baguazhang, and his biography has already been entered into the county gazetteer.

Born into an average agricultural family, from his youth he studied martial arts, first learning Baguazhang at age nine with his uncle. At age eighteen he was accepted by Gao Yisheng as an inner-chamber disciple and received instruction from Gao in his hometown for the next nine years. Because Liu was naturally intelligent, always a diligent student, and willing to train hard, Master Gao was extremely fond of him. In his last days Master Gao transmitted his complete experiences and understanding of this art to Master Liu. Because he received Gao's true and complete teaching, his skill advanced very quickly, and he had already attained notoriety in his hometown after only a few years. Liu often accompanied Gao on his many travels, assisting him in passing on this art. In 1936, when Liu turned twenty-eight, Gao established a place in Tianjin to transmit his art, and Liu again followed his teacher there to make his living, continuing to assist Gao in teaching Baguazhang. Not until he retired in 1983 did he leave Tianjin and return to his hometown, and even then he still continued to accept students and transmit his art in Binzhou City, Shandong.

For over sixty years, Liu was connected to Baguazhang through inseparable destiny. There was not one day that he did not practice; not one day that he did not teach. Aside from his time spent at work and in day-to-day activities, almost the entirety of his free time was devoted to the practice, teaching, and research of Baguazhang, practicing and contemplating morning and night without cease. Although not highly educated, he only needed someone to begin discussing Baguazhang and his words would come in volumes, like an unbroken flood, regarding Baguazhang's important points, poems, and stories of famous practitioners; he knew them by heart and could recite them backward and forward. He was adept in performance and skilled in fighting, his achievements in Baguazhang profound and deep. Because of this, his name was known in Baguazhang circles throughout Tianjin, Beijing, Hebei, Shandong, the whole of China, and overseas. In 1981, at the invitation of famous Baguazhang Masters Li Ziming and Kang Gewu, he attended, as a sponsor, the ceremony to celebrate relocating Dong Haichuan's tomb organized by the Beijing martial arts community, and was the only representative from Tianjin to have his name carved on Founding Master Dong's tomb in Beijing's Wan'an Cemetery as a permanent record.

Master Liu's Baguazhang basic skills were profound, his fighting art exquisite and complete, and he was renowned at home and abroad; The *Tianjin Daily*, Taiwan's *Li Yu Mei* and *Wulin* magazines, and the American *Bagua Journal* all published special pieces introducing his profound Baguazhang skill. The Chinese Wushu Research Institute's researcher and Baguazhang specialist Kang Gewu once praised him by saying, "Master Liu's movements are vigorous and, even in his advanced years, he can still outstandingly express the special flavor of Gao Style boxing; this is something rare and worthy of praise. Of all the elder-generation martial artists I have seen, none are able to surpass the exquisiteness of his postures."

Master Liu's performance of the Pre-Heaven Palms and Post-Heaven Palms as well as Baguazhang weapons and animals showed perfected artistic and martial flavor, and they serve as a model to be pursued by later practitioners of this style. His school brothers all considered watching his performances as a type of artistic appreciation. If he was still, they would observe the shape of his postures, extended and large; his manner still, full and complete with power, his energy abundant—inside and out all one qi. If he was moving, they would watch his exhibition, his tracks twisting and coiling like a dragon playing in the water, light but not floating, stable but not stiff, hard and soft blended and united in one body, all with a mystery that is only perceptible but cannot be expressed, causing applause and sighs when complete. After his death, people used their precious photos of his performances for reference and as a model for their practice. Several martial arts schools overseas, in Taiwan and the United States, have taken Master Liu's training photos and combined them into a large wall poster that, together with his portrait, are hung in the training hall to fully express their feelings of reverence for him, and to recognize him as one of the great lineage masters of Cheng School Gao Style Baguazhang.

During his life, Master Gao also lavished praise on Liu's performance style and abilities. When he first came to Tianjin, Master Gao remarked more than once to his disciples: "People say that Baguazhang is practical but not good-looking, but that's just because their skill is not complete. Go and watch Fengcai practice his circle; it's simply too beautiful." In his later years, he once evaluated Liu to his face, saying, "If we talk about crossing hands, you're still not as good as me when I was your age, but if we talk about your performance skill, you've already surpassed me by a lifetime." Master Gao later took the distillation of his life's efforts, his handwritten original Baguazhang manual, and passed it on to Liu, who, in his later years, used it as a great resource for preparing the *Cheng School Gao Style Baguazhang Manual.*

Master Liu's life undertaking was martial study in one vein, but he broadly selected from other strengths. He was adept at Wu Style Taijiquan, Wudang Taiji Thirteen Straight Sword, and Three Emperors Canon Fist, which he transmitted to many people. He also had deep and complete skill in Night-Fighting Saber and Double Rattan Sticks, rare treasures of Chinese martial arts, but he considered these his arts of self-protection and transmitted them to very few people.

In his Baguazhang training, Master Liu not only understood the postures but researched the theory, often saying: "The Pre-Heaven Palms are the foundation of the Post-Heaven Palms; the Post-Heaven Palms are the application of the Pre-Heaven Palms. If there are no Pre-Heaven Palms, your Baguazhang has no root; if there are no Post-Heaven Palms, your Baguazhang is not complete. The Pre-Heaven Palms are the precious method to cultivate, build, and strengthen the body; the Post-Heaven Palms are the mysterious art of self-protection, self-defense, and fighting."

He considered the Pre-Heaven Palms, including the moving posts, as the foundational skill of Cheng School Gao Style Baguazhang. What are called "internal skill posture-completion methods" mainly train whole-body power. One must truly feel "seeking flowing in the midst of opposing," and only after circularity is trained in the whole body—above and below—can one exhibit skill. Beginners must strictly adhere to the twenty-four points when walking the circle, and should be slow, not fast, like the saying "slowly issue the skill, but quickly issue the hands" ("hands" meaning practical fighting applications). The Post-Heaven Palms are the practical methods to utilize Gao Style Baguazhang, and they are the art of application, which must seek bidirectional force and train fierce explosive power that is issued at the first touch. The Post-Heaven Palms emphasize that application, response, development, and evolution must be approached step-by-step. In training the original posture and original application, one must not only know this application, but must also know how to dissolve it—this is response. Training the Dismantling Palms is two people working short sets that develop "perceptive power" and lead to understanding and manifesting "seeking cleverness within following." Only after combining skilled power with all types of fighting techniques, and understanding change and lively application, can one be victorious over others. This is what people mean with the common saying "Taijiquan utilizes the empty course; Xingyiquan utilizes the straight course; Baguazhang utilizes the evolving course." Here "course" means standing in an undefeatable position. Baguazhang primarily relies on changeability to be victorious over others.

Liu Fengcai's Study of Martial Arts

Master Liu felt that becoming stronger than others is *gongfu;* becoming faster than others is gongfu; using learned skill to attain victory is also gongfu. So in practicing martial arts, we primarily look at gongfu. Gongfu is time. Time does not cheat people, but gongfu can only come naturally.

On the study of all types of weapons, Master Liu also had considerable insight. He felt that any type of weapon is really just an extension of the arm. The key is to train long weapons close in, short weapons long-range, and to use the mind to train the weapon until it is a natural part of one's body. Only when it is integrated as one body and can be applied at will, the intention arriving with the power, does it express expert gongfu.

Master Liu's temperament was mild, and he was always benevolent toward others. He esteemed the martial and honored virtue. Although his art was high, his skill deep, and his applications completely exquisite, often "sending people off" with intention in the midst of no-intention, he never considered fighting and winning over others as a goal and did not believe in the strong bullying the weak. He felt that today, martial arts are primarily for health-building and making friends, and fighting is secondary. His whole life he stressed his guiding principle that "practicing martial arts is for building health and strengthening the body," and strongly opposed thoughtless fighters who only praised courage. Throughout his life, although he often tested hands with others, he always used virtuous skill to subdue them, just touching with a strike and then stopping. When he encountered one who loved to fight, he was thrice humble, and he never injured anyone in his whole life. Because of this, his disciples all praised him, calling him "the kindest toward others."

Master Liu began working as a farmer in his village and later entered the city as a laborer, throughout his life never seeking fame or fortune, seldom venturing out to show his face. In his almost fifty years residing in Tianjin, many times he gracefully declined invitations to attend all types of martial arts organizations, including once declining the personal invitation of Liu Wanfu, associate professor of martial arts at Tianjin University of Sport and former Tianjin Martial Arts Association vice chairman. Even less frequently did he attend any type of martial arts exhibition or competition. Later in life Master Liu once said to his students: "I've spent my whole life practicing and transmitting martial arts, and I only studied it as a hobby, transmitted it as an act of goodness; that is all. Aside from that, I was without other aspirations."

Master Liu saw "all martial arts under heaven as one family," and in making friends did not regard school or style. In receiving disciples he always taught according to the individual, and throughout his life continued to spend his nonwork time training students and transmitting his art. Moreover, he never accepted payment, and even further, did not seek to collect wealth from his students, deeply gaining the respect and endearment of his many disciples and students. Throughout his life his strictly held principle was, "In transmitting this art, virtue is first; benevolence and righteousness are the foundations of acting as a teacher to others. In studying this art, character is the highest; an empty heart and persevering nature are the basis for being a student." Master Liu's virtue was high, and he was widely esteemed. It is hard to count the number of people who studied with him due to his reputation. Many of them, in fact, came to him after studying other arts. His students worked in every profession and were ordinary people and high-level officials. There were intellectuals but also workers, farmers, businesspeople, students, and soldiers. Especially in the last century, in the 1960s, when he held an appointment as extracurricular martial arts coach at Nankai University for more than five years, the researchers, professors, students, and staff from Tianjin University and Nankai University who studied forms and weapons with him were numerous and could be said to be like "peaches and plums filling the world." Among Master Liu's followers, those who received his true teachings and reached some comparative attainment were also quite numerous. Well-known practitioners include his direct students Liu Shaochen, Wang Shusheng, Yang Zhisheng, Dong Jiegao, Lian Zhaolong, Wang Fuling, Gao Jinhua, Chen Baozhang, Liu Jitang, Pi Shuqiang, and Li Zhongfang. Liu Fengcai's only family-taught disciple, Liu Shuhang, is currently Eighth Duan in the Chinese Wushu Association, and he serves as secretary of the Cheng School Gao Style Baguazhang Research Committee. He completely and systematically inherited the Baguazhang taught by Liu Fengcai, once assisting Master Liu in organizing and editing the *Cheng School Gao Style Boxing Manual*, and he is a representative inheritor of Cheng School Gao Style Baguazhang. Liu Shuhang's well-known direct disciples Zhang Shoukun, Liu Yungang, Liu Lingjie, and Wang Xu have already achieved the rank of Sixth Duan in the Chinese Wushu Association.

In his later years Master Liu returned to his hometown, living in the home of his son Liu Zhenzhong in Binzhou City, Shandong Province. During this time, he still expended all efforts in promoting our ancestral traditional martial arts culture, wholeheartedly transmitting his art. He took many disciples there, and those that are well-known include Li Cang, Shi Jitao, Xiao Jun, Gao Guoyou, Liu Changzai, and Sun Shijun, Liu Gang, and Liu Anxiang.

Master Liu enjoyed an eminent reputation throughout his era, and he followed the course of researching and transmitting Baguazhang his entire life. In order to pass on and promote our motherland's traditional martial arts culture, wherever he went he brought Baguazhang to that place. Using a lifetime of passionate and hard-won research, he transmitted the results of Gao Yisheng's Baguazhang skills, using his own experience from study and practice to take all of the art that Master Gao passed on and push it toward a pinnacle of skilled art that would define an era. In his later years he strove to synthesize his own understanding and experience, wholeheartedly editing the *Cheng School Gao Style Baguazhang Manual*, leading Cheng School Gao Style Baguazhang to be recognized by related experts of the Chinese Martial Arts Research Institute, making more abundant the treasure-room of traditional Chinese martial arts, and leaving for later generations a legacy of extremely valuable martial studies. In establishing the academic position of Cheng School Gao Style Baguazhang, he made a significant and historical contribution. He also facilitated the uniting of domestic and foreign Gao Style Baguazhang practitioners, serving as a bridge for exchange and establishing a foundation for Cheng School Gao Style Baguazhang to be spread throughout the world. Today, the North American Tang Shou Tao Association in the United States, the

Hanshin Taijiquan Enthusiasts Club in Japan, the Tai Shi Yizong group in Taiwan, and the Guanghua Baguazhang group in Hong Kong all have historical origins in the Baguazhang taught by Master Liu, and individually they have established connections with Master Liu's students in China. Between 2002 and 2010, his family-taught disciple, Liu Shuhang, accepted invitations to transmit Cheng School Gao Style Baguazhang in Japan, the United States, and Thailand on eight separate occasions, and he has personally felt the deep feelings of esteem and respect that these overseas Baguazhang practitioners have toward Liu Fengcai.

To commemorate and cherish the achievements of Master Liu's lifetime of martial study, and to inspire future practitioners, on April 5, 1995, the day of the Qingming Festival, the Tianjin office of the International Baguazhang Friendship Association, with funds contributed by Cheng School Gao Style Baguazhang practitioners from Tianjin, Shandong, Taiwan, Hong Kong, Japan, and the United States, sponsored a grand headstone-raising ceremony, raising a large headstone on Master Liu's grave north of his home village. Experts and officials from the Chinese Martial Arts Research Institute, the Shandong Provincial Martial Arts Research Institute, and local, county, township, and village officials as well as domestic and foreign supporters, Master's relatives, and village residents all came out to attend the headstone-raising ceremony.

The front of the stele is inscribed "Grave marker of the famous Chinese martial artist and fourth-generation inheritor of Baguazhang Liu Fengcai." On the back are the names of forty-eight domestic and overseas Baguazhang practitioners inscribed as a permanent record. They are:

- From Tianjin: Wang Shusheng, Han Fengrui, Zhu Xiliang, Liu Jianying, Wang Dengjia, Gao Shuqing, Xu Li, Liu Shuhang, Ge Guoliang, Li Xueyi, Liu Jinwang, Zhao Junde, Li Xuemin, Zhang Li'an, Tian Qingping, Su Qingsheng.
- From Shandong: Pi Shuqiang, Li Cang, Shi Jitao, Xiao Jun.
- From Taiwan: Pan Yue, Liu Jinyu, Pan Zichao, Cai Rongguang, Lian Wanlai, You Shengming, Zhang Shibo.

- From Hong Kong: Deng Changcheng, Lei Rulin, Xu Guodong, Wu Baoquan, Xu Biao, Feng Senyuan, Huo Dongcheng, Wen Yaoji, Yeh Guansen.
- From Japan: Tsujita Noboru, Tsujimoto Saburomaru, Okuda Ryoichi, Gujyo Naoko, Azuma Miharu, Ikeda Ruriko.
- From the United States: Vincent Black, Kim Black, Tom Bisio, David Nicoletti, Chris Quayle, Marc Melton.

Kang Gewu, researcher at the Chinese Martial Arts Research Institute and executive director of the International Baguazhang Friendship Association, composed a grave marker inscription, the full text of which reads:

> Master Liu, given name Fengcai, courtesy name Junchen, a native of Wudi, Shandong, was born in 1908 and died in 1987 at age eighty. From a young age he enjoyed studying martial arts and took up the family teaching. At nineteen he began discipleship under his relative Gao Yisheng, researching Baguazhang, and in nine years' time received the true transmission. He had a miraculous understanding of fighting theory; his palm art was superb. He esteemed virtue and valued righteousness; in his dealings he was modest. After his art was complete, he moved to Tianjin and began teaching, and after more than fifty years his disciples are innumerable. He spent his life promoting Baguazhang, and in his later years edited the *Gao Style Baguazhang Manual* as a benefit to domestic and foreign fellow enthusiasts. To spread his fame for future generations, look up to him as a person of exemplary virtue, remember former times, and make friends, we solemnly compose this inscription to record our respect and admiration.

Compiled by Liu Shuhang
Revised October 2004
Reedited January 2010

WANG SHUSHENG'S STUDY OF MARTIAL ARTS

Wang Shusheng.

Wang Shusheng (1919–1995) was from Beiguan Village, Anxin County, Hebei Province. A famous Chinese martial artist and fifth-generation lineage holder in Baguazhang, he was one of the important representatives of Cheng School Gao Style Baguazhang. He loved martial arts from a young age and first studied Shaolin. In 1941 he came to Tianjin to seek employment, and there became a disciple of famed Bajiquan master Huang Qishan, studying for more than six years and attaining a deep grounding in the art. In the early days after the liberation of Tianjin, he entered into the Baguazhang school together with Liu Shaochen, Yang Zhisheng, and Dong Jiegao, becoming one of the four great kowtowed inner-chamber disciples of famous Baguazhang practitioner Liu Fengcai. Naturally clever and intelligent, and because of his grounding in Bajiquan, Wang's learning in Baguazhang was rapid. He was a strong favorite of Master Liu, who fully transmitted his life's art, allowing him to inherit the complete and true essence of Cheng School Gao Style Baguazhang. Through several decades of research, theorizing, and practice in Baguazhang, he became one of the most skilled of Liu Fengcai's students. He especially valued application, and he excelled in fighting. He was outspoken and straightforward toward others, with high martial virtue—never using strength to lead the weak—and he enjoyed the deepest respect from his school brothers and students. Wang Shusheng's contributions toward the promotion and continuation of Cheng School Gao Style Baguazhang are evident mainly in four areas:

1. Joining together with Liu Shuhang and others, he spared no effort in assisting Liu Fengcai to edit and publish the *Cheng School Gao Style Baguazhang Manual*, which made an important contribution

to establishing the academic standing of Cheng School Gao Style Baguazhang.

2. He made broad contributions to the fighting applications of Baguazhang. Working together with his school brother Yang Zhisheng, he completely reviewed the Post-Heaven Sixty-Four Dismantling Palms, carrying out meticulous research and repeated experimentation over three years. Adding to the foundation transmitted by Liu Fengcai, he dissected and added new concepts, adding to the completeness of the Sixty-Four Dismantling Palms, and greatly increasing the practical applications of the Post-Heaven Palms. Moreover, he organized the results of his research into a manual that was disseminated widely.

3. Joining with Liu Shuhang, Ge Guoliang, Li Xueyi, Ge Shuzhen, Ge Shuxian, Liu Jinwang, and others, he received many foreign Baguazhang practitioners and enthusiasts from Japan, the United States, Taiwan, and Hong Kong, exchanging and transmitting Baguazhang. In 1988 he was the first member of the Cheng School Gao Style Baguazhang family to travel east to Japan to teach, remaining there to teach for more than a month, receiving high praise from these Japanese friends, and inspiring the Hanshin Taijiquan Enthusiast Club to organize eleven visits to Tianjin to research and train in Baguazhang.

4. Wang's art was extraordinary, and he taught numerous students. Of all of Liu Fengcai's many disciples, Wang's disciples and students are the most numerous, and his influence is the greatest. He formerly held the position of Baguazhang instructor at the Heping District Zhenhua Martial Arts Academy and the Nankai District Martial Arts Academy, personally teaching several hundred students. His more outstanding inner-chamber disciples, including Ge Shuxian, Ge Shuzhen, Ge Guoliang, Li Xueyi, Liu Jinwang, Tian Qingping, Zhao Junde, Zhang Jinhe, Li Xuemin, and Pan Yue, and grand-student Yuan Pengfu, are all well-known practitioners at home and abroad whose impact on Cheng School Gao Style Baguazhang

has been great. Among them, Liu Jinwang serves as the president of the Cheng School Gao Style Baguazhang Research Association; Ge Guoliang, Li Xueyi, Ge Shuxian, and Ge Shuzhen serve as vice presidents; and Zhao Junde serves as deputy secretary. Additionally, Ge Guoliang, Li Xueyi, and Ge Shuxian have all traveled, together with Liu Shuhang, to exchange and teach Cheng School Gao Style Baguazhang in Japan and the United States. Especially in recent years, Wang's direct disciples and grand-students have many times attended domestic and international martial arts competitions, winning gold medals rather frequently. In summary, Wang Shusheng had an irreplaceable impact on the continued expansion of the Cheng School Gao Style Baguazhang family at home and abroad, the continued rise in its academic standing, and the continued expansion and reach of its influence, making an important contribution that cannot be overlooked.

Liu Shuhang
2010

Liu Fengcai Demonstrating the Eight Big Palms

1. Snake-Form Flowing-Posture Palm

2. Dragon-Form Piercing-Hand Palm

3. Turning-Body Tiger-Striking Palm

4. Swallow-Overturning Covering-Hand Palm

5. Spinning-Body Back-Covering Palm

6. Twisting-Body Forward-Searching Palm

7. Overturning-Body Backward-Inserting Palm

8. Stopping-Body Moving-Hooking Palm

Wang Shusheng Demonstrating Baguazhang Weapons

Bagua Body-Adhering Spear

Bagua Rolling-Hand Broadsword

Bagua Yin-Yang Mandarin Duck Knives

Bagua Heart-Height Staff

Bagua Connected Links Straight Sword

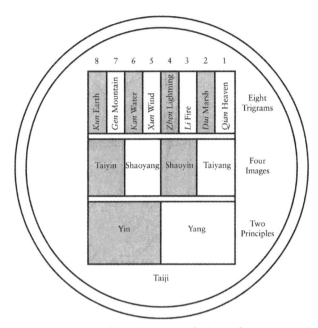

Figure 0.1. The divisions of yin and yang.

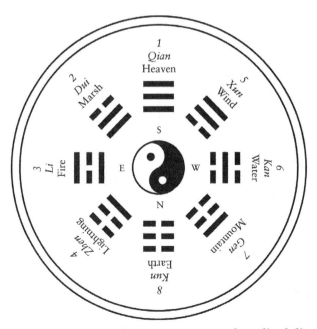

Figure 0.2. The Pre-Heaven Bagua sequence and cardinal directions.

Figure 0.3. The Pre-Heaven Bagua correspondences.

Figure 0.4. The Post-Heaven Bagua sequence and cardinal directions.

Baguazhang Theory Reference Charts

Figure 0.5. The Post-Heaven Bagua correspondences.

Figure 0.6. The Art-Training Tree.

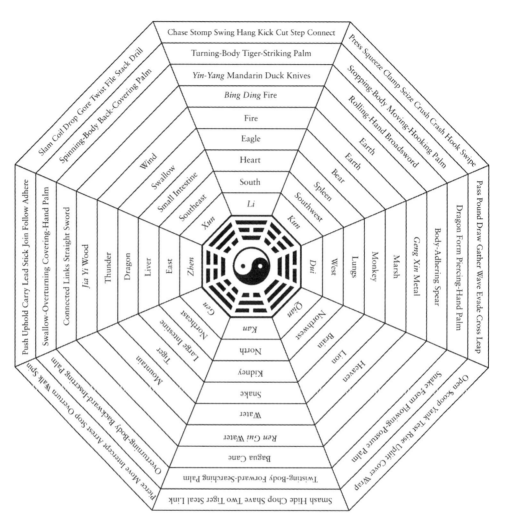

Figure 0.7. Cheng School Gao Style Baguazhang correspondence chart.

CHAPTER 1

Baguazhang History, Theory, and Performance

The song of Baguazhang performance and theory says:

Feet tread the Eight Trigrams upon the circle,
Pre-Heaven and Post-Heaven one qi connected,
Entering with yin and yang, exiting with He and Luo,[1]
the Xi and Zhou[2] *methods of change are the origin*
    of ten thousand principles.

The preface to the *Yijing,* the *Book of Changes,* says: "That which we call change is the way of yin and yang . . . this way is vast, and there is nothing it does not encompass; its application is miraculous, and there is nothing it does not contain." The "Explanation of the Trigrams" chapter of the *Yijing* says: "In ancient times, the sages created the changes, and used them to follow the principles of life. Therefore, they called that which established the way of Heaven as yin and yang, and that which established the way of earth as soft and hard." Our wise ancestors created the martial study of Baguazhang using the theory of the *Yijing* to explain boxing theory, an art modeled on yin and yang, united with numerology, with hard and soft mutually promoting, and with change at its core. The Pre-Heaven Eight Big Palms are the body; the Sixty-Four Post-Heaven Palms are the application; and the 384 movements are the adaptations. Truly, "within numerology is art, within art is numerology; using change as the pivot, changing ceaselessly." By following the principles of strengthening nature and cultivating life, one fully utilizes the way of change in fighting. Studying Baguazhang, one should understand its principles, study its postures, research its mechanisms, comprehend its transformations, and know the postures within the principles and the principles within the postures. The principles and postures are combined—this is where the art lies. Therefore this manual makes its purpose and theme clear from the very beginning, and with this first chapter states these principles.

Baguazhang's Origin, Development, and Transmission

Due to societal, historical, environmental, and many other factors, and additionally because the written record regarding Baguazhang is lacking, the numerous explanations of the origins and history of Baguazhang mostly rely on colorful legends and are confused. Some say Baguazhang was already transmitted before Dong Haichuan existed; some say Dong Haichuan was the first to transmit Baguazhang; some say Dong Haichuan created Baguazhang.

In 1981 noted martial arts scholar Kang Gewu began an investigation into and evaluation of the origins and history of Baguazhang. After gathering writings, material objects, and opinions from many sources and carrying out diligent systematic research, he publishing the article "Research on the Origin of Baguazhang," a text that served as Kang Gewu's master's thesis. In the text he confirms that Baguazhang was created by Dong Haichuan and that Bagua's schools were formed between 1866 and 1894, inferring that Baguazhang was the product of Dong Haichuan's combining of the Turning the Celestial Worthy practice of southern Chinese Daoists with the various Chinese boxing arts he already knew. Later, through the organizational and promotional efforts of Cheng Tinghua and his other disciples, Baguazhang attained its perfection and was transmitted broadly to the world.

Today, although there are still differing opinions regarding the origins of Baguazhang, almost all common lineages recognize Dong Haichuan as the art's founding master. According to the inscription recorded on Dong Haichuan's gravestone, the twenty-character lineage poem reads:

"As eternal as the blessed ocean and ancient mountains / Strong and resolute in establishing the foundation of the nation / Flourishing and bright, shining across this great continent / The way and its virtue building without limit."[3]

Since its founding by Dong Haichuan, Baguazhang has undergone transmission through successive generations until the present day, when, because of differences between individuals, it has formed into many different schools with their own methods of training and special characteristics. Firstly, this was because at the time that Master Dong transmitted his art, he carried out instruction according to the individual. Secondly, it reflects the fact that most of those who studied the art from Master Dong brought with them another art—like Cheng Tinghua, who had previously practiced Shuaijiao, and Yin Fu, who had earlier practiced Luohanquan. Additionally, a few well-known martial arts masters, who had received true instruction, deeply researched the principles and explored some subtlety, or borrowed from it broadly in order to perfect their own skills, or traveled far and wide promoting their art. One could say it is like a mother who bears nine sons, and each son is different.

The Cheng School Gao Style Baguazhang Origin and Transmission Chart (below) in this revised edition of the manual uses as its foundation the original version dictated and personally examined and approved by Liu Fengcai, which was published in the first edition of the manual in 1991. In line with the principle of "respecting history while seeking truth from facts," broad investigation was undertaken, soliciting the views of fellow practitioners and emphasizing the actual conditions of inheritance and transmission within Master Liu's school, and with careful consideration the many disciples listed under Master Liu's lineage were verified, resulting in minor additions and deletions. For example, Pi Shuqiang did not have his name listed in the first edition only because at the time he was not in Tianjin and communication with him had been broken. However, as everyone knows, he received the art's true transmission, first following Liu Fengcai in the research and study of Three Emperors Canon Fist and Baguazhang at twelve years of age, in early 1962, and after 1983, when Master Liu returned to his hometown, still seeking him out many times to request instruction. Moreover, in Jinxiang County, Shandong Province, he passed on broadly all that Master Liu taught him, and his influence was relatively great. Based on this, through general discussion with fellow practitioners, it was agreed that Pi Shuqiang's true aspirations should be respected, and it is suitable to place his name under Liu Fengcai's school.

Owing to the fact that Master Gao Yisheng's life work was the research, practice, and teaching of Baguazhang, the disciples in his school were numerous. Through the process of inheriting and passing on this art over nearly one hundred years, his disciples, grand-disciples, great-grand-disciples, and even great-great-grand-disciples have spread Cheng School Gao Style Baguazhang broadly, not only throughout our ancestral China but also extensively to inheritors overseas. Now, according to the author's knowledge, I solemnly record the fellow practitioners of Master Gao's branch at home and abroad:

Since the founding of the Cheng School Gao Style Baguazhang Research Association in 2006, branch chapters have been established one after another in Ji'nan, Binzhou, Dongying, Wuji, Jinxiang, and even Tianjin Wuqing. The main inheritors of Liu Fengcai's line of Cheng School Gao Style Baguazhang in Shandong Province include: Li Cang, Liu Gang, and Liu Anxiang (Ji'nan City); Shi Jitao, Xiao Jun, and Gao Guoyou (Binzhou City); Liu Changzai (Wuji County); Chen Demin (Yangxin County); and Pi Shuqiang (Jinxiang County). After returning to his hometown in retirement, Lian Zhaolong, a disciple from Liu Fengcai's early years in Tianjin, has in his later years dedicated himself to instructing disciples and transmitting this art, and his students are numerous. Li Yongfu, Jiang Xiafang, Du Zhigang, Li Shaolu, and Huang Guoqing are all well-known and important inheritors of Cheng School Gao Style Baguazhang in Dongying City, Guangrao County. The contact for the Tianjin Wuqing chapter is Gao Haihua.

Wu Huishan was one of the earliest disciples of Master Gao when he was teaching in his hometown in Shandong. He primarily taught people in Shandong, but his son, Wu Jinyuan, who also received instruction from Master Gao in Tianjin, later resided in Taiwan and formerly taught Baguazhang in Xinzhu. His well-known inheritors include Wu Guozheng (Wu Jinyuan's son) and Liu Bangzhuang. They are currently still in Taiwan and dedicated to maintaining the lineage and promoting the Baguazhang taught by Gao Yisheng.

Zhang Junfeng was a direct disciple of Master Gao in Tianjin and was fairly close with Liu Fengcai. In 1948 he first moved to Taiwan for business, and later gave up business for martial arts, taking up teaching boxing as his profession. In Taiwan he established the Shandong Yizong Guoshu Academy and publicly accepted students; his disciples were numerous, becoming well-known in the region. Because no one in Taiwan had seen Baguazhang at that time, distinguished locals inscribed a plaque calling him "Taiwan's Originating Yizong." Due to history, the two sides of the strait were separated for many years, and his disciples had little contact with the mainland. Based on written materials we have learned that Zhang Junfeng had forty-one main inheritors spread widely across the island, including Chen Ronggou, Huang Ahe, Xiao Muquan, Yang Tianshui, Hong Yiwen, Guo Endian, Hong Yimian, and Hong Yixiang. We also know that Hong Yimian once taught Baguazhang in the United States, while Hong Yixiang founded the Tang Shou Tao Association, and his disciples were numerous.

Zhang Junfeng's wife, Zhang Baomei, formerly maintained the Yizong Guoshu Academy. Zhang Junfeng's well-known grand-student Pan Yue gave up business for martial arts and has researched Cheng School Gao Style Baguazhang with great devotion. His research has produced accomplishment, and his study has gained achievement; he is one of the important contemporary inheritors of Cheng School Gao Style Baguazhang in Taiwan.

He Kecai was also a direct disciple of Master Gao in Tianjin. Shortly after the start of the Second Sino-Japanese War, he left Tianjin, and later in Hong Kong founded the Baguazhang Health-Building Society, teaching his art and accepting students; his disciples were numerous. Today, his well-known disciples Deng Changcheng and Lei Rulin have established the Hong Kong International Baguazhang Association. Additionally, his well-known disciple Wu Weiming has inherited his teaching business and maintains the Baguazhang Health-Building Society Incorporated. These two societies, although each has their own viewpoint, take equally as their mission the practice, research, transmission, and promotion of the Baguazhang taught by Master Gao, and they have all come to Tianjin at some point to exchange this art.

Yu Yixian was also a direct disciple of Master Gao in Tianjin who once taught Baguazhang in the United States. His well-known inheritor Huang Yaozhen maintains the Y. C. Wong Kung Fu Studio and teaches Baguazhang in California. The author once traveled to the United States and inquired after him but did not meet him.

Li Zhuangfei was also a direct disciple of Master Gao, and it is known he also once taught Baguazhang in the United States. His well-known inheritor is Wu Min'an. Sadly, we have not yet had contact with him.

Furthermore, those of Gao Yisheng's direct disciples, grand-disciples, and great-grand-disciples who have successively transmitted their art over seas are not few, and overseas inheritors are even more numerous. According to an incomplete reckoning, currently there are inheritors in Taiwan, Japan, the United States, France, and Italy. As an example, Pan Yue of the Yizong Yue Internal Arts Research Association, Liu Zhen, and Pan Yue's disciple Zhang Shibo have come to Tianjin many times to exchange their art and research Cheng School Gao Style Baguazhang.

As of October 2004, Tsujita Noboru and Tsujimoto Saburomaru, the president and secretary of the Hanshin Taijiquan Enthusiast Club in Japan, have already led eleven research groups to Tianjin. With the great support of the City of Tianjin Foreign Friendship Association and the Tianjin Martial Arts Association, Wang Shusheng, Liu Shuhang, Ge Guoliang, and Li Xueyi attended their visits and meticulously and systematically guided their members in their study and research of Cheng School Gao Style Baguazhang. In 1996 the Baguazhang Committee of the Tianjin Martial Arts Association, the Tianjin Office of the International Baguazhang

Friendship Association, and the Cheng School Gao Style Baguazhang Association all recognized Tsujita Noboru, Tsujimoto Saburomaru, Okuda Ryoichi, Ikeda Ruriko, Azuma Miharu, Gujyo Naoko, and Kato Chie as authentic inheritors of Cheng School Gao Style Baguazhang in Japan.

As another example, since 1991 the founder of the North American Tang Shou Tao Association, Vincent Black, has organized trips to Tianjin for association members and enthusiasts such as Kim Black, David Nicoletti, Miranda Warburton, Gail Derin, Peter Davis, John Tesi, Neil Clark, Steve Jax, Harmony Wagner, Ethan Murchie, Gregory Steerman, Jennifer Minor, Marc Melton, Jason Redinbo, Brandy Peterson, Ashton Wolfswinkel, John Groschwitz, Naoko Koike, Sylas Navar, Sean Orlando, Shawn Smolinski, Adrianna Gonzalez, and Josh Scheider to learn, research, and exchange Cheng School Gao Style Baguazhang. Wang Shusheng, Liu Shuhang, and others organized numerous exchange activities in Tianjin, and Liu Shuhang and others have frequently accepted Vincent Black's invitations to come to the United States and Thailand to teach and research. In 2003, Liu Shuhang, Ge Guoliang, and Li Xueyi toured the United States, teaching at North American Tang Shou Tao Association schools, and during this trip recognized the North American Tang Shou Tao Association as the official representative body of Liu Fengcai's Gao Style Baguazhang in North America. In 2011, Liu Shuhang requested that Vincent Black undertake the translation into English and publishing of the 2010 third edition of the *Cheng School Gao Style Baguazhang Manual*. At the same time, Vincent Black recommended several core members of the North American Tang Shou Tao Association to be taken as Liu Shuhang's direct disciples. In 2012, Liu Shuhang made his sixth trip to the United States, visiting the association headquarters in Tucson, and on May 5 solemnly performed his first discipleship ceremony outside China. The event was attended by Vincent Black as recommending master, Gao Jinhua as witness and master of ceremonies, and many honored guests and association members from across the United States and Canada. Fourteen disciples from the United States, Canada, and Japan—many of whom have a decade or more of training in Baguazhang and have traveled to China to study multiple times—were accepted, according to the Chinese tradition of kowtowing and exchanging certificates, as Liu Shuhang's direct inner-chamber disciples and sixth-generation (Qiang) inheritors of Cheng School Gao Style Baguazhang.

Cheng School Gao Style Baguazhang recognizes Dong Haichuan as the Founding Master, and its origin and transmission from teacher to student is as in the following charts, which list only representatives known to the authors:

Cheng School Gao Style Baguazhang Origin and Transmission Chart

Liu Qilan (Xingyiquan)

Dong Haichuan (first generation—Hai)

Li Cunyi

Cheng Tinghua (second generation—Fu)

Song Yiren—Family-Style Red Boxing

Zhou Yuxiang

Gao Yisheng (third generation—Shou)

Fourth Generation—Shan

Gao Fengming Wu Huishan Wu Hongshan Wu Xiudong Wu Chongwen Qiu Fengpei Guan Yunfa Gao Wencai Zhang Yufeng
An Jihai Li Yunzhang Zhang Junfeng Xu Mingqiao **Liu Fengcai** Qu Kezhang Yan Peilin Sun Zhenshan Wu Mengxia
He Kecai Zhao Baichuan Du Shaotang Li Zijin Yu Yixian Li Zhuangfei Liu Boyong

Fifth Generation—Yong

Liu Shaochen Lian Zhaolong Hao Runhua Li Zhongfang Chen Lianfa Liu Qingshan Liu Jitang Li Zhongxun Han Fengrui
Gao Shuqing Dong Jiegao Zhu Xiliang Wang Fuling Yang Zhisheng **Wang Shusheng** Gao Jinhua Sun Fude Chen Baozhang
Su Qingsheng Liu Jianying Xu Li Liu Gang Liu Anxiang Feng Huiyu Pi Shuqiang Li Cang Shi Jitao Xiao Jun
Gao Guoyou Sun Shijun Liu Changzai Chen Demin Zhang Liqing Gong Yufa Sun Shusen Vincent Black[4] **Liu Shuhang**

Sixth Generation—Qiang

Ge Shuxian Ge Shuzhen Liu Wenkun Tang Yao Qi Yongping Mu Yingchen Hao Baofa Feng Yuejie Li Hongsheng
Zhao Wenguang Jia Qijiang Ge Guoliang Li Xueyi Liu Jinwang Tian Qingping Zhao Junde Zhang Jinhe Li Xuemin
Li Baoyi Fu Baochang Zhang Li'an Zhu Yuncheng Pan Yue Yu Jiajian Yu Jiaquan Ren Jianming Liu Huizhong
Chen Weiguo Xie Quanyou

Bloodlines and Baguazhang Lineage Chart
of the Gao and Liu Families

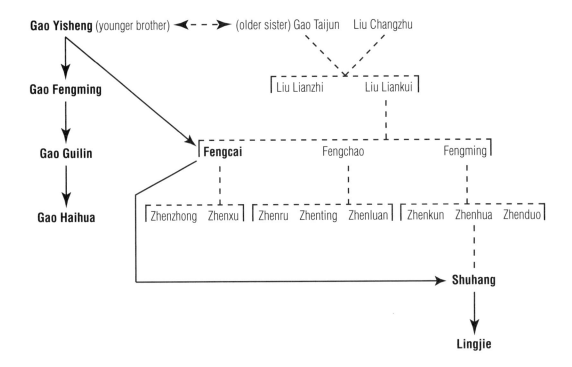

According to the records of the Liu-Clan Family Lineage Registry, Liu Changzhu was a 15th-generation ancestor of the Shandong Liu Clan Friendship Hall. In terms of blood relations, Gao Yisheng, Liu Fengcai, and Liu Shuhang represent five generations. When discussing Baguazhang relationships, Gao Yisheng, Liu Fengcai, and Liu Shuhang represent three generations. None of Liu Fengcai's immediate family— uncle, father, or two brothers—studied Baguazhang. Of Liu Fengcai's eight sons and nephews, only Liu Zhenhua was taken with him to Tianjin to make a living, where he remained; the other sons and nephews were not in Tianjin. Moreover, none of Liu Fengcai's eight sons and nephews studied martial arts, making Liu Shuhang the only family-taught disciple of Liu Fengcai.

Baguazhang Lineage Chart of the Gao and Liu Families

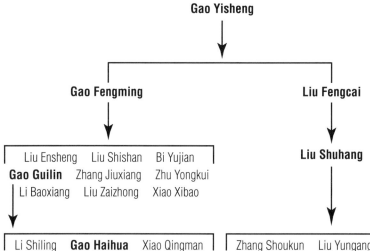

Gao Yisheng

Gao Fengming

Liu Fengcai

Liu Ensheng   Liu Shishan   Bi Yujian
Gao Guilin   Zhang Jiuxiang   Zhu Yongkui
Li Baoxiang   Liu Zaizhong   Xiao Xibao

Liu Shuhang

Li Shiling   **Gao Haihua**   Xiao Qingman

Zhang Shoukun   Liu Yungang   Zhang Yang   **Liu Lingjie**
Wang Xu   Liu Jianxin   Chen Tao   Wang Bin   Wang Gang
Liu Chunyuan   Yao Xiangkui   Lan Guangwei   Ou Weilin
Zhang Hualong   Su Mingchao   Yue Peng   Ma Jian
Gao Ming   Meng Xiangguo   Wang Qiang   Li Yan   Liu Xintian
Shi Chuanshi   Guo Jinming   Ren Jiwei   Wang Shiping
Miranda Warburton   David Nicoletti   Neil Clark
Gregory Steerman   Naoko Koike   Ethan Murchie
Jennifer Minor   John Groschwitz   Harmony Wagner
Sean Orlando   Benjamin Scharfenberger   Sylas Navar
Jarrod Lash   Eli Schwartz-Gralla
Ren Dongxiao   Chen Anji

The Naming and Meaning of Baguazhang

Baguazhang is one of the traditional styles of Chinese martial arts. It uses *Yijing* theory to explain boxing theory and borrows the Eight Trigrams for its name. It is a type of internal boxing art combining offensive and defensive fighting methods with Daoyin life-cultivating methods while turning-the-circle walking and spinning. It utilizes this unique walking and turning of the circle as its foundational movement form, and further uses the palm as a fist; because of this it is called Eight Trigram Palm, or Baguazhang.

Yijing theory comes from the *Yijing,* or *Book of Changes.* This book contains the theory, laid out by the ancient sages of China, regarding the universal evolution of the qi of yin and yang in the Eight Trigrams. This so-called *Yijing* theory is in fact the principles of the changes of yin and yang in the Eight Trigrams. The Eight Trigrams represent roundedness; "change" represents transformation; and "principles" represent regular patterns. Owing to this, one can say that Baguazhang is a martial style that takes as the foundation of its theory the changes of yin and yang within the trigrams—mutually producing and mutually controlling with opposites unified; substantial and insubstantial mutually aiding while spinning, advancing, and retreating—which, through the exercise of turning-the-circle walking and spinning, investigates the regular patterns of changes in yin and yang and movement and stillness within the human body. Using *Yijing* theory to explain boxing theory and using boxing postures to express *Yijing* theory is Baguazhang's unique inherent cultural quality.

The Eight Trigrams are the foundation of the *Yijing* and are pictorial forms comprised of yin lines (--) and yang lines (—). The eight trigram diagrams include the Fu Xi Pre-Heaven Bagua Diagram, the Sixty-Four Hexagrams Diagram, and the King Wen Bagua Diagram. The Bagua Diagrams used in Baguazhang contain the Taiji symbol in its middle, which arises from the precept that "Change contains Taiji, which gives rise to the Two Principles. The Two Principles give rise to the Four Images, and the Four Images give rise to the Eight Trigrams." The marks of the Bagua Diagram forms are called lines; those with a broken middle (--) represent

42

a yin line, while those that are connected and unbroken (—) represent
a yang line. Each set of three marks combined are called a trigram, and
altogether there are eight groupings, representing the Eight Trigrams. The
Qian trigram (☰) is called "Qian three connected." The Kun trigram (☷)
is called "Kun six broken." The Li trigram (☲) is called "Li middle empty."
The Kan trigram (☵) is called "Kan middle full." The Zhen trigram (☳)
is called "Zhen upturned cup." The Gen trigram (☶) is called "Gen overturned bowl." The Xun trigram (☴) is called "Xun lower broken." The Dui
trigram (☱) is called "Dui upper missing." When all possible sets of two
trigrams are stacked together, they form the Sixty-Four Hexagrams, which
evolve out of the 384 lines. One could say they represent generation without rest, and change that is inexhaustible. The Eight Trigrams represent
the eight directions and are also called the Eight Gates or Eight Palaces.

The *Yijing* is an important source of traditional culture for Chinese
people. It is one of the oldest classical writings in China and, according
to Bagua yin-yang theory, originated 6,500 years ago in the age of Fu
Xi. From antiquity until the present, the *Yijing* has been esteemed and
respected as the "first among all classics." Within the *Yijing*, the theory
of universal evolution of the qi of yin and yang in the Eight Trigrams
contains profound social science and natural science principles that have
consanguineous relationships with modern science. The ancients said that
the *Yijing* is expansive and exhaustive in its uses. It embraces the ten thousand images. At its most advanced, it is the study of the sages external-
ized; at its most base, it is the multitudinous images of all things. Nothing
exists that can be outside its bounds. Truly, one can say it is the great
way of heaven and earth, and the great way of humanity. This profound
Yijing theory has direct significance for the formation and development
of Baguazhang martial culture.

The explanation and meaning of the Eight Trigrams within the *Yijing*
reveal dialectical rules for the movements of human life and establish a
theoretical basis for the principles and methods of Baguazhang, such as
"begin in the place of yin and yang; advance in the boundaries of yin
and yang; change in the space between yin and yang," "train the internal

to foster the root, mutually cultivating nature and life," and "in fighting and struggle, use change to obtain victory." The study and practice of Baguazhang follows the same principles as cultivating and establishing oneself, which also requires hard and soft, movement and stillness.

1. Qian ($\equiv$) is heaven. Baguazhang's head-pressing skill is heaven; adopt its meaning of vigor and purity.
2. Kun ($\equiv\equiv$) is earth. Baguazhang's stepping method is earth; adopt its meaning of tranquility and supporting all things.

The *Yijing* text for the Qian hexagram says it is "the beginning, development, success, and completion of all things." The image says "heaven's movement is eternal; the gentleman should be self-improving without cease." The three lines of the Qian trigram are all yang, and thus it is the image of pure yang and has the meaning of "hard," "firm," and "unyielding." It could be called "complete hardness." Qian is heaven; the way of heaven is united qi flowing and moving, circulating without endpoints, traveling endlessly. Baguazhang's turning-the-circle walking and spinning adopts the way of heaven, moving eternally without limits. The way of heaven moves with complete hardness and complete yang, and there is nothing that can harm it. Those who practice boxing first must develop high martial virtue, be principled without question, and train until they are a vessel of completely expansive and completely hard vast qi, so the hundred evils cannot invade. Those who practice boxing must maintain and persevere, tenacious and unyielding, modeling the movement of heaven, eternally self-improving without cease. Regarding the way of heaven, in spring the ten-thousand things sprout forth; this is called "beginning." In summer the ten-thousand things flourish; this is called "development." In fall the ten-thousand things become full; this is called "success." In winter the ten-thousand things return to hibernation; this is called "completion." Spring, summer, fall, and winter cycle and begin again without exhaustion. The way of boxing is the same: when two people exchange techniques, and both parties first face off and show intention, it is called "beginning." Although the form has not been exhibited externally, the intention has already sprouted forth.

Obtaining the advantage or position and initiating an attack is called "development." Hard qi coalescing into force, issued fiercely, and hitting its mark is called "success." The opponent losing the advantage and being defeated, concluding the first round, is called "completion." The end of the first round is the beginning of the second round, cycling and beginning again like the movements of heaven, circulating without end. These are the rules according to which matters develop and change, and in which all matters show similarity. One must only flow with this and not resist it. The way of heaven is thus, and the boxing arts are also thus.

The *Yijing* text for the Kun hexagram says it is "beneficial like the loyalty of a mare." The image says "the earth's abundance is Kun; the gentleman should broaden his virtue to support all things." The three lines of the Kun trigram are all yin, and thus it is the image of pure yin and has the meaning of "soft" and "following." In terms of the way of people, "soft and following" is not hesitation but rather the ability to empty one's heart in tolerance. To possess tolerance is greatness, like the greatness of the earth's support for all things. There is nothing that is not shown tolerance, and nothing that is not supported. Baguazhang is also like this. When crossing hands with someone, one must also empty the heart and hold back; whether the opponent truly attacks or makes a feint, is fierce or crafty, one must always be able to follow what is natural—absorbing, yielding, being soft, dissolving, following, and then striking. This is the great method of "soft in changing and hard in striking, using soft and supple to overcome hard and strong." The *Yijing* says "hard with the ability to be soft is the method of heaven." Following can produce strength, and softness can dissolve hardness. Great softness is not softness; soft is actually hard. This is the way of heaven, of earth, and of people. The way of training in boxing has the same principle.

Heaven and earth, yin and yang, hard and soft are unified antagonists that mutually transform and are mutually necessary. Only when Qian and Kun are combined, with Qian leading Kun and Kun following Qian, is there accord with the great way of heaven and earth. The way of Baguazhang, then, is that within hard there is soft; within soft there is hard. Use hard to lead soft, and use soft to follow hard. Hardness is the root; softness is its transformation. Hard and soft are mutually beneficial. Hard can defeat soft; soft can dissolve hard. The fingers press, the neck twists, and the head presses up to heaven. The toes grip and the feet press, treading the ground—Qian above and Kun below. Qian and Kun are fixed positions, and the internal qi circulates within the body, like boiling water changing to steam in a cauldron, bubbling and roiling. Whenever striking with a hand, lift the anus and close the buttocks, sink the shoulders and drop the elbows, join the knees, the back like a bow and the hands like arrows, the internal qi rising from Haidi,[5] uniting the strength of the entire body and filling forward, issuing outward when it reaches the palms and fingers. This is the outline of Baguazhang.

3. Li (☲) is fire. Fire governs brightness. Baguazhang adopts its meaning of the brightness of theory.
4. Kan (☵) is water. Water flows downward internally. Baguazhang adopts its meaning of developing internal qi.

The *Yijing* text for the Li hexagram says it is "beneficent and steadfast; prosperous. A husbanded cow. Auspicious." The image says "the two brightnesses arise; the great man uses continual brightness to light the four directions." Li is pairing, as the sun and moon are paired in heaven. Its image is fire, and thus has the meaning of the sun's brightness. The treasure of humanity is the brightness of self-knowledge. This is brightness internally, and also brightness externally. When thorough and penetrating internally and externally, this brightness is inexhaustible; thus it is called "continual brightness." In training boxing, one must understand the postures and also understand the theory, and then one may understand themselves and also understand others. One may understand within the body and may also understand outside the body. The Li trigram is a yin line held between two yang lines, and it is the image of emptiness within containing the ability to enlighten. Li governs the heart, and the insubstantial numen of the Li Palace is a person's spirit. If insubstantial, then numinous; if numinous, then bright. If the heart is in chaos, it must be confused. Therefore one must know the way and utilize brightness and must be skilled in cultivating brightness; only then can one be "prosperous." Only through the orderly cultivation of one's nature, like the husbanding of a cow, can one be "auspicious." Only then can one internally develop their brightness. One must study broadly and inquire cautiously, contemplate carefully and discriminate clearly, and then put this learning into practice; only then can one be without blame. Training in boxing is also like this. If one does not themselves know but can empty their heart and exert their virtue through the brightness of seeking instruction from others and the abundance of honoring others, then although one does not know, one may know. Thus auspiciousness lies in softness, obedience, and emptying the heart. If one knows only the application in training but not cultivation, is only hard and cannot be soft and obedient, only knows striking and does not know change, then in the end they must be like the fading sun: their brightness has reached its peak and must turn dark. Those who train in Baguazhang should empty their hearts and persevere, training sincerely and intensely, understanding the internal and external, the flowing and the contending, and they will be both internally and externally bright and of utmost goodness.

The image of the Kan trigram is a yang line inserted between two yin lines. The outside is insubstantial, and inside substantial. Its usage in studying boxing is that when there are multitudes of distractions, one's way and mind constantly retain correct qi that cannot be scattered. Although mingling with the ordinary scenes and dirt of the world, one is not trapped by them. In this way skill may advance, and the way can become complete.

One may say that the two trigrams Kan and Li are used in unison and are the intention within the body. Kan is water and the kidneys; Li is fire and the heart. In the image of heart and kidney, fire and water, water should ascend, and fire should descend. This is why those who excel in the way of boxing and cultivation expound most strongly on developing the qi and regulating the water and fire. The Li trigram is solid outside but empty inside; its body is hard but it utilizes softness. Its image is of fire; fire's nature is to flare upward. It governs the heart and represents

47

fire and qi. The Kan trigram is empty outside and solid inside; its body is soft but it utilizes hardness. Its image is of water; water's nature is to move downward. It governs the kidneys and represents water and essence. Those who first study boxing seek only to increase their skills, gaining several punches and a few kicks, and always their conduct is like fire— always opposing, always trying to beat others, unrestrained and without fear, like the flaring upward of fire. However, their desirous heart is like water, with a hundred wild thoughts chasing the wind that blows the waves, without end and without break, easily becoming base, moving downward like water. These two conditions are the great prohibitions of learning boxing, for they lead to a dangerous path. Only in restricting this drying fire and obstructing this desirous heart can one cause the fire to reverse its nature and have an empty heart yet emit brightness, and cause the water to return to its origin, filling the belly without danger. If the original jing does not leak out and the true water and true fire both mutually aid each other, then the Pre-Heaven qi can naturally arise. The requirements of Baguazhang are to empty the chest and fill the belly, for the internal qi to sink to the dantian, the water ascending and the fire descending, the heart and kidneys mutually interacting, the two mutually aiding each other; then the true qi will condense, and jing, qi, and shen will gradually increase. Those who are skilled in boxing must not only study the postures and seek integrated power, but more importantly must also cultivate internal skill, fully nurture internal qi, and regulate water and fire. Guiding the qi and causing the kidney water to ascend and mix with the heart, and causing the heart qi to descend to the kidneys, is the true meaning of the idea "water and fire mutually aiding; Kan and Li active" sought after by high-level Baguazhang practitioners.

5. Zhen (☳) is thunder. Thunder governs movement. Baguazhang adopts its meaning of rolling and moving.

6. Gen (☶) is a mountain. Mountain is the image of stillness. Baguazhang adopts its meaning of moving when it is time to move, stopping when it is time to stop.

The text of the Zhen hexagram says "thunder is penetrating. Thunder arrives with a frightening din; greet it with a laughing smile and silence. Thunder startles for a hundred miles; do not lose the dagger and wine cup." The image says "the gentleman uses terror and fright to cultivate and self-reflect." Zhen is thunder and has the meaning of rolling and moving. For building health, strengthening the body, and training fighting movements, Baguazhang uses worldly methods to cultivate the way. Inexhaustible unending changing techniques all arise from movement. The *Yijing* says "Movement is change." Bagua adopts "changeability" in its fighting methods; as soon as one gains the advantage or gains the position, the force is issued like the startling explosion of shaking thunder. Therefore Zhen is penetrating. Those who study boxing and cultivation should at all times internally guard the way and mind. The thunder is heard for a hundred miles but does not startle or terrorize, and one "does not lose the dagger and wine cup." Speak and smile casually, keeping calm and steady as before. As people now often say, "whenever you encounter great troubles, have calm qi." "The gentleman uses terror and fright to cultivate and self-reflect" is a warning to students of boxing not to be self-satisfied. One must not fail to recognize others and feel as if they themselves are "the first and most esteemed under heaven." One must know that this art is limitless. Beyond your world is a greater world; beyond yourself is a greater self. One should always contemplate the deficiencies in one's being. Hold the terror and fright in your mind and be self-reflective. Speculate carefully and deeply, seeking its essence. When one uses terror and fright to cultivate and self-reflect in this way, in the end there will be no terror and fright; then one has entered the true way of Baguazhang.

The text of the Gen hexagram says "stop at his back, do not strike his body; enter his residence, but do not see his family; no blame." The image says "the rolling mountains are still; the gentleman uses contemplation not to exceed his position." Gen is the mountain, and its image is stillness. "Stopping at his back" is the image of stopping at things and preventing impulses. "Do not strike his body" is to forget oneself. "Do not see his family" is to forget other things. Without self and without

49

things, the two forgotten, the mind is calm and settled. A calm mind is beneficial in developing jing, qi, and shen. "The mind should be still" is the first of the Baguazhang requirements for practice. The *Yijing* says "the transformation of movement and stillness is the image of advancing and retreating." The image says "when time to stop, then stop; when time to move, then move. In movement and stillness do not miss the timing; this way is shining and bright." Therefore Bagua adopts "changeability" as its method. Change is slow transformation; transformation is the completion of change. Between these is the space of victory, where nothing is excessive and nothing is ill-timed. Baguazhang follows the way of heaven and earth and unites with the principles of the ten thousand things, always adopting the middle path within the changes of yin and yang, movement and stillness, and motion and rest. In movement and stillness, don't lose the opportunity. If still, then not controlled by movement; if moving, then issuing the hands without revealing the form, and striking without leaving a shadow. Beating an opponent lies between intention and nonintention, and only this is high-level boxing skill. Therefore it is said, "The way is shining and bright." Baguazhang adheres to the principles of movement and stillness of Gen and Zhen, waiting for the opportunity and changing, advancing without meeting the guard or losing one's measure; retreating without scattering one's qi or losing one's integrity; hard without being harmed by hardness; soft without being restrained by softness; the center stable, unmoved by the opponent's posture. Thus we use change as the middle way, with methods for advancing and retreating, and having a sequence for movement and stillness. Baguazhang's way of fighting excels through this.

7. Xun (☴) is the wind. It is the image of following and liveliness. Baguazhang adopts its meaning of following and being clever.
8. Dui (☱) is a marsh. It is the image of seeping water. Baguazhang adopts its sentiments of exchanging and collecting.

The image of Xun is wind. The nature of wind is soft and obedient yet active, as well as continuous and without pause. It travels everywhere under heaven: there is nowhere it does not reach, and there is nothing it does not caress. In Baguazhang usage, adopting this establishes the principle of "using the wind and following the wind; not hurried and not slow; hard and soft united; changing according to the situation, lively in application; picking up the hands when they appear, drilling in when there is an opening." The lines of the Xun trigram are a yang line at the top, a yang line in the middle, and a yin line at the bottom. This is softness lodged beneath hardness, the image of softness following hard yang, and the meaning of how in movement the ten thousand things must follow the rules of the circulation of heaven and earth. In Baguazhang this is following what is natural in response. For instance, in the Pre-Heaven Palms it is required to "seek following amid opposition" while the Post-Heaven Palms emphasize "in following seek subtlety." Both do not stray from the word *following.* In adhering to the following of Xun, one is lively.

The text of the Dui hexagram says it is "prosperous; beneficent and steadfast." The image says "the connected marsh is full; the gentleman uses friends to discuss and study." The lines of the Dui trigram are two yang lines below and one yin line above. It is empty outside but full inside. When training Baguazhang and testing hands with friends, one should be internally hard but externally soft. Internally there is an abundance, but externally it seems as if there is a deficiency. This is the attitude of presenting courtesy and not being strong-willed and obstinate. Dui adopts the image of the marsh whose seeping waters reach the ten thousand things. The image of the happy completion of the ten thousand things, the sentiment of the Dui marsh is like true and good friends meeting. In Baguazhang the holding of the knees, the closing of the arms and hands, the joining of the crotch and hips, and the internal and external three harmonies all contain this sentiment of Dui. Dui is happiness. This trigram means happiness in following the way. The way of Baguazhang is the study of nature and life, internal and external cultivated together, using *Yijing* theory to explain boxing theory. Its theory is the deepest, its skill the most perfect. In studying martial arts, one should be upright and not hypocritical. In attending people and drawing near animals, one should be gentle and not violent, have an ultimate skill in the heart, but not be forceful or insulting. All that one does and strives for should follow heaven and respond to people; then one may obtain the "happiness" and "beneficence and steadfastness" of boxing. Training in boxing, one must adhere to the ways of Xun and Dui, know their principles, understand their postures, cultivate their morality, train their skills, and know that yin and yang have a sequence. Movement and stillness must be clearly divided. Xun and Dui are harmony and following, hardness and softness used together. In time, the skill will naturally form.

Baguazhang uses *Yijing* theory to explain boxing theory; its forms are simple but their meaning broad, and their content is extremely rich. To summarize its essence, Baguazhang is a school of scientific study that uses *Yijing* theory as a theoretical foundation and researches movements that unite health-building with combat. During the process of building the body with the practice of Baguazhang, one's skills and power are increased, causing the health of the body and fighting ability to improve simultaneously. When continued, this will develop the body's latent abilities. It could be called a field of study in which body, usage, and art are completely integrated. In discussing the body, the essence of Baguazhang's health-building is in the requirements for practice and training methods. In adopting the principles of the formation of the ten thousand things, and the sequence of their growth and development, then—using this scientifically—one can receive the effects of building the body and removing illness, benefiting long life and lengthening the life span. In discussing its usage, the essence of Baguazhang's combat skill is in organizing and refining the essential fighting movements of every part of the body, and combining them with scientific rules through training, causing them to have order and not to be chaotic, thus raising one's abilities in fighting. In discussing its art, Baguazhang's cultural and artistic essence is in the fact that Baguazhang is an erudite martial endeavor, with theory incorporating and uniting the most outstanding traditional culture of the Chinese people. Its movement models are beautiful and pleasing to watch—exemplifying yin and yang turning and changing in rhythm, hard and soft uniting, integrated and rational—and can give practitioners feelings of beauty and power within themselves. Baguazhang can cause practitioners to feel the quintessence of Chinese traditional culture within their bodies while, through performance, also giving observers an appreciation of artistic beauty.

Baguazhang uses palm methods as analogies to trigram images, and also borrows the forms and images of the trigrams to describe parts of the body and represent technical requirements. As an example, in Cheng School Gao Style Baguazhang's Form Boxing, the Qian trigram is heaven and the form name is Lion Waves, taking as its image the lion. The Kan trigram is water and the form name is Snake Wraps, taking as its image the snake. The Gen trigram is a mountain and the form name is Tiger Crouches, taking as its image the tiger. The Zhen trigram is thunder and the form name is Dragon Form, taking as its image the dragon. The Xun trigram is wind and the form name is Swallow Overturns, taking as its image the swallow. The Li trigram is fire and the form name is Eagle Tears, taking as its image the eagle. The Kun trigram is earth and the form name is Bear Yanks, taking as its image the bear. The Dui trigram is marsh and the form name is Monkey Image, taking as its image the monkey. Similarly, like the Baguazhang skill method requirements, the head is Qian, taking the idea that Qian is above, evoking the image of pushing and suspension. The lower limbs are Kun, taking the idea that Kun is below, and the form is like six broken segments, taking the image of the three segments—hip, knee, and foot—of both legs, requiring the two feet to follow the intention, mud-wading as they step, giving rise to the postures, in the way that Kun follows Qian and gives rise to the ten thousand things. The lower abdomen is Kan. The form of the Kan trigram (☵) is full in the middle, taking the image of the center being substantial and requiring the abdomen to be full and enriched. The chest is Li, taking the image of the Li trigram (☲), empty in the middle, requiring the chest to be empty and unobstructed. The buttocks are Zhen, taking the image of the Zhen trigram (☳), where above is empty and below is solid, requiring the buttocks to sink and glide rounded. The back and neck are Gen, taking the image of the Gen trigram (☶), where the top is solid and the bottom is empty, requiring the neck to lift vertically and the shoulders to relax and hook inward, presenting the back as tight and rounded. The two feet are Xun, taking the image of the Xun trigram (☴), where there is wind beneath the feet, requiring the two feet to advance and retreat rapidly like the wind. The two shoulders are Dui, taking the image of the form of the Dui trigram (☱), where above is empty and below is full, requiring the two shoulders to relax and sink downward. Baguazhang also borrows the complete numerology of the Eight Trigrams, utilizing it to standardize the progression and systematization of fighting techniques. For example, Cheng School Gao Style Baguazhang uses the Eight Big Palms to represent the number of the trigrams, the Sixty-Four Post-Heaven Palms as an analogy for the sixty-four hexagrams, and the 384 movements of the Dismantling Palms as analogous to the 384 lines of the hexagrams.

Baguazhang uses *Yijing* theory to explain boxing theory, to standardize boxing skills, and as a complete theoretical basis for this art. *Yijing* theory is the explanation within the *Book of Changes* regarding the pictorial forms and implied meanings of the Eight Trigrams, and it includes three basic meanings of the character *yi* (易): "simple," "change," and "unchanging." As Zheng Xuan said in his *Praise of the Changes:* "Yi is one character with three meanings. Simple is first. Change is second. Unchanging is third."

Firstly, *Yijing* theory recognizes that "easy is easy to know; simple is easy to follow." The "Commentary on the Appended Phrases" says that the simpler a theory is, the easier it is to clearly understand. The simpler a method is, the easier it is to put into practice. This is the meaning of "simple." The introduction to Zhu Xi's *Original Meaning of the Zhou Changes* says "Change is the way of yin and yang." One yin and one yang is called change. Although yin and yang are simple, they can give rise to the ten thousand things and ten thousand images. Although the yin line (- -) and yang line (—) are simple, they can arrange and evolve into endless hexagram forms and images. Baguazhang models itself on this theory of simplicity, using turning-the-circle walking and spinning as the basic movement form. Turning left is yang, turning right is yin, and through this turning both left and right evolve the Eight Big Palms and every type of posture, including the Sixty-Four Palms and the 384 applications. This is the most evident characteristic of Baguazhang and its foundational movement that separates it from other boxing arts; therefore Baguazhang practitioners say "one yin and one yang is boxing."

Secondly, *Yijing* theory states that "birth upon birth is called change." This means that heaven, earth, and the ten thousand things and ten thousand images are in the midst of ceaselessly moving and transforming. This is the meaning of change. The change of yin and yang is the core of Eight Trigram theory, and also the most important foundational theory in Baguazhang. The *Yijing* lists many types of change between yin and yang, such as "hard and soft brush one another," "the Eight Trigrams sway together," "hard and soft push against each other and give rise to change," "one closed and one open is called change," "transforming and reducing is called change," and "change is the image of advancing and retreating." This recognizes that change is penetrating and creative. Baguazhang models itself on this mutual root of yin and yang and the idea of their changing growth and decline. The changes of yin and yang and offensive and defensive postures while turning-the-circle walking and spinning are blended into one body, the feet treading the Eight Trigrams with advancing, retreating, and coiling; the hand movements and palm skills extending and retracting, hard and soft; the body overturning and spinning with striking and receiving, opening and closing, like the movement of the heavens, ceaseless and ever-renewing, transforming hard to soft, transporting soft to hard, the postures unbroken and the movements one breath. When applying this to an opponent, it is even more crucial that hard and soft supplement each other, and yin and yang transform. Because pure yang is extreme hardness, it is too stiff and thus easily broken. Because pure yin is extreme softness, it is too supple and thus easily disintegrated. Only when yin and yang are combined and hardness and softness are mutually aiding and supplementing, stressing the importance of change, can one dissolve with softness but strike with hardness, arriving at the level of "hard before the opponent's force" (smothering the opponent's force and striking), "soft riding after his force" (borrowing the opponent's force and then striking). Only then can you encircle the enemy, avoiding the substantial and striking the insubstantial, avoiding the direct and striking the flanks, using movement to control nonmotion, using fast movement to control slow movement. Altogether, Baguazhang models itself on the idea of change and emphasizes that the method to control victory when facing an opponent lies in changing movement, forming the overall fighting principle of "using the circular as a method, and using change as the pivot."

Lastly, *Yijing* theory holds that movement and stillness are constant. This says that the changes of heaven and earth and the ten thousand things and ten thousand images all follow set rules in circulating endlessly. The rules are unchanging. This is the meaning of "unchanging"—like the movements of the heavenly bodies, the sun and moon waning and waxing, the seasons changing from winter to summer, the ten thousand things growing old and dying and being reborn anew. The rules of the cycles of nature will not change. Baguazhang adopts this idea of the unchanging principles of movement, and it forms unchanging rules of movement and techniques as postural requirements—such as the head presses up and the shoulders close; the body is upright; the chest is hollow and the belly full; the arms twist and the feet tread—as well as the requirements for techniques—such as Koubu and Baibu to walk and turn, the feet are like wading in mud—and requirements for energetic qualities, such as rolling, drilling, thrusting, and wrapping. These are all unchanging principles that must be followed in the practice of Baguazhang.

The introduction to Zhu Xi's *Original Meaning of the Zhou Changes* says: "the Pre-Heaven creates and initiates entities; the Post-Heaven sets in motion and completes their actions." The sixty-four hexagrams and 384 lines all follow the principles of life and are simply the way of change. Thus change is the way of yin and yang. The trigrams are the embodiment of yin and yang; the lines are the movement of yin and yang. The sages of

Baguazhang used *Yijing* theory to explain boxing theory, boxing theory to adopt *Yijing* theory, adopting the circle as the method and change as the constant. "If near, use the whole body; if far, use all things." According to the way of the changes of yin and yang, they took fighting techniques, health-building, and Daoyin and combined them while turning-the-circle walking and spinning. They adopted the images of the Eight Trigrams of the *Yijing* to name and create a boxing art. Baguazhang truly is a miraculous skill for the ages.

"If near, use the whole body" means the head, which is Qian; the abdomen, which is Kun; the feet, which are Zhen; the buttocks, which are Xun; the ears, which are Kan; the eyes, which are Li; the hands, which are Gen; and the mouth, which is Dui. Inside the body, the brain is Qian, the spleen is Kun, the kidneys are Kan, the heart is Li, the lungs are Dui, the liver is Zhen, the small intestine is Xun, the large intestine is Gen. This is the enumeration of the Pre-Heaven. If discussing the whole body, the lower abdomen is Wuji, the navel is Taiji, the buttocks are the two principles, the two arms and two legs are the four images. The two arms and two legs all have two sections, which are the Eight Trigrams. The thumbs and big toes of both hands and feet all have two sections, altogether eight sections; the three joints of the remaining sixteen fingers and toes together have forty-eight sections. The two arms and two legs have eight sections; adding to this the eight sections of the thumbs and big toes as well as the forty-eight sections of the remaining fingers altogether makes sixty-four sections. This is the numerology of the Post-Heaven. The principle of "if far, use all things" is that Qian is lion, Kan is snake, Gen is tiger, Zhen is dragon, Xun is swallow, Li is eagle, Kun is bear, Dui is monkey. The sages used the images of the Eight Trigrams in the body and the fighting movements of every type of animal, and in form and image used the Eight Trigrams to adopt an image and name, creating Baguazhang. As Sun Lutang said, Baguazhang "begins with Wuji and ends with the Eight Trigrams. In the middle it is divided into the two principles and the four images, and it contains Pre-Heaven and Post-Heaven, contracting power and following action, with the fixed and changing interwoven, and there is nothing it does not wholly possess. Those who know the changes can use it to great exquisiteness." Because of this, Baguazhang is also called a type of boxing art that "uses the body of the Eight Trigrams; follows the principles of the Eight Trigrams; trains the palms of the Eight Trigrams; and strengthens the substance of the Eight Trigrams."

The complete name for the Baguazhang taught by Gao Yisheng is Bagua Twisting-Body Connected Palm. The Eight Trigrams are positions. The Pre-Heaven palms follow the Pre-Heaven Bagua diagram in taking their names; the Post-Heaven Palms follow the Post-Heaven sixty-four hexagram diagram is taking their names. "Twisting-Body" is the body method and stepping method. The body method of Pre-Heaven Baguazhang takes softness as its focus, with steps like wading in mud. "Connected" means the postures connected one link after another. The Pre-Heaven palms use turning palm as the beginning and changing palm as the mother, creating eight paths of body-overturning Eight Big Palms. Each palm creates eight techniques that combined are the Post-Heaven Sixty-Four Palms. Each posture of the Post-Heaven Palms creates six techniques, altogether 384 techniques to accord with the 384 hexagram lines. In this way, palm after palm is connected and collected to form a boxing style. "Palm" means the hand methods. Baguazhang uses the palm as the primary focus, using the palm to represent the fist, with the intention of "the five fingers spreading open like a dragon's claw, the qi penetrating *Laogong* and reaching the tips of the fingers."

Gao Yisheng inherited the basic practice methods and basic palm posture (Dragon Claw Palm) of the Baguazhang taught by Cheng Tin-gua in Beijing, and he called this the Pre-Heaven Eight Big Palms. In addition, he also collected every type of free-fighting technique and solo exercise posture of Cheng School Baguazhang while adopting the Post-Heaven Baguazhang practice methods of Song Yiren from Shandong and, with this foundation and after decades of research and actual combat, undertook synthesis, organization, and creation, gradually forming his own distinctive practice forms and methods: Cheng School Gao Style Baguazhang. He caused the Bagua Pre-Heaven Palms and Post-Heaven

Palms to be divided and practiced separately, and took strengthening the tendons and bones and guarding the body as the main focus. He also combined health-building and fighting into one framework, with structure and application fully realized, internal and external cultivated together, until it possessed a rather strong health-building, self-defense, self-protection, and fighting value. Accordingly, it even more completely embodied the meaning of the Baguazhang saying "the feet tread the Eight Trigrams, combining yin and yang, moving Pre-Heaven qi, and transforming Post-Heaven strength."

In summary, Cheng School Gao Style Baguazhang formed its own system, beginning according to the Pre-Heaven Bagua diagram (fig. 0.2), where Wuji gives rise to Taiji, Taiji creates the two principles, the two principles create the four images, the four images create the five elements, the five elements create the six harmonies, the six harmonies create the seven stars, and the seven stars create the Eight Trigrams. This is Baguazhang's core, the Pre-Heaven Eight Big Palms. Further, following the Post-Heaven Bagua diagram (fig. 0.4), each trigram creates eight hexagrams—the eight palms giving rise to the Sixty-Four Palms. This is the application of this art, the Post-Heaven Sixty-Four Palms. Still further, adopting the Bagua's "transformation of yin and yang," where movement in its extreme becomes stillness and stillness in its extreme becomes movement, and uniting the way of yin and yang in Bagua with the five-element creative and destructive principles, each of the Sixty Four Palms can be divided into six applications, with 384 applications altogether. These are the transformations of the Post-Heaven Palms. Taking the idea that the Eight Trigrams are "variable without exhaustion," each posture of the 384 hands of Baguazhang can be utilized and practiced in any order one likes, the hands and eyes following each other, the body and feet connected, advancing and retreating with method, issuing the hands in application but the applications without fixed postures, coming and going unpredictably. Transformation without exhaustion, an art without limits—these are the general outlines of Baguazhang.

Basic Special Characteristics of Cheng School Gao Style Baguazhang

Baguazhang's primary special characteristics, which differentiate it from other types of boxing, manifest in five areas:

First, turning the circle. Most boxing arts move along straight or oblique lines. Only Baguazhang utilizes the unique Koubu and Baibu[6] steps to turn and walk the circle as a basic movement form, turning and walking the circle according to the four cardinal and four intercardinal points of the Eight Trigrams. It is said that Master Dong Haichuan once summarized turning the circle by saying: "The body is like the movements of a swimming dragon, a wild goose ascending the emptiness, a tiger crashing, a turtle diving, or a snake slithering, turning the circle at will in connected and united postures, angled or crossing, advancing or retreating while talking and laughing." This is the most evident special characteristic that differentiates Baguazhang from other types of boxing.

Second, use of the palm. Most other boxing styles primarily use the fist, as in Taijiquan, Xingyiquan, or Shaolinquan. Baguazhang primarily utilizes the palm, using the palm in place of the fist.

Third, the Mud-Wading Step. Most other boxing styles use advancing and retreating, striding and leaping as primary techniques. Only Baguazhang uses Koubu, Baibu, and Mud-Wading Step as its primary methods.

Fourth, left and right match. Each application and each posture in Baguazhang, if practiced on the left, must also have a right, emphasizing that left and right must match. Other types of boxing seldom emphasize left-right symmetry.

Fifth, it is simple and easy to learn. Most boxing forms are relatively complex, and a large number of indirect movements are used to connect postures. Moreover, more than a few of the movements are difficult, and to practice a form, one must have a large practice area. There is a folk saying, "When young, don't practice Taiji; when old, don't practice Shaolin," because Taiji is soft and slow, and Shaolin is hard and straight. Only Baguazhang postures are simple, may be practiced fast or slow, and can be trained "in the space of a lying cow." It is easy to learn for men and women, young and old. Just as the great Baguazhang Master Sun Lutang said, "Baguazhang does not have the bitterness of bent legs and folded waist, nor does it require the toil that causes the flesh to wear out. It is a truly an elegant thing among martial arts."

Aside from possessing these special characteristics, Cheng School Gao Style Baguazhang also has special characteristics different from the other styles of Baguazhang currently found in China and other countries:

First, the Pre-Heaven Palms and Post-Heaven Palms are divided and trained separately. This is the most evident special characteristic of Cheng School Gao Style Baguazhang that differentiates it from other styles of Baguazhang. In most Baguazhang currently taught in China and elsewhere, applications are contained in walking and turning the circle, known as the Pre-Heaven and Post-Heaven combined in training, or "sixty-four palms contained in the circle." Only Cheng School Gao Style Baguazhang divides the Pre-Heaven Palms and Post-Heaven Palms and trains them separately, emphasizing that "Pre-Heaven Palms are the basis for the Post-Heaven Palms; the Post-Heaven Palms are the application of the Pre-Heaven Palms; without the Pre-Heaven Palms, one's Baguazhang has no root; without Post-Heaven Palms, one's Baguazhang is not complete." The Pre-Heaven Palms use Turning Palm as the beginning and Single Palm Change as the mother, creating eight sets of body-overturning (the Pre-Heaven Eight Big Palms), and use Black Dragon Whips Its Tail Palm as a closing posture. The Post-Heaven Palms are sixty-four individually practiced techniques derived from the Pre-Heaven Eight Big Palms, called the Post-Heaven Sixty-Four Palms.

Second, the Pre-Heaven Palms inherit and preserve the original basic characteristic of Baguazhang: "using the circle as the method, winding along the Eight Trigrams, moving like flowing water, walking and changing posture while winding with Koubu and Baibu; the postures without pause, from beginning to end moving from the edge of the circle inward to advance and attack." The Post-Heaven Palms use palm methods and single applications as the focus, incorporating kicking and elbowing techniques, advancing on lines both straight and curved, exemplifying the special fighting characteristics of Baguazhang by "striking second to control someone (I arrive first); avoiding the solid and attacking the empty; first neutralizing and later creating; and attacking primarily from the flanks."

Third, the movement forms emphasize if still to manifest roundness, and if moving to possess roundness. Whether still or moving, and whether Pre-Heaven Palm or Post-Heaven Palm, it is always required that the four limbs seem bent but are not bent, seem straight but are not straight, causing the whole body above and below to be one undivided form, everywhere rounded, guaranteeing that qi and blood may circulate abundantly and without obstruction, expanding and contracting at will, absolutely without stiffness and clumsiness.

Fourth, the movements of the Pre-Heaven Palms utilize softness as their focus, but softness that contains hardness. "The Turning Palm is like a twisted string" emphasizes integrated energy and twisting and wrapping energy, causing the whole body above and below to be one connected qi, one undivided form, twisting into one mass, with the energy contained internally but not shown externally. The postures should be unbroken, reaching the level of seeking following in opposition. The Post-Heaven Palms use hardness as their focus, but hardness that contains softness, emphasizing following energy, reaching the level of seeking subtlety in following. The energy must be issued outward as much as possible, with the feet aiding the body, the body aiding the arms, the arms aiding the palms, the palms striking with the force to topple walls. The combination of the two aspects of Pre-Heaven Palms and Post-Heaven Palms fairly outstandingly embodies the special characteristic of "hard and soft mutually aiding" found in Cheng School Gao Style Baguazhang.

Fifth, Pre-Heaven Palms are the basis for the Post-Heaven Palms; the Post-Heaven Palms are the application of the Pre-Heaven Palms. The goal of the Pre-Heaven Palms is to train the internal and foster the root, and it is extremely beneficial in cultivating life, building health, increasing qi, and extending power. The Pre-Heaven Palm Internal Skill Posture-Completion Methods, which emphasize relaxed stillness and naturalness and are really a moving *qigong*. Aspects such as "the five toes claw the ground; the five fingers spread open," which can connect the twelve meridians and channels, five *zang* and six *fu* organs, brain and nervous system, and through this reach the level of effect where one can regulate qi and blood and prevent and treat disease; "all postures that have a left must also have right, left and right matching," which causes both the left and right hemispheres of the brain to simultaneously receive stimulation; and the Mud-Wading Step, which causes the soles of the feet and what the medical world calls the "second heart" to both reflexively receive strong stimulation and massage; all of these adhere to modern health-building and body strengthening theory.

The main goal of the Post-Heaven Palms is to train crossing hands and confrontation, and they are the application of the Pre-Heaven Palms. Every posture has a clear fighting intent, and one can say that "none of the palms are empty." There are no intermediate movements used to connect the forms, and the intention of each individual posture is evident; how it is trained is how it is applied. Primarily these are for self-defense and guarding against opponents, and they emphasize "apply, respond, develop, and evolve." "Apply" means the original application and posture. "Respond" means first transforming and then issuing. "Develop" means two-person dismantling palms practice according to established sets of movements. "Evolve" means free fighting, changing according to the situation, using change as the pivot, applying moves at will. Using many changes of movement and with subtlety of change, victory over the opponent lies between intention and nonintention. This is the true essence of Gao Style Baguazhang fighting.

Basic Hand Positions and Footwork

Cheng School Gao Style Baguazhang's basic hand positions adhere to those taught by Cheng Tinghua and use the Dragon Claw Palm (the five fingers spread open) as the main focus. The basic palm positions are explained as below:

Dragon Claw Palm

The five fingers spread open, the root of the palm bends at the wrist and presses forward. The thumb spreads outward, and the index finger presses up; hukou is rounded and full. The middle finger points to heaven, the ring and little fingers hook inward slightly. The lateral edge of the palm curls slightly inward, the heart of the palm is hollow, and the back of the palm is slightly bowed like a roof tile. This is the most basic palm position of Cheng School Gao Style Baguazhang, and all other palm positions evolve out of this (fig. 1.1).

Spiraling Palm

Changing from Dragon Claw Palm, the little finger, lateral edge of the palm, wrist, and forearm simultaneously rotate inward, with spiraling energy twisting and wrapping into the palm. This is called Spiraling Palm (fig. 1.2).

Downward Vertical Palm

Also called Downward Spiral Palm. Also changing from Dragon Claw Palm, the little finger, lateral edge of the palm, wrist, and forearm simultaneously rotate downward, with spiraling energy twisting and wrapping downward. This is called Downward Vertical Palm (fig. 1.3).

Upturned Palm

The heart of the palm faces up, the five fingers are spread open, the thumb presses outward and hooks inward, and hukou is full and rounded. The index and middle fingers press forward. The ring and little fingers wrap slightly inward, and the heart of the palm is hollow (fig. 1.4).

Overturned Palm

This palm position is the same as Upturned Palm, but with the heart of the palm is facing downward (fig. 1.5).

Uplifting Palm

The five fingers are open, the fingers pointing up, using pressing energy to pierce and uplift (fig. 1.6).

Embracing Palm

The five fingers are open with the thumb edge facing up, the heart of the palm facing inward, the elbows bent forward, and the palm energy pressing inward as if embracing (fig. 1.7).

Upholding Palm

Changing from Dragon Claw Palm, the little finger and ring finger press outward, hukou is rounded and full, the heart of the palm is facing up and hollow, the energy upholding forward (fig. 1.8).

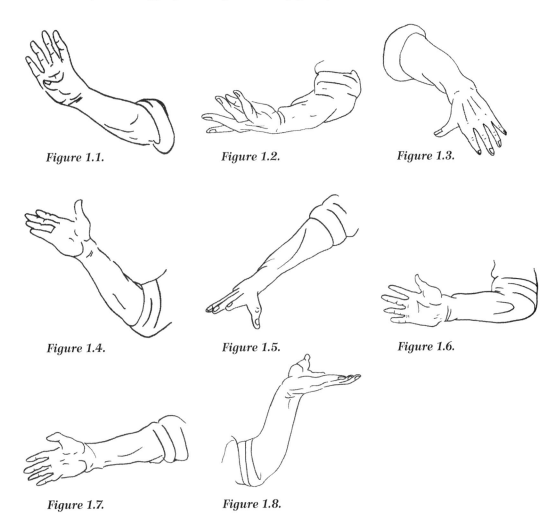

Figure 1.1.   *Figure 1.2.*   *Figure 1.3.*

Figure 1.4.   *Figure 1.5.*   *Figure 1.6.*

Figure 1.7.   *Figure 1.8.*

The basic stepping methods of Cheng School Gao Style Baguazhang are the turning and coiling of Koubu and Baibu, and the Mud-Wading Step.

- Outside foot inward Koubu (fig. 1.9).
- Inside foot outward Koubu (fig. 1.10).
- Outside foot outward Baibu (fig. 1.11).
- Inside foot inward Baibu (fig. 1.12).
- Mud-Wading Step

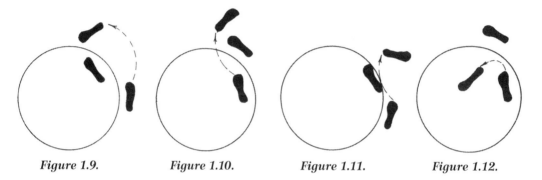

| *Figure 1.9.* | *Figure 1.10.* | *Figure 1.11.* | *Figure 1.12.* |

Mud-Wading Step is a stepping method unique to Baguazhang, and it runs through the basic stepping method of walking the circle. In the process of walking the circle, adhering to the principle of "using the circle as the method," within the circle is "inside," and outside the circle is "outside." Walking the circle counterclockwise the left foot is inside, and the right foot is outside. This is reversed in the opposite direction. The basic requirements are: when the rear foot strides forward, first use treading energy to lift the sole flat, no higher than the ankle. When setting the foot down, the toes and forefoot touch the ground first and slightly slide forward along the ground before stopping. All five toes grip the ground with pressing energy. The intention is as if walking in mud and water, not knowing the depth, testing with the steps as one walks, feeling the way to advance.

Baguazhang Post-Standing and Piercing the Nine Palaces

"Practice boxing without training basic skills, and in old age everything will be empty." Post-Standing is one of the basic skills of traditional Chinese martial arts. Generally speaking, all traditional Chinese martial arts have their own unique standing method. Experience has proven that those who, through perseverance and with concerted research and practice, can study Post-Standing and acquire its methods are always able to receive the effects of increasing internal power, developing the body's latent abilities, and developing the special abilities of the body's intelligence.

The inherent internal power of the average person is their original power. Only by training the power one receives through conscious special effort can this be called skilled power. Today, the power sought by modern competitive fighters is external power, which is easily increased but easily diminished, internally makes no change to the root, and is only used for competitive fighting. Baguazhang stresses that the internal and external are cultivated together, especially in the power sought by Post-Standing, which is an internal power and is used not only for fighting but more importantly in cultivating and building the body. The Post-Standing introduced in this manual is an important part of Cheng School Gao Style Baguazhang, and it is a traditional internal skill-cultivation and training method. It trains the internal, supplements the original, and increases the basic skills of inherent power. It is the guide to strengthening the being and building the body as well as actual combat. It is the inner-chamber foundation for training the Pre-Heaven and Post-Heaven Palms. The standing taught by Master Gao Yisheng is divided into standing posts (static posts) and moving posts (active posts); the names reflect the meaning of each type. The standing posts are training methods where one stands without moving according to fixed rules concerning proper posture. The moving posts are training methods where one turns the circle walking and spinning in accordance with set requirements, while also adhering to fixed rules concerning proper posture. This is also called

Turning Palm. This is the most archetypal movement of the Baguazhang created by Dong Haichuan and its most basic movement form. Piercing the Nine Palaces, then, is a type of relatively complex comprehensive method of moving posts.

Whether standing posts or moving posts, whether Pre-Heaven Posts —including the Pre-Heaven Eight Big Palms described below—or the Post-Heaven Post, it is only in the movement form that there are slight differences; the basic training aim is the same—all of these seek internal refined power. Because of this, the basic requirements for all are completely the same. All adhere to the Pre-Heaven Palm Twenty-Four Basic Requirements described later in this volume to complete the postures. Moreover, the requirement for training space is not great. One only requires clean fresh air—somewhere clear and quiet is best—and both indoors or outside are acceptable. To measure the length of practice, after training the entire body should feel light, relaxed, and comfortable. The basic standing requirements are that one must strictly adhere to the Twenty-Four Basic Requirements to complete the postures; gather the qi and collect the spirit; breathe naturally; relax the whole body, with the chest broad and the belly full; maintain intention in the tips of the fingers; and the body's form should—from outside in, and from beginning to end—maintain a relaxed, quiet, and natural state, full and abundant, with hardness and softness mutually aiding; above and below, left and right, front and back all mutually opposing and balancing to form complete power. Attention must be paid to alternating left and right postures. It must be especially emphasized—and beginners must pay attention—that breathing is the essence of heaven and earth. In the beginning one breathes naturally, and after a time this will naturally reach the level of breaths that are even, fine, deep, and long. Further practice will naturally reach the state of full belly breathing, and later finally reach the most exquisite state of whole-body breathing. This is communicating with nature, and it is also called "forget myself breathing," which causes the entire body to be integrated into the great qi, entering into the realm of heaven and earth united. This most exquisite realm can only be reached sequentially and gradually, obtained amid following what is natural, and absolutely must not be actively and forcefully sought out. Training in the post skills and practicing the Baguazhang forms is the same; the height of the postures must be based on each individual, appropriately selecting upper, middle, or lower basin. Usually middle basin is acceptable.

Standing Posts (Static Posts)

Modern science recognizes that quiet stillness is a special state of movement. All movement is related to the shift in position of some point, and the more refined the movement form, the more subtle this positional shift. The natural biological movements of each system in the human body are the highest-level forms of movement. According to this theory, Post-Standing utilizes a form of relative rest for the body; externally it is static, but internally it moves. Using stillness as the main focus, it seeks movement in stillness and primarily trains enlivening and enriching qi and blood throughout the body. Standing posts follow the Twenty-Four Basic Requirements to complete their posture. The joints of the entire body maintain a feeling of seeming bent but not being bent, seeming straight but not being straight; nowhere fully straight, nowhere fully bent; everywhere rounded and curved. Stand fast without moving, the intention in the tips of the fingers and concentrating on dantian, relaxed, quiet, and natural. Only with the intention quiet will the qi settle. If the qi settles, then yin and yang are united. If yin and yang are united, then the vessels and channels will be open and unobstructed. If the vessels and channels are open and unobstructed, then the qi and blood will be lively. The more lively and unobstructed the circulation of qi and blood, the faster skilled power will increase. According to Liu Fengcai's firsthand experience, Gao Yisheng viewed Post-Standing as very important, and when standing often would suspend from each wrist a light brick to increase the skilled power of seeking movement in stillness.

In summary, Static Posts are a type of traditional skill-training method that uses intention, not force; seeks movement in stillness; uses the mind to regulate movement; and cultivates and stores internal power. In the beginning, the intention is in the fingertips. After long practice, "extreme stillness leads to movement," and one day the fingertips will have a feeling or sensation of movement (including feelings of numbness, swelling, cold, or hot); this is the qi and blood within the body being invigorated. Then one must gradually, through intention and physical perception, guide the sensation step-by-step to the upper limbs, back, waist, and abdomen, and the lower limbs, until one has connected the entire body inside and out. Going through the process of changing quantity to changing quality, and following an increase in the length of Post-Standing, internal power will gradually increase and deepen. Over time, not only can one feel the cultivation of front-back, left-right, and upper-lower oppositional power, but one may also train forth extraordinary skilled power.

PRE-HEAVEN POST

Using the Pre-Heaven Palm opening posture as the foundational posture, and following the Pre-Heaven Palm Neigong Posture-Completion Methods, stand still, in middle basin, with the weight distributed thirty percent in the front leg, seventy percent in the back leg (fig. 1.13). Left and right postures are the same.

POST-HEAVEN POST

Using the Post-Heaven Palm opening posture as a foundational posture, stand still, in middle basin, with the weight distributed thirty percent in the front leg, seventy percent in the back leg (fig. 1.14). Left and right postures are the same.

Figure 1.13.   *Figure 1.14.*

Moving Posts (Active Posts)

Bagua Moving Posts are the Turning Palms, also called Spinning Skills. They are the most basic of all the methods that Dong Haichuan taught and train the fundamental skills of Pre-Heaven Baguazhang. These are the most important signature contents of Cheng School Baguazhang. Even though today each Baguazhang transmission has its own special characteristics, with dissimilar forms and different postural appearances, the Moving Posts and Turning Palms are basically the same across all branches.

The Moving Posts are movements built on the foundation of the Pre-Heaven Standing Posts, which use different postures while turning-the-circle walking and spinning according to fixed requirements. The Moving Posts are a skill that seeks stillness in movement, requiring the body and mind to relax in the midst of regulated movement. Amid the movement of the body one must seek stillness in the mind, and in all movements from beginning to end one must maintain the Twenty-Four Requirements, always "using intention, not using force." The intention can be in the dantian or in the feet, but the goal is to avoid floating qi and to train a complete, unified, whole-body energy and skilled power. While moving, the upper limb postures do not change. The steps must be stable as if wading in mud, traveling with slow steps like stepping on black ice. Stepping slowly is better than quickly, and one absolutely must not "run the circle." The common saying of the ancestors "Slowly bring out the skill; quickly issue the hands" is just this principle. In turning-the-circle walking and spinning with the Moving Posts, it is prohibited to float up and down or wobble side to side. Even more, one cannot obstruct the qi, use crude force, lift the chest and round the belly, or stick out the buttocks. These are all basic requirements of the Pre-Heaven Palms and must be carefully grasped and understood in practice.

FIERCE TIGER LEAVES THE MOUNTAIN

Using counterclockwise circle-walking to start, simultaneously walk, twist the waist, and turn the body, the heart of the two palms pressing downward, with hukou pointing to and level with the lower abdomen. The middle fingers of both hands point toward each other, the space between them about six inches. The chest is facing the center of the circle, the eyes looking level into the center of the circle (fig. 1.15). Without stopping, turn the circle walking and spinning utilizing Mud-Wading Step. Left and right are the same.

GREAT ROC SPREADS ITS WINGS

Following Fierce Tiger Leaves the Mountain, simultaneously walk and rotate the two palms upward, the hands leading the arms; pass the chest, rising until reaching the collarbone, then extend outward in front of the body to the sides, the hearts of the palms facing up, sinking the shoulders and dropping the elbows, the two shoulders hooking inward, the forearms twisting outward, the palms in Spiraling Palm (fig. 1.16). Continue walking. Left and right are the same.

LION OPENS ITS MOUTH

Following Great Roc Spreads Its Wings, simultaneously walk and rotate the left palm inward, the left arm seemingly bent but not bent, seemingly straight but not straight, the heart of the palm facing up, the fingers pointing into the circle. Raise the right hand and overturn it until above

Figure 1.15.   *Figure 1.16.*   *Figure 1.17.*

the crown of the head, the heart of the palm facing down, the two palms facing each other (fig. 1.17). Left and right are the same.

White Ape Offers Fruit

Following Lion Opens Its Mouth, simultaneously walk and retract the arms and bend the elbows, the wrists pulling in close. Sink the shoulders and drop the elbows, the hearts of the two palms inclining forward and upward, carried in front of the chest, the chest facing the center of the circle (fig. 1.18). Left and right are the same.

Strength to Push Eight Horses

Following White Ape Offers Fruit, simultaneously walk and rotate the palms and arms inward, then press outward with the two arms, the fingers of both hands pointing toward each other, the hearts of the palms pressing into the center of the circle (fig. 1.19). Left and right are the same.

Embrace the Moon

Following Strength to Push Eight Horses, simultaneously walk and over-turn the hearts of both palms inward, the thumbs facing upward, the heart of the palm facing the chest. The arms fill outward rounded (fig. 1.20). Continue walking the circle. Left and right are the same.

Figure 1.18. *Figure 1.18.* *Figure 1.20.*

POINT TO HEAVEN AND PIERCE EARTH

Following Embrace the Moon, simultaneously walk and pierce downward with the fingers of the left hand, the heart of the palm facing outward, the back of the palm sticking lightly to the outside of the right knee while the right palm pierces upward, fingers pointing toward the heavens, extending the arm, the heart of the palm spiraling to face backward (fig. 1.21). Continue walking the circle. Left and right are the same.

GREEN DRAGON EXTENDS ITS CLAWS
(SAME AS PRE-HEAVEN PALMS TURNING PALM)

Following Point to Heaven and Pierce Earth, simultaneously walk and move the left arm upward, the index finger pointing to the heavens, hukou rounded and full, the heart of the palm facing into the circle, the palm at the height of the shoulder, sinking the shoulders and dropping the elbows, bending the wrist and pressing with the fingers, extending in front of the chest. At the same time, the right palm hooks downward and guards below the left elbow, bending the wrist and pressing with the palm, the middle finger pointing at the left elbow. Twist the waist and turn the body, the chest facing the center of the circle, the eyes looking level across hukou of the left hand (fig. 1.22). Continue walking the circle. Left and right are the same.

Figure 1.21.   *Figure 1.22.*

The above eight types of Moving Posts may be practiced individually, connected and alternated in practice, or, if fully grasped, their sequence randomized.

Piercing the Nine Palaces

Also called Nine Palace Stepping or Flying the Nine Palaces, this is a fairly complex traditional method for training the Moving Posts. The Nine Palaces are the Eight Trigrams, representing the eight directions, and adding the central Taiji as the central palace, together making nine palaces. Piercing the Nine Palaces takes its name from its concept. Following the basic requirements of Baguazhang, one uses the form of walking and stepping to pierce and move between the Nine Palaces according to the sequence of the Nine Palaces Eight Trigram Tactics Diagram and—while in the process of piercing and moving—changes postures and applications at will, from big to small or slow to fast. This primarily trains the intention of attack and defense and the agility of advancing and retreating, evading and dodging. It is also called Forest-Piercing Palm. The piercing-walking path is like figures 1.23, 1.24, and 1.25 below. Because Piercing the Nine Palaces is fairly complex, it is difficult to gain familiarity and fully grasp it without special training, and currently few people practice according to the diagrams, instead using the piercing of Black Dragon Whips Its Tail instead, which can also lead to the same results.

Sequence	1	2	3	4	5	6	7	8	9
Nine Palaces	*Kan* Palace	*Kun* Palace	*Zhen* Palace	*Xun* Palace	Central Palace	*Qian* Palace	*Dui* Palace	*Gen* Palace	*Li* Palace
Symbol	☵	☷	☳	☴		☰	☱	☶	☲
Gate	Generate	Awaken	Close	Observe		Injure	Open	Rest	Expire

Figure 1.23. Nine Palace sequence diagram.

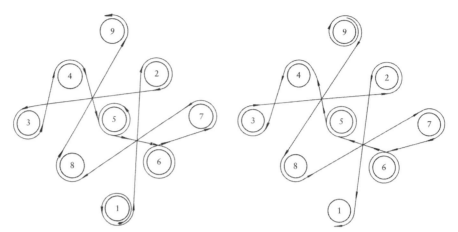

Figure 1.24. Forward-Moving Nine Palace diagram.

Figure 1.25. Backward-Moving Nine Palaces diagram.

An Explanation of the Art-Training Tree Diagram

In his original handwritten manuscript of the Baguazhang manual, the creator of Cheng School Gao Style Baguazhang, Gao Yisheng, meticulously drew a large tree with coiled roots and intertwined branches, calling it the Art-Training Tree (fig. 0.6). He also laid out the "Explanation of the Art-Training Tree," which will yield some understanding if assessed quietly and carefully at length.

Baguazhang describes its heroes by their depth of gongfu, and does not deceive with the falsehood and flattery of flowery fists and embroidered kicks. *Gongfu* means time. With perseverance, and through the passage of time, skill will naturally develop. Elder Baguazhang practitioners compared this art to a tree to inspire those who study Baguazhang to empty their hearts and with a perseverant nature diligently put forth great effort.

Baguazhang utilizes the circularity of the Eight Trigrams, and pointing to the roundness of a tree, compares training the art to a tree. To compare the art to a tree has the meaning that as a tree grows, so the art also grows. The roots of a tree are its source, its Pre-Heaven nature. The source of this art is the Pre-Heaven Palms. When a tree has not yet come out of the earth, it is like the state of Wuji chaos; when it emerges from the earth, it is like the Taiji differentiation of heaven and earth. The Pre-Heaven Palms exemplify the idea of Wuji giving rise to Taiji in the Turning Palms. The trunk of a tree will produce eight branches; the Turning Palms of this art produce eight sets of Pre-Heaven body-overturning to accord with it. Each branch of the tree will again produce eight twigs, totaling sixty-four twigs; each Pre-Heaven Palm of this art again produces eight related postures, which are the Post-Heaven Sixty-Four Palms. Each twig on the tree will produce six buds, and accordingly each Post-Heaven posture changes into six applications, totaling 384 applications in accordance with the 384 lines of the hexagrams. The leaves of a tree flourish and grow incalculably, and this art uses the inexhaustible changes of yin and yang and movement and stillness within the Eight Trigrams to accord with this. This is "self-improving without cease" in comparing the art to a tree. The song of the Art-Training Tree says:

> *Training the art compared with a tree, the meanings are connected,*
> *All contained within the Taiji and Bagua,*
> *Nine Palaces and Ten Methods produce change,*
> *Yin and yang and movement and stillness are miraculous without end,*
> *As the tree grows branches and twigs, so the art deepens,*
> *The tree roots coil and twist; the feet and eyes are complete,*
> *With roots deep and leaves full, the applications are vast,*
> *Meditate on the essential meaning of this broad study.*

Combat Applications of Cheng School Gao Style Baguazhang

The inherent essential character of the martial arts is their offensive and defensive use in fighting. The core principle of martial technique is that "the method relies on attack and defense." Whether or not one can employ their art in fighting and actual combat is the only standard by which to test whether a form is scientific in its design and whether a practitioner's level of skill and technique is high or low. The character "martial" (武) comes from the root "dagger-ax." The dagger-ax ruled the army; the army refers to matters of armed conflict and struggle. The character "arts" (艺) refers to skills, techniques, methods, and tricks. The character for "martial" is the combination of two root characters, "stop" (止) and "dagger- ax" (戈). "Stop the dagger-ax" contains the meaning of "use the martial to prohibit violence, impose order on chaos, and put an end to the use of arms," and it is not simply using the martial to be cruel to others. One can see that the sages of old created martial arts originally as a type of combat method used to stop violence and violation. Because of this, from antiquity until the present, generally every type of skill and every move and posture in the forms of all that can be called martial arts must have intention for attack and defense. Otherwise it can only be called physical exercise or a type of dance. The core materials for basic movement in Cheng School Gao Style Baguazhang almost all have strong intention in attack and defense, and every type of skill trained is in the service of raising the practitioner's offensive and defensive abilities. Especially with the Post-Heaven Sixty-Four Palms used directly in fighting, each move and each posture contains evident offensive and defensive intent. Moreover, how you train is how you apply the technique. Because of this, offensive and defensive character and fighting intent are together the essential nature of Cheng School Gao Style Baguazhang. The basic tenet is "follow the opportunity and change accordingly, using change as a constant." "Follow the opportunity" means the opportunity that arises from following the opponent's incoming force. "Change accordingly" means flowing with the incoming force and changing to respond to it. "Using change as a constant" means meeting change with change; using change to stand in an undefeatable position. Practical fighting techniques commonly used "amid change" include the concepts of "using movement to control stillness and avoiding the direct, and attacking from the angle"; "emptying as it approaches, and solidifying as you respond, changing with softness as hardness approaches, avoiding the solid and attacking the empty"; "using change to meet change, issuing last but arriving first"; "being hard before they have issued their power, being soft to ride after they have issued their power, first neutralizing softly and then issuing hard"; and "if vertical, using horizontal to dissolve, and if horizontal, using vertical to attack."

The rule of using change as the constant in attack and defense comes from the guidance of *Yijing* theory and has been gradually developed and formed from being put to the test in actual combat. The *Yijing* says: "one yin and one yang is called the Way; the subtlety of yin and yang is called the Divine." The changes of yin and yang are the core of the Eight Trigrams of the *Yijing*. In applying this to the art of Baguazhang, they are called empty and full, hard and soft, advance and retreat. In actual fighting and combat, applying the changes of empty and full, hard and soft, and advance and retreat at the appropriate time, when meeting the force of the opponent, will cause the opponent to be unable to successfully block an attack, and allow one to stand in an undefeatable position, snatching victory in the end. This is the essence of Baguazhang fighting theory.

The *Yijing* says: "Change is the image of advance and retreat"; "transforming and cutting off is called change"; "hard and soft are mutually promoting, and change is between them." In the "Virtue of Water" chapter of the *Dao De Jing* it says: "Under Heaven nothing is more soft and yielding than water. Yet for attacking the solid and strong, nothing is better; it has no equal. The weak can overcome the strong; the supple can overcome the stiff."[7] Within the Eight Trigrams and the five elements, water's nature is the most soft and supple; the remaining metal, wood, fire, and earth elements are all harder than water. Yet when fire meets water, it is extinguished; when wood meets water, it floats; when metal meets water, it erodes; when earth meets water, it becomes weak. One can see that within the ultimate softness of water hides an ultimate hardness; ultimate suppleness contains ultimate unyieldingness. The past sages of Baguazhang were applying exactly this principle found in the *Yijing* of the changing of yin and yang and the formlessness of water and its ability to adapt. Through long experimentation they established the Baguazhang fighting principle of using change as the constant, thus arriving at the goal of using softness to overcome hardness, using suppleness to overcome strength.

The *Yijing* says: "The blessings and abundance from heaven are auspicious, and there is nothing they do not aid." "Blessings" means assistance. The *Yijing* continues, "That which heaven assists is flowing." "Flowing" means following the natural course; following the force and changing. Sunzi's *The Art of War,* in the chapter titled "Weak Points and Strong," says:

> Military tactics are like unto water; for water in its natural course runs away from high places and hastens downward. So in war, the way is to avoid what is strong and to strike at what is weak. Water shapes its course according to the nature of the ground over which it flows; the soldier works out his victory in relation to the foe that he is facing. Therefore, just as water retains no constant shape, so in warfare there are no constant conditions. He who can modify his tactics in relation to his opponent and thereby succeed in winning, may be called a heaven-born captain.[8]

Sunzi's insightful analysis from two thousand years ago was also an important theoretical basis for the former sages in establishing the Baguazhang fighting principles of follow the opportunity and change accordingly, using change as a constant. The famous Baguazhang practitioner Sun Lutang wrote:

> If the opponent is hard, I am soft. If the opponent is soft, I am hard. If the opponent is low, I am high. If the opponent moves, I am still. If the opponent is still, I move. If I look at the topography, I may differentiate and utilize expanding and contracting back and forth. Observe the height of the opponent's body, measure the situation to see whether substantial or insubstantial; investigate the opponent's depth and breadth of disposition, knowing in your heart the opponent's craftiness, solidity, or emptiness; deliberate and, following the opportunity, act.

Sun Lutang's analysis expresses in depth that in fighting with Baguazhang one must pay attention to changes in the physical body by watching the opponent's postural and positional changes and, at the appropriate time, changing one's own posture and position, seeking a corresponding countermeasure. At the same time, upon this foundation one must also continually change one's own mentality and intention; this is what is meant by "the body leans but the mind does not lean." Sunzi's *The Art of War,* in the chapter titled "Weak Points and Strong," also says: "O divine art of subtlety and secrecy! Through you we learn to be invisible, through you inaudible: and hence we can hold the enemy's fate in our hands." And also: "In making tactical dispositions, the highest pitch you can attain is to conceal them: conceal your dispositions, and you will be safe from the prying of the subtlest spies, from the machinations of the wisest brains." Clearly, winning through intention is the highest level of fighting. Dong Haichuan strongly emphasized the uniting of intention and physical form, and viewed as especially important intention's leading effect in regard to fighting. The form changes, and so the intent changes; if the intent changes, then the form changes. This is the true fighting characteristic of Baguazhang's phrase "follow the opportunity and change accordingly, using change as a constant."

Combat Application of the Pre-Heaven Palms

Walking the circle is the key to not being controlled by others.

That which is called "victory" in combat, speaking from principle, means to control others and to not be controlled by them. Cheng School Gao Style Baguazhang retains the special characteristic of traditional Baguazhang, moving from the periphery of the circle toward the center when attacking, amid walking and spinning. The fundamental Turning Palm posture (Green Dragon Extends Its Claws) is broadly applicable in actual combat. Whether talking of boxing, Karate, Tae Kwon Do, Thai Boxing, Jeet Kun Do, or Chinese-style Shuaijiao, all utilize this stance, but only Baguazhang uses this method as its foundational skill. The reasons for this are primarily as follows:

- The Turning Palm posture is movement within stillness, and also still-ness within movement. The arms are static and fixed, but the body moves at a regular or variable speed, and does not give the opponent a fixed point to strike, while amid constant motion one continually seeks to be able to aim at a striking point, and can change postures and issue a strike at any time.

- Using an angled line to face the opponent, the arms find the most perfect blocking angle, as in boxing's orthodox stance.
- One can adopt the most active retreat (using retreating as advancing). One should say that by itself, Turning Palm posture is purely defensive. But from another point of view, without a stable guard in advancing to attack, one takes on a comparatively greater risk.

The changes of postures while walking and spinning form three-dimensional topological spheroids moving in three-dimensional space.

While walking and spinning, the changes of the head, hands, elbows, shoulders, hips, knees, and feet form a three-dimensional sphere with the Du channel as its axis. In shifting along the circumference of the circle while turning around one's own axis, and following the changes of the hands and feet, the radius of the sphere expands and contracts, forming a three-dimensional topological sphere. With this sphere, any point on the surface is determined by seven parameters: four more than in simple rotation.

Looking at it from the aspect of the guard, this sphere is comprised of three levels with a shared center, and these three levels are the so-called three gates. The wrists and ankles make up the first gate; the elbows and knees make up the second gate; the shoulders and hips make up the third gate. The opponent must break down these three gates to drive on to the yellow dragon.[9] The defender must defend each gate and only then will not lose. However, because of the topological property of the sphere, with each level changing through expansion and contraction, it is like a flexible steel ball. Speaking from intention, it is something that can expand until there is nothing outside of it, and contract until these is nothing inside of it.

Clearly this sphere, from the point of view of the guard, is perfect in all respects. We can see this from the following imaginary experiment. Place a ball on a flat surface, and when it is completely still, use a bamboo stick to poke it. One must consider that causing the ball to move in the direction of the push, even in a state without any rotational movement, is very difficult. One can then imagine, if the sphere were rolling, shifting, and spinning in three dimensions and at the same time expanding and contracting, that finding the ideal striking point in an instant would be even more difficult. This is Baguazhang's defensive model.

In the chapter titled "Energy" in *The Art of War,* Sunzi says: "Amid the turmoil and tumult of battle, there may be seeming disorder and yet no real disorder at all; amid confusion and chaos, your array may be without head or tail, yet it will be proof against defeat." This precisely describes Baguazhang's defensive mysteriousness.

Furthermore, from the aspect of attack, this type of sphere's power is great. In the same chapter, Sunzi also says:

> The clever combatant looks to the effect of combined energy and does not require too much from individuals. Hence his ability to pick out the right men and utilize combined energy. When he utilizes combined energy, his fighting men become, as it were, like unto rolling logs or stones. For it is the nature of a log or stone to remain motionless on level ground, and to move when on a slope; if four-cornered, to come to a standstill, but if round-shaped, to go rolling down. Thus the energy developed by good fighting men is as the momentum of a round stone rolled down a mountain thousands of feet in height. So much on the subject of energy.

In reality, a rotating sphere's attacking power can be broken down in three ways: the radiant energy from the center of the sphere to a point on its surface, the tangent force from the sphere's surface, and the curved power within the sphere. If the sphere undertakes attack, the opponent will have difficulty in instantaneously determining resistance to three forces of equal magnitude but different direction.

Combat Application of the Post-Heaven Palms

Gao Yisheng's Post-Heaven Palms were created specifically for combat, and from middle age until the end of his life, he never lost a match relying on the Post-Heaven Palms. The Pre-Heaven use softness as its focus, and the Post-Heaven uses hardness as its focus, but this type of hardness is like cotton wrapped around iron. It's a type of explosive energy that in an instant goes from nothing to something, from extremely small suddenly changing to extremely large, from extremely soft to extremely hard. The issuing power of the Post-Heaven Palms, which all utilize drawing in to the extreme and only then issuing power, is just this principle. The trick is to remain extremely round and flexible in this extreme position, without leaving a trace, and only then will you not be followed by the opponent. This must be accomplished by walking and turning. The elder generation's saying, "winning is in this; losing is in this," is completely relevant.

The Post-Heaven Palms mostly move in zigzag patterns, with some moving in a straight line. The former comes from Three-Points Post-Standing (Post-Heaven Post-Standing), the latter from practicing outward-radiating power. Three-Points Post-Standing is used in fighting by almost every type of pugilistic art like this, but the angled attack of Baguazhang's twisting waist and hips is unique. Only in this way can one exhibit mysteriousness in the midst of change and move freely and change quickly. A zigzag attack issues power after opening, pulling, or leading to the left or right and is used when the opponent's center of balance is shifted to the left or right; only then can one achieve great force. The straight line is not the same as in Xingyiquan. Baguazhang usually uses this after pulling down, cutting off, or similar hand movements, when the opponent has formed a plane with the practitioner and has been controlled; only then can one achieve great force. Of course, if there is only one power, it is not doubtful that one will be defeated. Every posture of Baguazhang maintains the six harmonies, presses to the eight sides, and changes to the eight directions; only then can one not be defeated.

The Post-Heaven Palms are not simply an appendage of the Pre-Heaven Palms but are a further elaboration upon the foundation of the Pre-Heaven Palms. Looked at from any angle, one can say they are a necessary supplement and an interesting reinforcement. For instance, the elbow sets and leg sets are creation and development, and the palm skills are mainly elaboration.

The Pre-Heaven Palms attack and defend relying on softness, using dissolving as their exemplary character, are completed without leaving a trace, and are nonintention in action. The Post-Heaven Palms attack and defend having form and intention, and are intention in action. This is why, when discussing combat, the Pre-Heaven Palms are discussed frequently and the Post-Heaven Palms are discussed less. The Pre-Heaven Palms have many indescribable mysterious elements, while the Post-Heaven Palms have form that everyone can see and learn. The elder generations first taught the Post-Heaven and then trained the Pre-Heaven; this is similar to first diving for pearls and then later threading them together into a necklace. But one must pay attention to the fact that the necklace is certainly not the pearls, but the pearls organically form a part of the necklace. Lastly, the authors must strongly emphasize that even though, for the ease of explaining combat theory and special characteristics, we separate the Pre-Heaven and Post-Heaven in discussion, in reality they are closely connected and cannot be separated, and they are an organic whole.

Gao Yisheng on Combat

Gao Yisheng had a great knowledge of Baguazhang combat, and he presented his theories many times. They are summed up as follows:

Quickness, Ruthlessness, Changeability

The songs of Baguazhang combat say:

> *The mind is the commander-in-chief of the troops,*
> *The hands and feet are the troops of the four armies,*
> *The body sets up the fortifications,*
> *The eyes are the forward scouts,*
> *Mysterious like the thousand infantry and ten thousand horsemen,*
> *The scouts lead the masses to the enemy,*
> *Coordinated like three armies acting as one,*
> *When meeting the enemy call out the old encampment.*

Baguazhang exhibits yin and yang,
One rises, one falls, and the body hides,
Wave the head and advance with the sound of wind and thunder,
Connected rolling palms guarding above and below.

Movement like a dragon and palms like the wind,
Employing the palms, one cannot retain compassion or emotion,
With kind heart and weak visage in the end there is no victory,
The intention ruthless and hands black, causing the opponent fright.

Seizing hands like an ox's tongue,
Striking like a tiger's mouth,
Hands go out like steel files,
Hands return like steel hooks.

Hands like lightning and feet like a dragon,
When two enemies meet, it is like a blazing fire,
Hands like poison arrows and the body like a bow,
The information is all in the pressing of the rear foot,
Rise without form or shadow and land without a trace,
The hands and feet as if chasing the wind,
The five elements issued as one with the power complete,
Hands strike and feet kick without retaining emotion.

As a result of footwork that coils, walks a curve, and seldom walks a straight line, Baguazhang energy is like spirally wrapping silk. The energy of the entire body above and below is concentrated in the palms and issued outward, lengthening and striking far. Because of this, the special characteristics of Baguazhang fighting are clearly exemplified in three words: quickness, ruthlessness, changeability.

Quickness. Exceeding swiftness. The eyes quick, the hands quick, the feet quick. Not moving, like a mountain. Moving, like thunder. Speaking in common terms, this is the quick beating the slow. Every move and every posture of the Baguazhang Post-Heaven Palms contains clear offensive and defensive combative intent, with left and right postures the same, and practice and application completely in accord. Because of this, in application they are very useful. Upon meeting an adversary, with one look the four limbs follow the command and swiftly advance. Furthermore, Baguazhang emphasizes footwork skills, increasing the agility of the lower body, which has a promoting effect on the level of quickness in fighting. Just as Gao Yisheng said:

> When the common people cross hands and compete, most use sealing, closing, withdrawing, evading, hooking, pulling, toppling, and striking as their specialty, but do not consider the value of the palm's miraculous speed. Baguazhang palms move without casting a shadow. As soon as they move, they arrive, with a mechanism that is miraculous and movements that are nimble. Like the wind blowing the grass, they respond after only a touch; within this is miraculousness. Those not skilled in contemplating this through actual practice cannot accept it.

"The speed of surging water can even float stone; this is force." One's level of quickness is mainly determined by the degree to which one is familiar in everyday training. The idea of "familiarity produces cleverness, cleverness produces subtlety, subtlety produces miraculousness" is this very principle.

Ruthlessness. The heart is ruthless, and the hands are ruthless. Move without moving lightly, and from the first movement, be ruthless. Issuing each palm, if not seeking the enemy's life, must at least seek to injure them. Of course, ruthlessness can only be used when actually facing an enemy; when testing hands in training, one cannot be ruthless. Speaking about the offensive and defensive intent of Post-Heaven Baguazhang when facing an enemy, the striking target of almost every posture is a vulnerable part of the body, like the head, neck, chest, abdomen, ribs, crotch, and knees. Furthermore, when discussing issuing power in Baguazhang, power unification is emphasized, with the power of the whole body focused in the finger, hand, arm, foot, knee, or leg. In this way, issued power must naturally be ruthless. Of course, to reach the level of ruthlessness depends primarily on the depth of one's skill. This is the principle of the hard beating the soft.

Changeability. This is the main special characteristic that differentiates Baguazhang from other pugilistic fighting arts. In the introduction to his *Study of Baguazhang,* Sun Lutang writes: "Taijiquan is the empty course; Baguazhang is the changeable course; Xingyiquan is the straight course. 'Course' means standing in an undefeatable position." Because of this, Baguazhang is called remarkable by utilizing lively crisscrossing changes. The main combat principles of Baguazhang fighting are: avoid the straight, and attack from the angle; use the straight to expel the angled; surround the target; follow the opportunities and change accordingly; avoid the substantial, and attack the insubstantial; withdraw the body and become a shadow; block and intercept, then advance to attack; borrow energy and utilize it. The power of changeability is being soft in transforming but hard in issuing, using following to seek cleverness, and using cleverness to destroy a thousand pounds. One must judge the postures and move. This is exactly the principle of "when practicing there are fixed rules; in application there are no fixed methods." In sum, Baguazhang fighting methods, like utilizing tranquility to lead movement, first transforming and later initiating, storing energy and then issuing, striking with borrowed energy, and striking last but arriving first, all exemplify "changeability" and the principle of following the opportunity and responding with change. Cheng School Gao Style Baguazhang utilizes single postures or small sets of offensive and defensive movements as materials to train in fighting, to temper the ability of responding with change when meeting an enemy; these are the Dismantling Palms, and they are the essence of Cheng School Gao Style Baguazhang. The true opportunity for changeability and transformation comes from practical experience, and therefore it is difficult begin teaching with the concept of changeability when meeting an enemy.

The Six Harmonies, Seven Stars, and Nine-Character Rhyme

The six harmonies are the hands harmonized with the feet, the elbows harmonized with the knees, the shoulders harmonized with the hips, the mind harmonized with the intention, the intention harmonized with the qi, and the qi harmonized with the power. Baguazhang emphasizes the six harmonies in daily training and when facing an opponent. This is the harmony of internal and external, beginning with the intention moving, continuing with the internal moving, and only then the form moving, using the internal movement to carry the external form, the external form harmonized with internal movement, from internal to external, using the external to draw out the internal, until in the end internal and external are mutually harmonized. Qi is a formless power; power is a skill with shape and form. The muscles, blood, tendons, and bones of the entire body are aided by qi. When the four limbs move, the internal qi presses and arrives. The harmonization of internal and external in this way is the subtle aspect of Cheng School Gao Style Baguazhang fighting.

The seven stars are metal, wood, water, fire, earth, yin, and yang. In relation to the body, they are the head, hand, elbow, shoulder, hip, knee, and foot. The seven stars of the body are the weapons used by martial artists to harm an opponent when crossing hands. The rhyme-song says:

The head strikes, intending to crash to the face,
The hands rise and fall, striking, moving at will,
The elbows intend to seek the chest and ribs,
The shoulders strike as one yin becomes one yang,
The hips strike as the three segments unite,
The knees strike using strong force, like a tiger,
The feet strike treading and kicking, not settling on air,
The seven stars in unison show remarkable ability.

When speaking of the nine palaces, Baguazhang has nine skill methods that must be known. This is the nine-character rhyme of fighting: "follow, brave, straight, clever, subtle, connected, ruthless, immediate, and skilled." "Follow" means natural. "Brave" means resolute. "Straight" means issuing must be heavy. "Clever" means borrowing the opponent's energy, destroying a thousand pounds with no wasted energy. "Subtle" means change has many aspects; issue hands without leaving a shadow. "Connected" means adhering and changing; advancing without cease.

"Ruthless" means moving without showing emotion. "Immediate" means issuing as soon as touching, close and fast. "Skilled" means internal skill. The nine skills use the hands and feet as their specialty, the body and footwork as the keys. In fighting one must advance with the body, raise the hands and issue the palms, lift the feet to tread and strike, the palms arriving when the body arrives. This is exactly the principle that when the body moves, the feet move first.

Gather the Qi and Consolidate the Spirit

"Gather the qi" means the qi sinking to dantian. "Consolidate the spirit" means the mind is unified. Gathering the qi and consolidating the spirit, then, is the mind and intention united with the six harmonies, achieving unanimity in the whole body, above and below, inside and out. Especially when crossing hands with someone, one must calm the three functions. The eyes are the function of vision and must constantly judge timing, angle, and force. The ears are the function of perception and must constantly be vigilant. The heart is the function of bravery and must maintain alertness. This is the intention of spirit.

Rising and Falling, Advancing and Retreating, Reversing and Turning, Receiving and Issuing

These eight words are key elements of Baguazhang's adaptability in fighting. "Rising" is brave crossing force. "Falling" is following, natural. "Advancing" is advancing with the feet, advancing with the body, advancing with the hand. "Retreating" is retreating with the feet, retreating with the body, changing postures. "Reversing" means turning around, spinning the body, guarding the rear. "Turning" means an active body, evasive body, drawing in and transforming. "Receiving" means stepping back and restraining oneself like a crouching cat. "Issuing" means leaping forward like a tiger pouncing on prey. Those who study the art today have terms such as explosive energy, attacking energy, springy energy, and tenacious energy. In reality, explosive energy is too simple, and difficult to use in rising and falling. Attacking energy is too dead, and difficult to use in changing.

Springy energy is too crude, and difficult to use in a lively manner. Tenacious energy shows the form and causes it not to be nimble. Only with Baguazhang's eight energies of grasp, seize, lead, carry, stick, join, follow, and adhere can one rise and fall, advance and retreat, reverse and turn, and receive and issue at will.

Three Gates, Three Segments, Height and Gaze Direction

Comparing the three gates: "Comparing" means comparing power and testing hands. The three gates are the wrist, elbow, and shoulder. Baguazhang fighting emphasizes the three gates. The wrists are the outer gate, the elbows the second gate, and the shoulders the third gate. Passing the third gate, one reaches the inner courtyard, and then one may enter the chambers. Therefore, when comparing hands, first have a reaction at the wrists, flexing and extending back and forth, changing at will. Reaching the hands and advancing past the outer gate, one seizes the initiative. Passing the elbows is entering the second gate and endangering the opponent. Only continuing to advance to the third gate is victory. Entering only to the first or second gates, the opponent can still change, and one cannot hold the key to certain victory. The three gates cannot not be known.

The three segments are above, middle, and below. Speaking of the whole body, the hands and elbows are the tip segment, the chest and waist are the middle segment, and the legs and feet are the root segment. When raising hands, attack the opponent in the upper and middle segments; when raising the feet and legs, attack the middle or root segments. Above, middle, and below coordinate to attack the opponent's whole body. If the upper segment is not understood, the hands and elbows will be stiff and brittle. If the middle segment is not understood, the entire body will be insubstantial and empty. If the lower segment is not understood, the footwork will be chaotic. Only if the three segments are understood will cleverness and subtlety arise.

Height and gaze direction. When crossing hands, one encounters high and low. If high, one should look low. If low, one should look high. "Gaze" means observing movement and stillness, insubstantial and substantial.

In order to attain victory, one must attack the opponent's unprepared places, seeking points of inattention. This is striking the opponent with three unknowns: without moving, gain the advantage in advance. Observe until prepared, and then move. When moving, be rapid. One move and then victory. The song says:

> Meeting an enemy, one must observe closely,
> Inspect the face and gauge the posture, and do not hesitate,
> If hesitant with ten opponents, then ten dangers,
> With one opponent, gaze until prepared, and then move first.

The Ten Losses in Crossing Hands

When martial arts practitioners cross hands, whether they are of internal or external schools, there must be a division of victorious and defeated. Defeat has many causes. Speaking of the important points of fighting, there are generally ten ways to lose with all attacks. Not knowing how to gather the qi and consolidate the spirit when crossing hands is the first loss. Having nothing within the chest and skill that is too shallow, issuing palms with no power is the second loss. The hands not differentiating between front and rear while covering in front of the chest, only concentrating on charging in to attack is the third loss. Choosing too high a stance with evident gaps is the fourth loss. Jumping, leaping, evading, and dodging too frequently, working without rest is the fifth loss. Crossing hands only at the wrist, without knowing to advance the feet and advance the body is the sixth loss. When crossing hands, if the two combatants seize each other and wrestle together and only then try to strike, this is the seventh loss. Bending the body to change postures and lifting the chest when facing the enemy is the eighth loss. Only guarding above and not guarding below, only knowing how to use the hands but not knowing how to use the feet is the ninth loss. Failing to understand the requirements of grasping, seizing, leading, and carrying or the methods of sticking, joining, following, and adhering is the tenth loss.

The Ten Methods in Fighting

Generally, those who pass on a martial art must first talk of its theory and second understand its postures. Today, those who understand the postures are many, but those who talk of its theory are very few. They already know each move and each posture, but when investigating their meaning, they are at a loss. If those who pass on a martial art do not pass on its theory, how are those who study able to grasp its truth? In lacking the smallest part, they mistake it by a thousand miles and are replete with errors. Here we briefly explain the ten methods of Baguazhang fighting, as an admonishment to martial enthusiasts.

STEPPING METHODS

People often say that Taijiquan talks of the waist, Xingyiquan talks of the hands, and Baguazhang talks of the stepping. This makes sense. In crossing hands with someone, Baguazhang especially stresses stepping methods. There is a rhyme-song that says:

> *Without having moved the tip, first move the root,*
> *Quick hands are not as good as a half-Following Step,*
> *Advancing and retreating and leaving and entering with only a half*
> *   step,*
> *Controlling the opponent and advancing in attack is miraculous, like*
> *   a god,*
> *When power is concentrated on the opponent, their root is already*
> *   gone,*
> *Wishing to again gather power, they find it difficult,*
> *The opponent's force is like a thousand pounds and quick like a shuttle,*
> *Evading the strong must use quick stepping,*
> *Evading, dodging, drawing in, and changing all rely on stepping,*
> *With feet and eyes coiling, the mystery is everywhere.*

There are eight stepping methods: advance, retreat, shuffle, skip, steal, bound, jump, and dart. Advancing step means stepping forward. Advancing steps in Baguazhang usually start with the front foot first. Retreating step means the opponent comes with fierce force, and the practitioner takes a retreating step and evades with the body. This is avoiding the substantial and striking the insubstantial. Retreating steps in Baguazhang usually start with the rear foot first. Shuffling step means the opponent retreats backward and the practitioner immediately advances and attacks with a shuffle, the step and palm arriving simultaneously. Skipping step means when the two opponents are separated by four or five feet and one wants to advance and attack, with a skip forward one can arrive. Stealing step means when the opponent leads the practitioner's hand horizontally, they take a stealing step and miraculously spin the body. A stealing step and spinning the body can change opposing to following. It is an excellent fighting move to spin the waist and change to a flowing step, and more contemplation and usage should be sought through practical experience. Bounding step means when the opponent is six or seven feet away, one advances with the front foot and bounds with the rear foot, arriving in one movement. Jumping step means when the opponent is eight or nine feet away, one jumps and leaps, arriving like the wind. It is too late for the opponent to dodge and evade, and the practitioner's palm has already struck the opponent's body. Darting step advances with the front foot and carries the back foot, which leaps and flies horizontally. Of these eight types of steps, Darting step is the most difficult. If one's art is not complete, then this cannot be trained lightly, even though the other fine stepping methods may be easily practiced and applied.

Body Methods

Body methods also contain eight words: draw, evade, wave, twist, turn, spin, overturn, and stop. Drawing body means the opponent advances with an attack and the practitioner sucks the body back, transforming and opening and changing postures to advance. Evading body means the opponent advances with a very fierce attack that the practitioner cannot adhere to, and then the practitioner uses lively stepping to evade and dodge. Waving body means one is grabbed by the opponent with strength that is difficult to escape from, and then the practitioner uses lively stepping and waves the body to dissolve and open. Twisting body means the opponent advances, seeking the center, and the practitioner uses lively stepping to twist the body and change the posture. Turning body means the opponent and the practitioner cross hands, and the practitioner first flashes a false Piercing Palm and then escapes, turning around quickly and again seeking an attack. Spinning body means the opponent leads the practitioner horizontally, and the practitioner spins the body with a clever change and advances with an attack. Overturning body means that when facing opponents on both sides, the practitioner overturns the body and guards the rear. Stopping body means when joining hands, the practitioner carries the opponent behind, steps forward, stops the body, and looks to the rear.

When crossing hands with someone, the body methods must exemplify liveliness in application.

Hand Methods

Hand methods are both single-handed and double-handed. The hands rise like tigers pouncing on prey, fall like eagles tearing at a catch. They are quick in rising, quick in falling like a swallow skimming the water, pressing and moving. The applications of the hand methods are contained in the changes of the Sixty-Four Palms. The key is trained power. The palms rise like lifting a cauldron, fall with the ability to split stone. When crossing hands with someone, the two hands are like gate sentries; issuing the hands is like holding a spear—one forward, one in rear, one above, one below, seemingly straight but not straight, seeming bent but not bent, one hand in front to meet the opponent at any time, one hand in back to guard oneself and assist the front hand at any time. The two hands are used in unison, striving for the initiative.

Foot Methods

Foot methods are kick, stomp, step, and tread. Kick the leg, kick the knee, kick the abdomen, kick the head. Stomp the waist, stomp the hip, stomp the knee, stomp the leg. Step on the leg, step on the foot. Tread on the foot. The feet kick like a bow releasing an arrow and stomp like a bullet hitting a bird, and they should issue and retract quickly. The feet step like a whirlwind sweeping the ground and tread like a stone hitting the water, taking aim and applying. When crossing hands with someone, the two feet are placed one in front, one behind, the front empty and the back solid, the energy thirty percent in front and seventy percent in back. In this way one may advance, retreat, and change at will.

Intercepting Methods

One must know intercepting methods when crossing hands with others. Intercepting methods include intercepting the hands, intercepting the body, intercepting the legs, intercepting the face, and intercepting the mind. Intercepting the hands means the opponent moves their hands first, and the practitioner uses their own hands to block and intercept, then changes postures and advances with an attack. Intercepting the body means the opponent has not yet moved and the practitioner uses the body to block the opponent; when the opponent moves, the practitioner again changes postures and intercepts. Intercepting the legs means using the changing of the legs to intercept leg to leg. Intercepting the face means the opponent's face shows the intention. If smiling, then one intercepts with a smile; if fierce, then one intercepts with ferocity. Intercepting the mind means observing the opponent's movement and stillness, inviting an opportunity and then intercepting it. Knowing the intercepting methods, even with equal opportunity, one may still gain the first strike.

Leading Methods

Leading is grabbing the opponent's wrist with one hand and moving forcefully left or right, and it is differentiated between inward leading and outward leading. The left hand leading the opponent's left hand, and the right hand leading the right hand, forcefully moving outward, is outward leading. The left hand leading the opponent's right hand, and the right hand leading the left hand, forcefully moving toward the chest, is inward leading. Outward leading steps forward and advances to attack from outside. Inward leading draws back with the body, steps back or switches hands, and then advances to attack. When leading, one must lead the opponent's arm horizontally, causing the hand, foot, and back power to be useless while one follows the energy and moves at will. Leading is one of the important hand methods of Baguazhang.

Carrying Methods

Single-handed is leading, double-handed is carrying. Carrying is when one hand grabs the wrist, one hand grabs the elbow and pulls forcefully behind the body. The left hand grabbing the left wrist, the right hand grabbing the left elbow and pulling forcefully backward to the left with the right foot in front is called left carrying. Reversed, it is called right carrying. If the left comes, carry left; if the right comes, carry right; left and right are the same. Carrying must follow the energy and use hard force. The method to apply carrying is to issue the hands like a snake devouring its prey. If the opponent is higher, carry and throw; if the opponent is lower, carry and dislodge. Carrying is also an important hand method for Baguazhang fighting.

Yanking Methods

Yanking method is similar to carrying method. Either single-handed or double-handed, grab the opponent's wrist and pull downward forcefully, with a violent energy. If the opponent's hands are near and held high, drill up, then yank. If the opponent's hands are near and level, pierce and then yank. If the left comes, yank left; if the right comes, yank right. Yank violently causing the opponent to shake, the body to move, and the spirit to disperse. Although the opponent has methods, they are of no use, and the practitioner can act at will.

Following Methods

Following methods are following the opponent's energy and then moving. If the opponent retreats, follow with an advance. If the opponent advances, follow with a retreat. If struck high, follow high; if struck low, follow low. If struck left, follow left; if struck right, follow right. If coming quickly, block quickly; if coming slowly, meet slowly. As soon as the opponent issues a hand, the practitioner follows using silk-reeling energy, wrapping the opponent's hand, sticking, joining, following, and adhering at will. Regardless of what attack is used, the opponent cannot escape the practitioner's influence.

CHASING METHODS

Chasing methods are one unified qi, known as chasing and following the body. When crossing hands with someone, if the opponent wants to escape, one uses a chasing method. Chasing methods must be fast, moving like a dragon, jumping like a tiger, chasing the form and following the shadow, the eyes ever moving, chasing the wind and catching the moon without relaxing, causing the opponent—although wanting to escape—to be shackled and unable to flee.

In sum, when martial artists compare skills, it's like a general leading troops; if a practitioner has fine troops but a poor general, one cannot gain victory. If one has good art but no skill, one cannot attack someone. After long practice of Baguazhang, in comparing hands with someone, one need not use too many postures. This is what is described by "an army is not in numbers but in bravery." This art is not in volume but in refinement. Refinement is the name for deep skill. If all of the elements above are understood, one's Baguazhang fighting will be supernatural.

Cheng School Gao Style Baguazhang's Health-Building Benefits

The song of life-cultivation says:

Moving in Turning Palm removes the hundred diseases,
To keep the body soft and supple, study the Single Palm Change,

Snake-Form Flowing-Posture relieves heart fire,
Dragon-Form Piercing-Hand regulates the San Jiao,
Turning-Body Tiger-Striking soothes the liver and lungs,
Swallow-Overturning Covering-Hand solidifies the kidneys and waist,
Spinning-Body Back-Covering increases power,
Twisting-Body Forward-Searching balances the spleen and stomach,
Overturning-Body Backward-Inserting strengthens tendons and bones,
Stopping-Body Moving-Hooking, and the hundred maladies disperse,
For the five overexertions and seven harms, use Black Dragon Whips
*   Its Tail,*
To strengthen and bolster the body, training the palms is the highest art.

According to modern economic theory, Baguazhang's practical value is its utility—that its natural attributes are able to satisfy every type of need of the masses in our society. Baguazhang can be used not only for fighting, self-protection, and opposing violence; it can also be used for building health. Increasing and strengthening internal power and raising combat technique ability while building health is the evident special characteristic of Baguazhang. Because of this, strengthening the being and building the body is the essential physical education value of Baguazhang.

"Move and do not decline" is an outstanding traditional Chinese life-cultivation concept. The ancient centenarian doctor Sun Simiao wrote: "If the body is often worked lightly, then reaching one hundred will be gentle and pleasant, the qi and blood strong and cultivated, the spirit contained. If the meridians and channels are exercised, external evils have difficulty invading, just as flowing water is not polluted, and the doors rot but the hinges do not decay." Modern scientists recognize that a human's vitality has an extremely close relationship with both genetic inheritance and exercise. In comparing the two, exercise is even more important to vitality than inheritance. Because of this, the concept that vitality lies in exercise has already been closely linked scientifically with human vitality and physical exercise. Exercise has benefits for health and benefits in raising the quality of life. This conclusion is not only acknowledged by modern doctors and health science practitioners but is becoming accepted more and more by the general public. Experience shows that, in general, physical exercise must be of suitable duration, according to the proper method, and maintained regularly in order to receive health-building effects. If the exercise form and methods are different, the health-building effects are different. The commonality of all physical exercise is that it can not only promote internal metabolism, increase and strengthen new vitality in the body, maintain the internal yin-yang balance of qi and blood, and prevent or eradicate microorganisms invading the body, but can moreover dredge the qi-blood, digestive, and lymphatic pathways of the body, maintain the free flow of all vessel systems in the body, and take the wastes produced by the body's physiological processes, including every type of poisonous and harmful substance, and quickly remove them from the body, thus reducing the internal factors that result in bodily illness, achieving the health-building goal of preventing and curing disease. But it must be clear: physical exercise is a teaching that takes as its primary duty developing bodily strength and building one's constitution. Physical education studies should be health-building education studies. Physical exercise must train the body to increase the constitution and have building health and strengthening the body as the goal of exercise. Exercise must be able to promote growth and development in youth, must be able to stave off all types of degenerative changes in the middle-aged and elderly, and must be the type of exercise that has the intention of raising the quality of life. It should not contain those types of sporting exercises where winning over others is the only goal, and training and competition border on brutality to the point of surpassing the limits of life; not only is this not beneficial to health-building, it will in fact create harm for the health of the body, to the point of inducing disability or early death. Baguazhang exercises, then, are one of the traditional physical education regimens where the health-building effects are obvious.

In 1994 the World Health Organization revised its definition of the word *health*. This new meaning recognizes that a person must not only have correct physiological and psychological function, adapting well to the society, but must also have high moral character. The research of

Brazilian medical expert named Martinez[10] discovered that people who habitually embezzle and accept bribes are prone to cancer, brain hemorrhages, heart disease, neuroses, and other illnesses, and have shortened life spans. A good mental state can encourage the secretion of more beneficial hormones, enzymes, and acetylcholine within the body. These substances can regulate the rate of blood flow and excite neurons to their most optimal state, thus increasing the body's disease-fighting ability, promoting the body's vitality and health, and lengthening life. For those who act contrary to societal moral norms, their conduct will inevitably lead to nervousness, fearfulness, and guilt, leading the function of the central nervous and endocrine systems to lose balance, disturbing the body's normal physiological processes, weakening their immune system's defensive ability, and in the end, under the stress of an evil state of mind and every type of disease torment, will lead to early decline or loss of life.

Baguazhang is a study in balanced movement and stillness, training the internal to foster the root, nature and life trained together, body and mind jointly cultivated. Moreover, it especially emphasizes that "in training, virtue is first," and strongly attaches importance to the cultivation of morals in addition to the meticulous requirements and rich content of its special characteristics of form movement. Because of this, the theory and practical effects of strengthening the being and building the body through Baguazhang also have unique character.

In his *Study of Baguazhang,* Sun Lutang writes: "The nature of this art [Baguazhang] is that it simply takes cultivating correct qi as its aim. Therefore the many types of heresy and black magic cannot compare with it." He also says, "the art of Bagua boxing has an impact on the whole body and spirit, can stave off illness and lengthen life, and is not only for studying fighting;" and "Baguazhang practice is very easy, its application the most refined, implementing the natural principles of heaven and earth, utilizing one complete and pure qi. Whether male, female, women, or children, or those in middle age, anyone can practice it."

If Baguazhang is practiced as far as the miraculous level, then it possesses "the true image of miraculous transformation and skillful application, clarity of the spirit, strengthening of the essence, the form and countenance pure and correct, smooth and beautiful. With awareness of mind and subtlety of method, the origins of its theory are profound, quiet, and deep and cannot be measured. The qi is vast like the heavens and broad without measure. This is the description of a boxing art which is profound, subtle, and miraculous." Master Sun's Baguazhang treatise vividly describes the dialectical relationship between Baguazhang practice and a person's correct qi. It relates how, in the process of ceaseless turning and changing movements, Baguazhang gives rise to health-building effects. This point has already been acknowledged around the world.

An English researcher named Sitman[11] says: "utilizing walking to consume heat and bring about weight loss can achieve good results." Halalide,[12] also of England, says: "For those who work with their minds, especially speaking of those who undertake creative work, walking is the best method of physiological exercise." Baguazhang's walking is a high-level form of walking. This is walking and spinning, which is walking cyclically eight steps along the edge of the circle, with the single requirement of circulating while walking and spinning. The length of each step is approximately the length of one side of an octagon inscribed within the circle, with the angle between two adjacent sides roughly 135 degrees. This way inevitably causes the line of the inside foot's outer edge and the line of outside foot's inner edge to coincide with the tangent line at the place of stepping down with a Baibu and Koubu step while walking and spinning. In order to make walking with this type of Baibu-Koubu stepping seem like walking on clouds or in flowing water, the center of gravity should move level and at an even speed. The two legs should be slightly bent, the two feet rise and fall level. The back foot presses and lifts, the front foot tests and treads, this way forming the famous Mud-Wading Step. In actuality, this type of walking method evolved from Daoist walking cultivation methods and, tracing it back even farther, is very likely connected to the ancient Yu Stepping.[13] According to legend, the first generation of famous Bagua practitioners could place a bowl of water on their heads and hold bowls of water in each hand while walking and spinning for a long period without spilling even a drop. To reach this type of state, the entire body must be relaxed and open, using intention as the guide and spirit as the application, harmonious like a fish that has forgotten the water. This is the Moving Posts. This is Baguazhang's unique specialty, and a rare moving qigong.

This type of walking and spinning opens the three yin and three yang meridians of the foot. In walking and spinning with Koubu and Baibu, the three yang meridians of the outside leg and the three yin meridians of the inside leg are correspondingly opened. In spinning to change direction, the two legs again switch, with the inside leg becoming the outside leg, and the outside leg becoming the inside leg. While walking and spinning, the two legs must seek to rub shins, causing the two legs to rub and knead each other and thus receive conditioning. This type of meridian-opening method is a training method particular to Baguazhang, seeking to simultaneously develop and naturally coordinate yin and yang through walking and spinning.

While walking and spinning, it is required that the five toes grasp the ground, the heel pushes forward, the center of the foot is drawn up, and the intention follows *yongquan*. In this way it will cause the jing well points of the three yin and three yang meridians of the feet to first open and then roil like waves, the *shu* stream points to open, and thus traveling upward open the jing river and he sea points. In this way the five shu stream points are completely opened. The "Basic Questions" portion of the *Huangdi Neijing* has the related theory of treating diseases of the entire body with the five shu stream points. Baguazhang's training method of causing the five shu points to open naturally while turning and walking is, in reality, a high-level Daoyin art.

When walking and spinning, setting aside the requirements for stepping methods, it is also required to extend the arms toward the center of the circle, one palm attending to the outside, one palm attending to the inside. The index finger of the front palm extends vertically to lead up, each finger slightly bent like holding a ball, with the form like a dragon claw. The tip of the middle finger of the back palm is placed on the inside edge of the elbow of the front arm, with the same shape as the front palm. Walking and spinning must maintain natural and open breathing, the front arm opening outward, the back arm wrapping inward, the heels of the palms pressing out, the hearts of the palms pulling back. In this way the three yin and three yang meridians of the hand will be completely opened. Of course, first to open are the five shu points, as described above.

To maintain this type of posture, the waist must twist, with the spine twisting but remaining vertical. In this way the Dai channel is opened, and above and below, the meridians and channels are connected horizontally; the back shu points are opened, which has a direct benefit for the zang-fu organs. The head presses up and the anus is lifted, causing the *Baihui* and *Huiyin* points to correspond above and below; connecting the Heavenly Circuit is a matter of intention. Those who regularly practice the walking and spinning of Baguazhang will have the feeling of being unwilling to stop. The reason for this is in the hundred channels being opened, causing the great system, which is the entire body, to be placed in a high-level state of dynamic equilibrium. Changes of palm position, body position, and leg position will even further ensure that in the entire body, above and below, there is nothing that is not moving. Having all places in the body receiving training attains the level of the best whole-body exercise.

The paragraphs above only discusses walking and spinning. There are countless books dealing with qigong, and so the formless aspects such as intention and qi will not be discussed further here.

When modern people talk of the health-building effects of Baguazhang, some discuss it from the aspect of biology according to systems like the digestive system or the reproductive system; some discuss it according to disease type, such as high blood pressure or diabetes. The authors feel that all of Baguazhang's abilities to cause one to be healthy, prevent disease, and remove disease are founded in its holistic and systematic concepts. The reason for the body to have disease is the imbalance of yin and yang. This imbalance is not in a specific part but is the overall system not being in coordination, with symptoms at specific locations. If one is to treat the disease, then one must regulate the larger system and not treat the constituent part. This high-level treatment principle model is the Taiji Diagram, which portrays both static balance and active balance. In summary, Master Dong Haichuan said, "Of the many training methods, walking is first." If one can persevere and strictly adhere to the Baguazhang requirements, stepping with yin and yang, treading the Eight Trigrams while turning-the-circle walking and spinning, over time one will receive the miraculous effects of training the internal and fostering the root.

Eight Trigram yin-yang theory is an important component part of the body of ancient Chinese philosophy. According to Chinese medical theory, "if yang flourishes, then it's a yin disease; if yin flourishes, then it's a yang disease." Only when yin and yang are balanced and united can the body maintain health. Baguazhang utilizes exactly this yin-yang theory to reach the effects of strengthening the vital qi and eliminating pathogenic factors, strengthening the being and building the body. For example, Baguazhang uses the circle as the method, with walking left as yang and walking right as yin. Walking and spinning left and right with changing movements opens the meridians and channels and regulates the qi and blood, thus causing the body inside and outside to unite, yin and yang to balance, the qi and blood to harmonize, reaching the effect of building health. The main health-building effects are prominently exhibited in the following several aspects:

Skill Is in Training the Internal and Fostering the Root

Chinese medicine has an important principle, "strengthen the vital qi and eliminate the pathogenic factors," that emphasizes that in treating illness, first treat the cause, then treat the symptoms. Training Baguazhang is an important method to strengthen the vital qi. The Pre-Heaven Baguazhang Posture-Completion Methods, or Twenty-Four Requirements, all embody the special points of internal skill training. Because of this, regularly practicing Baguazhang has beneficial strengthening and regulating effects for each tissue system—especially the internal zang-fu organs—for which it has a very strong massaging effect, thus reaching the level of efficacy that trains the internal and fosters the root, builds the constitution, strengthens the vital qi and eliminates pathogenic factors, improves health, guards against disease, and cures disease.

Chinese medicine also recognizes that the body has twelve meridians and eight extraordinary channels, which connect internally to the zang-fu organs and wrap the four limbs, skin, and muscle. The fingers and toes are all the origins or termini of the meridians. The Hand Taiyin Lung Meridian terminates on the inner side of the thumb. The Hand Jueyin Pericardium Meridian terminates at the tip of the middle finger. The Hand Shaoyin Heart Meridian terminates at the tip of the little finger. The Hand Yangming Large Intestine Meridian originates at the tip of the index finger. The Hand Shaoyang Sanjiao Meridian originates at the tip of the ring finger. The Hand Taiyang Small Intestine Meridian originates on the side of the tip of the little finger. The Foot Taiyin Spleen Meridian originates at the inside tip of the large toe. The Foot Jueyin Liver Meridian originates at the outer edge tip of the big toe. The Foot Shaoyin Kidney Meridian originates at the Bubbling Well point on the foot. The Foot Yangming Stomach Meridian terminates at the side of the tip of the second toe. The Foot Shaoyang Gallbladder Meridian terminates at the tip of the fourth toe. The Foot Taiyang Urinary Bladder Meridian terminates at the outer edge of the tip of the little toe. The requirements for Baguazhang practice especially and noticeably emphasize that the five toes grip the earth and the wrist is bent with the five finger spread open and pressing. In this way the results of practice are to foster the synchronized movement of every meridian and channel, causing the twelve meridians all to receive relatively strong stimulation, subsequently influencing the movement of the zang-fu organs, reaching the goal of training the internal and fostering the root.

Efficacy Is in Strengthening the Legs and Solidifying the Waist

A common saying is that "when people age, they age first from the legs. When age comes, the waist bends, and one must grasp a cane to stand." Due to the singular training methods of Baguazhang—such as walking-the-circle spinning and turning while bending the legs and twisting the waist, the five toes grasping the ground as if treading in mud—the waist is twisted toward the center of the circle from beginning to end. In changing movements, the intention leads the qi, the qi penetrates the power. Power starts from the feet and transfers to the waist, using the waist to carry the shoulders, and the shoulders to carry the arms, palms, and fingers. Because of this, regularly practicing Baguazhang is important training for the legs and waist, and it produces beneficial effects to stop the decline of leg and waist function, strengthen the legs, and solidify the waist.

Ingenuity Is in Building the Body and Strengthening the Mind

Baguazhang has a special characteristic different from other boxing arts, which is that in both the Pre-Heaven Palms and the Post-Heaven Palms, for every posture, if there is a left, there must be a right, and left and right are the same. This special characteristic of practice can not only promote coordination and enliven the body but also has the special effect of improving brain function. Medical experts think that the brain is divided into two hemispheres, with the left hemisphere controlling the right side of the body and the right hemisphere controlling the left side of the body. The level of activity in most average people is greater in their right hand and right leg, and so their left hemisphere is relatively more developed. Regular practice of Baguazhang can greatly strengthen the level of activity in the left hand and left leg, thus causing the right hemisphere to receive ample training, which is greatly beneficial in maintaining the vitality of the brain and especially in developing the intelligence of the right hemisphere.

Benefit Is in Holistically Building the Body

Within the Cheng School Gao Style Baguazhang system, Post-Standing skills and the Pre-Heaven Palms can, while building health, produce internal power and a unified body uniting movement and stillness. Due to

Baguazhang's seeking movement in stillness and stillness in movement, and whole-body exercises balancing movement and stillness, its health-building efficacy is complete.

First, moving in the Pre-Heaven Palms and Turning Palms require hard and soft to be mutually aiding, but more emphasis is placed on softness as the focus, as low-intensity movement. When practicing, "the form is worked without being exhausted; one sweats but does not pant," which is greatly beneficial to the health of the body and mind.

"Working the form" can promote the metabolism and circulation of the blood, and it can encourage the development of every organ and system in the body, increasing one's internal vitality. "Without being exhausted" then means the right degree. Scientific research shows that exercise of excessive intensity will not only exceed one's limits and consume one's energy, but the body's immune system will be affected first, causing the functions of the body's white blood cells and antibodies to be interrupted, increasing the burden on the nervous system. Because of this, some people call exercise of excessive intensity "self-crippling exercise." Baguazhang is a health-building exercise that uses an appropriate degree of activity.

Exercise that induces sweating is beneficial in building health. Scientific study shows that the surface of the body has more than five thousand sweat glands, and every sweat gland contains immunoglobulin A, which can effectively stop viruses and bacteria from entering the body through the hair follicles. Exercise that induces sweating can not only expel waste and harmful substances from the body but can also safeguard the smooth function of the sweat glands, increasing the vitality of the immunoglobulin A in the glands and, from this, achieve a health-building result. Not panting can reduce the burden on the heart and lungs, which shows that Baguazhang is an exercise of appropriate degree.

At the same time, not being exhausted and not panting also have the meaning of arousing the nervous system. The practice of Baguazhang can regulate and correct the emotions, causing the optimal arousal of the cerebral cortex. Scientific research shows that this type of arousal can promote the activity of the hypothalamus and, through secretion of related hormones, stimulate the pituitary gland, causing the brain to produce substances that bring pleasure to the body (endorphins), which can alleviate the harm done to the mind and body through mental stress, depression, and worry, thus training the will and raising the ability to adapt and adjust to harmful stimuli, reaching the goal of holistically training the body and mind.

Second, Baguazhang Post-Standing and Pre-Heaven Palms both emphasize natural breathing, gradually transitioning to abdominal breathing. Abdominal breathing is the most advantageous breathing method for health. At birth, everyone's first mouthful of air is inhaled using abdominal breathing, which is whole-lung breathing. However, after children's bodies are upright and they learn to walk, they gradually change to thoracic breathing. Scientific research shows that humanity's learned thoracic breathing method causes the middle and lower four-fifths of the entire pulmonary alveoli of the lung to become useless in the long-term. The result of this long-term biased use and disuse is that the upper lungs become overused, and the lower lungs become overstagnated. This is the reason that degenerative lung diseases in the middle-aged and elderly mostly invade the lower lobe of the lung. Regular practice of Baguazhang utilizing abdominal breathing methods can cause the pulmonary alveoli of the middle and lower lobe of the lungs to receive passive exercise, which can prevent and cure many lung diseases. Utilizing abdominal breathing while undertaking Baguazhang exercises, one can inhale from several times up to a dozen times more oxygen than the average person who is sedentary, thus benefitting the health of the heart and the physiological function of the whole body.

Third, our ancestral medical studies and modern medicine all recognize that people and all living systems are holographic, and every discreet part carries in it the germ of the whole. "Holographic" means that each discreet part of a person's body reflects complete information about the whole body. For example, a person's palms are the "information centers" reflecting the functions of the internal zang organs, and the zang-fu organs all have reflective zones on the palms. Similarly, the feet reflect complete information about the whole body, and the zang-fu organs also have reflective zones on the soles of the feet. According to this principle, as a result of Baguazhang's requirements for gripping toes, spreading fingers, and Mud-Wading Step, and the effect of using intention but not using power, the hands and feet are important areas of training in Baguazhang. During exercise, this causes the qi and blood to directly fill the fingertips and soles of the feet, thus arousing the zang-fu organs, promoting and improving microcirculation of the blood, benefitting the nervous system, and achieving whole body health-building effects.

Fourth, in the process of practicing Post-Standing skills and Pre Heaven Palms, under the effects of the basic requirements and intention, the mouth cavity will be moist and produce more *jin-ye* fluids (saliva), which should be regularly swallowed. This jin-ye originates in the essence of food and water and is also a treasure of the body. It not only has the ability to aid in digestion, irrigate the zang-fu organs, and beautify and moisten the skin, but also has antibacterial and antiviral effects, benefits growth and development, and fights decline and old age. Modern medical research has discovered that many types of enzymes and hormones, as well as immunoglobulin A, are contained within the jin-ye fluids. These can cause carcinogenic materials like nitrosyl compounds, aflatoxin, tobacco tar, and soot to lose their cancer-causing abilities within thirty seconds, and thus saliva can be viewed as the body's natural cancer-preventing and cancer-fighting preparation. It has been reported that scientists have also discovered that jin-ye contains a type of secreted white blood-cell inhibitory protein enzyme that can be effective in inhibiting the HIV virus from infecting the body's immune cells. Because of this, multiplying the jin-ye is also an important effect of Baguazhang's health-building.

Gao Yisheng on Building the Body

Regarding the health-building effects of Baguazhang, Gao Yisheng wrote the "Life Cultivation Treatise" portion of his manual, summarized below:

Those who study this art mostly use cultivating the bodily form as their intent and do not take crossing hands with others and contesting strength as their goal. Only Baguazhang takes health-building, strengthening the body, and cultivating the body as its main aim. As an art that uses the martial but conducts itself civilly, cultivating the bodily form and protecting qi and blood, none is better than this.

Within the body, jing, qi, and shen are the foundation. Shen is produced from qi, qi is produced from jing, jing is produced from blood, and the blood and qi are the body of life. The strength or weakness, life or death of the body all depend primarily on qi and blood. Ordinary people training in this art is like the sages training the treasures. Regular practice of Baguazhang can lengthen tendons, pull the bones, increase qi, enliven the blood, promote the metabolism, and, because training in Baguazhang will increase eating and drinking, qi and blood naturally proliferate. If the qi and blood are sufficient, it will develop the bodily form and enhance power and energy, causing it to circulate, reaching everywhere back and forth, returning the body to balance, and building the being and form. If the internal and external are strong, illness cannot arise. With continued practice of Baguazhang, the skill becomes even greater, and it can protect the bodily form completely and fully; cold and heat cannot invade the body; wind and rain cannot damage the body; toil and disease cannot harm it internally.

Qi and blood originate in the middle *jiao*, commanded by the heart and lungs, externally guarding at the surface, internally moving in the core, coming and going, rising and falling, and circulating throughout the whole body. This is the work of the *ying qi* and *wei qi*. The ying qi is the essential qi of transformed water and food. Wei qi is the ferocious qi of transformed water and food. The ying controls the blood, and wei controls the qi. Qi and blood irrigate the body, regulate the five zang organs and moisten the six fu organs, and join the internal and external, moving without cease, nourishing and protecting the body. When the eyes receive, them they can see; when the ears receive them, they can hear; when hands receive them, they can grasp; when the feet receive them, they can walk; when the zang organs receive them, they can produce fluids; when the fu organs receive them, they can produce qi. Repeatedly training palm skill to increase and nurture qi and blood, the eyes can see and are doubly bright and clear; the ears can hear and are doubly aware and agile; the hands can grasp and are doubly strong; the feet can walk and are doubly quick; the zang organs can produce fluids and are doubly moistened; the fu organs can produce qi and are doubly filled. When the qi and blood are moistened, promoted, and connected, there can be no greater benefit. If the qi and blood are abundant, the form is abundant. If the qi and blood decline, the form declines. For the desire to cultivate the bodily form, protect the qi and blood, prevent and remove disease, extend one's years, and lengthen life, there is really none more miraculous than the art of Baguazhang, a treasure of treasures.

Toward Scientific Tests and Conclusions about Building the Body

Modern medicine thinks that declining with age is the path that the body's vital movement must follow. As a result of the fact that Baguazhang is a type of training method with the unique characteristic of uniting intention, qi, and the body, regular practice of Baguazhang can cause the body to increase oxygen intake, cause the meridians and channels of the body to be aroused, can promote increased speed of blood circulation, and can increase qi and lengthen power, balancing the yin and yang of qi and blood and regulating and correcting one's thought processes and emotions. These effects all have positive ramifications for fighting decline and aging. In 1996, expert scholars from Beijing Sport University, including Gao Qiang, director and associate professor of the Physiological Sciences Teaching and Research Laboratory, Kang Gewu of the Martial Arts Research and Training Laboratory, Xian Hanzhao of the Sports Medicine Teaching and Research Laboratory, and Chen Minyi of the Exercise Analysis Teaching and Research Laboratory together used modern scientific methods for research and experimentation to prove Baguazhang's health-building and life-extending effectiveness.

They organized one group of older people who regularly trained in Baguazhang (the practice group comprised thirty people, average age

69.43) and one group of older people who had never practiced Baguazhang but who were of healthy body and took part in other daily exercise (the comparison group comprised thirty people, average age 69.67). Under similar conditions, they carried out repeated physiological target measurements on the two groups of people, including X-rays of the brain, lower back, and hips; measurements of shoulder, hip, and spinal column movement angle; respiratory function measurements; circulatory function measurements; and tests of muscle workload capacity, aural acuity, visual acuity, balance, and range of motion of the four limbs. They took the resulting numbers and carried out computerized statistical analysis of participants above age 60.69, above age 70, and of the entire group as a whole. The results showed that in each type of measurement there was a clear distinction that the practice group was better than the comparison group.

Conclusion one is that practicing Baguazhang can delay degenerative changes of the bones, including osteoporosis and osteoproliferation, and through training produce the beneficial adaptation of strengthening tendons and bones.

Conclusion two is that practice of the qi sinking to the dantian and the breath naturally becoming fine, even, deep, and long in Baguazhang causes the depth of inhalation and exhalation to increase, and especially increases the range of movement of the diaphragm, thus improving lung function. Utilizing rhythmic belly breathing can also promote the return flow of blood in the veins, and increased practice of Baguazhang can promote the systolic function of the four limbs and muscles, causing the capillaries of the heart, lungs, and muscles to open and their volume to increase, and blood circulation to increase; and can reduce deposits of fatty material plaque on the vascular walls, improving nutrition of the heart muscle and skeletal muscle, increasing the function of the heart and lungs.

Conclusion three is that study of Baguazhang has a beneficial effect on movement ability. For example, in endurance, thrust force, reaction time, waist and hip range of motion, aural acuity, visual acuity, balance, number of teeth, and many other measurements, the practice group was also clearly superior to the comparison group. From deep personal understanding arising from the research experiment process, Gao Qiang said: "Even we strong middle-aged people could not match some measurement standards." Through this experiment, the results amply show that the practice of Baguazhang can delay or prevent all types of degenerative changes related to decline and aging of the body, and moreover can cause the body to develop beneficial adaptations to training. This provides scientific theory and a practical experiential basis for Baguazhang's effects in building health and removing illness, lengthening years, and benefiting life.

Required Introductory Knowledge of Cheng School Gao Style Baguazhang
Ten Rules for the Practice of Baguazhang

The successive generations of great Baguazhang masters all wholly emphasized martial virtue. The Ten Rules for the Practice of Baguazhang passed on by Gao Yisheng condense and embody the main tenet that "in practicing the arts, virtue is the foremost." Those who study Baguazhang should know and observe them.

Rule one: be filial and honor your father and mother. One's father and mother are the origin of one's body. Without parents, how can you exist? Someone acting unfilial is less than a beast and cannot be taught or interacted with. Even more, they cannot be entered into the Baguazhang school.

Rule two: be harmonious in the village. "The village" means those living near the central well. "Harmonious" means showing mutual respect, being mutually polite, mutually aiding in difficulty, and mutually caring for others in illness.

Rule three: respect the elderly and aid the weak. "Elderly" means the previous generation or the aged, who on principle should be respected. "The weak" means women, children, or those in distress. "Aid" means to assist, care for, and take care of.

Rule four: do not drink liquor to the point of getting drunk. Drink liquor in the appropriate measure for one's body and not excessively. When inebriated, it is extremely easy to injure oneself, and one will lose dignity and commit errors. Because of this, one should not train Baguazhang when inebriated.

Rule five: avoid gambling and drugs. Since antiquity, gambling has led to theft, and gambling and theft are connected. One should add a strong prohibition against gambling. Drugs harm the body, destroy the family, and cannot lead to gain.

Rule six: respect the teacher's instruction. The instructor is the master. The student is the disciple. Master and disciple are like father and son. "Instruction" means words of training and guidance. Obtaining the art relies solely on the teaching of the master. If there was no master to instruct, the art would be like water with no source. The master's instructions cannot not be obeyed.

Rule seven: practice carefully. There is no difficultly in the world that does not fear a careful person. A common saying is "The teacher leads one through the gate; cultivation depends on the student." If the teacher transmits one application, carefully practice it with modesty and perseverance. With long days and years, the art will naturally become complete.

Rule eight: do not allow wild speech or excessive talk. Wild speech means exaggeration. Excessive talk means ridiculing and mocking words. When practicing, definitely do not forget that gongfu is without limits, and outside this heaven is another heaven; outside the self is a greater self.

Rule nine: be loyal and sincere, straightforward and honest. "Loyal and sincere" means true and virtuous. "Straightforward and honest" means steady in all matters, without being frivolous and unreliable.

Rule ten: seek trust from others, and make friends widely. Trust is the foundation on which a practitioner becomes established. To conduct oneself as a human being, one must take action on the words they speak; actions must have results. Friends are one of the five human relationships. Friends should be made widely but also selectively. The finest birds select their trees before perching; the gentleman selects people before befriending them.

The Three Unacceptables for Teaching and Interacting When Practicing Baguazhang

According to the opinions of the older generation, Dong Haichuan often advised his disciples: "Those who study this art must transmit it to virtuous and trustworthy gentlemen, and not teach the small-minded, who are without propriety or righteousness. In transmitting the art, one must always be selective in teaching." Gao Yisheng felt that those who teach must use loyalty and sincerity as the framework and treat others with compassion and righteousness. Those who study the art, then, must observe good behavior, with extreme morality and upright conduct. Teachers should have a soft spot for endurance; students should have modesty and perseverance. Teachers should regularly demonstrate, often explain, and diligently make corrections. Students should regularly practice, often ask questions, and diligently receive instruction. Teachers should first discuss the principles, and second explain the postures. Students should first understand the principles, and second train the postures. Understand the principles and know the subtlety. Train the postures and develop the power. Moreover, it is a rule that all who practice our Baguazhang must know the "three unacceptables" in serving as an instructor and in interacting as a friend.

In this world there are three types of people that cannot be taught and cannot be interacted with. These are the unrighteous, the violent, and thieves. The unrighteous are the type of person who has forgotten kindness. They often ignore the aspirations of the teacher, turn their backs on the desires of friends, act quickly when they see benefit and flee when they see righteousness, and are small-minded. The violent are those who, before they have any understanding, flaunt their own abilities, bully the weak, and clash with the strong, always causing trouble. Not following the instructions of the teacher and always talking of the low skill of others in the school while boasting of their own high abilities is also the conduct of the violent. If individuals are unbalanced, there will eventually come a time when they are disgraced, and their teacher and friends will also lose face. Thieves are profligates who covet wealth, steal, rob, and engage in other illegal activities. Because of this, those who serve as teachers are forbidden to teach these three types of people, and as friends it is advised that these three types of people not be interacted with.

Avoiding the Three Harmful Errors

When first studying Baguazhang, it is easy to commit three types of errors. The harm from these three errors is great, and because of this, the older generation warned later practitioners that when training in Baguazhang, one must avoid the three harmful errors. If the three harmful errors are not avoided, not only can one not build health, but sometimes health will actually be injured. The three harmful errors are: first, avoid crude power. Using crude, awkward power, it is easy to restrict the qi. Second, avoid anger, which is suppressed qi. Using angry power, it is easy to injure the original qi. Third, avoid puffing out the chest and sticking out the belly. Puffing out the chest and sticking out the belly means the qi does not return to the dantian, and the feet have no root. In practicing Baguazhang, one must strenuously adhere to the requirements of movement, maintaining relaxation, quiet, and naturalness, and not commit the three harmful errors.

Required Knowledge for Beginning Baguazhang Study
Know the Goal of Training

Baguazhang is a martial study possessing form, application, and art with health-building, fighting, and cultural arts united in one. Fighting skill is Baguazhang's essential martial nature. The basic function of Baguazhang is to increase martial skill and fighting ability through strengthening the being and building body. In addition, Baguazhang has a very strong artistic nature, watchability, and flavor, and it can be used for entertainment, recreation, and performance. Because of this, when beginners enter the gate to study Baguazhang, they can pursue it from five different perspectives. First is life-cultivation and eradicating illness, strengthening the being and building the body, benefiting life and extending life span, and through practical experience deeply exploring and developing the potential of the human body. Second is to pursue fighting abilities, skills, and methods to raise self-protection and self-defense capabilities. Third is seeking the coordinated and model beauty of the uniting of strength and power within performance. Fourth is seeking its flavor for use in recreation and entertainment, in the midst of recreation and entertainment raising the level of health of the body and mind. Fifth is pursuing its profound cultural connotations used in molding sentiment, cultivating the body, nurturing the nature, and cultivating the spirit while simultaneously using modern scientific theory and techniques to explore and research, seeking Baguazhang's scientific principles and the true essence and profundity of its health-building and fighting aspects, revealing the patterns not yet recognized by others. This is the most difficult goal to reach, and the highest level of pursuit in studying Baguazhang. In their pursuit, these five goals are inter-connected. Beginners will have different goals depending on their own nature and may have primary or secondary aims. From simple to complicated, from shallow to deep, seek one but take others into consideration; become proficient in one, but select broadly from others; only if the goal is clear may one then attain benefits.

Know That Famous Teachers Produce Good Students

"Famous teachers" also means teachers with understanding. Beginners should seek instruction with well-known and accomplished practitioners with understanding. First, understanding of the postures; second, understanding of the theory; and third, understanding of the methods, to avoid the spreading of falsehoods and being led astray. The saying "Study from the superior and achieve middling skill; study with the middling and achieve low-level skill; study with the low-level and achieve nothing" is also applicable in studying Baguazhang.

Know How to Advance Gradually and Sequentially

Baguazhang's form is simple but its meaning deep, especially emphasizing the word *change*. Change has many aspects, and its meaning is very rich. Studying the postures and understanding its theory requires a relatively long time period and must be a process of advancing sequentially. Differentiated according to experience, this process can be divided into three levels:

At the first level, the form is like the teacher. The beginner should diligently imitate the teacher's movements, experientially understanding each and every main point from the teacher, and each application and each posture should, as much as possible, resemble those of the teacher.

At the second level, the spirit looks like the teacher. On the foundation of form, one should try to figure out the expression, spirit, and intention of the teacher, striving to have a spirit like the teacher.

At the third level, the form and spirit look like oneself. Also on the foundation received from the teacher, study the past, but do not be bound by the past in developing one's own strong points, pursuing one's own style, attaining a form and style that is unique and different from all others. Just as green comes from blue but surpasses blue, each generation should surpass the previous, accordingly moving Baguazhang toward an even more refined, sophisticated, and scientific level of development.

These three levels can be summarized in five words: study, learning, skill, mastery, and transformation. Study and learning are beginning-level skills, meaning studying the main points, learning the forms, and fully investigating its shapes. Skill and mastery are mid-level skills, meaning being skilled in the art, comprehending the theory, and mastering the spirit. Transformation is a high-level skill, meaning changing the form, blending the grace and charm with some new creation and development, finally forming one's own unique style and self-systematized school.

Know That Learning Has No Limits

Baguazhang bases its theory on the *Yijing,* and its changes are without end and inexhaustible. Learning the forms is easy; mastering them is difficult. Transforming them is more difficult. Because of this, whether one is practicing health-building arts, fighting skill, or martial cultural arts, the performance and practice of Baguazhang is forever without an end.

Know Following the Natural

Humans model the earth, the earth models heaven, heaven models the Way, the Way models the natural. The most important principle in Baguazhang is to unite heaven and human as one and follow what is natural. "Natural" means releasing tension. Not only must the entire body internally and externally release tension, but the spirit and intention must also release tension. One must be relaxed but not disconnected; within relaxation is tautness. Natural means that heaven, earth, and human beings are one entity. Place one's body within nature, and exchange with and derive from nature its essence. "Natural" means comfortable. One should feel comfortable not only during the process of training, but after training should feel even more comfortable. Not only is the whole body comfortable; the spirit should also feel comfortable. "Natural" means following regular patterns. Generally speaking, all health-building and physical exercise movements have this regularity of pattern. One can only adhere to scientific principles in following the patterns, but definitely cannot exceed these patterns.

Know That Movement and Stillness Have Limits

Movement and stillness both have their limits, and Baguazhang movements are the same. This means one must not doggedly pursue some type of extranatural state, cannot pursue "skill" with rough force, and especially cannot exceed one's biological limits to pursue a nonexistent "ultimate skill." Movement and stillness must accord with the middle way. According with the middle way means not being extreme. The mind must be still; the body must move. The middle way is beneficial; excess is injurious. This is the secret to training in this art.

Know the Demands of Training

Baguazhang material is rich and its contents deep. It is able to fulfill different levels of need for different individuals. Speaking of the usually generally accepted requirement levels, humanity's requirements fall into five levels: survival, safety, social interaction, respect, and self-fulfillment.

Upon the foundation of fully learning and grasping the main requirements and movements of Baguazhang, one can, according to one's own interest, enthusiasm, and actual strong points, practice with emphasis on some aspect, making every effort at constant improvement, to fulfill different individual requirements.

Know Modesty and Perseverance

"The teacher leads one through the gate; cultivation depends on the student." Knowing modesty in study will allow one to obtain the art; only with perseverance can one train completely and produce skill. Those who train must not only use the body and four limbs to study diligently and intensely, but even more importantly must be resolute to remain constant in purpose—persistently, carefully, and diligently contemplating, and repeatedly physically experiencing the subtlety. In this fashion, after the accumulation and passage of time, moving from quantitative change to qualitative change, one may finally have some achievement. Nowhere in the world is there an ultimate skill that can be studied once and mastered. Only something singular may be called "ultimate." The elder generations and former sages of Baguazhang have left us many valuable training methods, and only through modesty and the perseverance of a hundred forgings and a thousand hammer blows can one have results. Familiarity brings cleverness; cleverness brings subtlety; subtlety brings mysteriousness. Mysteriousness is the "ultimate skill."

CHAPTER 2

Pre-Heaven Baguazhang

The Naming of Pre-Heaven Baguazhang

The Song of Pre-Heaven Baguazhang says:

> *The head pressing and shoulders joining is Qian three connected,*
> *Finger and elbow aligning is Dui upper missing,*
> *Filling the belly and emptying the chest is Li empty middle,*
> *Relaxing the shoulders and dropping the elbows is Zhen upturned cup,*
> *Holding the knees and covering the groin is Xun lower broken,*
> *Qi sinking to the dantian is Kan middle full,*
> *Tongue curling to upper palate is Gen overturned bowl,*
> *Swinging left and coiling right is Kun six broken.*[1]

Pre-Heaven Baguazhang is the traditional practice method Gao Yisheng inherited from all of the Baguazhang taught by Cheng Tinghua. Using Turning Palm as the source and Single Palm Change as the mother, it produces eight sets of body-overturning, each taking its image and name according to the Pre-Heaven Bagua diagram arrangement (fig. 0.3).

1. Heaven: Snake-Form Flowing-Posture Palm
2. Marsh: Dragon-Form Piercing-Hand Palm
3. Fire: Turning-Body Tiger-Striking Palm
4. Thunder: Swallow-Overturning Covering-Hand Palm:
5. Wind: Spinning-Body Back-Covering Palm
6. Water: Twisting-Body Forward-Searching Palm
7. Mountain: Overturning-Body Backward-Inserting Palm
8. Earth: Stopping-Body Moving-Hooking Palm

Pre-Heaven Baguazhang's
Twenty-Four Requirements
(Neigong Posture-Completion Methods)

- Mind and intention must be still.
- Breath must be even.
- Head must press.
- Tongue must curl.
- Neck must twist.
- Eyes must follow.
- Dantian must be full.
- Anus must lift.
- Shoulders must sink.
- Elbows must drop.
- Chest must hollow.
- Waist must twist.
- Hips must sit.
- Knees must join.
- Arms must extend.
- Legs must bend.
- Wrists must settle.
- Fingers must spread.
- Finger must point to elbow.
- Elbow must cover heart.
- Feet must be sprung.
- Toes must grasp.
- Steps must wade.
- Walking must be stable.

Mind and intention must be still; breath must be even. The Pre-Heaven Palms primarily train the internal to foster the root, taking internal skill as their primary concern. Because of this, when practicing, the mind must absolutely be still, and should remove all types of extraneous thoughts, amassing essence and gathering spirit. At the same time, respiration must be natural, gradually reaching a state of "even, fine, deep and long," and it is absolutely forbidden to force the breath. All movements must use intention to drive them, the internal movement leading external movement, and absolutely must not use crude and unyielding strength. The energy must take softness as its main focus and maintain reserves without displaying this outwardly. The force is continuous, and walking is like flowing water.

Head must press; tongue must curl. Taking the lower jaw and pulling back slightly, the head presses lightly upward. At the same time, the tongue curls to the upper palate, connecting the two Ren and Du meridians, producing saliva that is gradually swallowed, moistening the five zang and six fu organs.

Neck must twist; eyes must follow. The neck extends straight and turns toward the inside of the circle. The eyes accordingly gaze level at the index finger of the forward hand, with the Tiger's Mouth open level at the height of the mouth.

Dantian must be full; anus must lift. The dantian is located in the area three *cun* (about two inches) below the naval, and is the site of storing jing and developing qi. "The dantian must be full" indicates lightly gathering the qi of the abdomen and letting it sink to the dantian, causing the dantian to be full and enriched. "The anus must lift" is the coccyx tilting forward, gathering the anus, and causing the Ren and Du meridians to connect and the qi and blood to join. To lift the anus, one must gather the buttocks, thus avoiding the phenomenon the buttocks sticking out.

Shoulders must sink; elbows must drop. The shoulders must relax and sink downward, and they must not lift. The elbows must drop downward, the hollows of the elbows slightly bent, forming arcs. This can foster the qi sinking to the dantian.

Chest must hollow; waist must twist. The shoulders wrap inward slightly, causing the chest to be hollow, which requires contracting slightly and not lifting, maintaining a broad and relaxed chest and free-flowing qi and blood. The chest lifting outward will impact the qi sinking to dantian, and the chest contracting inward to the extreme will compress the heart and lungs, obstructing the free flow of qi and blood. Twisting the waist uses the waist as a pivot, causing the front aspect of the upper body to face toward the inside of the circle. This primarily trains waist strength and increases the agility of the waist.

Hips must sit; knees must join. In the movements of turning-the-circle walking and spinning, the hips must sit downward, the knees bending and joining together; this is the intention of joining the knees to protect the groin. The knees seem close but are not close. This posture is the Bagua Yin-Yang Post, and it trains the body's balance. It increases leg strength extremely quickly, but attention must be paid to ensure the knee joints are relaxed. The knee joint cannot bear weight while twisting and turning, and one should use comfort as a guide.

Arms must extend; legs must bend. The forward hand seems bent but is not bent, seems straight but is not straight, and as much as possible stretches and extends but contains twisting energy. The meaning of "bent legs" is that during movement, the legs should maintain a fixed degree of bend, selecting as appropriate upper, middle, or lower basin.

Wrists must settle; fingers must spread. The roots of the palms settle downward as much as possible, the five fingers spreading open to different directions, the index finger pointing toward heaven and falling straight toward the ground. The heart of the palm maintains a hollow and the Tiger's Mouth makes a half circle, in order to guarantee that the qi and blood fill and permeate the five fingers.

Finger must point to elbow; elbow must cover heart. The middle finger of the rear hand points toward the elbow of the forward arm while the elbow point of the back arm is aligned with the hollow of the chest. The back arm hooks inward but does not hug the body, causing the rear hand and rear elbow to serve to guard the chest and ribs. This is called Heart-Covering Elbow or Rib-Guarding Palm.

Feet must be sprung; toes must grasp. The soles of the feet must be sprung, the five toes gripping the ground and the hearts of the feet maintaining a hollow, causing qi and blood to reach the yongquan acupuncture point.

Steps must wade; walking must be stable. In Baguazhang stepping, the back foot must press, and the front foot must tread. The steps must rise level and fall level, and the foot must not rise too high, like walking in muddy water or wading in mud, walking using intention with testing steps. In moving, the steps must be stable, and each movement must follow the rhythmic changes of respiration. Usually the speed of turning-the-circle walking and spinning should be three steps for one inhale and three steps for one exhale, thus reaching Baguazhang's unique effect of "perspiring slightly but not panting."

These twenty-four requirements are a framework for the practice of the Pre-Heaven Palms and are also called Neigong Posture-Completion Methods. Following this framework, to complete the postures will cause the whole body to be connected as one, with qi and blood penetrating to the four termini and the whole body above and below, internal and external in absolute unity, twisting to form one energy, concentrated and embodying Baguazhang's special characteristic of whole-body energy. Practicing Baguazhang according to the framework of the Twenty-Four Requirements over days and years can produce internal skill. Training until they are completely familiar, one can follow one's heart, the intention moving and the form following, winding back and forth, connected as one qi. When practicing, be like a swimming dragon or flying phoenix, light but not floating, stable but not rigid, beautiful and elegant. In building the body and strengthening the being, increasing qi and lengthening power, and especially in regulating qi and blood, opening the meridians, and increasing the power of all parts of the body, the Twenty-Four Requirements have very excellent effects.

For those who are first studying Baguazhang, to completely and freely grasp the Twenty-Four Requirements requires having a process. Because of this, we have taken the main principles contained within the Twenty-Four Requirements and summed them up simply as three pressings, three hollows, three rounds, three twists, three drops, steps like wading in mud, and using the circle as the method.

Three pressings. The head presses, the tongue presses (curls upward to the palate), and the fingers press (spread open). If the head presses, the body is upright. If the tongue presses, the kidney qi descends and the mouth will have saliva, raising the clear and dropping the turbid. If the fingers press, the power fills the tips of the fingers.

Three hollows. The heart of the hand is hollow, the heart of the foot is hollow, and the heart of the chest is hollow.

Three rounds. The back between the shoulders is round, the Tiger's Mouth is round, and the crooks of the elbows are round. Power comes from the waist and is issued through the back. If the power can be transmitted externally, qi has filled the entire body.

Three twists. The neck twists, the waist twists, and the arms twist. This causes the whole body above and below to twist, forming one energy. Not only must attention be paid to the twisting and rotation of the hands, arms, and shoulders, but more importantly it must be paid to the twisting and rotation of the waist, hips, and body.

Three drops. The wrists drop, the shoulders and elbows drop, and the hips drop. This causes the qi to sink to the dantian, and above and below to be connected, filled with one qi.

Steps like wading in mud. Koubu and Baibu coil and rotate while walking with testing steps as if wading in muddy water. Firm and calm while light and fast, not clumsy and heavy but not floating, the source of power is from the feet.

Using the circle as the method. The inside foot making an inward Baibu and the outside foot making an inside Koubu, walking without interruption, will naturally form a circle. The size of the circle varies by the person, but it is usually eight steps to make one circuit. If the bodily form is rounded when walking, the qi can penetrate throughout the body, increasing *mingmen* fire. Using the circle as the method is definitely not simply walking a circle, and that's it. It requires force without breaks, forming a circular path with only one movement and in changing postures requires maintaining circle upon circle within the whole body above and below, containing circular movement within roundness, and roundness within circular movement, taking the circle and training it into the entire body above and below. Only then can it really be considered reaching the requirement of using the circle as the method. Without fluent skill, this cannot be attained.

The Pre-Heaven Palms are a type of whole-body movement in which when one moves, nothing does not move. In their totality, the requirements take softness as their main focus, but softness that contains hardness. While moving, the postures are continuous without break, the energy is spiraling, containing but not showing, in order to attain seeking flowing in opposition, the internal and external three harmonies training a unified power. The Twenty-Four Requirements are the framework for the Pre-Heaven Palms. While moving, one must stress "using intention, not using force." This is a common and undisputed principle in training the internal arts, and it is an important sign of development toward a higher level Baguazhang fighting method. Using intention is the mind method. Using power means crude power. In all movements in Baguazhang, intention is first, using intention to command and control the movements of the bodily form, without using crude power. Having intention is having skill; lacking intention is lacking skill and using crude power, which is stiff. As Master Liu Fengcai often said:

> Training Baguazhang not only uses the body to train, but even more importantly uses the mind and uses the intention to train. One must use the mind to feel at all times whether or not the requirements are in the body, and use intention to recognize the rolling, drilling, opposing, and wrapping contained within the spiraling energy of the limbs when in motion. Only by using the mind and using intention to control the movements can one achieve the goals of strengthening the being and building the body, increasing qi and lengthening power. In the end, after the accumulation of days and months, from quantitative change to qualitative change, one can develop a deep, resonant whole-body power uniting intention, qi, and strength—skilled power.

Master Gao Yisheng viewed the Twenty-Four Requirements as vitally important, calling them Neigong Posture-Completion Methods. He used the Twenty-Four Requirements as a foundation, specifically including the "Discussion on Neigong" in his handwritten original manual. We can view the Twenty-Four Requirements not only as a framework for the research and practice of the Pre-Heaven Palms, but also as the requirements for the research and practice of post skill and Neigong, and as the guiding principles for research and practice of the Cheng School Gao Style Baguazhang system. The keys to grasping the Twenty-Four Requirements in actual movement are "relaxed, calm, and natural, using intention, not using force." In the first month of the *dingchou* year (1997), the author used his own insight to write a scroll for Japanese friends visiting to research and train Cheng School Gao Style Baguazhang, which read: "Inheriting direct teaching of the great methods of Bagua, relaxation and calm nourish jing, qi, and shen. Partaking of the miraculous martial way, Neigong uses intention to cultivate water, fire, and wind." The words *relaxation, calm,* and *using intention,* emphasized in this scroll, exactly reflect the spirit of the main points of Pre-Heaven Bagua Neigong research and practice.

Actual experience has proved that only by strictly grasping the main points, keeping "relaxed, calm, natural, and using intention, not using force," and persevering in training until one is fluent, can one gradually achieve the ability to change at will from a natural state to a training state, and for the training state to be a standard of high-level art that is like a natural state. This is the closely-held secret of the former generations. Enthusiasts must deeply research and thoroughly contemplate this while making persistent efforts in training through practical experience. Only then can they unravel its mysteries. To achieve this, one can only feel it, and it is hard to describe in words.

A Pictorial Explanation
of Pre-Heaven Baguazhang
Opening Postures
(Turning and Changing Palms)
Turning Palm

The Song of Turning Palm says:

Bagua Turning Palm is the root and the source,
Using the circle as method walking must be round,
Inside the circle is inner; outside the circle outer,
The circle is the Pre-Heaven Bagua basin,
Training the internal to foster the root is the main aim,
After long days and years, deep skill must develop,
Regulating yin and yang, uniting qi and blood,
Benefiting and cultivating the being and body,
*   miraculous like an immortal.*

Explanation:

- The index finger of the forward hand points to Heaven at the height of the eyes, and the eyes look at the tip of the index finger. The mouth is aligned with the Tiger's Mouth of the forward hand. Using the waist as a pivot, the upper body twists toward the middle of the circle, the forward palm in Dragon Claw Palm turned toward the inside of the circle, the root of the palm toward the center of the circle from beginning to end.

- The rear elbow covers in front of the heart, the rear palm also forming Dragon Claw Palm, with the middle finger pointing to the elbow of the forward arm, the palm covering near the ribs.

- Walking the circle must be round, with the inside step an inside Baibu and outside step an inside Koubu; respiration must be natural; and the circle's size must be appropriate, normally eight steps per circle.

- When beginning to practice walking the circle, one should not be too fast but should walk with slow steps, the rear foot pressing, the front foot treading, walking while adhering to the Twenty-Four Requirements to correct one's movements. Generally the speed for walking the circle should be one inhalation every three steps, one exhalation every three steps. Waiting until after movements are correct and fluent, one can appropriately increase speed, but one must absolutely avoid "running the circle," where the heel of the foot sets down first.

- The whole body above and below is one form, open and rounded, and everywhere must feel oppositional energy.

Turning Palm constitutes the most basic movement form of Pre-Heaven Baguazhang. It is the core of the Baguazhang created by former Master Dong Haichuan, and it is the basic skill required to train in Pre-Heaven Baguazhang well. Because of this, Baguazhang begins with Turning Palm, so Gao Yisheng called Turning Palm the head of all Pre-Heaven Palms. The Turning Palm Rhyme-Song:

Bagua Turning Palm is the first skill,
Hide the crotch, sink the qi, and close the front of the chest,
Two feet grasp the ground with the toes, using force,
The forward hand opens outward like twisting a rope,
The rear elbow hooks inward in line with the center of the chest,
The fingertips closely following the forward elbow's movement,
The palms are like dragon claws, and steps wade in mud,
The thousand types of changes are born within.

1. Preparatory posture: stand with feet together, eyes gazing level, shoulders hanging down, respiration natural, the whole body relaxed (fig. 2.1).

2. Following the above posture, sit in the hips, bend the two legs, extend the left foot in front, the body's center of gravity shifted to the right leg and, using the waist as a pivot, twist the upper body toward the center of the circle and complete the posture according to the Twenty-Four Requirements (fig. 2.2).

3. Without changing any of the requirements of the entire body, begin Mud-Wading Stepping, following the circle, walking and turning; this is called Turning Palm. Turning left and turning right are the same.

Figure 2.1.   *Figure 2.2.*

Single Palm Change

Single Palm Change, as the name implies, is the palm posture used individually in changing direction. Because all changes of posture in the Pre-Heaven Palms are built upon the foundation of this posture, and rely on this posture to change directions, Gao Yisheng called this palm the mother of the Pre-Heaven Palms. The Changing Palm Rhyme-Song:

> *Changing Palm is the mother, a beginning without end,*
> *Eight roads of body-overturning born from within,*
> *One road of body-overturning creates eight postures,*
> *Eight roads giving birth to sixty-four names,*
> *The sixty-four postures create change,*
> *Yin and yang movement and stillness miraculous without end,*
> *Eight roads of body-overturning to accord with Eight Trigrams,*
> *Black Dragon Whips Its Tail creating a whirlwind.*

1. Following from Turning Palm, the left hand in front, the right hand in back, walking the circle counterclockwise (fig. 2.3), step left with an inward Baibu into the circle and step right with an inward Koubu, striding into the circle; twist the left hand outward and twist the right hand inward, the waist turning toward the left, the upper body continuing in the direction of the turn as the left arm continues to twist and open outward horizontally, the heart of the palm facing out, and insert the right hand under the left armpit (fig. 2.4). Following this, the left foot continues and steps with a Baibu toward the edge of the circle as the left arm wraps inward and the right foot steps onto the edge of the circle and walks with the right palm following the left arm piercing upward.

2. Following this posture, the hands are positioned as if holding something in the air (Tiger Embraces Head), crossing in front of and above the crown of the head, the arms extending upward as much as possible as the hips sit downward, creating oppositional force (fig. 2.5). Continue walking and turning as the left hand twists inward, following the crook of the right arm and sinking below the right elbow,

and the right arm overturns outward, twisting toward the inside of the circle (fig. 2.6).

3. Following this posture, the right hand overturns outward, becoming a vertical palm extended toward the inside of the circle, the back hand now becoming the front hand as the left hand settles downward, guarding below the ribs, the front hand now becoming the back hand and, through uninterrupted movement, completing the change of direction. Continue walking clockwise, turning-the-circle walking and spinning in Turning Palm (fig. 2.7).

4. The reverse is the same, and will again change to walking the circle counterclockwise. Use this repeatedly in practicing turning the circle, walking the circle in Turning Palm in the two directions, each changing to become Single Palm Change.

Figure 2.3.   *Figure 2.4.*   *Figure 2.5.*

Figure 2.6.   *Figure 2.7.*

Explanation:

- When the two arms twist and rotate, internally they must contain wrapping soft power.
- When the forward hand wraps inward and the rear hand follows the forward elbow and forearm piercing upward, one must pierce upward as much as possible, then open horizontally.
- Internally one must maintain the four energies of inward wrapping, upward piercing, twisting and rotating, and horizontal opening. In shorthand this is expressed as wrap, pierce, twist, open. Within the changing movements, one must use intention to feel oppositional force.

Eight Big Palms

The Pre-Heaven Palms are altogether eight big postures, also called Eight Big Palms, and are the main body of Pre-Heaven Baguazhang. The Song of the Eight Big Palms says:

The inside foot hooking outward, Flowing Posture is born,
Inward Baibu Piercing Palm like the Dragon Form,
Spinning outward, turning the body, Tiger-Striking Palm,
Stealing step covering palm is called Swallow Overturns,
Inward hooking spinning the body Back-Covering Palm,
Stepping back Forward-Searching causes the waist to twist,
Inside Baibu Waving-Body Backward-Inserting Palm,
Turning Body Moving-Hooking causes the body to stop.

Palm 1: Snake-Form Flowing-Posture Palm
(Qian Posture)

1. Following the Single Palm Change posture, walking counterclockwise in Turning Palm (fig. 2-8), the right foot steps outward with a Baibu, as the left palm covers inward, and the right palm follows below the left elbow (fig. 2.9).

2. Following this posture, the left foot steps outward with a Koubu, passing in front of the right foot, and the right foot steps out onto the edge of the circle, turning the front of the body to face inside the circle, as the left hand continues to cover inward in front of the face, becoming a Spiraling Palm; the right hand from below the ribs following the right leg and piercing down as much as possible near the lower leg, becoming a Spiraling Palm (fig. 2.10).

3. Following this posture, from in front of the face the left hand pulls downward, opening outward below the abdomen (fig. 2.11).

4. Following this posture, the left hand twists and wraps inward, the right palm wraps inward toward the inside of the circle as the palm overturns; the left hand follows the right arm piercing upward from below the armpit and overturning inward, forming the Single Palm Change posture; the left foot walks the circle first, returning to Turning Palm walking counterclockwise (fig. 2.12).

Explanation: For all of the postures of the Pre-Heaven Palms, if there is a left, there must be a right, and left and right are the same. The first palm is Flowing-Posture Palm, starting in counterclockwise Turning Palm and returning to counterclockwise Turning Palm. To practice in the other direction requires changing direction through the use of Single Palm Change, and then following the same movement sequence practiced on the opposite side.

Figure 2.8.

Figure 2.9.

Figure 2.10.

Figure 2.11.

Figure 2.12.

Palm 2: Dragon-Form Piercing-Hand Palm
(Dui Posture)

1. Following Snake-Form Flowing-Posture Palm, walk counterclockwise in Turning Palm (fig. 2.13).
2. Following this posture, step forward with the right foot, then Baibu with the left foot into the circle as the left palm overturns upward, Dragon Claw Palm becoming Upturned Palm, extending into the circle, the heart of the palm facing up; the right palm also follows this overturning upward to become Upturned Palm, guarding below the left elbow in preparation for piercing up (fig. 2.14).
3. Following this posture, the right foot takes an inward Koubu step as the right hand follows the left elbow and arm piercing upward. Bend the left leg, the left hand pointing downward, the right hand pointing upward (Pointing to Heaven and Piercing Earth), the two hands both twisting outward forming Spiraling Palms, half-kneeling with the left knee, lowering the body downward, forming a coiling-leg Resting Stance (fig. 2.15).
4. Following this posture, raise the body, the right hand becoming an Overturned Palm, pressing downward; the left hand overturning inward to become an Overturned Palm; the two hands crossed in front of the abdomen as the waist spins toward the back left; the left foot following the force striding toward the circle's edge; the right leg forming a Bow Stance; the two hands ending in Divided Center Palm (fig. 2.16).
5. Following this posture, the right hand wraps inward and pierces upward, and the left hand overturns outward and wraps inward, both Overturned Palms becoming Upturned Palms; the right foot begins stepping onto the circle, the right hand piercing past the left hand like Single Palm Change; advance with three linked steps into clockwise Turning Palm, the left hand becoming the rear hand, the left foot become the outside foot (fig. 2.17).

Explanation: From clockwise Turning Palm, as in figure 2.17, continue to practice Dragon-Form Piercing-Hand Palm in the opposite direction; all of the movements are the same, and after completing all movements, one will return to counterclockwise Turning Palm.

Figure 2.13.   *Figure 2.14.*   *Figure 2.15.*

Figure 2.16.   *Figure 2.17.*

Palm 3: Turning-Body Tiger-Striking Palm
(Li Posture)

1. Following Dragon-Form Piercing-Hand Palm, walking counter-clockwise in Turning Palm with the left foot in front (fig. 2.18), the right foot steps outward in Baibu as the left hand wraps and covers inward (fig. 2.19).

2. Following this posture, the left foot passes the right foot with a Koubu toward the outside of the circle, spinning the body 180 degrees as the left hand continues to cover, and the right hand follows the elbow and arm piercing upward, left hand below, right hand above, the right foot setting down on the edge of the circle in an Empty Stance (fig. 2.20).

3. Following this posture, the right hand uplifts and overturns, Upturned Palm becoming Overturned Palm, and the left hand overturns upward, settling the wrist, Upturned Palm becoming Dragon Claw Palm (fig. 2.21).

4. Following this posture, the right hand strikes downward at an angle with Pressing Palm, the left hand guarding at the ribs; step out with the right foot, becoming a right forward-weighted Bow Stance (fig. 2.22).

5. Following this posture, the left palm becomes an Overturned Palm, opening outward into Divided Center Palm; the right hand pulls, and the left hand wraps inward; the right hand pierces upward, following from below the left armpit along the elbow and forearm; advance with three linked steps like Single Palm Change, following the circle in clockwise Turning Palm, the left hand becoming the rear hand, the right hand becoming the forward hand (fig. 2.23).

Explanation: From clockwise Turning Palm, as in figure 2.23, continue to practice Turning-Body Tiger-Striking Palm in the opposite direction; the movements are all the same, and return to walking counterclockwise in Turning Palm.

Figure 2.18.

Figure 2.19.

Figure 2.20.

Figure 2.21.

Figure 2.22.

Figure 2.23.

Palm 4: Swallow-Overturning Covering-Hand Palm
(Zhen Posture)

1. Following Turning-Body Tiger-Striking Palm, walking counterclockwise in Turning Palm (fig. 2.24), step forward with the right foot, then with the left foot enter into the circle with an inward Baibu step, the left Dragon Claw Palm overturning inward and inserting downward, becoming Overturned Palm, the right hand overturning outward, becoming Upturned Palm, stopping below the armpit of the left hand (fig. 2.25).

2. Following this posture, the right hand follows the left elbow and arm piercing downward as the left palm pulls back; advance with right Koubu step, and step behind with the left foot, twisting the body to complete the posture (fig. 2.26).

3. Following this posture, the right arm and palm press downward forcefully while using the right foot as the pivot and overturning the body with twisting energy of the waist; the left palm overturns and passes over the head, extending in front of the face and becoming Spiraling Palm. While lifting the left knee, the right palm pulls back, becoming Spiraling Palm, guarding near the right ribs (fig. 2.27).

4. Following this posture, step out with the left foot, the right hand piercing past the left hand, the left hand wrapping inward, the right hand piercing upward and opening outward; with several linked advancing steps, like Single Palm Change, change to clockwise Turning Palm, the left hand becoming the rear hand, the right hand becoming the forward hand (fig. 2.28).

Explanation: From clockwise Turning Palm, as in figure 2.28, continue to practice Swallow-Overturning Covering-Hand Palm in the opposite direction. The movements are all the same. Return to walking counterclockwise in Turning Palm.

Figure 2.24.

Figure 2.25.

Figure 2.26.

Figure 2.27.

Figure 2.28.

Palm 5: Spinning-Body Back-Covering Palm (Xun Posture)

1. Following Swallow-Overturning Covering-Hand Palm, walk counterclockwise in Turning Palm (fig. 2.29).
2. Following this posture, step right with an inward Koubu, the left palm overturning downward to become Overturned Palm, pressing downward; the right palm twisting upward, becoming Upturned Palm, the arms crossing in front of the chest (fig. 2.30).
3. Following this posture, the left foot steps 180 degrees with an outward Baibu, spinning the body, the left hand covering over the back; Overturned Palm becoming Spiraling Palm, sitting into a half coiling step (fig. 2.31).
4. Following this posture, advance with a right step, the right palm following the left elbow, opening outward, the left palm becoming Overturned Palm, striking and pressing into the circle (fig. 2.32).
5. Following this posture, step forward with the right foot, advancing into the circle, the right palm striking downward in Overturned Palm, the left palm opening outward (fig. 2.33).
6. Following this posture, the right hand seizes, becoming an Upturned Palm piercing upward, the left palm becoming an Upturned Palm wrapping inward as the right foot takes a Baibu step and treads on the edge of the circle; with several linked advancing steps, the right hand pierces past left hand like Single Palm Change, becoming clockwise Turning Palm (fig. 2.34).

Explanation: From clockwise Turning Palm, as in figure 2.34, continue to practice Spinning-Body Back-Covering Palm in the opposite direction. The movements are all the same. Return to walking counterclockwise in Turning Palm.

Figure 2.29.

Figure 2.30.

Figure 2.31.

Figure 2.32.

Figure 2.33.

Figure 2.34.

Palm 6: Twisting-Body Forward-Searching Palm
(Kan Posture)

1. Following Spinning-Body Back-Covering Palm, walk counterclockwise in Turning Palm (fig. 2.35).

2. Following this posture, advance with the right foot, enter into the circle with a left inward Baibu step; the left palm overturns upward and becomes Upturned Palm, heart of the palm facing up, extending into the circle; the right palm also follows this, overturning upward and becoming Upturned Palm, guarding below the left elbow (fig. 2.36).

3. Following this posture, take a right Koubu step toward the inside of the circle, the right hand following the left arm piercing upward; the left foot steps behind with a Backward-Inserting Step, the left hand inserting backward from below the left ribs and pressing as the body twists and spins 360 degrees, the right hand extending downward from above, the left hand pressing outward (fig. 2.37).

4. Following this posture, the right Overturned Palm becomes an Upholding Palm, pulling back and uplifting; the left hand becomes Upholding Palm, striking forward and uplifting, the body sitting backward (fig. 2.38).

5. Following this posture, extend the body forward, the right palm again striking and the left palm pressing outward, repeating movement 3 (fig. 2.39) and returning to movement 4 (fig. 2.40).

6. Following this posture, step back with the left foot forming a high Bow Stance, the right hand pulling inward toward the chest, Upholding Palm becoming Embracing Palm, the left hand overturning outward (fig. 2.41).

7. Following this posture, the right foot steps toward the rear with a Baibu, and the left foot takes a big Koubu step; both hands form Ball-Embracing Posture, overturning and twirling at the same time as the body spins; then again step with a right Baibu onto the edge of the circle, the left palm below forming Embracing Palm, the right palm above forming outward Moving Palm (fig. 2.42).

Figure 2.35.

Figure 2.36.

Figure 2.37.

Figure 2.38.

Figure 2.39.

Figure 2.40.

Figure 2.41.

Figure 2.42.

8. Following this posture, repeat the above movements in the opposite direction. The left foot steps toward the rear with a Baibu; the right foot takes a big Koubu step, both hands forming Ball-Embracing posture, overturning and twirling at the same time as the body spins; then again step with a left Baibu onto the edge of the circle, the right palm below forming Embracing Palm, the left palm above forming outward Moving Palm (fig. 2.43).

9. Following this posture, the right hand pierces past the left hand; the right step begins several linked advancing steps like Single Palm Change, following the clockwise Turning Palm (fig. 2.44).

Explanation: From clockwise Turning Palm, as in figure 2.44, continue to practice Twisting-Body Forward-Searching Palm in the opposite direction. The movements are all the same. Return to walking counterclockwise in Turning Palm.

Figure 2.43.　　　　　*Figure 2.44.*

Palm 7: Waving-Body Backward-Inserting Palm
(Gen Posture)

1. Following Twisting-Body Forward-Searching Palm, walk counter-clockwise in Turning Palm (fig. 2.45).

2. Following this posture, advance with a right step, and advance into the circle with a left Baibu step, the left palm overturning upward, becoming Upturned Palm, extending into the circle, the right palm overturning upward, becoming Overturned Palm, guarding below the left elbow (fig. 2.46).

3. Following this posture, take a right inside Koubu step toward the middle of the circle, twist the body, and step behind with the left foot in a Backward-Inserting Step, the right hand piercing past the left hand, the left hand pulling back (fig. 2.47).

4. Following this posture, overturn the body and twist the waist, the right hand coming from behind the back over the head, inserting forward and downward, the heart of the palm facing into the circle as the body waves, overturns, and spins 180 degrees, the left hand pulling back below the right armpit and the left leg lifting and extending forward, the right leg slightly bent, the right Overturned Palm inserting beside the left foot (fig. 2.48).

5. Following this posture, set the left foot down and step behind with the right foot in a Backward-Inserting Step, the left palm piercing

Figure 2.45.   *Figure 2.46.*   *Figure 2.47.*   *Figure 2.48.*

past the right palm, the right palm pulling back, twisting the body (fig. 2.49).

6. Following this posture, the left arm pushes downward with force; the right palm overturns and passes over the head; using the left foot as the pivot, twist the waist and overturn the body, lift the right foot, the right palm becoming Spiraling Palm, extending in front of the face, the left palm becoming Spiraling Palm guarding near the left ribs, in posture movements like Swallow-Overturning Covering-Hand Palm (fig. 2.50).

7. Following this posture, set the right foot down and advance with a left step, the left hand piercing past the right hand, the right palm wrapping inward, the left hand opening outward like Single Palm Change, and with several linked advancing steps, return to counterclockwise Turning Palm (fig. 2.51).

Explanation: This palm does not naturally change direction. One must add a Double Palm Change to change counterclockwise Turning Palm to clockwise Turning Palm, and then continue to practice Waving-Body Backward-Inserting Palm in the opposite direction. The movements are the same, but this time will still return to clockwise Turning Palm. If continuing to Palm 8, below, a Double Palm Change must again be added, changing clockwise Turning Palm to counterclockwise Turning Palm (fig. 2.51).

Figure 2.49.   *Figure 2.50.*   *Figure 2.51.*

Palm 8: Stopping-Body Moving-Hooking Palm
(Kun Posture)

1. Following Waving-Body Backward-Inserting Palm, walk counter-clockwise in Turning Palm (fig. 2.52).
2. Following this posture, the right foot takes an outward Baibu outside the circle; the left foot takes a big outward Koubu step; the body spins 360 degrees; the right hand seizes; the left hand hooks and strikes, the right hand becoming an empty fist, the left hand becoming an Overturned Palm, the right leg in an angled Bow Stance (fig. 2.53).
3. Following this posture, at the same time the left and right hands hook inward and swipe outward with overturning palms, both becoming Spiraling Palms, with the right hand above and left hand below, as the left leg lifts (fig. 2.54).
4. Following this posture, set the left foot down and advance with a right step as the left hand opens outward to the rear, the right hand striking deeply downward from above (fig. 2.55).

Figure 2.52.   *Figure 2.53.*   *Figure 2.54.*   *Figure 2.55.*

5. Following this posture, the left Upturned Palm becomes an Overturned Palm inserting downward; the right palm twists inward, becoming Upturned palm; the right palm piercing past the left palm, the left palm pulling back, take a right Koubu step and step behind left with a Backward-Inserting Step as the body twists (fig. 2.56).

6. Following this posture, like a swallow overturning, make a big turn with the body, the left palm overturning and passing over the head from above; using the right foot as the pivot, twist the waist, overturn the body, and lift the left leg, the left palm becoming a Spiraling Palm extending forward, the right hand becoming a Spiraling Palm guarding near the right ribs (fig. 2.57).

7. Following this posture, set the left foot down, the right hand piercing past the left hand, the left hand wrapping inward; the right hand pierces upward and opens out, with several linked advancing steps like Single Palm Change, returning to clockwise Turning Palm, the right palm becoming the forward hand, left palm becoming the rear hand (fig. 2.58).

Explanation: From clockwise Turning Palm, as in figure 2.58, continue to practice Stopping-Body Moving-Hooking Palm in the opposite direction. The movements are all the same. Return to walking counterclockwise in Turning Palm.

Figure 2.56.

Figure 2.57.

Figure 2.58.

Closing Posture: Black Dragon Whips Its Tail Palm

Using Black Dragon Whips Its Tail as a closing posture is an important special characteristic of Cheng School Gao Style Baguazhang. Is also a clear symbol of the difference from all other families of Baguazhang both domestically and abroad. Black Dragon Whips Its Tail is also called Black Dragon Locking Tail and is the ending of the Pre-Heaven Palms. This palm follows closely on Palm 8, Stopping-Body Moving-Hooking Palm. After setting the foot down, piercing, and walking in Turning Palm, there is no need to pause; simply directly continue to practice this palm. This palm is carried out turning the circle completely without stopping, and speed may be increased appropriately, moving at will to the four corners and eight directions, crisscrossing, coming and going, weaving back and forth, and overturning and rolling above, below, left, and right. The Rhyme-Song of Black Dragon Whips Its Tail says:

Black Dragon Whips Its Tail fast like the wind,
Swirling hands inserting downward like a dragon's form,
Walking steps piercing the forest quick and fast,
Great Python Overturns Its Body miraculously without cease,
Front and back left and right threading the eight directions,
Advancing, retreating, entering, and leaving with remarkable skill,
Containing within the sixty-four changes,
For Pre-Heaven Bagua, this is the end.

1. Closely following on Stopping-Body Moving-Hooking Palm, walk counterclockwise in Turning Palm (fig. 2.59). There is no need to walk a full circle; just begin practicing Black Dragon Whips Its Tail from the above posture, advancing with a right step, the left hand wrapping downward, becoming Overturned Palm, inserting into the circle; at the same time the left foot makes a Baibu step into the circle, the right palm becoming Overturned Palm, guarding below the left arm (fig. 2.60).

Figure 2.59.

2. Following this posture, take a right Koubu step as the right palm pierces past the left palm and inserts downward, the left palm pulling back in front of the right shoulder (fig. 2.61).

3. Following this posture, the right arm presses downward with force; using the right foot as the pivot, the waist twists and the body overturns, the left hand overturning and passing over the head, forming Spiraling Palm, extending forward; the left leg lifts, the left elbow aligned with the left knee, the right palm pulling back, forming Spiraling Palm, guarding near the right ribs (fig. 2.62).

4. Following this posture, set the left foot down and advance with the right foot, as the right hand pierces past the left hand like Single Palm Change, returning to clockwise Turning Palm (fig. 2.63).

5. According to figures 2.63 through 2.66, repeat the previous movements (figs. 2.59–2.62) in the opposite direction, returning to counterclockwise Turning Palm (fig. 2.67). Between the postures, there are no pauses; only their direction is different.

6. Following this posture, advance with a right step, the left palm overturning downward and wrapping inward, the right palm piercing upward and opening outward, as the left foot takes a Baibu step into the circle and the right foot again advances, stepping on the edge of the circle (fig. 2.68).

7. Following this posture, shuffle back with the right foot, spin the body, and advance with a left step along the edge of the circle, the right palm overturning downward and wrapping inward; advance with a left step as the left hand pierces upward and opens outward (fig. 2.69).

8. Following this posture, in a left Bow Stance, step behind and right with a Backward-Inserting Step, overturn the left palm outward, as the right palm follows the right leg, inserting downward (fig. 2.70).

Figure 2.60.

Figure 2.61.

Figure 2.62.

Figure 2.63.

Figure 2.64.

Figure 2.65.

Figure 2.66.

Figure 2.67.

Figure 2.68.

Figure 2.69.

Figure 2.70.

155

9. Following this posture, twist the hips and raise the body, advancing with the left foot and stepping onto the edge of the circle, the right hand wrapping inward, the left hand piercing past the right hand, now facing counterclockwise (fig. 2.71).

10. Following this posture, take a right Koubu step, overturn the left palm above the head, and strike forward with the right palm (fig. 2.72).

11. Following this posture, Great Python Overturns Its Body; using the right foot as a pivot, twist the waist and overturn the body, the left palm wrapping inward, overturning and passing over from above the head, becoming a Spiraling Palm extending forward, the right palm overturning outward, becoming Spiraling Palm, guarding near the right ribs while lifting the left leg (fig. 2.73). Similar to piercing and walking in Single Palm Change, this completes the movements in one direction.

12. Following this posture, set the left foot down, and step into the circle with the right foot, as the right had pierces past the left hand (fig. 2.74).

13. Following this posture, according to figures 2.74 through 2.80, repeat the previous movements (figs. 2.67–2.73) in the opposite direction, returning to counterclockwise Turning Palm (fig. 2.81). The direction is different, but the movements are all the same.

14. Following this posture, in the process of counterclockwise Turning Palm, with several linked advancing steps, both hands draw arcs, the two feet come together, and the hands fall to the sides of the body, fixing posture and returning to the origin (fig. 2.82).

Explanation: The Pre-Heaven Palms all change and move while walking in Turning Palm, especially the Black Dragon Whips Its Tail Palm, which should even more clearly exemplify the special characteristic of "postures without pause." When performing the Black Dragon Whips Its Tail closing postures, speed should be increased appropriately.

Figure 2.71.

Figure 2.72.

Figure 2.73.

Figure 2.74.

Figure 2.75.

Figure 2.76.

Figure 2.77.

Figure 2.78.

Figure 2.79.

Figure 2.80.

Figure 2.81.

Figure 2.82.

CHAPTER 3

Post-Heaven Bagua
Sixty-Four Palms

The Song of the Post-Heaven Palms says:

Post-Heaven is born of the Pre-Heaven principles,
The Pre-Heaven is the source, the Post-Heaven its application,
The Pre-Heaven and Post-Heaven are separated in training,
The Sixty-Four Palms are profound and inexhaustible.

The sixty-four individually practiced postures of the Post-Heaven Palms are the most evident special characteristic of Cheng School Gao Style Baguazhang that differentiates it from all other families of Baguazhang passed on today. The Post-Heaven Palms are all based on the Pre-Heaven Palms, with each of the Pre-Heaven Eight Big Palms producing eight postures, creating the Post-Heaven Sixty-Four Palms, in accordance with the sixty-four hexagrams (see fig. 0.5). Master Gao especially emphasized that "the Pre-Heaven Palms are the basis for the Post-Heaven Palms; the Post-Heaven Palms are the application of the Pre-Heaven Palms." Because of this, the Post-Heaven Palms are mainly used in crossing hands, free fighting, and combat. Each move and posture of the Post-Heaven Sixty-Four Palms contains the intention of facing an enemy, and according to the four principles of application, response, development, and evolution, each palm can be broken down into six hands, altogether 384 hands, in accordance with the 384 lines of the hexagrams. "Application" means the basic application and basic posture. "Response" means to dissolve an attack. "Development" means two people breaking down applications according to fixed sets in a "you go, I go" fashion. "Evolution" means following the opportunity and responding with change.

Application and response are the foundations of Post-Heaven Bagua-zhang; development and evolution are the essence of Post-Heaven Bagua-zhang. The dismantling and changing methods introduced in this book are built upon all that was taught by Master Gao Yisheng, but they have been enriched and developed by two generations of inheritors—Liu Feng-cai and Wang Shusheng—who have advanced them toward greater refine-ment and balance and made their fighting practicality now even stronger. The Post-Heaven Palms use individually trained movements as their main focus, using straight lines or zigzag lines as their basic movement pat-terns. The same movement is trained repeatedly on the left and right, the stepping primarily utilizing "Advancing-Following Step"[1] (hereafter "Fol-lowing Step"), the rear foot pressing, the front foot treading, advancing like plowing a field.

Post-Heaven Palm breathing usually is inhaling when gathering energy and exhaling when issuing energy, using the nose, not the mouth, with the internal qi sinking to Dantian. When striking, the energy is issued from the rear foot, directed by the waist, driven by the shoulders and arms, and flows through the root of the palm and tips of the fingers. This energy is primarily hard—but a hard that contains soft—and issued outward as much as possible, projecting long and striking far. Each posture of the Sixty-Four Palms should be repeated in practice, and left and right are the same.

The fundamental movement requirements of the Post-Heaven Palms Opening Posture are basically the same as the Pre-Heaven Turning-Palm Posture-Completion Methods. Only the arms and hands do not overturn outward, but rather extend forward, the heart of the forward palm fac-ing inside, the index finger of the rear palm aligned with the elbow and guarding near the ribs, the arms extending forward as much as possible, the eyes looking forward, the hips sitting downward, the center of grav-ity between the feet balanced thirty percent forward and seventy per-cent back. This is called the method of pulling the body and lengthening the arms, gathering qi and accumulating spirit. Amid the movements of changing postures in the Sixty-Four Palms, one must pay special attention to feeling oppositional force. The Post-Heaven Palms Opening Posture is the Post-Heaven static post. The movement stances of the Opening Posture are seen in figures 3.1 and 3.2, below.

The Post-Heaven Palms are the skills for use in actual combat and thus emphasize movements of the hands, arms, and shoulders and stress utilization of the waist, hips, and body; they especially attach importance to application of stepping methods. The sayings "The hands are like two gates; without footwork it is difficult to defeat others," and "Strike someone like giving them a kiss" both explain the importance of footwork. Only by gaining the advantage, gaining the force, advancing with the steps, and advancing with the body can one be victorious over others. The Post-Heaven Palms primarily utilize Following Step, where the back foot presses, the front foot advances, and the back foot follows; the front foot treads and strides forward like plowing a field. The Sixty-Four Palms all begin with an Opening Posture with the left hand in front, however if there is a left, there must also be a right, and left and right are the same. In this book there are a few postures that begin with an Opening Posture with the right hand in front, but this is solely for the ease of the reader in clearly seeing the movements of the application.

The Post-Heaven Palms Twenty-Four Requirements

- Eyes must understand.
- Ears must be nimble.
- Hands must be quick.
- Elbows must be close.
- Legs must be springy.
- Inside must be covered.
- Outside must be opened.
- Above must intercept.
- Below must arrest.
- Leading must cross.
- Carrying must follow.
- Seizing must be stable.
- Grasping must be full.
- Yanking must pull.
- Upholding must be accurate.
- Pressing must be linked.
- Squeezing must stick.
- Holding must be explosive.
- Crushing must be rapid.
- Crashing must draw near.

- Moving must be fierce.
- Hooking must be vicious.
- Stepping must be clear.
- The body must be lively.

Post-Heaven Palm Heaven (Qian) Eight Postures

The Pre-Heaven Heaven trigram produces a method of body-overturning called Snake-Form Flowing-Posture Palm, and from this palm eight Post-Heaven postures are developed: Opening Palm, Scooping Palm, Yanking Palm, Testing Palm, Rising Palm, Uplifting Palm, Covering Palm, and Wrapping Palm. These are the eight Heaven postures of the Post-Heaven Palms, which are the framework for all the Post-Heaven Palms, and are throwing methods. When training these eight postures, first the footwork must be trained clearly; second, the body method must be trained to be lively; third, the qi and power must be trained sufficiently; fourth, the hand methods must be understood. The Song of the Eight Heaven Postures says:

> *Covering hand Flowing-Posture like a snake's form,*
> *Advancing step Opening Palm qi and power skill,*
> *Outward leading Scooping Palm and Yanking from on high,*
> *Golden Dragon Tests Its Claws quick like the wind,*
> *Inward leading Rising Palm advances from outside,*
> *Outward leading Uplifting Palm meets with an angled strike,*
> *Double Carrying with advancing step using Covering Palm,*
> *Wrapping Hand's crushing fist does not relent.*

1. Opening Palm

Begin standing with the feet together, turn and step back right into the Post-Heaven Palms Opening Posture (figs. 3.1–3.2). With the left hand and foot in front, hook inward with the left hand as the right hand pierces past the left, both hands opening outward, overturning, and closing inward, the right hand in front, the left hand guarding near the right wrist, as the right foot steps forward and crashes forth with a Following Step (figs. 3.3–3.4). Move in a straight line. Left and right are the same. The Rhyme-Song of Opening Palm Dismantling says:

The Opening Palm method is miraculous,
With a shuffle step open outward striking to the chest,
B uses vertical post to deflect the attack,
A uses flowing energy and is victorious striking upward at the face,
B uses Part the Clouds to See the Sun to strike,
A uses crossing leading and double shoulder Crashing,
B quickly twists the body and leads outward to deflect,
A and B use piercing palms to change places and walk.

Figure 3.1.   *Figure 3.2.*   *Figure 3.3.*   *Figure 3.4.*

2. Scooping Palm

From the Opening Posture, with the left hand in front, lead outward with the right hand as the left foot steps diagonally to the left, step up with the right foot, and advance with a Following Step with both hands crashing forth in Scooping Palm (figs. 3.5–3.7). Move in a zigzag pattern. Left and right are the same. The Rhyme-Song of Scooping Palm Dismantling says:

> *Lead outward with an advancing step using Scooping Palm,*
> *B follows and lifts outward, striking with Pressing Palm,*
> *A uses Double Carrying, striking to the face,*
> *B uses Part the Clouds to See the Sun to be victorious,*
> *A uses outward Leading with a double crash to the shoulder,*
> *B dissolves Leading outward with skillful footwork,*
> *A uses Piercing Hand to dissolve the attack,*
> *A and B switch positions and walk.*

Figure 3.5.   *Figure 3.6.*   *Figure 3.7.*

3. Yanking Palm

From the Opening Posture, with the left hand in front, step up with the left foot and bring the right foot into an empty stance; lift the right hand and follow with the left hand uplifting and upholding above the crown of the head; grasp and seize with both hands and yank downward, advance with a Following Step and Double Crashing Palms (figs. 3.8–3.11). Move in a zigzag pattern. Left and right are the same. The Rhyme-Song of Yanking Palm Dismantling says:

Yanking Palm with one touch pulls down with force,
Shuffle step with Crashing Palm striking to the sternum,
B dissolves by opening outward and strikes with Hooking Palm,
A uses the many changes of Double Carrying,
Advancing and changing postures, striking the face,
B uses Part the Clouds to See the Sun to uphold,
A quickly seizes the hand and leads outward,
B uses Piercing Hand walking in unison.

Figure 3.8.   *Figure 3.9.*   *Figure 3.10.*   *Figure 3.11.*

4. Testing Palm

From the Opening Posture, with the left hand in front, pull the left hand back and extend the right hand to seek the opponent's hand, step up with the right foot as the right hand seizes backward and the left hand tests, then seize with the left hand and advance in a Following Step as the right palm strikes out in Heart-Pounding Palm (figs. 3.12–3.15). Move in a straight line. Left and right are the same. Also called Golden Dragon Extends Its Claws. The Rhyme-Song of Testing Palm Dismantling says:

> *Golden Dragon Extends its Claws fast like the wind,*
> *Seize the hand with an advancing step seeking the two eyes,*
> *B dissolves uplifting upward quick and fast,*
> *A changes to Pulling the Ridgebeam striking to the chest,*
> *B uses vertical post to dissolve the attack,*
> *A changes to uphold the arm, and Hide the Flower is victorious,*
> *B uses outward lifting and Single Crashing Palm,*
> *A changes to outward lifting and walks, changing positions.*

Figure 3.12.   *Figure 3.13.*   *Figure 3.14.*   *Figure 3.15.*

5. Rising Palm

From the Opening Posture, with the left hand in front, step out left and bring the right foot into an empty stance, as the left hand rises up and leads inward and the right hand draws a circle and inserts below the left, the left hand overturned up, the right palm below; then align left and right palms and advance with a Following Step and Double Crashing Palm (figs. 3.16–3.18). Move in a zigzag line. Left and right are the same. The Rhyme-Song of Rising Palm Dismantling says:

Rising Palm leads outward, upholding the upper arm,
B uses Insert the Flower to strike to the ear,
A changes with upward Rising using inward leading,
Switching hands to downward Rising Crashing Palm is victorious,
B uses outward hooking and strikes to the back,
A pushes B's elbow and spins the body to advance,
B quickly spins the body overturning above and below,
A uses a single fist to guard above and below.

Figure 3.16.   *Figure 3.17.*   *Figure 3.18.*

6. Uplifting Palm

From the Opening Posture, with the left hand in front, lead outward with the left hand, step up with the right foot, uplift with the right hand, advance with a Following Step as the left hand strikes out with a Vertical Palm toward the chest; without stopping the movement, uplift with the left and shuffle step, changing to Pull Out the Ridge Beam to Change the Post, the right hand striking to the face (figs. 3.19–3.22). Move in a straight line. Left and right are the same. The Rhyme-Song of Uplifting Palm Dismantling says:

> *Uplifting Palm with advancing step striking to the chest,*
> *B then steps back using the hand to uphold,*
> *A advances shuffling changing palms to strike,*
> *B uses dissolving steps and changes hands to uphold,*
> *A uses circular spinning, changing to Hide the Flower,*
> *B dissolves and opens inward, advancing with Pressing,*
> *A uses Double Carrying and strikes to the face,*
> *B uses Part the Clouds to See the Sun to meet.*

Figure 3.19.   *Figure 3.20.*   *Figure 3.21.*   *Figure 3.22.*

7. Covering Palm

From the Opening Posture, with the left hand in front, both hands seize to the rear as the body draws back with Double Carrying; step forward with the right foot as the right hand covers the face (figs. 3.23–3.25). Move in a straight line. Left and right are the same. The Rhyme-Song of Covering Palm Dismantling says:

> *Withdrawing the body with Double Carrying, Covering Palm is strong,*
> *Advancing step and meeting the face using Covering Palm,*
> *B uses dissolving steps and double Seizing Hands,*
> *Advancing and repeating Covering Palm striking to yintang,*
> *A again steps back with double Seizing Hands,*
> *Then steps up changing to face-striking palm,*
> *B uses Part the Clouds to See the Sun to strike,*
> *A uses Yanking and walks with Piercing Palm.*

Figure 3.23.   *Figure 3.24.*   *Figure 3.25.*

8. Wrapping Palm

From the Opening Posture, with the left hand in front, draw the body back, sink the left hand down and outward vertically, and then wrap inward to Embrace the Moon to the Bosom; advance with the right foot in a Following Step, and strike with the right hand (figs. 3.26–3.28). Move in a zigzag pattern. Left and right are the same. The Rhyme-Song of Wrapping Palm Dismantling says:

> *Withdrawing the body, Wrapping Palm hides beneath the arm,*
> *B uses outward leading and advances with Scooping Palm,*
> *A then uses Wrapping Palm and strikes with crushing fist,*
> *B dissolves with seizing hands and changes to horizontal Crashing,*
> *A changes leading outward quick and fast,*
> *B uses circular spinning, Upholding the Arm Palm,*
> *A quickly spins the body using Double Crashing,*
> *B dissolves with downward Rising and walks with Piercing Palm.*

Figure 3.26.   *Figure 3.27.*   *Figure 3.28.*

Post-Heaven Palm Water (Kan) Eight Postures

The Pre-Heaven Marsh trigram produces a method of body-overturning called Dragon-Form Piercing-Hand Palm, and from this palm eight Post-Heaven postures are developed: Rib Smashing Palm, Hide the Flower Palm, Chopping Palm, Shaving Palm, Two Immortals Preach the Dao, Tiger Pouncing Palm, Phoenix Steals the Nest, and Linking Palm. These are the eight Water postures of the Post-Heaven Palms, which are striking methods. After training them diligently until well-versed, the hands and eyes will be fast, and one can issue a technique without seeing the form, strike without casting a shadow. The Song of the Eight Water Postures says:

Dragon-Form Piercing-Hand tests above and below,
Inward posting, Smashing the ribs, moving left and right,
Advancing step Hide the Flower quick and fast,
Outward Chopping, inward Shaving, fast like the wind,
Outward Leading advancing step, the Two Immortals Way,
Fierce Tiger Pounces on the shoulder causing the body to twist,
Phoenix Steals the Nest turns the body to strike,
Advancing step Linking Palm leaves one victorious.

9. Rib Smashing Palm

From the Opening Posture, with the left hand in front, draw the body back and block downward vertically with the left hand; seize with the right hand and advance with a Following Step as the left hand strikes the ribs with a crushing fist; step forward right, pull the left hand back, and punch with a right crushing fist (figs. 3.29–3.32). Move in a straight line. Left and right are the same. The Rhyme-Song of Rib Smashing Palm Dismantling says:

> The Rib Smashing Palm method is called heroic,
> B advances with Opening Palm, striking to the chest,
> A uses inward posting to check the attack,
> Changing hands grasping and seizing strike to the ribs,
> B dissolves with retreating step and uses the hand to smother,
> A changes and advances switching hands to crush,
> B again retreats and uses the hand to smother,
> A changes to Hide the Flower quick like the wind.

Figure 3.29.   *Figure 3.30.*   *Figure 3.31.*   *Figure 3.32.*

10. Hide the Flower Palm

From the Opening Posture, with the left hand in front, lead outward with the left hand, and uphold with the right hand as the right foot advances and the left hand attacks with Heart-Pounding Palm; seize backward with the left hand into Embrace the Moon posture as the right fist strikes (figs. 3.33–3.35). Move in a straight line. Left and right are the same. The Rhyme-Song of Hide the Flower Palm Dismantling says:

> *The Hide the Flower Beneath the Leaf method is fierce,*
> *Grasp the wrist and uphold the arm striking the center chest,*
> *B uses Dropping Elbow to dissolve the attack,*
> *A uses Stealing the Peach and striking with the upper fist,*
> *B follows Uplifting, and A upholds the arm,*
> *Closely following, turning the waist, and striking the Jade Belt,*
> *B dissolves with lower Arresting and Single Crashing Palm,*
> *A dissolves with outward lifting and walks parting ways.*

Figure 3.33.   *Figure 3.34.*   *Figure 3.35.*

11. Chopping Palm

From the Opening Posture, with the left hand in front, cover inward with the left hand, bringing the elbow in front of the chest as the right foot steps behind in a Stealing Step; pluck and seize with the right hand, step out left as the left hand chops the face, pull the left hand back, covering inward and pierce upward; step forward with the right foot as the right hand pierces past the left hand (figs. 3.36–3.39). Move in a straight line. Left and right are the same. The Rhyme-Song of Chopping Palm Dismantling says:

> *Chopping Palm stealing step fast like the wind,*
> *Plucking and seizing and stepping out, Chopping to the neck,*
> *B meets and A changes to Dropping Elbow and pierces,*
> *Again meeting change postures and pierce to the eyes,*
> *B dissolves one after another with upholding hand,*
> *A changes to Yanking Palm and Double Crashing to be victorious,*
> *B dissolves evading outward and uses Hooking Palm,*
> *A follows with outward leading and walks parting ways.*

Figure 3.36. *Figure 3.37.* *Figure 3.38.* *Figure 3.39.*

12. Shaving Palm

From the Opening Posture, with the left hand in front, lead outward with the left hand as the right foot steps up and shave down from above with the right hand; advance with a Following Step as the right arm whips outward; open the right hand outward and uplift, advancing with a Following Step and striking with a left Heart-Pounding Palm (figs. 3.40–3.43). Move in a straight line. Left and right are the same. The Rhyme-Song of Shaving Palm Dismantling says:

Shaving Palm advancing step usage must be refined,
Leading outward advancing step Shaving to the neck,
B changes and intercepts up with reverse Insert the Flower,
A changes and intercepts up striking to the chest,
B dissolves with outward lifting and Rib Pressing Palm,
A meets and changes Arresting and striking to the waist,
B changes upholding the elbow Arresting and striking to the waist.
A dissolves with outward lifting and walks parting ways.

Figure 3.40.   *Figure 3.41.*   *Figure 3.42.*   *Figure 3.43.*

13. Two Immortals Preach the Dao

From the Opening Posture, with the left hand in front, lead out with the left hand, step forward right, and strike with a right fist behind the heart; advance with the left foot, and strike with the left fist in front of the heart; draw the body back as the left hand intercepts downward, advance with a Following Step and Double Crashing Palm, step forward with the right foot as the right hand pierces past the left, changing sides (figs. 3.44–3.48). Move in a straight line. Left and right are the same. The Rhyme-Song of Two Immortals Preach the Dao Dismantling says:

> Two Immortals Preach the Dao fast like a spirit,
> Leading outward advancing step striking behind the heart,
> B lifts outward with the elbow quick and fast,
> A quickly changes hands and strikes in front of the heart,
> B dissolves inward with vertical posting and Rib Pressing Palm,
> A uses outward lifting changing to Scooping Palm,
> B hangs and follows uplifting to double striking hammers,
> A changes to Squeezing Palm and B leads apart.

Figure 3.44.

Figure 3.45.

Figure 3.46.

Figure 3.47.

Figure 3.48.

14. Tiger Pouncing Palm

From the Opening Posture, with the left hand in front, step out diagonally left and bring the right foot up; twist the body and grasp the shoulder with both hands; draw the body back and carry toward the bosom;
advance with a Following Step and Double Crashing Palm (figs. 3.49–
3.52). Move in a zigzag. Left and right are the same. The Rhyme-Song of
Tiger Pouncing Palm Dismantling says:

> *Fierce Tiger Pouncing on the Shoulder is called heroic,*
> *B uses Double Carrying and Covering Palm to attack,*
> *A uses Tiger Pouncing and meets with Double Crashing,*
> *B dissolves with Seizing Hand and a drilling fist,*
> *A changes and intercepts high advancing with Goring Elbow,*
> *B dissolves cutting the elbow attacking with a low punch,*
> *A dissolves with lower lifting and Single Crashing Palm,*
> *B dissolves with outward lifting and walks parting ways.*

Figure 3.49.   *Figure 3.50.*   *Figure 3.51.*   *Figure 3.52.*

15. Phoenix Steals the Nest

From the Opening Posture, with the left hand in front, advance with the right foot and Double Carrying; advance with the left foot; spin the body to the right into Double Crashing Palm; turn the body to the right; advance with the right foot, and open outward with the right arm (figs. 3.53–3.56). Move in a straight line. Left and right are the same. The Rhyme-Song of Phoenix Steals the Nest Dismantling says:

Advancing step Double Carrying Phoenix Steals the Nest,
Spin the body quickly using Double Crashing Palms,
B follows seizing downward using Hooking Palm,
A meets uplifting in accordance,
B follows lifting upward and advancing with inner Crashing,
A changes to Squeezing Palm crashing to the sternum,
B dissolves leading outward A reverse pierces,
A and B separate walking in unison.

Figure 3.53.   *Figure 3.54.*   *Figure 3.55.*   *Figure 3.56.*

16. Linking Palm

From the Opening Posture, with the right hand in front, grasp and seize outward vertically with the right hand, and lock with the left hand; twist the body into a coiling stance; advance left as the left hand strikes the ribs, draw the body back with a Double Carrying; advance right and slap to the face; lift the left leg and swipe the eyebrows with the left palm; set the foot down and continue practicing on the other side (figs. 3.57–3.63). Move in a straight line. Left and right are the same. The Rhyme-Song of Linking Palm Dismantling says:

> *The Linking Palm method is like qinna,*
> *A locks and B rolls cutting the elbow and striking,*
> *B lifts outward with the elbow and advances with Pressing Palm,*
> *A carries with Hooking Palm and B Parts the Clouds,*
> *A uses retreating step upholding the arm to dissolve,*
> *B changes plucking and upholding striking with Hide the Flower,*
> *A uses lower Arresting and Single Crashing Palm,*
> *B changes and lifts outward and the two separate.*

Figure 3.57.

Figure 3.58.

Figure 3.59.

Figure 3.60.

Figure 3.61.

Figure 3.62.

Figure 3.63.

Post-Heaven Palm Mountain (Gen) Eight Postures

The Pre-Heaven Fire trigram produces a method of body-overturning called Turning-Body Tiger-Striking Palm, and from this palm eight Post-Heaven postures are developed: Rib Piercing Palm, Horizontal Moving Palm, Arm Intercepting Palm, Arm Arresting Palm, Body Stopping Palm, Hand Overturning Palm, Walking Stepping, and Spinning Body Palm. These are the eight Mountain postures of the Post-Heaven Palms, which contain precision. The wind blows, and the grass moves; with one touch, react. The movements are extremely nimble, and one technique can strike a thousand pounds without overexerting. The Song of the Eight Mountain Postures says:

> *Turning-Body Tiger-Striking hides at the ribs,*
> *Piercing Hand, flowing step, spin and change strongly,*
> *Stealing Step using Moving Hooking to the face,*
> *Intercepting and Arresting left and right and Crashing to the chest,*
> *Double Carrying Stopping Body turn the head and look,*
> *Seizing Hand Overturning Palm engaging above and below,*
> *Walking step Piercing Palm changes at will,*
> *Spinning Body Scooping Palm crashes to the ribs.*

17. Rib-Piercing Palm

From the Opening Posture, with the left hand in front, the left hand becomes a hook and uplifts as the right foot advances and the right hand pierces the ribs with Upturned Palm; the right hand circles and upholds; advance with a Following Step and left Heart-Pounding Palm; seize backward with the left hand, and punch with the right fist (figs. 3.64–3.67). Move in a straight line. Left and right are the same. The Rhyme-Song of Rib-Piercing Palm Dismantling says:

Piercing Palm advancing step like Dragon Form,
B dissolves downward rising fast like the wind,
A changes spinning a circle to Hide the Flower Palm,
B dissolves with Dropping Elbow A punches upward,
B follows piercing upward dissolving with Rising Palm,
A changes disengaging and Squeezing, fierce and ferocious,
B leads with Goring Elbow Tiger-Striking Palm,
A changes to Double Carrying and meets with Hooking Palm.

Figure 3.64. *Figure 3.65.* *Figure 3.66.* *Figure 3.67.*

18. Horizontal Moving Palm

From the Opening Posture, with the left hand in front, cover inward with the left hand; step behind with the right foot in inserting step; peel the wrist with the right hand; twist the waist and turn back as the left foot steps out, the left hand swiping at the eyebrows; step back left with double-handed carrying; advance with a Following Step as the right fist strikes the ribs (figs. 3.68–3.72). Move in a straight line. Left and right are the same. The Rhyme-Song of Horizontal Moving Palm Dismantling says:

> *Stepping behind the Horizontal Moving Palm method is strong,*
> *B uses outward leading upholding the arm, and Hiding,*
> *A follows with a stealing step peeling seizing and Swiping,*
> *B changes and intercepts high striking to the ribs,*
> *A carries and strikes the ribs B lifts outward,*
> *Overturning the palm upholding the elbow and Crashing on the angle,*
> *A leads with upholding elbow and strikes with Hide the Flower,*
> *B dissolves with outward lifting and uses single Crashing.*

Figure 3.68.

Figure 3.69.

Figure 3.70.

Figure 3.71.

Figure 3.72.

19. Arm Intercepting Palm

From the Opening Posture, with the left hand in front, wrap inward with the left hand, the palm overturning and rising up; advance with a Following Step as the right hand strikes with Heart-Pounding Palm; pull the left hand back, and uplift with the right hand as the left hand strikes with Heart-Pounding Palm (figs. 3.73–3.76). Move in a straight line. Left and right are the same. The Rhyme-Song of Arm Intercepting Palm Dismantling says:

> *Intercepting Palm changes are profound and inexhaustible,*
> *B uses outward leading upholding the arm,*
> *A changes to Intercepting Palm, shuffling with a strike,*
> *B uses outward leading Inserting the Flower to attack,*
> *A quickly advances and strikes with Uplifting Palm,*
> *B dissolves with Double Carrying and is victorious with Hooking Palm,*
> *A changes striking with Part the Clouds to See the Sun,*
> *B dissolves with downward seizing and walks parting ways.*

Figure 3.73.   *Figure 3.74.*   *Figure 3.75.*   *Figure 3.76.*

20. Arm Arresting Palm

From the Opening Posture, with the left hand in front, the left hand arrests upward, downward, then upward again; advance with the right foot, and uplift with the right hand; strike with both hands in Double Crashing Palm (figs. 3.77–3.80). Move in a straight line. Left and right are the same. The Rhyme-Song of Arm Arresting Palm Dismantling says:

Arresting Palm issues overturning above and below,
Arresting high and wrapping low while drilling inward,
Advance quickly using Double Crashing Palm,
B dissolves with inward leading the method is not hard,
A changes peeling and seizing to Eyebrow-Swiping Palm,
B uses Part the Clouds crashing to the chest,
A steps back plucking and upholding B Hides the Flower,
A dissolves with downward Rising and replies with single Crashing.

Figure 3.77.   *Figure 3.78.*   *Figure 3.79.*   *Figure 3.80.*

21. Body Stopping Palm

From the Opening Posture, with the left hand in front, Double Carrying in the same stance, step up with the right foot, and pierce with the right hand; stop and turn the head, looking back; spin the body with double Yanking and crash forward; turn the body, and open forward with the right hand (figs. 3.81–3.86). Move in a straight line. Left and right are the same. The Rhyme-Song of Body Stopping Palm Dismantling says:

The method of Body Stopping Palm uses guarding to attack,
A seizes B advances striking the ribs,
A follows with Double Carrying and walks with Piercing Palm,
Spinning the body quickly guarding against the rear attack,
B strikes A seizes using Goring Elbow,
B changes upholding the elbow with refined Hide the Flower,
A dissolves with Dropping Elbow B back-fists,
A changes intercepting upward and striking to the chest.

Figure 3.81.

Figure 3.82.

Figure 3.83.

Figure 3.84.

Figure 3.85.

Figure 3.86.

22. Hand Overturning Palm

From the Opening Posture, with the left hand in front, lead with the left hand as the right hand strikes the ribs and overturns to the face; step forward with the right foot as the right hand spins, upholding the arm; advance with a Following Step as the left hand strikes with Heart-Pounding Palm; seize backward with the left hand as the right hand punches upward (figs. 3.87–3.91). Move in a straight line. Left and right are the same. The Rhyme-Song of Hand Overturning Palm Dismantling says:

> *The Hand Overturning Palm method is like magic,*
> *Lead outward striking the ribs and overturning upward with a back-fist,*
> *B dissolves with lower intercepting and upward Arresting hands,*
> *A changes upholding the elbow and refined*
>   *Hide the Flower,*
> *B uses Dropping Elbow to dissolve the attack,*
> *A changes to Drilling Fist, striking to the face,*
> *B dissolves seizing the hand and striking with*
>   *Testing Palm,*
> *A changes to outward leading and is victorious*
>   *with horizontal Crashing.*

Figure 3.87.

Figure 3.88.

Figure 3.89.

Figure 3.90.

Figure 3.91.

23. Walking Stepping

From the Opening Posture, with the left hand in front, draw the body back as the left hand arrests downward and wraps inward; advance with the right foot as the right hand pierces past the left hand (figs. 3.92–3.94). This may move in a straight line or may pierce to the eight directions; it is also called Walking Stepping Forrest-Piercing Palm. Left and right are the same. The Rhyme-Song of Walking Stepping Dismantling says:

Walking Stepping Piercing Palm walks the Nine Palaces,
B uses a straight punch to the middle basin,
A then steps forward piercing to the ribs,
B changes stepping back to attack the middle basin,
A again lifts outward and walks piercing the ribs,
B changes withdrawing the body and upholding the elbow posture,
A changes peeling and seizing to Eyebrow-Swiping,
B changes intercepting upward and walks parting ways.

Figure 3.92.   *Figure 3.93.*   *Figure 3.94.*

24. Spinning Body Palm

From the Opening Posture, with the left hand in front, overturn the left hand upward, Koubu with the right foot as the right hand pierces upward, drilling at the neck; turn the body, and step out left into Double Crashing Palms; uplift with the left hand, and advance with a Following Step as the right hand strikes with Heart-Pounding Palm; step forward with the right foot as the right hand opens horizontally to change sides (figs. 3.95–3.99). Move in a straight line. Left and right are the same. The Rhyme-Song of Spinning Body Palm Dismantling says:

Spinning Body Palm method is extremely wise,
B leads A overturns and pierces to the face,
B dissolves with covering elbow leading inward,
A quickly spins the body attacking to the ribs,
B dissolves with outward lifting and Inserts the
*   Flower upward,*
A changes to Uplifting Palm striking to the
*   chest,*
B dissolves meeting the hand, A Hides the
*   Flower,*
B dissolves with downward lifting and walks
*   parting ways.*

Figure 3.95.

Figure 3.96.

Figure 3.97.

Figure 3.98.

Figure 3.99.

Post-Heaven Palm Thunder (Zhen) Eight Postures

The Pre-Heaven Thunder trigram produces a method of body-overturning called Swallow-Overturning Covering-Hand Palm, and from this palm eight Post-Heaven postures are developed: Push the Mountain into the Sea, Strength to Uphold a Thousand Pounds, Carrying Hooking Palm, Leading Hand Palm, Sticking Hand Palm, Advancing Joining Palm, Following Hand Palm, and Adhering Hand Palm. These are the eight Thunder postures of the Post-Heaven Palms, which conceal cleverness, following opportunity and responding with change. As soon as the mind moves, the hands and feet respond; as soon as the eyes see, the heart and spirit are already prepared. To become well-versed, they must be trained over time, and those who are not skilled in contemplating them cannot fully understand them. The Song of the Eight Thunder Postures says:

> *Swallow-Overturning Covering-Hand moves overturning the body,*
> *Push the Mountain into the Sea striking method is lively,*
> *Advancing step Plucking the Moon Heaven-Upholding Palm,*
> *Double Carrying Tiger Embrace method is refined,*
> *Leading method must twist and Sticking must be fast,*
> *Joining Palm is continuously profound and inexhaustible,*
> *Following method covering elbow Leading the body at an angle,*
> *Hide the Flower with Adhering Hand without retaining emotion.*

25. Push the Mountain into the Sea

From the Opening Posture, with the right hand in front, step out half a step to the left corner with the left foot; bring the right foot up into an empty stance in front of the left foot as the right hand seizes and yanks downward; advance with a Following Step as both palms crash forward; advance right and bring the left foot up into an empty stance as the left hand seizes and yanks; advance with Double Crashing Palms (figs. 3.100–3.106). Move in a zigzag pattern. Left and right are the same. The Rhyme-Song of Push the Mountain into the Sea Dismantling says:

> *Push the Mountain into the Sea the application is not hard,*
> *Lead outward and yank down Crashing obliquely to the shoulder,*
> *B dissolves with leading outward and oblique Crashing Palm,*
> *A uses outward leading and answers with Hide the Flower,*
> *B dissolves with downward Arresting A strikes up,*
> *B follows Rising upward trying to steal first,*
> *A gives up and withdraws the body plucking with Upholding Hand,*
> *B changes upholding the elbow retreating with Hide the Flower.*

Figure 3.100.

Figure 3.101.

Figure 3.102.

Figure 3.103.

Figure 3.104.

Figure 3.105.

Figure 3.106.

26. Strength to Uphold a Thousand Pounds

From the Opening Posture, with the left hand in front, arrest downward and uphold upward with the left hand; advance the right foot with a Following Step, striking with a right Upholding Palm (figs. 3.107–3.110). Move in a straight line. Left and right are the same. The Rhyme-Song of Strength to Uphold a Thousand Pounds Dismantling says:

> *Advancing step Upholding Palm walking must be harmonized,*
> *A uses Seizing Hand B lifts the leg,*
> *A changes to Arresting below using plucking and upholding,*
> *B quickly pulls the leg and uses the hand to block,*
> *Closely following changing hands, using Chopping Palm,*
> *A dissolves upholding the elbow just in time,*
> *B changes spinning the body entering with Goring Elbow,*
> *A changes to Hide the Flower B lifts to escape.*

Figure 3.107.   *Figure 3.108.*   *Figure 3.109.*   *Figure 3.110.*

27. Carrying Hooking Palm

From the Opening Posture, with the left hand in front, double-handed carry; hook with the right hand and a right Koubu step; step behind with the left foot, and spin the body; left punch to the ribs; advance with a right step and a right crushing fist to change sides (figs. 3.111–3.115). Move in a straight line. Left and right are the same. The Rhyme-Song of Carrying Hooking Palm Dismantling says:

Carrying Palm must flow and hooking must be fierce,
A seizes B advances with a punch to the middle basin,
A is quick with Double Carrying and hooks around the neck,
B retreats and leads outward A spins and punches,
B retreats meeting the hand A punches straight,
B again meets the hand fast like the wind,
A changes to Dropping Elbow and pierces to the face,
B upholds and A changes victorious with Upholding Palm.

Figure 3.111.

Figure 3.112.

Figure 3.113.

Figure 3.114.

Figure 3.115.

197

28. Leading Hand Palm

From the Opening Posture, with the left hand in front, withdraw the body as the left hand leads inward; advance right, and bring the left foot up to an empty stance as the left hand leads outward; advance with a Following Step and Double Crashing Palm (figs. 3.116–3.119). To change sides, step back with the left foot as the right hand leads inward. Move in a zigzag pattern. Left and right are the same. The Rhyme-Song of Leading Hand Palm Dismantling says:

Leading method must be horizontal the energy must twist,
B advances with Insert the Flower A leads inward,
B changes following the body switching hands, and seizing,
A meets with outward leading and Crashing is victorious,
B changes seizing the hand A strikes the ribs,
B dissolves Arresting downward A attacks upward,
B uplifts and crashes inward A uses Squeezing Palm,
B follows and leads outward, moving and changing places.

Figure 3.116.   *Figure 3.117.*   *Figure 3.118.*   *Figure 3.119.*

29. Sticking Hand Palm

From the Opening Posture, with the left hand in front, advance with a right step and seize with the left hand as the right palm strikes upward from below toward the ear (Insert the Flower Palm); circle the right hand and uphold the upper arm, advancing with a Following Step, striking with Hide the Flower; shuffle forward with a right Reverse Tossing Palm (figs. 3.120–3.123). Move in a straight line. Left and right are the same. The Rhyme-Song of Sticking Hand Palm Dismantling says:

Sticking Hand Palm method truly can be praised,
Seize the hand advance the step with regular Insert the Flower,
B quickly changes postures Rising to dissolve,
A changes upholding the arm striking with Hide the Flower,
B again changes tack dissolving with downward Rising,
A changes Stealing the Peach and reverse Inserting the Flower,
B quickly waves the body Crashing obliquely to the shoulders,
A seizes B pierces returning to original position.

Figure 3.120.　　*Figure 3.121.*　　*Figure 3.122.*　　*Figure 3.123.*

30. Advancing Joining Palm

From the Opening Posture, with the left hand in front, shuffle forward and lead inward with the left hand; step forward with the right foot as the right hand grabs the upper arm; advance left as the left hand swipes the eyebrows; advance right with Double Crashing Palms (figs. 3.124–3.127). Move in a straight line. Left and right are the same. The Rhyme-Song of Advancing Joining Palm Dismantling says:

> *Joining Hand Palm method is called the strongest,*
> *B advances with Insert the Flower A Climbs the Wall,*
> *B uses outward leading advancing with Goring Elbow,*
> *A changes cutting the elbow with no haste,*
> *B reverses the body and chops A uplifts and strikes,*
> *B uses connected Shaving as the most appropriate,*
> *A changes intercepting up with reverse Insert the Flower,*
> *B dissolves with Insert the Flower A crashes obliquely.*

Figure 3.124.   *Figure 3.125.*   *Figure 3.126.*   *Figure 3.127.*

31. Following Hand Palm

From the Opening Posture, with the left hand in front, withdraw the body and cover inward with the left hand; advance with a Following Step, the right hand guarding at the left wrist, joining and pressing outward; peel and seize with the right hand, and lead outward while advancing the right foot, opening outward with the left arm (figs. 3.128–3.131). Move in a straight line. Left and right are the same. The Rhyme-Song of Following Hand Palm Dismantling says:

Following Hand Palm method follows the force and moves,
B uses Affix the Seal striking to the chest,
A follows covering inward replying with joined palms,
B uses outward leading and oblique Crashing Palm,
A changes to outward leading attacking to the ribs,
B follows disengaging lifting and punching with a pounding fist,
A changes to upholding the elbow with refined Hide the Flower,
B quickly arrests and lifts and walks parting ways.

Figure 3.128.   *Figure 3.129.*   *Figure 3.130.*   *Figure 3.131.*

32. Adhering Hand Palm

From the Opening Posture, with the left hand in front, draw the body back as the left hand arrests downward and wraps inward; kick with the right heel as the right hand seizes and the left hand extends; set the right foot down, and advance with the left foot as the left hand circles and upholds the upper arm; advance with a Following Step as the right palm strikes the center (figs. 3.132–3.135). Move in a straight line. Left and right are the same. The Rhyme-Song of Adhering Hand Palm Dismantling says:

> *Adhering Palm specifically controls attacks to the ribs,*
> *A dissolves and lifts outward B Inserts the Flower,*
> *A follows adhering and wrapping meeting the hand and Testing,*
> *B dissolves uplifting with Part the Clouds method,*
> *A changes upholding the elbow using Hide the Flower,*
> *B uses retreating pulling and punches to the ribs,*
> *A dissolves with outward lifting B strikes up,*
> *A changes switching hands returning to original position.*

Figure 3.132.   *Figure 3.133.*   *Figure 3.134.*   *Figure 3.135.*

Post-Heaven Palm Wind (Xun) Eight Postures

The Pre-Heaven Wind trigram produces a method of body-overturning called Spinning-Body Back-Covering Palm, and from this palm eight Post-Heaven postures are developed: Slamming Elbow, Coiling Elbow, Dropping Elbow, Goring Elbow, Twisting Elbow, Filing Elbow, Stacking Elbow, and Drilling Elbow. These are the eight Wind postures of the Post-Heaven Palms. If the eight elbows are trained diligently, and made familiar in the mind, one can follow the opportunity and respond with change, quickly and ferociously, adhering to the opponent's body in applying them. The Song of the Eight Wind Postures says:

Koubu and spin the body with Back-Covering Palm,
Opening Palm and spinning the body Slamming Elbow is strong,
Lead with an advancing step entering with Coiling Elbow,
Below using Dropping Elbow the intercepting method is strong,
Advancing step Goring Elbow is quick and fast,
Outward Leading with the front hand Twisting Elbow injures,
Filing Elbow and Stacking Elbow must be fierce,
Waving the body with Drilling Elbow is difficult to defend.

33. Slamming Elbow

From the Opening Posture, with the left hand in front, overturn outward and press down with the left hand, advancing with a Following Step like Opening Palm; step behind right and spin the body, slamming horizontally with the right elbow; with the right hand now in front, use Opening Palm to continue to the next repetition (figs. 3.136–3.139). Move in a straight line. Left and right are the same. The Rhyme-Song of Slamming Elbow Dismantling says:

> *Slamming Elbow changes are called strongest,*
> *Shuffle step with Opening Palm striking to the chest,*
> *B dissolves with outward leading quick and fast,*
> *A spins with Slamming Elbow difficult to defend,*
> *B follows cutting the elbow striking to the ribs,*
> *A changes to Double Carrying checking and injuring the ribs,*
> *B dissolves with Dropping Elbow A overturns upward,*
> *B uses outward leading and oblique Crashing to the shoulders.*

Figure 3.136.   *Figure 3.137.*   *Figure 3.138.*   *Figure 3.139.*

34. Coiling Elbow

From the Opening Posture, with the left hand in front, press downward and pierce horizontally with the left hand; advance with a Following Step; bend the elbow (coil the elbow) and strike forward; advance with the right foot as the left hand turns over at the wrist and seizes downward, and the right hand pounces downward; advance with a Following Step with Double Crashing Palms (figs. 3.140–3.144). Move in a straight line. Left and right are the same. The Rhyme-Song of Coiling Elbow Dismantling says:

The mystery of the Coiling Elbow method startles others,
B leads A follows advancing with Coiling Elbow,
B follows and withdraws the body quickly upholding the elbow,
A changes locking upward with double pouncing strikes,
B dissolves switching hands plucking and upholding the elbow,
A drops the elbow down as the hand extends above,
B upholds A leads using Goring Elbow,
B uses Hanging Palm A carries and hooks.

Figure 3.140.

Figure 3.141. *Figure 3.142.* *Figure 3.143.* *Figure 3.144.*

35. Dropping Elbow

From the Opening Posture, with the left hand in front, draw the body back; bend the elbow of the left arm and drop down; advance with a Following Step as the left hand lifts upward and the right palm issues from below the left elbow (called Hammer under Elbow); step forward with the right foot as the right hand pierces past the left hand to change sides (figs. 3.145–3.148). Move in a straight line. Left and right are the same. The Rhyme-Song of Dropping Elbow Dismantling says:

> *Dropping Elbow Palm method differentiates yin and yang,*
> *B uses seizing the hand and Rib Checking Palm,*
> *A dissolves with Dropping Elbow B strikes up,*
> *A uses Intercepting Palm striking to the chest,*
> *B changes to Double Carrying A to Coiling Elbow,*
> *B follows freeing the grab A uses Wiping Palm,*
> *B again uses Double Carrying and A Coiling Elbow,*
> *B intercepts A changes to injure with Goring Elbow.*

Figure 3.145.   *Figure 3.146.*   *Figure 3.147.*   *Figure 3.148.*

36. Goring Elbow

From the Opening Posture, with the right hand in front, seize with the right hand; advance with the left foot, and gore with the left elbow; strike up with a back-fist using the left hand; overturn the fist, and block downward vertically; advance with a Following Step and Double Crashing Palms (figs. 3.149–3.154). Move in a straight line. Left and right are the same. The Rhyme-Song of Goring Elbow Dismantling says:

> *Goring Elbow changes are hard to defend,*
> *Seizing hand Goring Elbow injures the ribs,*
> *B dissolves withdrawing the body upholding the elbow in haste,*
> *A changes and overturns upward striking for yintang,*
> *B changes with intercepting above and Wiping Palm below,*
> *A changes to outward lifting Crashing to the chest,*
> *B dissolves upholding the elbow leading inside,*
> *A then spins the body injuring with Slamming Elbow.*

Figure 3.149.   *Figure 3.150.*   *Figure 3.151.*

Figure 3.152.   *Figure 3.153.*   *Figure 3.154.*

37. Twisting Elbow

From the Opening Posture, with the right hand in front, seize with the right hand as the left foot steps up, and the left hand smashes downward from above; when the forearm comes horizontal at the level of the waist, overturn the palm and twist the forearm, rolling outward horizontally, the right hand assisting at the left forearm, while simultaneously sticking to the body, advancing with a Following Step (figs. 3.155–3.156). This is also called Rolling Elbow. Move in a straight line. Left and right are the same. The Rhyme-Song of Twisting Elbow Dismantling says:

Shaving Hand splitting and advancing Twisting Elbow injures,
B dissolves with Filing Elbow as appropriate,
A quickly spins the body splitting chopping and shaving,
B dissolves again Filing the force must be strong,
A again spins the body splitting chopping and shaving,
B dissolves with Double Carrying and Spreading Wings Palm,
A dissolves with outward leading B spins and chops,
A changes intercepting upward and injures the ribs.

Figure 3.155.　　*Figure 3.156.*

38. Filing Elbow

From the Opening Posture, with the left hand in front, the right foot steps behind the left as the right hand peels and seizes and twists inward; step out left and use the left forearm to file; the left hand seizes as the right foot steps up and the right forearm files (figs. 3.157–3.160). Move in a straight line. Left and right are the same. The Rhyme-Song of Filing Elbow Dismantling says:

> *Flowing hand upholding the elbow Filing Elbow is lively,*
> *As B dissolves Filing and cutting the force must be increased,*
> *A changes and switches hands using Filing Elbow,*
> *B again files and cuts just as before,*
> *A changes entangling and locking grasping and throwing,*
> *B steps back with angled leading that must prop up,*
> *A changes to Goring Elbow striking to the chest,*
> *B uses cutting the elbow striking to the ribs.*

Figure 3.157.   *Figure 3.158.*   *Figure 3.159.*   *Figure 3.160.*

39. Stacking Elbow

From the Opening Posture, with the left hand in front, pull the left hand back, overturning the Tiger's Mouth; extend the rear hand forward, meeting the hand and seizing; advance with the right foot in a Following Step as the left hand presses and the right hand stacks downward; seize backward with the left hand, and strike the ribs with a right fist (figs. 3.161–3.164). Move in a zigzag pattern. Left and right are the same. The Rhyme-Song of Stacking Elbow Dismantling says:

Stacking Elbow changes are profound and inexhaustible,
B uses seizing the hand and Testing Palm to be victorious,
A follows seizing hand changing to Stacking Elbow,
B dissolves with Drilling Elbow striking to the chest,
A cuts B changes lifting, striking, and throwing,
A changes closing and squeezing, responding with angled Uplifting,
B locks A spins with moving hooking and throwing,
B changes and intercepts upward with refined Insert the Flower.

Figure 3.161.   *Figure 3.162.*   *Figure 3.163.*   *Figure 3.164.*

40. Drilling Elbow

From the Opening Posture, with the left hand in front, lead outward and twist inward with the left hand as the right foot steps behind the left; spin the body and strike with a right Goring Elbow (figs. 3.165–3.167). Move in a straight line. Left and right are the same. The Rhyme-Song of Drilling Elbow Dismantling says:

A uses outward leading B leads inward,
A advances with Drilling Elbow striking to the chest,
B upholds A changes lifting striking and throwing,
B uses Goring Elbow advancing with a lively body,
A follows cutting the elbow striking to the ribs,
B follows escaping and lifting stepping back to punch,
A changes uplifting and striking in a cross-step,
B dissolves seizing downward clutching the neck.

Figure 3.165.   *Figure 3.166.*   *Figure 3.167.*

Post-Heaven Palm Fire (Li)
Eight Postures

The Pre-Heaven Water trigram produces a method of body-overturning called Twisting-Body Forward-Searching Palm, and from this palm the eight Fire Post-Heaven postures are developed: Forward Chasing Leg, Backward Stomping Leg, Outward Swinging Leg, Inward Hanging Leg, Upward Kicking Leg, Downward Cutting Leg, Angled Stepping Leg, and Straight Crashing Connected Leg. If these eight kicks are trained diligently, each set contains three kicks, enabling twenty-four methods of intercepting kicking legs. Seizing the opportunity and applying them, meeting an opening and issuing, the mysteries of the eight legs are deep. The Song of the Eight Fire Postures says:

> *Stepping behind twisting the body is called Forward-Searching,*
> *Seizing the hand and Chasing forward below the knee is victorious,*
> *Turn the body and kick back using Stomping Leg,*
> *Outward Swinging Inward Hanging to the front and back of the chest,*
> *Upward Kicking to the back of the head or forward to the face,*
> *Outward Leading Downward Cutting with Linking kicks,*
> *Seize the hand and hasten forward with Angled Stepping Leg,*
> *Double Carrying, Crashing to the face, without using emotion.*

41. Forward Chasing Leg

From the Opening Posture, with the left hand in front, the right hand pierces past the left hand and seizes downward; raise the right leg, and kick below the knee; set the right foot down, and seize with the left hand; raise the left leg with a kick; set the left foot down in Koubu, and spin the body; raise the right foot, and kick to the rear with a Cutting Kick; set the right foot down, and advance with a Following Step and Opening Palm to change sides (figs. 3.168–3.171). Move in a straight line. Left and right are the same. The Rhyme-Song of Forward Chasing Leg Dismantling says:

> *Forward Chasing Leg method truly is unique,*
> *One posture with three kicks fast and quick,*
> *Touching hands Forward Chasing is applied below the knee,*
> *B then steps back dissolving Forward Chasing,*
> *A follows seizing the hand changing legs to kick,*
> *B uses outward leading dissolving must be quick,*
> *Spinning the body A uses Downward Cutting Filing,*
> *B dissolves arresting downward with a low Cutting Kick.*

Figure 3.168.   *Figure 3.169.*   *Figure 3.170.*   *Figure 3.171.*

214

42. Backward Stomping Leg

From the Opening Posture, with the left hand in front, press down with the left hand; advance with a Following Step with Opening Palm; spin the body, and advance with the left foot as the left hand pierces past the right; turn the body, raise the right leg, and stomp backward; set the right foot down, and spin the body as the left and right hands part, intercepting downward, and hook kick with the left leg; turn the body and set the foot down, right Cutting Kick; set the right foot down, and advance with a Following Step, the right hand now forward with Opening Palm (figs. 3.172–3.175). Move in a straight line. Left and right are the same. The Rhyme-Song of Backward Stomping Leg Dismantling says:

Back Stomping Leg method is clever and fast,
Plucking victory amid defeat guarding against B's advance,
Shuffle step with Opening Palm turn the body and walk,
As B follows issue the leg using Backward Stomping,
B uses withdrawing the body and lower arresting to dissolve,
A turns seizing the hand with a fast hooking leg,
B then lifts the leg to dissolve the attack,
A uses circling steps cutting to the knee.

Figure 3.172.   *Figure 3.173.*   *Figure 3.174.*   *Figure 3.175.*

43. Outward Swinging Leg

From the Opening Posture, with the left hand in front, the right hand pierces past the left hand, meeting the hand and leading inward as the right leg lifts with an outward kick, striking the front of the chest; change to the left hand leading outward as the left leg lifts with an outward kick, striking the back; set the foot down in a Koubu, and turn the body, kicking to the rear with a Cutting Kick; set the foot down as advancing with a Following Step and Opening Palm (figs. 3.176–3.179). Move in a straight line. Left and right are the same. The Rhyme-Song of Outward Swinging Leg Dismantling says:

> *Outward Swinging Leg method is called the strongest,*
> *Outward leading outward kicking injures the back,*
> *B quickly leads outward dissolving the attack,*
> *A switches to inward leading kicking to the chest,*
> *B then withdraws the body arresting downward to dissolve,*
> *A changes with circular stepping injuring with Cutting Leg,*
> *B quickly steps back lifting the leg fast,*
> *A shuffles seizing the hand and Opening to the chest.*

Figure 3.176.   *Figure 3.177.*   *Figure 3.178.*   *Figure 3.179.*

44. Inward Hanging Leg

From the Opening Posture, with the left hand in front, skip forward as the left hand seizes; raise the right foot Forward Chasing; set the foot down and twist the body; arrest outward with the right hand and lift the left foot with an inward hanging kick; set the foot down in a Koubu and spin the body; lift the right foot with a Cutting Kick; set the right foot and right hand down in front, and advance with Opening Palm (figs. 3.180–3.183). Move in a straight line. Left and right are the same. The Rhyme-Song of Inward Hanging Leg Dismantling says:

Inward Hanging Leg method changes are strong,
Shuffle step seize the hand and injure with Forward Chasing,
Switch hands arrest the arm with Inward Hanging Leg,
Horizontally hanging and kicking the chest is truly hard to defend,
B uses Arresting Palm to dissolve the attack,
A changes to circling steps with a hasty Cutting Kick,
B then lifts the leg and punches upward,
A uses Hide the Flower striking to the chest.

Figure 3.180.   *Figure 3.181.*   *Figure 3.182.*   *Figure 3.183.*

45. Upward Kicking Leg

The main requirements are similar to Outward Swinging Leg, only here one must kick as high as possible (kicking the head). From the Opening Posture, with the left hand in front, the right hand pierces past the left, meeting the hand and seizing downward; lift the right leg and kick to the face; switch hands and seize downward left; lift the left leg, kicking upward to the back of the head; set the foot down in Koubu, turn the body, and lift the leg in a right Cutting Kick; set the right foot and hand down in front, and advance with Opening Palm (figs. 3.184–3.187). Move in a straight line. Left and right are the same. The Rhyme-Song of Upward Kicking Leg Dismantling says:

> *Upward Kicking Leg method is difficult to defend,*
> *Lift the legs and kick hurriedly to their front and back,*
> *Upward Kicking to the back of the head on the Fengfu[2] point,*
> *Switch legs and front kick seeking the Chengjiang point,[3]*
> *B first leads outward and then cuts the elbow,*
> *A uses Backward Stomping injuring the hip,*
> *B uses lower arresting advancing with Crashing Palms,*
> *A quickly leads out with Rib Checking Palm.*

Figure 3.184.   *Figure 3.185.*   *Figure 3.186.*   *Figure 3.187.*

46. Downward Cutting Leg

From the Opening Posture, with the left hand in front, lead outward with the left hand, and pierce upward with the right hand; lift the left leg and use springing force to cut downward like a stone falling to the ground; change to the right hand leading outward and left hand piercing upward; lift the left leg and cut down; set the foot down in a Koubu and spin the body; lift the right leg with a springing Cutting Kick; set the right hand and foot down in front, shuffling forward with Opening Palm (figs. 3.188–3.193). Move in a straight line. Left and right are the same. The Rhyme-Song of Downward Cutting Leg Dismantling says:

Downward Cutting Leg method is cruel and unique,
Kicking like flaying the skin alive,
Lead outward stepping up with a downward Cutting Kick,
B changes to Outward Swinging returning kicking legs,
A arrests stepping up changing legs to cut,
B quickly lifts the leg and walks with Linking Kick,
A changes with circling steps and Cutting Kick,
B uses lower arresting and both separate and leave.

Figure 1.188.   *Figure 1.189.*   *Figure 1.190.*

219

Figure 1.191.   *Figure 1.192.*   *Figure 1.193.*

47. Angled Stepping Leg

From the Opening Posture, with the left hand in front, skip forward half a step with the left foot; seize downward with the left hand, and hasten forward with the right leg; set the right foot down and raise the left leg with an Angled Stepping Kick, sweeping horizontally, Koubu, and spin the body; lift the right leg with a springing Cutting Kick; set the right hand and foot down in front and advance with Opening Palm (figs. 3.194–3.197). Move in a straight line. Left and right are the same. The Rhyme-Song of Angled Stepping Leg Dismantling says:

> *Angled Stepping Leg method is quick and unique,*
> *Treading forward like a plow,*
> *Seize downward, step up with Forward Chasing Leg,*
> *B dissolves stepping back fast and quick,*
> *A quickly steps up with Angled Stepping Leg,*
> *B quickly lifts the leg and kicks with Cutting Leg,*
> *A quickly circles the steps turning the body to cut,*
> *B dissolves with lower arresting drawing the body back.*

Figure 3.194.   *Figure 3.195.*   *Figure 3.196.*   *Figure 3.197.*

48. Straight Crashing Connected Leg

From the Opening Posture, with the left hand in front, seize into Double Carrying; lift the right leg with a horizontal stomp kick to the opponent's front knee; set the right foot down; lift the left foot and heel-kick forward; set the foot down in Koubu and spin the body; lift the right leg with a Cutting Kick; set the right hand and foot down in front; shuffle with Opening Palm (figs. 3.198–3.201). Move in a straight line. Left and right are the same. The Rhyme-Song of Straight Crashing Connected Leg Dismantling says:

> Straight Crashing Connected Leg method is strong,
> Like a fierce tiger descending a mountain ridge,
> Double Carrying advancing step with Straight Crashing Leg,
> The knee of B's forward leg must be strongly injured,
> B then steps back to dissolve the attack,
> A closely kicks the knee B again retreats,
> A quickly turns the body with a side Cutting Kick,
> Eight sets of kicking methods spread to the four seas.

Figure 3.198.   *Figure 3.199.*   *Figure 3.200.*   *Figure 3.201.*

Post-Heaven Palm Earth (Kun)
Eight Postures

The Pre-Heaven Mountain trigram produces a method of body-overturning called Overturning-Body Backward-Inserting Palm, and from this palm the eight Earth Post-Heaven postures are developed: Pressing Palm, Squeezing Palm, Clamping Palm, Seizing Palm, Crushing Palm, Crashing Palm, Hooking Palm, and Eyebrow-Swiping Palm. After training these eight postures over time, there will be a method in stepping and walking, and extending the hands will have an application. These eight postures are the methods of the hands and eyes following together, the body and footwork connecting. The movements must be vicious, power must be issued fiercely, and when crossing hands, one cannot retain any kind sentiments; these admonishments must be carried in the heart. The Song of the Eight Earth Postures says:

> *Overturning-Body Backward-Inserting Palm method is lively,*
> *Advancing step Pressing Palm attacks the ribs,*
> *Cross-stance Seizing Hand using Squeezing Palm,*
> *Advancing step Clamping Palm strikes to the chest,*
> *Advancing step Seizing Hand with horizontal Crashing Palms,*
> *Step forward cutting and insert with Crushing fist,*
> *Outward Leading inward Rising inward Crashing Palm,*
> *Inside Hooking Outside Swiping fast like the wind.*

49. Pressing Palm

From the Opening Posture, with the left hand in front, advance with Opening Palm, but do not issue force, and as the opponent meets the hand, the left palm quickly overturns and rolls downward. Advance with a Following Step, and crash forth with Pressing Palm; advance on the right as the right hand pierces past the left, switching postures to Opening Palm with the right hand in front (figs. 3.202–3.204). Move in a straight line. Left and right are the same. The Rhyme-Song of Pressing Palm Dismantling says:

> *Pressing Palm opens upward, changing to attack below,*
> *B dissolves with downward Smashing and strikes to the face,*
> *A changes to uplift the elbow striking straight to the heart,*
> *B dissolves with downward lifting A rises up to meet,*
> *B uses White Crane Spreads Its Wings to strike,*
> *A changes hooking inward with a cross-step crushing fist,*
> *B changes intercepting up and downward Wiping Palm,*
> *A follows, lifting outward, separating palms, and walking.*

Figure 3.202.   *Figure 3.203.*   *Figure 3.204.*

50. Squeezing Palm

From the Opening Posture, with the left hand in front, seize downward with the left hand; test forward with the right hand in a cross-step; press down in an arc with the right hand; advance with the right foot into Double Crashing Palms (figs. 3.205–3.207). Move in a straight line. Left and right are the same. The Rhyme-Song of Squeezing Palm Dismantling says:

Squeezing Palm changes are profound and inexhaustible,
A uses seizing the hand and Testing to the forehead,
B uses upward Rising to dissolve the attack,
A changes to seizing and Squeezing to be victorious,
B leads with Goring Elbow A guides and leads,
B then spins the body and Splitting Palm is victorious,
A changes upholding the elbow using Hide the Flower,
B dissolves with outward lifting and walks parting ways.

Figure 3.205.   *Figure 3.206.*   *Figure 3.207.*

51. Clamping Palm

From the Opening Posture, with the left hand in front, advance the right foot as the left hand leads outward; pierce and uplift with the right hand seizing backward; advance with a Following Step and left tearing palm strike (striking with violent shaking power); advance with a Following Step and right palm-heel strike (figs. 3.208–3.211). Move in a straight line. Left and right are the same. The Rhyme-Song of Clamping Palm Dismantling says:

> *Clamping Palm method is fierce and terrible,*
> *Advancing step tearing and shaking to the chest,*
> *B dissolves stepping back with inward Covering Palm,*
> *A changes switching hands shaking the central palace,*
> *B again intercepts inward A strikes up,*
> *B follows uplifting striking to the chest,*
> *A lifts B heel-strikes A Spreads Wings,*
> *B advances with oblique Crashing as A walks away.*

Figure 3.208.   *Figure 3.209.*   *Figure 3.210.*   *Figure 3.211.*

52. Seizing Palm

From the Opening Posture, with the left hand in front, take a right Baibu step and bring the left foot up into an empty stance as the left hand seizes and yanks; shuffle step left and bring the right foot up into an empty stance as the right hand seizes and yanks; advance with a Following Step and Double Crashing Palms (figs. 3.212–3.217). Move in a zigzag pattern. Left and right are the same. The Rhyme-Song of Seizing Palm Dismantling says:

> *Seizing Palm begins first with cross-step Seizing,*
> *B uses Testing Palm piercing to the face,*
> *A follows with Seizing Hand again Seizing and Yanking,*
> *Shuffle step quickly using oblique shoulder Crashing,*
> *B leads striking the ribs A punches straight,*
> *B cuts A hooks overturning to the face,*
> *B hooks A changes to striking reverse to the back,*
> *B uses angled pushing and oblique shoulder Crashing.*

Figure 3.212.   *Figure 3.213.*   *Figure 3.214.*

Figure 3.215.   *Figure 3.216.*   *Figure 3.217.*

53. Crushing Palm

From the Opening Posture, with the right hand in front, seize with the right hand and advance with the left step as the left hand cuts downward from above, back-fist, uplift with the left hand as the right hand strikes with Hammer Below Elbow, advancing with a Following Step (figs. 3.218–3.221). Move in a straight line. Left and right are the same. The Rhyme-Song of Crushing Palm Dismantling says:

Using Crushing Palm seizing the hand must be refined,
Touching hands B seizes A uses springy Crushing,
B uplifts A uses changing hands and punches,
B pulls and Inserts the Flower A strikes with the palm heel,
B dissolves seizing and lifting with angled Single Whip,
A changes cutting the head fierce and terrible,
B uses upholding the elbow Arresting and striking the waist,
A changes arresting downward and chopping upward nimbly.

Figure 3.218.   *Figure 3.219.*   *Figure 3.220.*   *Figure 3.221.*

54. Crashing Palm

From the Opening Posture, with the left hand in front, lead outward with the left hand; advance with the right foot as the right elbow lifts the crook of the opponent's elbow; advance with a Following Step as both hands crash to the chest (figs. 3.222–3.224). Move in a straight line. Left and right are the same. The Rhyme-Song of Crashing Palm Dismantling says:

Inward Crashing Palm method is unique and refined,
Touching lifting outward and Crashing to the chest,
B covers with angled Squeezing A punches up,
B follows and uplifts with double strikes to the chest,
A follows covering inward again with angled Squeezing,
B changes intercepting upward with a palm heel pressing down,
A changes to outward leading and B uses reverse smash,
A changes upholding striking to the ribs.

Figure 3.222.   *Figure 3.223.*   *Figure 3.224.*

55. Hooking Palm

From the Opening Posture, with the left hand in front, lead outward with the left hand; advance with the right foot, and grab the upper arm with the right hand; advance the left foot as the left palm hooks to the face; step back left with double seizing hand; shuffle step with the right hand in front, striking the ribs (figs. 3.225–3.229). Move in a straight line. Left and right are the same. The Rhyme-Song of Hooking Palm Dismantling says:

Hooking Palm method is called heroic,
Leading outward and grasping the arm Hooking Palm is
    victorious,
B intercepts A carries striking to the ribs,
B seals A uplifts Crashing to the chest,
B dissolves upholding the elbow and leading inward,
A changes peeling and seizing responding with Eyebrow-
    Swiping,
B dissolves Filing and Drilling A seizes upward,
B locks A spins and Splitting Palm is victorious.

Figure 3.225.

Figure 3.226.

Figure 3.227.

Figure 3.228.

Figure 3.229.

56. Eyebrow-Swiping Palm

From the Opening Posture, with the left hand in front, lead outward with the left hand; advance the right foot as the right hand swipes the eyebrows, pressing downward; advance with a Following Step and strike with Double Crashing Palms (figs. 3.230–3.233). Move in a straight line. Left and right are the same. The Rhyme-Song of Eyebrow-Swiping Palm Dismantling says:

Eyebrow-Swiping Palm method is enlightened,
Seizing the hand advancing step swiping to tianting,[4]
B rises A changes seizing the hand and Crashing,
B dissolves stepping back and Stacking Palm is victorious,
A gores B smothers A upholds and locks,
B follows peeling and seizing Swiping Palm is nimble,
A follows propping and pushing and B spins and splits,
A carries with forward Crashing fierce and terrible.

Figure 3.230.   *Figure 3.231.*   *Figure 3.232.*   *Figure 3.233.*

Post-Heaven Palm Marsh (Dui) Eight Postures

The Pre-Heaven Earth trigram produces a method of body-overturning called Stopping-Body Moving-Hooking Palm, and from this palm eight Post-Heaven postures are developed: Arm Passing Palm, Wild Tiger Pounds the Heart Palm, Drawing-Body Palm, Gathering Palm, Waving-Body Palm, Evading-Body Palm, Crossing-Body Palm, and Leaping-Body Palm. These are the eight Marsh postures of the Post-Heaven Palms. If trained diligently, the body method will be agile, the hands will be rapid, and the eyes fast, and the transformations of movement and stillness and yin and yang within the internal zang and fu organs will be inexhaustible. The Song of the Eight Marsh Postures says:

Turning Body Moving-Hooking Palm causes the body to stop,
Ape and monkey Passing Arm attacking to the back,
Wild Tiger Pounds the Heart striking to the chest,
Drawing-Body with oblique Crashing causes victory,
Bend the body Plucking and Gathering using a coiled stance,
Waving-Body Crashing Palm must twist the waist,
Evading-Body twisting the body quick and fast,
Fierce tiger leaps the mountain fast like the wind.

57. Arm Passing Palm

From the Opening Posture, with the left hand in front, draw the body back as the left hand blocks vertically downward and overturns (Tiger's Mouth facing inward); lead inward; advance the left foot, and bring the right foot up into an empty stance; switch to the right hand and lead outward, advancing with a Following Step and striking with Double Crashing Palms (figs. 3.234–3.237). Move in a zigzag pattern. Left and right are the same. The Rhyme-Song of Arm Passing Palm Dismantling says:

A seizes B advances attacking with a straight punch,
A uses Passing Palm and Double Crashing is victorious,
B escapes and seizes downward using Heaven Thrusting Cannon,
A quickly uplifts striking to the chest,
B uses Double Carrying striking with Hooking Palm,
A quickly leads outward attacking with Single Crashing Palm,
B spins and advances with an elbow A cuts with an elbow,
B reverses A posts and chops lively to the ribs.

Figure 3.234.   *Figure 3.235.*   *Figure 3.236.*   *Figure 3.237.*

58. Wild Tiger Pounds the Heart Palm

From the Opening Posture, with the left hand in front, seize with the left hand and extend and strike with the right hand while raising a left heel kick; set the left foot down and advance with the right foot, stepping behind with the left foot as the right hand circles downward and upholds the arm, and the left hand becomes a fist and strikes to the center; step out right with a right crushing fist to the ribs (figs. 3.238–3.241). Move in a straight line. Left and right are the same. The Rhyme-Song of Wild Tiger Pounds the Heart Palm Dismantling says:

> *Wild Tiger Pounds the Heart is like a cat's form,*
> *Seize the hand in cross-stance striking to tianting,*
> *B rises A changes to Pound the Heart,*
> *B dissolves with Dropping Elbow A punches up,*
> *B changes intercepting upward with a lower palm press,*
> *A opens outward with an angled palm B draws close to attack,*
> *A evades and crashes inward B upholds the elbow,*
> *B advances with a straight punch and A arrests to meet.*

Figure 3.238.   *Figure 3.239.*   *Figure 3.240.*   *Figure 3.241.*

59. Drawing-Body Palm

From the Opening Posture, with the left hand in front, draw the body back with lively stepping; arrest downward and uphold with the left hand as the right palm strikes; overturn the right forearm and press with the right elbow; advance the right foot and crash forth with a Following Step (figs. 3.242–3.245). Move in a straight line. Left and right are the same. The Rhyme-Song of Drawing-Body Palm Dismantling says:

Drawing-Body Palm method is miraculous,
B uses reverse palm Insert the Flower to attack,
A dissolves with upward parry B strikes below,
A arrests B overturns A upholds and crashes,
B leads A uses close Pressing Palm,
B leads A changes to Bear Yanks Crashing,
B uplifts with Part the Clouds A Offers the Fruit,
B uplifts with oblique Crashing A leads and separates.

Figure 3.242.   *Figure 3.243.*   *Figure 3.244.*   *Figure 3.245.*

60. Gathering Palm

From the Opening Posture, with the left hand in front, lead outward with the left hand; lower the body into a resting stance; pluck and gather with the right hand; advance with the right foot and right hand, using force to lift up with the right hand (figs. 3.246–3.248). Move in a straight line. Left and right are the same. Move in a zigzag pattern. The Rhyme-Song of Gathering Palm Dismantling says:

B uses outward leading kicking below the knee,
A then plucks and scoops B spins and splits,
A uses uplifting striking B seizes and yanks,
A then waves and overturns with Double Crashing Palms,
A uses Double Carrying and Covering Hand is victorious,
B uses Part the Cloud to See the Sun to strike,
A uses Hide the Flower the usage must be refined,
B uses downward rising and walks parting ways.

Figure 3.246.   *Figure 3.247.*   *Figure 3.248.*

61. Waving-Body Palm

From the Opening Posture, with the left hand in front, seize with the left hand; advance the right foot and strike with the heel of the right palm downward from above; spin the body and advance with a Following Step; twist the right arm and carry backward; take a left Koubu step and right Baibu step; overturn the right hand and twist as the left hand pounces; wave the body toward the front and shuffle step with Crashing Palm (figs. 3.249–3.252). Move in a zigzag pattern. Left and right are the same. The Rhyme-Song of Waving-Body Palm Dismantling says:

Waving-Body Crashing Palm is called heroic,
Seize the hand with palm-heel striking to the abdomen and chest,
B carries A pierces changing to Waving Palm,
B quickly spins the body and Splitting Palm is victorious,
A cuts B seizes advancing with Testing Palm,
A changes upholding and responds with angled Crashing,
B uses outward leading and Hide the Flower Palm,
A follows lifting outward and walks parting ways.

Figure 3.249.   *Figure 3.250.*   *Figure 3.251.*   *Figure 3.252.*

62. Evading-Body Palm

From the Opening Posture, with the right hand in front, advance the left foot as the right hand opens outward; hook with the right step and right hand, spin the body with Hooking Palm, and step out with the left foot, the left hand striking horizontally to the ribs (figs. 3.253–3.256). Move in a straight line. Left and right are the same. The Rhyme-Song of Evading-Body Palm Dismantling says:

Evading-Body Palm method is miraculous,
B advances with Opening Palm striking to the chest,
A spins evading and hooking B leads outward,
A spins using a straight punch to attack,
B connects and reverse Pulls the Nine Oxen to dissolve,
A changes to Green Dragon Removes the Helmet to be victorious,
B changes to uplifting with a downward pressing strike,
A seizes Crashing obliquely B leads and walks.

Figure 3.253.   *Figure 3.254.*   *Figure 3.255.*   *Figure 3.256.*

63. Crossing-Body Palm

From the Opening Posture, with the left hand in front, the left hand seizes, and the right hand tests; step forward to the left corner with the left foot meeting the hand, and lead horizontally as the right foot comes up to an empty stance; advance with a Following Step, striking with Crashing Palms (figs. 3.257–3.260). Move in a zigzag pattern. Left and right are the same. The Rhyme-Song of Crossing-Body Palm Dismantling says:

> Seize the hand with Testing Palm crossing Crashing is refined,
> B dissolves with outward leading and pierces to the ribs,
> A changes to outward lifting and Yin Slapping Palm,
> B opens changing upward Inserting the Flower to attack,
> A uplifts with Part the Clouds to See the Sun to strike,
> B dissolves with lower Rising and a reverse back-fist,
> A uplifts again using Part the Clouds to strike,
> B rises A opens and walks parting ways.

Figure 3.257.   *Figure 3.258.*   *Figure 3.259.*   *Figure 3.260.*

64. Leaping-Body Palm

From the Opening Posture, with the left hand in front, both hands press downward; shuffle with the left foot, skip with the right leg past the left foot, and advance with the left foot, leaping forward with both palms pouncing forth; spin the body and advance with the left foot, the left hand piercing past the right hand; turn the body and advance with a Following Step and double pounce (figs. 3.261–3.267). Move in a straight line. Left and right are the same. The Rhyme-Song of Leaping-Body Palm Dismantling says:

> *Fierce Tiger Leaping the Mountain cruel and fierce,*
> *With a straight punch coming in pounce to the chest,*
> *B dissolves with inward leading A spins and pounces,*
> *B leads downward changing with refined lifting and throwing,*
> *Draw close squeezing and locking again pressing the arms,*
> *Bend the elbows for lively White Horse Rolls its Hooves,*
> *A locks B locks A spins the arm,*
> *B seizes and treads on the leg A lifts and walks.*

Figure 3.261.   *Figure 3.262.*   *Figure 3.263.*   *Figure 3.264.*

Figure 3.265.   *Figure 3.266.*   *Figure 3.267.*

Post-Heaven Palms Closing Posture

Like the last two movements of the Pre-Heaven Palms closing posture, the two hands pull back, drawing an arc upward from the sides of the body and pressing down in front of the face, fixing the posture and returning to the origin. One may close after each posture, or close after completing a set of eight postures, according to the person and according to the location; this is without set rules.

CHAPTER 4

Baguazhang Weapons

The Cheng School Gao Style Baguazhang weapons curriculum originally included five forms: broadsword, spear, straight sword, double knives, and cane. It is said that the first four forms were created by Dong Haichuan, with movement shapes dictated by turning the circle and changing postures as one walked, while the Bagua Cane—which does not turn the circle—was Gao Yisheng's creation, based on the Heart-Height Staff taught by Cheng Tinghua.

The Double Rattan Sticks and Night-Fighting Saber forms were not originally traditional Bagua weapon forms but were viewed by masters Gao and Liu as treasured self-protection arts, and they have actually now become an important part of the Cheng School Gao Style Baguazhang weapons curriculum.

Additionally, when Liu Fengcai first arrived in Tianjin, he used Night-Fighting Saber techniques to defeat the techniques of his school brother Qu Kezhang's well-known Daoist Wudang Straight Sword form and, after this, the two exchanged their arts. Liu Fengcai had always greatly admired Wudang Straight Sword, saying that this sword technique was elegant and extremely practical, "completely without empty elements." Liu Fengcai not only practiced this form regularly but taught it very broadly. Because of this, Wudang Straight Sword has also become an important component of the Cheng School Gao Style Baguazhang curriculum.

Within Gao Yisheng's original handwritten manual, there was no record of Bagua weapon forms. The first published edition of this book also had not yet listed weapon forms. After repeated deliberation by fellow disciples, it was proposed to include the Double Rattan Sticks,

Night-Fighting Saber, and Wudang Straight Sword in the Cheng School Gao Style curriculum in the revised second edition in order to preserve the completeness of the material taught by masters Gao and Liu, and ensure the continuation and furthering of the essence of these weapon forms as taught by these two generations.

These eight types of weapon forms have been ordered and organized according to Liu Fengcai's personal instruction, as a reference for fellow enthusiasts when they practice.

Bagua Yin-Yang Mandarin Duck Knives

Bagua Yin-Yang Mandarin Duck Knives are unusual weapons and are unique to Baguazhang. They have three pointed tips and eight sharp edges, and their name is derived from their shape. They are also known as Sun-Moon Heaven-Earth Swords or Deer-Horn Knives. The Duck Knives are a paired weapon, with two identical knives differentiated as male and female or yin and yang. The left-hand knife is female and yin; the right is male and yang. It is said that Dong Haichuan specialized in their use and was always victorious. Although they are small, they can spread out quite large and are excellent for controlling long weapons. Their practice method is to change postures based on the foundation of Baguazhang's Turning Palm, and their methods are difficult to practice without fluency in the Pre-Heaven Palms. Contained within the postures are eight principles: hook, hang, capture, seize, cut, pull, uplift, and thrust. All moves must have a left and right, with both sides mirror images. The form has eight gates, with eight moves in each gate, totaling sixty-four postures. Circle-walking counter-clockwise is the yang direction; clockwise is the yin direction.

Figure 4.1. Liu Fengcai's grand-student Zhang Shoukun.

Opening Posture: each hand holds a knife, the left knife lowered into the circle, the right knife raised outside the circle. Walk the circle counterclockwise.

First Gate: Qian—Clutch

1. Lower the right foot, downward hanging hook with the right knife. Spin the body toward the center of the circle; lift the left foot; downward hanging hook with the left knife.
2. Set the left foot down into the circle; advance with the right foot; clutch downward with the right knife.
3. Horizontal thrust to the chest with the back edge of the right knife.
4. Uphold with the center edge of the right knife.
5. Horizontal thrust to the chest with the back edge of the left knife.
6. Spin the body; lift the left leg; downward hanging hook with the left knife.
7. Set the left foot down; advance with the right foot; clutch with the right knife.
8. Horizontal thrust to the chest with the back edge of the right knife.

Step back left; both knives carry to the rear; twist the body and lift the right leg as the right knife hangs and hooks outward, both knives aligned level at the height of the abdomen; circle-walk clockwise with pushing knives. All postures in the opposite direction are the same. Return to circle-walking counterclockwise.

Second Gate: Kan—Seize

1. Continuing from the first gate, circle-walk counterclockwise with pushing knives. Left foot inside Baibu, right foot inside Koubu, left foot outside Koubu, overturn the body and seizing, deflect with the left knife.
2. Advance with the right foot, push with the right knife.
3. Advance with the left foot, push with the left knife.
4. Right seizing, deflect; double separation (advancing with the right foot).
5. Drawing step and double squeeze.
6. Right downward hanging hook.
7. Shuffle step, outward pulling cut with the left knife.

8. Step back left; both knives carry to the rear; hanging hook with right knife; lift the right leg; circle-walk clockwise with pushing knives.

All postures in the opposite direction are the same. Return to circle-walking counterclockwise.

Third Gate: Gen—Uphold

1. Continuing from the second gate circle-walking counterclockwise; left inward Baibu; uphold left.
2. Advance with the right foot; uphold right.
3. Step behind with the left foot and spin the body; thrust to the chest with the rear edge of the left knife.
4. Advance with the right foot; right downward hanging hook.
5. Left chop.
6. Advance with the left foot; both knives slice up.
7. Step back with the left foot; turn the body; left horizontal hang.
8. Advance with the right foot; thrust to the center with the rear edge of the right knife; hang right while lifting the right foot, and circle-walk clockwise.

All postures in the opposite direction are the same. Return to circle-walking counterclockwise.

Fourth Gate: Zhen—Embrace

1. Continuing from circle-walking counterclockwise with pushing knives, lift the left foot; left knife seizing embrace; raise the right knife outside the circle; back edge of the right knife facing up.
2. Set the left foot down in front; skipping step as the right knife seizes downward; sit into coiling posture.
3. Advance with the right foot; left hanging hook.
4. Right chop.
5. Double upholding knives.
6. Spin the body and lift the left foot; left downward hanging hook.

7. Set the left foot down in front as the left knife uplifts.
8. Step behind with the right foot; right hanging deflect; push left; hang right while lifting the right foot; circle-walking clockwise.

All postures in the opposite direction are the same. Return to circle-walking counterclockwise.

Fifth Gate: Xun—Slice

1. Continuing from circle-walking counterclockwise, left inside Baibu into the circle; left downward intercepting hook.
2. Advance with the left foot; slicing cut with the right knife.
3. Right downward intercept, then Uplifting hook.
4. Advance with the left foot; push left.
5. Overturn the body and lift the right foot; right embracing hang; lift the left knife, with the back edge of the left knife facing up.
6. Set the right foot down; left seize.
7. Left Baibu; right horizontal hang.
8. Right Koubu; left outward wiping; right inward cut; outward hang into pushing knives, lifting the right foot and circle-walking clockwise.

All postures in the opposite direction are the same. Return to walking counterclockwise along the circle.

Sixth Gate: Li—Spiral

1. Continuing circle-walking counterclockwise with pushing knives; left Baibu into the circle; left downward intercept.
2. Left spiraling uphold.
3. Advance with the right foot and right upward push; lower hanging hook.
4. Left chop.
5. Left Baibu and spin the body; left seizing deflect.
6. Advance with the right foot and right push.
7. Advance with the left foot and left push.

8. Left Baibu; right horizontal hang; right Koubu; left wiping hang; right slicing cut and inward hang; raise the right leg and circle-walk clockwise with pushing knives.

All postures in the opposite direction are the same. Return to circle-walking counterclockwise.

Seventh Gate: Kun—Slice Up

1. Continuing circle-walking counterclockwise, left Baibu into the circle; left downward intercept and uplift.
2. Advance with the right foot and right slice up.
3. Right drawing step; right downward intercept and uplift.
4. Advance with the left foot and left slice up.
5. Spin the body and lift the right foot; right embracing hang; left knife above; back edge of the knife facing up.
6. Set the right foot down; left seize.
7. Left horizontal hang; left wiping hang; spin the body into White Crane posture (left foot in front, right reverse Bow Stance, left knife below, right knife above).
8. Left Baibu; right horizontal hang; right Koubu; left wiping hang; right slicing cut and inward hang; lift the right foot and circle-walk clockwise with pushing knives.

All postures in the opposite direction are the same. Return to circle-walking counterclockwise.

Eighth Gate: Dui—Push

1. Continuing from circle-walking counterclockwise with level pushing knives, in one continuous motion, left downward intercept and vertical upward hook with the back edge of the knife facing up; right push, continuing to turn and walk.
2. Left Baibu; right Koubu; overturn the body; left seize and upward push.

3. Advance with the right foot; right knife pierces upward.

4. Left Baibu; overturn the body; left seize.

5. Advance with the right foot; horizontal smash with the tip of the middle blade.

6. Left Baibu; right horizontal hang; left horizontal hang.

7. Advance with the right foot into a low posture; right upward slicing pulling cut.

8. Right hang; lift the right leg and circle-walk clockwise.

All postures in the opposite direction are the same. When closing, the eighth posture should be: left drawing step; left knife hooks downward and lifts up; right Koubu; right knife pierces up as the body overturns; left knife below; right knife above as in the opening posture; again circle-walking counterclockwise, then settle the posture and return to the origin.

Bagua Rolling-Hand Broadsword

The Bagua single broadsword is a weapon of the Bagua school used specifically for training basic skills. The broadsword preserved by Liu Fengcai's family was crafted in the Qing Dynasty, weighs five pounds, and measures four feet seven inches, with the words *Bagua Steel Broadsword* engraved on it. Due to the Bagua sword's unusually heavy weight,

and because it is longer than normal broadswords, it is often mistaken as a double-handed weapon. Practicing broadsword opens the gallbladder channel. Its form changes postures while turning the circle, rolling above and below with big attacks and large chops; hence it is named Bagua Rolling-Hand Broadsword. There are eight gates containing the eight principles: mow, chop, draw, pull, intercept, slice up, uplift, and thrust. Each gate contains eight sword movements, with sixty-four movements

Figure 4.2. Liu Fengcai's grandstudent Liu Lingjie.

altogether to accord with the Eight Trigrams. The form is divided into yin and yang sword; walking counterclockwise with a raised sword is yin, walking clockwise with an upholding sword is yang.

The beginning posture is embracing the sword. Circle-walk clockwise with an upholding sword.

First Gate: Qian—Mow

1. Right Baibu into the circle; advance with a left step, and mow to the right.
2. Advance with a right step; chop to the left.
3. Heart-stabbing sword.
4. Left rear cross-step; pierce the ribs; spin the body.
5. Right Koubu; left rear cross-step; coiling stance with horizontal blocking sword.
6. Spin the body to have the right foot in front; advance with a left step and lift up with the tip and back edge of the sword.
7. Left skipping step and right kick, then chop to the rear.
8. Set the right foot down and uphold the sword; left Koubu and horizontal sweep with the sword; circle-walk counterclockwise in yin-posture lifting sword.

Second Gate: Kan—Chop

1. Continuing from circle-walking counterclockwise in yin posture with raised sword, left Baibu into the circle; advance with a right step; chop to left.
2. Advance with a left step and mow to the right.
3. Advance with a right step and heart-stabbing sword.
4. Spin the body into coiling stance with lower splitting sword.
5. Advance with a right step; slice up to the yin.
6. Spin the body; lift the left foot with hanging hooking sword.
7. Set the left foot down; advance with a right step and splitting sword.

8. Spin the body; raise the left foot in fisherman's sword. Set the left foot down; right Koubu and hooking sword; raise the right foot and circle-walk clockwise into yang-posture upholding sword.

Third Gate: Gen—Draw

1. Continuing from circle-walking clockwise in yang posture with upholding sword, right Baibu into the circle; advance with a left step, and chop the wrist toward the right.
2. Step back left; draw the sword and spiral slice to the armpit.
3. Advance with a left step and mow right.
4. Advance with a right step and chop left.
5. Heart-stabbing sword.
6. Spin the body, jumping step, and beat down with the sword.
7. Twist the body and intercept upward to the rear, then hang the sword into fixed posture.
8. Right Koubu, and sweep and overturn the sword. Left Koubu, and cover over the head to the right. Right Baibu; left with the left foot; circle-walk counterclockwise in yin-posture lifting sword.

Fourth Gate: Zhen—Pull

1. Continuing from circle-walking counterclockwise in yin posture with raised sword, left Baibu; advance with a right step; left pull to the wrist.
2. Advance with a left step; right pull to the wrist.
3. Advance with a right step; twist the sword and forward wipe.
4. Horse stance and horizontal pulling sword.
5. Following Step and slice up to the groin.
6. Drawing step and reverse split.
7. Heart-stabbing sword.
8. Withdraw the body and become a shadow; turn the body with splitting sword, the right foot in front. Baibu left; Koubu right; step back left; raise the right foot and circle-walk clockwise into yang-posture upholding sword.

Fifth Gate: Xun—Intercept

1. Continuing from circle-walking clockwise in yang posture with upholding sword, right Baibu into the circle; downward intercepting sword.
2. Upper closing sword; shuffle step with pushing sword.
3. Left Baibu; right Koubu; and spiral slice to the armpit.
4. Overturn the body; lift the left foot; and flick with the sword tip.
5. Set the left foot down; spin the body and downward intercept.
6. Upper closing sword; shuffle step with pushing sword.
7. Spin the body and head-covering posture.
8. Left Baibu and right Koubu with waist-wrapping sword; left Koubu; right Baibu; lift the left leg; circle-walk counterclockwise in yin-posture lifting sword.

Sixth Gate: Li—Slice Up

1. Continuing from circle-walking counterclockwise in yin posture with raised sword, left Baibu into the circle; advance with a right step; left upper slicing-up sword.
2. Advance with the left foot; right draping sword.
3. Overturn the body and lift the right foot; horizontal sword and Hold the *Pipa* Backward; then jumping step into Downward Waters Push the Boat.
4. Spin the body; step and beat down with the sword.
5. Spin the body and leaping step; cover over the head (right foot in front).
6. Turn around with sweeping and overturning sword.
7. Advance with a right step with splitting sword.
8. Heart-stabbing sword. Koubu and circle-walk clockwise into yang-posture upholding sword.

Seventh Gate: Kun—Uplift

1. Continuing from circle-walking clockwise in yang posture with upholding sword; right step into the circle; left Baibu into coiling stance and uplifting sword posture.
2. Advance with a right step with sweeping and overturning sword.
3. Advance with a left step and split to the wrist.
4. Right Koubu; turn around with pressing sword.
5. Step back left with left sweeping and overturning sword.
6. Drawing step with cover over the head to the right.
7. Right Koubu and spin the body; lift the left foot; Searching the Sea sword.
8. Leaping step and splitting sword; circle-walk counterclockwise in yin-posture lifting sword.

Eighth Gate: Dui—Thrust

1. Continuing from circle-walking counterclockwise in yin posture with raised sword; inside-foot Baibu; outside-foot Koubu; advance with a left step and thrust to the ribs.
2. Left Baibu; right Koubu; spin the body; lift the foot and flick with the sword tip.
3. Right pressing sword; set the left foot down.
4. Left slicing-up sword; advance with a right step.
5. Step back left with left splitting sword.
6. Tornado sword (posture of Carrying the Broadsword on the Back).
7. Cross-form sword, and advance with a right step.
8. Heart-stabbing sword; embrace the sword; and close returning to the origin.

Bagua Connected Links Straight Sword

Figure 4.3. Liu Fengcai's grand-student Liu Yungang.

Bagua straight sword is also a weapon used specifically in Baguazhang for training basic skills. It is famous for its excessive weight and is longer and broader than usual blades. The sword preserved by Liu Fengcai's family weighs 5.5 pounds and measures four feet three inches long. The special characteristic of practicing Bagua Connected Links Straight Sword is that the form changes postures while turning the circle. Training the straight sword opens the heart with large open movements that are martial but also cultivated and elegant. Contained within are eight principles: thrust, mow, embrace, open, stab, slice up, lift, and wipe. The form is divided into yin and yang; walking counterclockwise with a hanging sword is yin, walking clockwise with an upholding sword is yang. There are eight gates, with each division containing eight sword moves, for a total of sixty-four movements to accord with the Eight Trigrams.

First Gate: Qian—Thrust

The beginning posture is carrying the sword on the back.

1. Immortal Points the Way.
2. Golden Silk Enwraps the Wrist.
3. Turn the Body and Slice the Groin.
4. Golden Rooster Nods Its Head.
5. Cloud Flowers Cover the Peak.
6. Horizontal Snake Blocks the Road.
7. Planting Flowers on Level Ground.
8. Downstream Waters Push the Boat.

Lift the sword in yin posture, and circle-walk counterclockwise.

Second Gate: Kan—Mow

1. Strength to Split Mount Hua.
2. White Snake Spits Out Its Tongue.
3. Precious Sword Enters the Scabbard.
4. Hooking, Hanging, and Splitting Sword.
5. Fierce Tiger Spins Its Body.
6. Golden Rooster Nods Its Head.
7. Second Son Carries the Mountain.
8. Single Wing Shakes the Feather.

Uphold the sword in yang posture, and circle-walk clockwise.

Third Gate: Gen—Embrace

1. Embrace the Moon.
2. Old Moon Leaves the Embrace.
3. Wang Liang Whips the Horse.
4. Hide the Flowers in the Sleeves.
5. Pluck the Moon from the Sea Bottom.
6. Downstream Waters Push the Boat.
7. Hooking, Hanging, and Splitting Sword.
8. Fierce Tiger Shakes Its Head; Old Tree Coils Its Roots.

Lift the sword in yin posture, and circle-walk counterclockwise.

Fourth Gate: Zhen—Open

1. White Crane Shows Its Wings.
2. Part the Grass to Search for Snakes.
3. Yaksha Searches the Sea.
4. Lift the Clothes on One Side.
5. Golden Rooster Shakes Its Feathers.
6. Jade Maiden Threads the Shuttle.
7. Yellow Dragon Lies in the Road.

8. Old Gentleman Shoots the Arrow.

Uphold the sword in yang posture, and circle-walk clockwise.

Fifth Gate: Xun—Stab

1. Yaksha Searches the Sea.
2. Lift the Clothes on One Side.
3. Right Draping Sword.
4. Holding the Pipa Upside Down.
5. Downstream Waters Push the Boat.
6. Speed the Horse by Adding the Whip.
7. Red Apricot Comes Out of the Wall.
8. Hide the Flowers in the Sleeves.

Lift the sword in yin posture, and circle-walk counterclockwise.

Sixth Gate: Li—Slice Up

1. Lift the Clothes on One Side.
2. Right Draping Sword.
3. Reverse Splitting Mount Hua.
4. White Ape Offers Fruit.
5. Insert the Golden Needle into the Ground.
6. Black Dragon Sways Its Tail.
7. Hooking and Hanging Continuously.
8. Jade Maiden Threads the Needle.

Uphold the sword in yang posture, and circle-walk clockwise.

Seventh Gate: Kun—Lift

1. Step Up and Lift the Brazier.
2. Horizontally Push Eight Horses.
3. Cloud Flowers Cover the Peak.
4. Hold the Boots to Ascend the Palace.
5. Reverse Splitting Mount Hua.

6. Qin Qiong Walks the Horse.

7. Rock Sinks into the Ocean.

8. Remove the Body and Become a Shadow.

Do not circle-walk; continue directly to the eighth gate.

Eighth Gate: Dui—Wipe

1. Fierce Tiger Shakes Its Head.

2. Wave the Body and Double Wipe.

3. Green Dragon Overturns Its Body.

4. Yellow Dragon Lies in the Road.

5. Bend the Bow to Shoot the Wild Goose.

6. Reverse Splitting Mount Hua.

7. Spring Wind Scatters the Willows.

8. Strange Python Enwraps the Wrist.

Pass the sword to the left hand; carry the sword on the back; fix the posture; and return to the origin.

Bagua Body-Adhering Spear

The spear used in Bagua Body-Adhering Spear is different from other spears, and it is also a special weapon practiced in Baguazhang to train basic skills. Both ends of the spear have triangular bladed edges, so it is also called "Double-Headed Snake." Practicing spear stimulates the large intestine channel internally and strengthens the waist and arms externally. "Body-Adhering" means that the spear does not leave the body. The form uses circle-walking as its basic movement, and the postures change while turning the circle, walking in both yin and yang

Figure 4.4. Liu Fengcai's grand-student Ge Guoliang.

257

directions with Upholding Spear. The form emphasizes practical applications, with straight-line attack and defense devoid of showy movements, unlike other flowery spear forms. Each movement has a meaning, and contained within are the thirteen points of spear practice: cover the top, slice up to the eyebrows, stab to the chest, thrust to the middle, slice up to the groin, pierce to the ribs, poke the groin, thrust to the knee, seek the ears, stab the foot, uplift the shoulders, scoop the hands, and search for the throat. Circle-walking counterclockwise is yin; clockwise is yang. The form has eight gates, with eight spear moves in each gate, totaling sixty-four moves to accord with the Eight Trigrams. All moves must have a left and a right, with each side a mirror image.

The opening posture is circle-walking counterclockwise with spear-upholding posture, left hand inside the circle, right hand outside the circle. The spear tip inside the circle is the front; the spear tip outside the circle is the back. The back tip is high; the front tip is low.

First Gate: Qian—Slice Up to the Eyebrows and Seek the Ear

1. The left foot steps into the circle; slice up to the eyebrows.
2. Step behind right; reverse the spear, and intercept downward.
3. Advance with a left step; hook the spear and pierce forward, seeking the ear.
4. Step behind left; stab with the back tip.
5. Advance with a left step; stab with the front tip.
6. Embrace the spear and hang with the front tip.
7. Left Baibu; right Koubu; sweep the lower basin with the back tip.
8. The front tip covers the head; reverse the grip so the front hand becomes back hand; left Baibu and raise the right foot, the left hand inside the circle; circle-walk clockwise in spear-upholding posture.

All postures are the same in the opposite direction. Return to circle-walking counterclockwise.

Second Gate: Kan—Covering Staff Coiling at the Neck

1. The left foot steps into the circle; parry high.
2. Following the energy, cover and intercept downward to the left.
3. Advance with a right step; cover the staff with the back tip.
4. Drawing step; twist the body and coil at the neck (with the back tip).
5. Left Baibu; right Koubu; spin the body and stab with the front tip.
6. Stab to the rear with the back tip.
7. Spin the body and raise the right foot; hang downward with the back tip.
8. Set the foot down and slice up to the groin. Advance with a left step with upward-slicing spear; reverse the hands; circle-walk clockwise in spear-upholding posture.

All postures are the same in the opposite direction. Return to circle-walking counterclockwise.

Third Gate: Gen—White Snake Spits Out Its Tongue

1. Lift the left foot and intercept downward.
2. Set the foot down and pierce the throat.
3. The right foot steps out horizontally with a low intercept.
4. The left foot shifts forward; hooking spear and left upper uplift.
5. Advance with a right step and slice up to the groin with the back tip.
6. Step back right and stab with the front tip.
7. Spin the body and advance with a left step with upward slice to the groin (with the front tip).
8. Cover with the spear; reverse the hands; circle-walk clockwise in spear-upholding posture.

All postures are the same in the opposite direction. Return to circle-walking counterclockwise.

Fourth Gate: Zhen—Iron Ox Plows the Earth

1. The left foot steps into the circle; parry upward.
2. Following the energy, intercept downward.
3. Shuffle step and stab the hips (Iron Ox Plows the Earth).
4. Upholding blocking spear.
5. Hook the spear and stab the center.
6. Drawing step; embrace the spear and hang with the front tip.
7. Left Baibu; right Koubu; sweep the middle basin with the back tip.
8. The front tip covers the head; reverse the grip and raise the right foot; circle-walk clockwise in spear-upholding posture.

All postures are the same in the opposite direction. Return to circle-walking counterclockwise.

Fifth Gate: Xun—Pierce the Ribs and Stab to the Chest

1. Left Baibu into the circle; twist the spear; right hook; strike and stab.
2. Outward hang and upper flick to the eyebrows.
3. Spin the spear and again flick to the eyebrows.
4. Drawing step with vertical intercept to guard the ribs (front tip on top).
5. Strike the ears with the front tip.
6. Downward cover; reverse hook; pierce the ribs and stab the chest.
7. Spin the body and attack the chest with the back tip.
8. Advance with a left step; upward-slicing spear with the front tip; reverse the grip and raise the right foot; circle-walk clockwise in spear-upholding posture.

All postures are the same in the opposite direction. Return to circle-walking counterclockwise.

Sixth Gate: Li—Embrace the Moon and Pierce the Forest

1. Upward parry.
2. Downward intercept.
3. Embrace the spear and hang in the middle.
4. Right Koubu; slice up to the groin with the back tip and fierce staff.
5. Step back left; turn the body and stab with the front tip.
6. Left drawing step; hang outward and flick upward.
7. Outward hanging embracing spear; sweep the upper basin with the back tip.
8. The front tip covers the head; reverse the grip and raise the right foot; circle-walk clockwise in spear-upholding posture.

All postures are the same in the opposite direction. Return to circle-walking counterclockwise.

Seventh Gate: Kun—Lateral Staff

1. Upward parry (left foot entering the circle).
2. Lower intercept.
3. Vertical intercept outside the limbs (front tip on the bottom).
4. Advance with a right step, the back tip crossing the staff; attack the chest.
5. Shuffle step; cover the staff with the front tip.
6. The back tip stabs backward beneath the elbow.
7. Left Koubu; spin the spear and sweep horizontally.
8. The front tip slices up to the groin; reverse the grip and raise the right foot; circle-walk clockwise in spear-upholding posture.

All postures are the same in the opposite direction. Return to circle-walking counterclockwise.

Eighth Gate: Dui—Yanking Staff

1. Upward parry (left foot entering the circle).
2. Following the energy, parry low in Embrace the Moon posture.
3. The front tip covers outward, advance with a right step and smash the staff with the back tip.
4. The rear tip parries above; escape with a jumping step, the front tip yanking and splitting on the staff, the left foot in front.
5. Stab the middle.
6. Left Koubu; turn the body; stab with only the right hand holding the spear.
7. Upward-slicing spear; reverse the grip and raise the right foot; circle-walk clockwise in spear-upholding posture.

All postures are the same in the opposite direction. Fix the posture and return to the origin to close.

Bagua Cane

The Bagua Cane form was derived from the Heart-Height Staff, which is shorter and thinner than a common staff and is made of filled bamboo. Its length is exactly heart high from the ground, hence the name Heart-Height Staff. In practice this short staff should be wielded like a long weapon. It is said that the Heart-Height Staff was created by Cheng Tinghua, who usually carried a filled bamboo staff as a defensive weapon when he went out. Later he passed the Heart-Height Staff form on to Gao Yisheng. Gao usually carried a gentleman's cane when he went out to teach, and he often used this cane to teach the form, so over time he added moves utilizing the cane's hook. Later he changed the name of the form to Bagua

Figure 4.5. Liu Fengcai's grand-student Li Xueyi.

Cane. The Bagua Cane form does not turn the circle, but comprises sixty-four movements, in accordance with the Eight Trigrams. Although he taught the cane more frequently, the staff and cane forms taught by Liu Fengcai were essentially the same, and one may recover the Heart-Height Staff form through practice of the cane form.

The opening posture is standing naturally with the right hand holding the cane. Extend the left foot outward to the side of the body, the right hand gripping the cane head, the left hand holding the middle of the cane body. The right hand is the back hand, the left hand is the front hand, similar to holding a bayonet.

1. Right strike the eyebrows.
2. Left downward cover.
3. Hook the neck; reverse splitting; and switch hands (the front hand becomes the back hand).
4. Left strike the eyebrows.
5. Right downward cover.
6. Hook the neck; reverse splitting; and switch hands (the front hand becomes the back hand).
7. Right downward parry.
8. Right upward parry.
9. Hook the leg; reverse splitting; and switch hands.
10. Left downward parry.
11. Left upward parry.
12. Hook the leg; reverse splitting.
13. Spin the body; downward intercept; and slap inward.
14. Upward cover.
15. Strike the eyebrows.
16. Hook the neck; reverse splitting; and switch hands.
17. Downward intercept and slap inward.
18. Upward cover.
19. Strike the eyebrows.
20. Hook the neck; reverse splitting.

21. Spin the body; embrace the cane.

22. Downward press; strike and stab.

23. Smash with the hook.

24. Hook and pull the neck.

25. Turn the body and strike the center; reverse hands.

26. Embrace the cane.

27. Strike and stab.

28. Smash with hook.

29. Hook and pull the neck.

30. Turn around and strike the center.

31. Neutralize downward and outward.

32. Embrace the cane and hang in the middle.

33. Retreating jumping step; reverse splitting; switch hands; spin the body.

34. Neutralize downward and outward.

35. Embrace the cane and hang in the middle.

36. Retreating jumping step.

37. Right single-hand horizontal sweep to right; downward strike.

38. Right bow stance; uplift the cane backward; and hide the cane behind the back.

39. Left hand catches the cane tip under the right ribs; sweep horizontally to the left with the hook.

40. Downward strike.

41. Jump backward; left bow stance; hide the cane behind the back.

42. Right hand catches the cane hook under the left ribs; sweep horizontally right with tip.

43. Both hands uphold the cane (the left hand grasps at the tip, the right hand grasps at the middle, the hook facing upward); right bow stance; pause.

44. Both hands hold the cane; left horizontal block.

45. Coil overhead and pull the shoulder with the hook.

46. Right blocking cane.

47. Coil overhead; right horizontal sweep.

48. Pull downward on the head with the hook.

49. Right cover; pull the neck.

50. Spin the body; left block.

51. Coil overhead; sweep to the left.

52. Reverse the hands and hook downward on the head.

53. Following the energy, gore to the chest with the hook.

54. Spin the body; right blocking cane.

55. Coil overhead and pull the shoulder with the hook.

56. Left blocking cane.

57. Coil overhead; left horizontal sweep.

58. Hook downward on the head.

59. Left cover; hook and pull the neck.

60. Spin the body; right blocking cane.

61. Coil overhead; right horizontal sweep.

62. Reverse the hands; hook downward on the head.

63. Pull out the hook and reverse-hook the groin.

64. Spin the body; embrace the cane; closing posture, and return to the origin.

Double Rattan Sticks

Double Rattan Sticks are paired weapons that employ two short sticks made of rattan. It is said that that the best rattan sticks had iron placed inside. The length is dependent on the individual, but they should be light and easily controllable. This Double Rattan Sticks form originated with the Purple Hammer School and was regarded by Gao Yisheng as his self-protection skill; it was the last part of the art he passed on to Liu Fengcai. While teaching in Tianjin, Gao taught this to a few students under the name "Double Iron Clubs," so it is also known as Bagua Double Iron Clubs. The Double Rattan Sticks form is divided into four lines or sections, with sixteen staff techniques as fundamental points: seize, push, slice up, uphold, uplift, chop, block, cut, thrust, stack, deflect,

Figure 4.6. Liu Fengcai's student Liu Shuhang.

mow, stab, lift, clutch, and pinch. In practice, the movements are like drumming, and the postures are like scissors; one up and one down, one attacking and one defending; when defense is complete, the attack is complete, striking simultaneously. It is effective against long weapons and is very practical.

In the opening, the body posture is similar to the beginning posture of the Post-Heaven Palms, the stance also light in front and solid in back. The hands each hold one stick, the right hand joined with the left at the level of the abdomen. These are yin and yang sticks.

First Line

1. Right seize; left push.
2. Left seize; right uphold.
3. Left inward cover; right cut.
4. Return to the origin; downward x-block pinch.
5. Spin the body; right seize; left push.
6. Left seize; right uphold.
7. Right cover; left thrust; spin the body and double slice up.
8. Right seize; left push; right push.
9. Right uplift; left block; right horizontal chop.
10. Left cover; right cut.
11. Spin the body; right and left x-blocks.
12. Spin the body; left cover and uplift; right block; left thrust.
13. Spin the body; right downward cover and uphold; left chop.
14. Left cover; right stab.
15. Right cover; left stab.
16. Left downward cover and uphold; right chop.
17. Right cover; left stab.
18. Left cover; right stab.
19. Right downward cover and uplift; left block; right thrust.
20. Spin the body and return to the origin. Cross both sticks in an X shape, both hands in front of the abdomen at the level of the navel.

Second Line

1. Left seize; right slice up.
2. Left outward cover; right cut.
3. Right seize; left push; right push.
4. Spin the body; left cover; right cut.
5. Spin the body; double parry posture.
6. Leap forward; right downward cover; left draw to the face.
7. Spin the body; left block; right stab to the wrist.
8. Spin the body; right cover; left thrust; left cover; right cut.
9. Left seize; right cut.
10. Spin the body; double parry posture.
11. Leap forward; left downward cover; right draw to the face.
12. Spin the body; right block; left stab to the wrist.
13. Right cover; left cut.
14. Right seize; left slice up.
15. Overturn the body; left chop; right cut.
16. Right block; left uphold.
17. Left block; right uphold.
18. Right cover; left cut.
19. Left seize; right cut.
20. Spin the body and return to the origin.

Third Line

1. Left cover; right cut.
2. Right cover; left cut.
3. Right seize; left slice up.
4. Right cover; left cut.
5. Left cover; right cut.
6. Left seize; right slice up.
7. Left parry; right lift.
8. Right parry; left lift.
9. Spin the body; left seize; right push; left push.

10. Spin the body; right cover; left cut.

11. Right wrapping uphold; left cut.

12. Left downward cover and uphold; right cut.

13. Right press; left draw.

14. Right stab; X-shape double-seize to the neck.

15. Spin the body; left cover; right cut.

16. Left uphold; right cut.

17. Right downward cover; left cut.

18. Left press; right draw.

19. Left stab; X-shape double-seize to the neck.

20. Spin the body into fixed posture and return to the origin.

Fourth Line

1. Left seize; right thrust.

2. Right seize; left thrust.

3. Left seize; right thrust.

4. Spin the body; left downward cover and uphold; right cut.

5. Right downward cover and uphold; left cut.

6. Left uplift; right block; left horizontal chop.

7. Spin the body; right cover; left cut.

8. Spin the body; left uphold; right chop to the foot.

9. Right uphold; left chop to the foot.

10. Spin the body; right seize; left push.

11. Left stacking covers; double pinch to the neck.

12. Left block; right uphold.

13. Left drawing backslap; right stab; X-shape double-seize to the neck.

14. Spin the body; left seize; right push.

15. Right stacking covers; double pinch to the neck.

16. Right block; left uphold.

17. Right drawing backslap; left stab; X-shape double-seize to the neck.

18. Spin the body to closing posture; right hand covers left hand into fixed posture, and return to the origin.

Night-Fighting Saber

Legend has it that the Night-Fighting Saber was passed down by a great highwayman. In Yangxin County, Shandong Province, it was transmitted for four generations only within the family of Wang Maolin. Wang Maolin excelled in this art, and in his early years attended a large martial competition where he quickly gained fame. He was nicknamed "Single-Broadsword Wang" and was subsequently asked to teach six lines or sections of this sword art in Ji'nan. When Gao Yisheng was in Shandong spreading his own art, he learned of and greatly admired this art of Night-Fighting Saber. Around 1935, at the direction of Gao, Liu Fengcai visited Wang Maolin and spent great amounts of money to learn this art. Gao and Liu considered Night-Fighting Saber to be their ultimate skill for self-protection, and they seldom taught it to others. This art is for two-person fighting practice, and

Figure 4.7. Liu Fengcai's student Gao Jinhua (left) and grand-student Wang Xu.

it mimics fighting at night. Its movements are unique, and with long practice they become almost miraculous. All its movements are extremely practical. The two practitioners facing each other are required to maintain low postures yet have agile footwork, like two butterflies plucking flowers—flying up and down continuously—while guarding against double injury. Altogether, the Night-Fighting Saber form has twelve lines.

First Line: Inward Cutting Sword

A1. Angled split to the left shoulder.

B1. Inward cut.

A2. Horizontal dueling sword.

B2. Pressing sword; cut to the head.

A3. Drawing sword; chop to the hip.

B3. Lower intercepting wrist.

A4. Jumping step; flick to the upper arm.

B4. Outward hang and cut upward to the head.

A5. Downward pulling sword; sword-hiding posture.

B5. Outward hanging sword; Bow Stance with the sword at the back.

A6. Stab the hip.

B6. Horizontal hang; slice the wrist.

A7. Vertical sword; leaping step; return to the origin.

B7. Leaping step; return to the origin.

Second Line: Outward Cutting Sword

A1. Angled split to the right shoulder.

B1. Outward cut.

A2. Turn the wrist outward to horizontal hang; slice the wrist.

B2. Upward vertical thrusting sword.

A3. Bow Stance with sword at the back.

B3. Sword-hiding posture.

A4. Pause.

B4. Advance and pierce the hip.

A5. Forward Fishing.

B5. Reverse Fishing.

A6. Lift the sword and pierce the ear.

B6. Swallow Skims the Water.

A7. Speed the Horse by Adding the Whip.

B7. Horizontal block.

A8. Sword-hiding posture.

B8. Bow Stance with sword at the back.

A9. Advance and pierce the hip.

B9. Forward Fishing.

A10. Reverse Fishing.

B10. Lift the sword and pierce the ear.

A11. Swallow Skims the Water.

B11. Speed the Horse by Adding the Whip.

A12. Leaping step; return to the origin.

B12. Leaping step; return to the origin.

Third Line: Low Intercepting Sword

A1. Chop the hip.

B1. Lower intercept.

A2. Raise the sword and flick the upper arm.

B2. Horizontal hang.

A3. Chop the foot.

B3. Downward press.

A4. Lever up and sweep the feet.

B4. Jumping step and following sword.

A5. Head-cutting sword.

B5. Following the energy and pulling sword.

A6. Outside hanging sword.

B6. Leaping step; return to the origin.

A7. Leaping step; return to the origin.

Fourth Line: Upholding Hands Sword

A1. Frontal vertical split.

B1. Coiling stance; uphold the hands.

A2. Raise the sword and kick the wrist.

B2. Raise the body and chop the foot.

A3. Downward point to the wrist.

B3. Upward point to the wrist.

A4. Raise the sword and open the door.

B4. Sword-hiding posture.

A5. Pause.

B5. Heart-stabbing sword.

A6. Leaping step; outward cut.

B6. Leaping step; inward cut.

A7. Leaping step; inward cut (high stance).

B7. Low posture hiding the sword; pierce the hip.

A8. High Fishing.

B8. Reverse Fishing.

A9. Lift the sword and close swords.

B9. Close swords and inward point at the wrist.

A10. Stealing sword, horizontal opening.

B10. Thrusting sword.

A11. Leaping step; return to the origin.

B11. Leaping step; return to the origin.

Fifth Line: Insert the Sword and Grasp the Wrist

A1. Frontal vertical split.

B1. Vertical intercepting sword; insert inside.

A2. Thrusting sword.

B2. Grab the wrist.

A3. Draw downward; hide the sword.

B3. Backward retreating step and open the door.

A4. Heart-stabbing sword.

B4. Seek the wrist.

A5. Sink the wrist; Koubu; spin around; foot-sweeping sword.

B5. Vertical intercepting sword.

A6. Leaping step; outward cut.

B6. Horizontal hang; slice the wrist.

A7. Thrusting sword; leaping step; return to the origin.

B7. Leaping step; return to the origin.

Sixth Line: High Hanging Sword

A1. Frontal vertical split.

B1. High hanging sword.

A2. Reverse flick; retreating-sword posture.

B2. Sword-hiding posture.

A3. Pause.

B3. Stab the knee.

A4. Leaping step; outward cut.

B4. Leaping step; inward cut.

A5. Leaping step; inward cut; high ready posture.

B5. Low ready posture; stab the hip.

A6. High Fishing.

B6. Reverse Fishing.

A7. Lifting sword.

B7. Join swords.

A8. Join swords; pierce the ribs; thrust and pull.

B8. Pierce the ribs; thrust and pull.

A9. Leaping step; return to the origin.

B9. Leaping step; return to the origin.

Seventh Line: Waist-Inserting Sword

A1. Frontal vertical split.

B1. Inward block; insert to the waist.

A2. Horizontal intercept across the chest.

B2. Right foot kicks the wrist.

A3. Chop the foot.

B3. Jumping step; intercepting sword; left hand grabs the opponent's handle.

A4. Overturn the wrist and chop the hand.

B4. Jumping step; sink the wrist.

A5. Lifting sword; Koubu; spin the body; foot-sweeping sword.

B5. Vertical intercepting sword.

A6. Leaping step; outward cut.

B6. Horizontal hanging sword; slice the wrist.

A7. Vertical sword; leaping step; return to the origin.

B7. Leaping step; return to the origin.

Eighth Line: Oppositional Cutting

A1. Frontal stab to chest.

B1. Opposing cut.

A2. Reverse flick; backward retreating step; open the door.

B2. Sword-hiding posture; heart-stabbing sword.

A3. Leaping step; outward cut.

B3. Leaping step; inward cut.

A4. Leaping step; inward cut; high ready posture.

B4. Low ready posture; stab the hip.

A5. High Fishing.

B5. Reverse Fishing.

A6. Lift the sword; pierce the ear.

B6. Swallow Skims the Water.

A7. Speed the Horse by Adding the Whip; leaping step; return to the origin.

B7. Leaping step; return to the origin.

Ninth Line: Frontal Cutting

A1. Frontal vertical split.

B1. Vertical intercepting splitting sword (frontal cut).

A2. Evade with the body; reverse flick; open the door.

B2. Sword-hiding posture; heart-stabbing sword.

A3. Lower intercept to the wrist.

B3. Lift the sword; inward horizontal test to the upper arm.

A4. Horizontal hang; close swords.

B4. Close swords.

A5. Koubu; spin the body; left-handed sword sweeps the feet.

B5. Vertical intercepting sword; pierce the ear.

A6. Upward blocking sword.

B6. Drawing sword; stab the middle.

A7. Koubu; spin the body; grab the sword with the right hand and point downward; leaping step; return to the origin.

B7. Low retreating-sword posture; uplift; leaping step; return to the origin.

Tenth Line: Slap the Hand and Drape the Sword

A1. Left angled split to the head.

B1. Vertical hanging sword; slap the hand; drape the sword; chop the wrist.

A2. Horizontal pulling sword.

B2. Advance and cut to the head.

A3. Drawing sword; chop the waist.

B3. Lower intercept to the wrist.

A4. Flick the upper arm; close swords.

B4. Horizontal hang; close swords.

A5. Drawing sword; spin the body; left-handed sword sweeps the feet.

B5. Vertical intercepting sword; pierce the ear.

A6. Blocking sword.

B6. Drawing sword; stab the middle.

A7. Spin the body; transfer the sword to the right hand; point downward; leaping step; return to the origin.

B7. Sink the wrist; low retreating-sword posture; uplift; leaping step; return to the origin.

Eleventh Line: Lead the Hand and Kick the Sword

A1. Right angled spilt to the head.

B1. Evade with the body; uplift to the wrist with the back edge of the blade.

A2. Retreating sword; kick the wrist.

B2. Chop the foot.

A3. Leaping step; outward cut.

B3. Leaping step; inward cut; sword-hiding posture.

A4. Leaping step; inward cut; high covering sword.

B4. Advance and stab the hip.

A5. High Fishing.

B5. Reverse Fishing.

A6. Lift the sword; close swords; thrust and pull.

B6. Close swords; thrust and pull.

A7. Leaping step; return to the origin.

B7. Leaping step; return to the origin.

Twelfth Line: Thrusting Sword and Seize behind the Back

A1. Frontal vertical split.

B1. Right opening; thrusting sword; stab the shoulder.

A2. Upward thrusting sword.

B2. Grab the wrist; twist inside; lift the shoulder.

A3. Following the energy, spin the wrist.

B3. Thrust upward to the head.

A4. Evade with the head.

B4. Pierce the ribs.

A5. Evade with the body.

B5. Lift the leg; downward thrust to the leg.

A6. Lift the leg.

B6. Loosen the hand; overturn the body; split.

A7. Turn the wrist outward to horizontal hang, slice the wrist.

B7. Vertical upward thrust.

A8. Leaping step; return to the origin.

B8. Leaping step; return to the origin.

Wudang Straight Sword

The Wudang Straight Sword form, formally called Wudang Taiji Thirteen Straight Sword, is a famous Daoist sword form said to have been transmitted at Wudang Mountain during Gao Yisheng's era. Liu Fengcai obtained this form using Night-Fighting Saber to exchange arts with his school brother Qu Kezhang. Qu, a Daoist priest that people called "Daoist Uncle," was a close friend of Liu, and also, with Liu, one of the "eight great loyals," sworn brother disciples of Gao Yisheng. Qu was skilled in sword arts and had formerly defeated numerous famous martial artists. When Liu first came to Tianjin, he followed Master Gao to teach. One day after a practice session everyone gathered around to talk about martial arts. Qu held a sword in his hand, took a stance, and said: "My Wudang Straight Sword is genuine and includes the three treasures of heaven,

earth, and human. Among short weapons, it is unbeatable."
Everyone knew his swordplay was extraordinary, so they only
looked at one another, remaining silent. At that moment,
Gao stroked his long beard and said, "You are exactly right.
Your swordplay is excellent. However, we have someone here
today who can test with you, who I'm afraid you might not
be able to defeat." After hearing this, everyone's interest was
piqued, and Qu especially wanted to know who the person
was, so he excitedly asked, "Who is it that you are referring
to?" Gao pointed with a laugh, saying, "It's him, your elder
school brother Liu Fengcai." After hearing this, Qu and the
others almost simultaneously turned to look at Liu in surprise. Liu said hurriedly, "No, no, don't listen to Master Gao.
How can I compare?" But, unable to bear everyone's pressure, Qu's sincere entreaties, and Gao's encouragement, he
could only agree to a test match. At this, everyone formed a
big circle, and Liu and Qu, holding a wooden broadsword
and a wooden straight sword, entered the ring and faced off.

Figure 4.8. Liu Fengcai.

First, Qu took a stance, and Liu attacked. In a flash Liu swung his
broadsword, leaped lightly in front of Qu, and the tip was already pointing at the wrist of Qu's sword hand. Qu and the others were all astonished. Liu then quickly leaped backward into a Night-Fighting Saber ready
stance, inviting Qu to attack. Qu calmed his spirit, searched for an opening, then leaped forward with a straight thrust. Liu evaded, raised his
hand, and struck down. Again, the blade tip flicked Qu's wrist. The two
continued like this back and forth several times until every side of Qu's
wrist had been struck by the tip of Liu's broadsword. Seeing this, everyone cheered, including Qu, and the two ended their contest. Qu quickly
approached Liu and asked, "Great broadsword play, but I don't know
what it's called?" By this time, the others had also gathered close, and
Gao answered for him, saying, "This art is called Night-Fighting Saber. It
originates from Shaolin, and Liu learned it in Shandong. This is the first
time Liu has used it against someone since coming to Tianjin."

Afterward, due to Qu's continual requests, Liu and Qu exchanged arts. Master Liu truly loved the Wudang Straight Sword form and, after long practice and experimentation, gradually incorporated into it some applicable skills from the Night-Fighting Saber. Because the Wudang Straight Sword form is extended and open, graceful and beautiful to watch, and it is faster than Taiji Sword but slower than the Night-Fighting Saber, it is suitable for both old and young, and therefore Liu taught it widely. Wudang Straight Sword includes thirteen fundamentals: slice, chop, split, evade, cut, slide, lift, flick, flip, cloud, slice up, stab, and wipe. Therefore it is also known as the Wudang Thirteen Sword. There are two sections in the form. The first section consists of 108 moves, and the second has 99. Every move is practical. The sword poem says:

The precious sword was passed down from ancestors,
Attack and defense seem miraculous,
Split, chop, slice, and cut like a broadsword,
To make the old sword sage Sanfeng laugh.

First Section

1. Opening Posture.
2. Immortal Points the Way.
3. Golden Youth Wooden Fish.
4. Jade Pillar Uplifting Hand.
5. Golden Rooster Nods Its Head.
6. Pluck the Moon from the Sea Bottom.
7. Wisteria Hangs on the Wall.
8. Nesting Bird Enters the Forest.
9. Embrace the Moon.
10. Old Moon Leaves the Embrace.
11. Easily Leading the Sheep.
12. Green Dragon Extends Its Claws.
13. Left and Right Spreading Wings.
14. Winter Duck Plays with Water.

15. The Four Stars Abandon the Dipper.
16. The Four Stars Return to Origin.
17. The Old Gentleman Closes the Brazier.
18. White Crane Shows Its Wings.
19. Green Dragon Lifts Its Hand.
20. Black Dragon Sways Its Tail.
21. Phoenix Stretches Its Wings.
22. Phoenix Searches for Its Nest.
23. Golden Youth Wooden Fish.
24. Jade Pillar Uplifting Hand.
25. Strength to Split Mount Hua.
26. Holding the Pipa in the Arms.
27. Flowing Waters Push the Boat.
28. Closing Sword Posture.
29. Jade Maiden Brushes the Sleeves.
30. Shooting Star Chases the Moon.
31. The Youth Worships Buddha.
32. Closing Sword Posture.
33. Step Back to Ambush.
34. Embrace the Moon.
35. Old Moon Leaves the Embrace.
36. Wang Liang Whips the Horse.
37. Green Dragon Lifts Its Hand.
38. Left and Right Wheel.
39. Falling Goose Stretches Its Wings.
40. Nesting Bird Enters the Forest.
41. Embrace the Moon.
42. Two Dragons Play with Pearls.
43. Pluck the Peach Beneath the Leaves.
44. Jade Maiden Works the Shuttle.
45. Wiping Out a Thousand Soldiers.
46. Jade Belt Enwraps the Waist.
47. Wiping Out a Thousand Soldiers.

48. Turn the Head to See the Shore.

49. Throwing Out a Brick to Attract Jade.

50. Hungry Tiger Pounces on Its Prey.

51. The King of Heaven Upholds the Pagoda.

52. Green Dragon Lifts Its Hand.

53. Present a Flat Peach on the Birthday.

54. Phoenix Spreads Its Wings.

55. Green Dragon Lifts Its Hand.

56. Closing Sword Posture.

57. The Wind Sweeps the Lotus Leaves.

58. Swallow the Elixir and Spit Out a Treasure.

59. Left and Right Embrace the Moon.

60. The Hornet Comes Out of the Cave.

61. Golden Flower Falls to the Ground.

62. White Ape Hangs on the Branch.

63. Part the Clouds to Look at the Moon.

64. Winter Duck Pecks the Snow.

65. Golden Silk Enwraps the Wrist.

66. The Hegemon Lifts the Whip.

67. Strike Backward at the Purple and Gold Cap.

68. Yellow Dragon Turns Its Body.

69. Serpents and Dragons Emerge from the Water.

70. The Hegemon Lifts the Whip.

71. Pluck the Star to Patch the Moon.

72. Wisteria Hangs on the Wall.

73. Pagoda Hanging on a Single Peak.

74. Great Roc Spreads Its Wings.

75. Striding Tiger Ascends the Mountain.

76. White Snake Spits out Its Tongue.

77. Closing Sword Posture.

78. Fierce Tiger Shakes Its Head.

79. Snatch Victory from Defeat.

80. White Ape Searches for Fruit.

81. Rein in the Horse to Lift the Hoof.
82. Ge the Immortal Spits Fire.
83. The Nimble Cat Pounces on the Rat.
84. Bend the Bow to Shoot the Goose.
85. Golden Silk Enwraps the Wrist.
86. Embrace the Moon.
87. Flowing Waters Push the Boat.
88. Fierce Tiger Enters the Cave.
89. Strength to Split Mount Hua.
90. Golden Youth Wooden Fish.
91. Jade Pillar Supports the Sky.
92. Praying Mantis Catches the Cicada 1.
93. Praying Mantis Catches the Cicada 2.
94. Praying Mantis Catches the Cicada 3.
95. Purple Lightening Soars in the Air.
96. Wiping Out a Thousand Soldiers.
97. Winter Duck Plays with Water.
98. Knock Loose the Golden Cicada.
99. Golden Needle Enters the Ground.
100. Wang Liang Whips the Horse.
101. Remove the Body and Become a Shadow.
102. Jade Maiden Extends the Sleeve.
103. Jade Maiden Lifts the Brazier.
104. Lift the Clothes on One Side.
105. Striding Tiger Ascends the Mountain.
106. White Snake Spits out Its Tongue.
107. Push the Window to Gaze at the Moon.
108. Immortal with Shepherd's Flute; Fixed Posture and Return to Origin.

Second Section

1. Opening Posture.
2. Immortal Points the Way.
3. Golden Youth Wooden Fish.

4. Jade Pillar Supports the Sky.
5. Golden Needle Enters the Ground.
6. The Youth Worships Buddha.
7. Reverse Splitting Mount Hua.
8. The Boy from Xiang Lifts the Basket.
9. Qin Official Whips the Stone.
10. Golden Needle Enters the Ground.
11. Vermillion Phoenix Strokes the Eyebrow.
12. Green Dragon Lifts Its Hand.
13. Wisteria Hangs on the Wall.
14. Shooting Star Chases the Moon.
15. Wiping Out a Thousand Soldiers.
16. Left Coiling Knee.
17. Dragonfly Touches the Water.
18. Face the Wind and Brush Away the Dirt.
19. Vermillion Phoenix Faces the Sun.
20. Black Dragon Sways Its Tail.
21. Green Dragon Lifts Its Hand.
22. The Wind Sweeps the Sparse Clouds.
23. The Youth Worships Buddha.
24. Reverse Splitting Mount Hua.
25. Great Grandfather Goes Fishing.
26. Snatch Victory from Defeat.
27. Poisonous Scorpion Flips Its Tail.
28. Hide the Flower in the Sleeves.
29. Guardian Wei Sweeps the Threshold.
30. Open the Door to Catch the Thief.
31. Close the Door and Seal the Household.
32. Clever Swallow Pierces the Clouds.
33. Phoenix Stretches Its Wings.
34. Phoenix Searches for Its Nest.
35. Separate the Sun and Moon.
36. White Ape Searches for Fruit.

37. Rein in the Horse to Lift the Hoof.
38. Ge the Immortal Spits Fire.
39. Serpents and Dragons Enter the Sea.
40. Jade Belt Enwraps the Waist.
41. Clever Maiden Threads the Needle.
42. Wiping Out a Thousand Soldiers.
43. Right Coiling Knee.
44. The Fisherman Spreads the Net.
45. Reverse Splitting Mount Hua.
46. Rhino Gazes at the Moon.
47. Clear Frost Covers the Ground.
48. Embrace the Moon.
49. Old Moon Leaves the Embrace.
50. Yaksha Searches the Sea.
51. The Boy from Xiang Lifts the Basket.
52. Xiang Yu Wields the Whip.
53. Strange Grass Insert and Sting.
54. Face the Wind and Brush Away the Dirt.
55. Golden Silk Enwraps the Wrist.
56. Wind Whips the Lotus Leaves 1.
57. Wind Whips the Lotus Leaves 2.
58. Golden Cicada Sheds Its Shell.
59. Golden Rooster Shakes Its Feathers.
60. Golden Rooster Nods Its Head.
61. Wisteria Hangs on the Wall.
62. Shooting Star Chases the Moon.
63. Fixed Tornado.
64. Fierce Tiger Comes Out of the Cave.
65. Three Rings Trap the Moon 1.
66. Three Rings Trap the Moon 2.
67. Three Rings Trap the Moon 3.
68. Wheel Sword 1.
69. Wheel Sword 2.

70. Wheel Sword 3.
71. Black Dragon Sways Its Tail.
72. Strange Python Enwraps the Wrist.
73. Holding the Pipa in the Arms.
74. Flowing Waters Push the Boat.
75. Hide the Flower in the Sleeves.
76. Great Grandfather Goes Fishing.
77. Immortal Pushes the Millstone.
78. Vermillion Phoenix Searches for Its Nest 1.
79. Vermillion Phoenix Searches for Its Nest 2.
80. Vermillion Phoenix Searches for Its Nest 3.
81. Spring Wind Strokes the Willows 1.
82. Spring Wind Strokes the Willows 2.
83. Green Dragon Crouches on the Ground.
84. The Following Wind Rips the Flag.
85. Yellow Dragon Lies on the Road.
86. Lone Goose Leaves the Flock.
87. Following Wind Sweeps the Leaves.
88. Immortal Leans on the Cane.
89. Flying Kick Seeks the Wrist.
90. Golden Silk Enwraps the Wrist.
91. Sparrow Hawk Overturns Its Body.
92. White Ape Hangs on the Branch.
93. Wheel Sword 1.
94. Wheel Sword 2.
95. Insert the Flower on Level Ground.
96. Immortal Lies in Bed.
97. Push the Window to Gaze at the Moon.
98. Immortal with Shepherd's Flute.
99. Fixed Posture and Return to Origin.

CHAPTER 5

Baguazhang Form Boxing

Form Boxing[1] is Image-Form Boxing. Cheng School Gao Style Baguazhang Form Boxing was created by Gao Yisheng and is unique content of the Cheng School Gao Style Baguazhang system. Altogether there are eight boxing routines named for the form, image, and fighting posture of eight types of animals. They follow the Eight Trigrams, arranged according to the order of the Bagua Map: Qian—Lion Waves; Kan—Snake Wraps; Gen—Tiger Crouches; Zhen—Dragon Form; Xun—Swallow Overturns; Li—Eagle Tears; Kun—Bear Yanks; Dui—Monkey Image. Former masters Gao and Liu called Form Boxing internal Bagua: lion belongs to heaven and connects to the brain; snake belongs to water and connects to the kidneys; tiger belongs to mountain and connects to the large intestine; dragon belongs to wood and connects to the liver; swallow belongs to wind and connects to the small intestine; eagle belongs to fire and connects to the heart; bear belongs to earth and connects to the spleen; monkey belongs to marsh and connects to the lung.

Baguazhang Form Boxing routines are short and concise. The first four sets contain the methods of the Pre-Heaven Palms, while the latter four sets contain the methods of the Post-Heaven Palms and kicking postures, blending together the essence of Cheng School Gao Style Baguazhang's Pre-Heaven and Post-Heaven Palms. Not only are they appropriate for building the body and fighting, but the animals are also lively and possess great flavor and watchability, with active movements whose power comes from mutually supporting hard and soft, and showing yin and yang clearly in rhythm.

Briefly recorded below are the basic movements of all eight Form Boxing routines as taught directly by Liu Fengcai, as a reference for enthusiasts in research and practice.

Routine 1: Qian—Lion Waves

Post-Heaven Palms opening posture, left hand and left foot in front.

1. Lion Pounces on the Prey.
2. Lion Opens Its Mouth.
3. Lion Rolls the Ball (left).
4. Lion Rolls the Ball (right).
5. Lion Rolls the Ball (left).
6. Left palm wraps inward; right palm pierces up and opens out into Pre-Heaven Turning Palm posture; circle-walk clockwise (one or two circles are adequate).
7. Pre-Heaven Palms Double Palm Change, changing to circle-walk counterclockwise.
8. Lion Spins Its Body (similar in form to Swallow-Overturning Covering-Hand Palm).
9. Hide the Flower Palm. Shuffle step; left hand lifts; right palm attacks the ribs.

Figure 5.1. Ge Guoliang in Lion Opens Its Mouth.

10. Lion Waves Its Claws.
    Left Eyebrow-Swiping Palm.
11. Same as move 6; circle-walk clockwise.
12. Lion Spins Its Body. Repeat move 8 on the opposite side.
13. Hide the Flower Palm.
    Right hand lifts; left palm attacks the ribs.
14. Lion Waves Its Claws.
    Right Eyebrow-Swiping Palm.
15. Lion Rolls the Ball (left).

16. Lion Rolls the Ball (right).
17. Lion Upholds the Ball. Left hand leads; advance with a right step; right hand upholds. Right hand leads; advance with a left step; left hand upholds.
18. Lion Wipes and Crashes.

    Left hand leads; advance with a right step; right Eyebrow-Swiping Palm. Advance with a left step; Double Crashing Palm.
19. Lion Shakes Its Head.

    Spin the body; right hand leads; advance with left step; left Eyebrow-Swiping Palm. Left hand leads; advance with right step; right Eyebrow-Swiping Palm.
20. Lion Leaps.

    Both hands pounce forward with leaping step and Crashing Palm.
21. Wrapping-Hand Palm.

    Right hand wraps; advance with a left step; left Beng Quan.
22. Left hand wraps inward; right palm pierces up and opens out into Pre-Heaven Turning Palm. Circle-walk clockwise, right hand inside the circle.
23. Lion Overturns Its Body (right).

    Right Baibu into the circle; step through left and Following Step right (feet together); right palm slices horizontally. Retreat right; left Koubu; left hand pierces the right palm; large Overturn the Body; the right hand twists; the left hand files; raise the right leg.
24. Set the right foot down; right hand wraps inward; left hand pierces and opens outward. Starting with the left foot, circle-walk counter-clockwise, left hand inside the circle.
25. Lion Overturns Its Body (left).

    Repeat move 23 on the opposite side.
26. Fixed Posture and Return to Origin.

    Set the left foot down to the rear; spin the body and advance right, the right hand piercing the left. Again turn the body into fixed posture and return to the origin.

Routine 2: Kan—Snake Wraps

Figure 5.2. Li Xueyi in Snake Lifting.

Post-Heaven Palms opening posture, left hand and left foot in front.

1. White Snake Spits Out Its Tongue.

    Turn the left palm outward; advance right; right hand files. Turn the right palm outward; advance left; left hand files. Turn the left palm outward; advance right; right hand files.

2. Golden Snake Wraps the Waist.

    Right hand leads horizontally; advance left. Left hand arrests the waist, wrapping and gathering. Right foot inserts forward (Scissor Legs); right hand pierces the left hand. Place the left step as both hands strike in Heart-Dividing Palm.

3. Pre-Heaven Turning Palm.

    Left wraps; right pierces and opens outward; circle-walk clockwise, right hand inside the circle.

4. Green Snake Pierces the Forest.

    Right Baibu into the circle; right hand inserts downward and wraps upward. Advance left; left hand pierces. Left Baibu; left hand inserts downward and wraps upward. Advance right; right hand pierces. Right Baibu; right hand inserts downward and wraps upward. Left Koubu; left hand pierces; spin the body; Double Crashing Palm (right foot in front).

5. Snake Lifting Moving Step.

    Lift the right foot; right hand seizes; left piercing palm. Step down right; right arm opens horizontally. Right hand parries downward and wraps upward; advance left; left hand pierces. Left hand parries downward and wraps upward; advance right; right hand pierces.

6. Step Back Spit Out the Tongue.

    Step back right; left hand pierces. Step back left; right hand pierces. Step back right; left hand pierces. Jumping step into scissor-legs and strike with Heart-Dividing Palm (White Snake Parts the Grass).

7. Pre-Heaven Turning Palm.

    Right hand wraps; left hand pierces and opens out to form Pre-Heaven Turning Palm; circle-walk counterclockwise, left hand inside the circle.

8. Repeat moves 2–7 on the opposite side (left becomes right; right becomes left). Return to circle-walking clockwise, right hand inside the circle.

9. Python Enters the Cave.

    Pre-Heaven Palms Spinning-Body Back-Covering Palm, until the left palm's testing strike.

10. Fixed Posture and Return to Origin.

    Post-Heaven Palms Piercing Palm; advance left; right hand pierces; spin the body into fixed posture and return to the origin.

Routine 3: Gen—Tiger Crouches

Post-Heaven Palms opening posture, left hand and left foot in front.

1. Fierce Tiger Pounces on the Shoulder (left).

    Advance with a right step; both hands seize downward; step up left; pounce toward the left.

2. Fierce Tiger Pounces on the Shoulder (right).

    Advance with a left step; both hands seize downward; step up right; pounce toward the right.

3. Vicious Tiger Pounces on the Prey.

    Step back right and spin the body; advance with left step; left hand pierces the right hand; turn around and double pounce, then leaping step with Double Crashing Palm (right foot in front).

Figure 5.3. Zhang Shoukun in Wildcat Climbs the Tree

4. Pre-Heaven Turning Palm.

Right palm wraps inward; left palm pierces upward and opens outward; circle-walk counterclockwise in Turning Palm.

5. Stopping-Body Moving-Hooking Palm.

Right Baibu; right hand leads out; left Koubu; left Hooking Palm; both hands overturn upward in spiraling palms; lift the left leg. Step down left; advance with a right step; the right hand moves from above to below with Pressing Palm.

6. Overturn the Body Tiger Embraces.

Advance with a right step; left hand parries downward; right hand pierces; overturn the body with the right hand on top, the left hand underneath; lift the left leg into a ready posture similar to Tiger Embraces the Ball.

7. Double Crashing Palm.

Step down left; left hand leads inward; advance right; right elbow hangs; shuffle step and Double Crashing Palm.

8. Tiger Crouches to Enter the Cave.

Step back right; right hand waves and seizes; left Eyebrow-Swiping Palm. Step back left; left hand waves and seizes; right Eyebrow-Swiping Palm.

9. Fierce Tiger Pounces on the Mountain.

Right foot in front; both hands pounce downward; then leaping step with Double Crashing Palm.

10. Leading-Step Beng Quan.

Advance left; left Beng Quan.

11. Pre-Heaven Turning Palm.

Left palm wraps inward; right hand pierces upward and opens outward; circle-walk clockwise in Turning Palm.

12. Repeat moves 5–9 on the opposite side. Return to the left foot in front.

13. Wildcat Pounces on the Rat.

Spin the body so the right foot is forward; advance with a left step; step up right; right Yanking Palm and left Testing Palm. Advance with a right step; step up left; left Yanking Palm; right Testing Palm;

right Yanking Palm. Shuffle step with Double Crashing Palm. Wild-cat Pounces on the Rat three times.

14. Wildcat Climbs the Tree.

Left hand seizes; left foot stomps forward; right hand tests forward. Step down left, the right palm pressing down into a coiled stance.

15. Wild Tiger Beats the Heart.

Right hand upholds; advance with a right step; step behind with the left; left fist strikes the heart; step out right; right horizontal Beng Quan.

16. Fixed Posture and Return to Origin.

Spin the body and return to Post-Heaven Palms Opening Palm posture; close.

Routine 4: Zhen—Dragon Form

Post-Heaven Palms opening posture, left hand and left foot in front.

1. Golden Dragon Comes out of the Cave.

Left hand covers inward; step right with feet together; the right hand follows the left hand lifting up; step back right; both hands carry toward the rear.

2. Green Dragon Comes out of the Water.

Advance right; left hand seizes; right hand upholds; advance left; right hand seizes; left hand upholds; advance right; left hand seizes; right hand upholds.

3. Green Dragon Waves Its Claws.

Eyebrow-Swiping Palm. Right hand seizes; advance left; left palm swipes the eyebrow; advance right; Double Crashing Palm.

4. Lazy Dragon Overturns Its Body.

Spin the body so the left foot is in front. Left palm parries downward and wraps upward; advance with right step; right hand pierces downward. Right hand parries downward and wraps upward; advance with

Figure 5.4. Liu Yungang in Double Palm Change.

left step; left hand pierces upward. Step behind with the right foot; spin the body; Double Crashing Palm; right foot in front. Repeat this posture on the opposite side. Return to left foot in front.

5. Green Dragon Turns Its Head.

Step back left and spin the body, the left arm opening horizontally, left foot in front.

6. Yellow Dragon Spins Its Body.

The form is similar to Post-Heaven Spinning-Body Palm. Left palm turns outward; right Koubu; right palm pierces up; step behind left; spin the body; Double Crashing Palm; left foot in front. Step forward right, the right arm opening horizontally. Right palm turns outward; left Koubu; left palm pierces up; step behind right; spin the body; Double Crashing Palm; right foot in front.

7. Spin the body so the left foot is in front. Two Green Dragon Extends Its Claws, to left foot in front.

8. Spin the body so the right foot is in front. Two Green Dragon Seizes the Helmet, to right foot in front.

9. Right hand wraps inward; left hand pierces the right hand; return to counterclockwise Turning Palm.

10. Two Double Palm Changes, returning to counterclockwise Turning Palm.

11. Golden Dragon Entwines the Jade Pillar (left and right), returning to counterclockwise Turning Palm.

12. Black Dragon Whips Its Tail.

The first two moves from the Pre-Heaven Palms Black Dragon Whips Its Tail (wrapping-hand downward-inserting, like Dragon Form). Two overturn-the-body.

13. Fixed Posture and Return to Origin.

After the large overturn-the-body and lifting the right leg, first step down right, then spin the body and close.

Routine 5: Xun—Swallow Overturns

Post-Heaven Palms opening posture, left hand and left foot in front.

1. Single Crashing Palm, a.k.a. Taiji Palm.

   Left hand leads; step forward right; right hand grabs the upper arm; shuffle-step with left Single Crashing Palm; shuffle-step; right Beng Quan.

2. Reverse-step Opening Palm.

   Step forward left, right hand in front for Opening Palm.

3. Back Stomp Kick.

   Left Koubu; left hand pierces the right hand, and back stomp after turning the body.

4. Outward Swinging Legs.

   Set the right foot down; left Outward Swinging; right Outward Swinging; turn the body; left side-stomp; set the foot down; left foot in front.

5. Hiding the Flower Palm.

   Left hand leads; advance right; right hand upholds the upper arm; shuffle-step; left palm strikes the ribs; right Beng Quan.

6. Overturn the Body with Slicing Palm.

   Step back right and overturn the body (spin the body); advance with the left foot. Right hand seizes; left palm slices downward and opens upward; shuffle-step; right Crashing Palm.

7. Inside Hanging Leg.

   Right hand seizes; right forward Hastening Kick; left hand parries; left Inside Hanging Kick; Koubu and spin the body; right side-stomp kick. Set the foot down, right foot in front.

8. Right hand seizes; advance with a left step; left hand grabs the upper arm; right hand Covering Palm; left foot in front.

Figure 5.5. Liu Yungang in Inward Hanging Leg.

9. Spin the body to right foot in front; repeat moves 1–8 on the opposite side. Return to right foot in front.
10. Double Phoenix Cools Its Wings.

    Spin the body to left foot in front. Double-Handed Carrying Palm; right Koubu; right Hooking Palm. Step behind left; overturn the body; reverse left Hooking Palm. Step forward right; Double-handed Carrying Palm; left Koubu; left Hooking Palm. Step behind right; overturn the body; reverse right Hooking Palm, to right foot in front.
11. Spin the body to left foot in front; right hand seizes downward; right Forward Chasing Kick. Left hand seizes downward; left Forward Chasing Kick.
12. Post-Heaven Advancing Joining Palm.

    Left hand seizes; advance right step; right hand grabs the upper arm; advance left; left palm swipes the eyebrows with downward pressure; advance the right foot into Double Crashing Palm.
13. Spin the body; fixed posture and return to the origin. Close.

Routine 6: Li—Eagle Tears

Post-Heaven Palms opening posture, left hand and left foot in front.

1. Powerful Eagle Spreads Its Wings (Post-Heaven Clamping Palm).

    Left hand leads; step forward right; right hand pierces, uplifts up, and reverse-seizes; shuffle-step; left palm shocking strike (Clamping strike); shuffle-step; right palm pressing strike.
2. Post-Heaven Advancing Joining Palm.
3. Toppling pulling. Left hand leads; step forward right; right hand grabs the leg for toppling pulling; left Heart-Pounding Palm; right Beng Quan. Step forward left; left hand pierces and uplifts; right hand single crash.
4. Spin the body and advance left; left palm pierces the right palm; turn around into Double Crashing Palm; right foot in front.
5. Upward Straight Kick.

Advance with a left step; right hand seizes; right foot kicks up to the *houhai;* left hand seizes; left foot to kicks the *mianmen.* Spin the body to the right; right side-stomp kick.

6. Powerful Eagle Catches the Chicken.

    Set the right foot down; right hand seizes; advance left; left hand grabs the upper arm; shuffle-step; right hand clutches the neck; leading-step Beng Quan with left fist.

7. Opening Palm; Rib Checking Palm.

    Spin the body to right leg in front; shuffle-step with Opening Palm; right hand seizes; advance left; left fist strikes the ribs.

Figure 5.6. Liu Lingjie in Powerful Eagle Catches the Chicken.

8. Downward Cutting Leg.

    Pierce with the right hand; raise the right leg and cut downward. Pierce with the left hand; raise the left leg and cut downward. Left Koubu and turn the body; right side-stomp kick.

9. Powerful Eagle Catches the Chicken.

    Right hand seizes downward; advance left; left hand grabs the upper arm; shuffle-step; right hand clutches the neck; straight-step Beng Quan with left fist.

10. Spin the body to right hand and right foot in front. Repeat moves 1–9 on the opposite side, returning to right foot in front.

11. Spin the body to left foot in front; Eagle Tears (two Eyebrow-Swiping Palms). Left hand leads outward; advance right; right hand swipes the eyebrow. Advance left; Double Crashing Palm. Spin the body; advance left; left hand pierces the right. Turn around; right hand leads outward; advance left; left hand swipes the eyebrows; advance right; Double Crashing Palm.

12. Leading-step Middle Springing Kick.

    Spin the body to left foot in front; left palm parries low and wraps high; springing right kick; right Beng Quan. Set the foot down; right palm intercepts low and wraps high; springing left kick; left Beng Quan.

13. Yellow Eagle Cools Its Wings.

Set down the left foot; left hand leads outward; advance right; right hand upholds the upper arm; left Koubu; left Hooking Palm; overturn the body; double Yanking Palm; right foot in front; shuffle-step with Crashing Palm.

14. Spin the body; fixed posture and return to the origin. Close.

Routine 7: Kun—Bear Yanks

Post-Heaven Palms opening posture, left hand and left foot in front.

1. Hand-Overturning Palm.

Left hand leads; right hand strikes with Hand-Overturning Palm, first low, then high.

2. Heart-Pounding Palm.

Right palm presses down; advance right; left Heart-Pounding Palm; right leading-step Beng Quan.

3. Angled Stepping Leg.

Right hand seizes downward; left foot Forward Chasing Kick; right foot Angled Stepping Kick; turn the body; left foot side-stomp kick.

4. Hooking Hanging Connected Leg.

Spin the body to right foot in front; step back right; Double Carrying Palm; left hand presses; right hand flicks outward; raise the right foot into Hooking Hanging Connected Leg. Set the foot down, right foot in front.

5. Black Bear Climbs the Tree.

Spin the body; left hand seizes; left forward heel kick; right palm strikes the face.

6. Hide the Flower Palm.

Set down the left foot; advance right; right palm upholds; left palm strikes the ribs; right leading-step Beng Quan.

7. Bear Yanks.

Spin the body to left foot in front; both hands seize and yank downward; Opening Palm. Advance right; right hand pierces and lifts up; shuffle-step; Double Crashing Palm. Step behind with left; left hand stealing grasp; step out right; right palm swipes the eyebrows.

8. Forward Crashing Connected Leg.

Double Carrying Palm; lift the left foot and stomp the knee; right side-stomp kick. Right Koubu; turn the body; left rear stomp kick. Set the left foot down; left leading-step Beng Quan.

9. Spin the body to right hand and right foot in front; repeat moves 1–8 on the opposite side, returning to right hand and right foot in front.

Figure 5.7. Gao Jinhua in Angled Stepping Leg.

10. Hooking Hanging Connected Leg.

Pierce with the left hand; left Koubu; spin the body; right Baibu into coiling stance; rise up and left Hooking Hanging Connected kick.

11. Cripple Leg.

Set the left foot down; right rear stomp-kick.

12. Set the right foot down and spin the body; right hand leads outward; advance left; left hand grabs the upper arm; shuffle-step; right palm hooks; left leading-step Beng Quan.

13. Repeat moves 10–12 on the opposite side, returning to right leading-step Beng Quan.

14. Spin the body; fixed posture and return to the origin. Close.

Routine 8: Dui—Monkey Image

Post-Heaven Palms opening posture, left hand and left foot in front.

1. Monkey Clutches the Neck.

Left hand seizes; right hand tests; step up right to empty stance, left hand filing across the right wrist; step out with the right foot;

right hand clutches the neck. Right hand seizes; left hand tests; step up left to empty stance, right hand filing across the left wrist; step out with the left foot; left hand clutches the neck.

2. Monkey Climbs the Wall.

    Left hand leads inward; step forward right; right hand grabs the upper arm; step forward left as the left hand swipes the eyebrows; hopping step with two connected Beng Quan (right, left); left foot in front.

3. Monkey Gazes at the Scenery.

    Spin the body to the right into a coiling stance, right hand turned backward covering above the eyebrows, eyes looking to the rear.

4. Monkey Snap-Kick.

    Right hand parries downward; right side-stomp kick.

5. White Ape Enters the Cave.

    Spin the body right; three retreating steps with Seizing Palms; Double Crashing Palm; right foot in front.

6. Back Stomping Leg and Angled Step-Kick.

    Spin the body and step forward right; right Piercing Palm; left rear stomp kick; right leg angled step-kick. Spin the body, left foot in front.

7. Left snap-kick; left Beng Quan.

8. Monkey Claws the Face.

    Right hand tests and seizes; pounce forward as the left hand claws the face; right Heart-Pounding Palm; right foot in front.

9. White Ape Enters the Cave.

    Spin the body; three retreating steps with Seizing Palms; Double Crashing Palm; left foot in front.

10. Spin the body and pierce with the left hand; step forward left; right rear stomp kick.

11. Set the right foot down; seize with right hand; left Forward Chasing Kick; right Forward Chasing Kick.

12. Monkey Punches.

    Jumping step in place with three connected Beng Quan—right, left, right; right hand and right foot in front.

13. Monkey Gazes at the Scenery.

    Spin the body to the left into a coiling stance, left hand turned backward covering above the eyebrows, eyes looking to the rear.

14. Left hand parries down; left side-stomp kick.

15. White Ape Enters the Cave.

    Spin the body; three retreating steps with Seizing Palms; Double Crashing Palm; left foot in front.

16. Back Stomping Leg and Angled Step-Kick.

    Spin the body and pierce with the left hand; step forward left; right rear stomp kick; left leg angled step-kick. Spin the body; right foot in front.

17. Right snap-kick; right Beng Quan.

18. Monkey Claws the Face.

Figure 5.8. Wang Xu in Ape Gazes at the Scenery.

    Left hand tests and seizes; pounce forward as the right hand claws the face; left Heart-Pounding Palm; left foot in front.

19. White Ape Chews the Peach.

    Step back left; left hand parries downward and lifts up, wrapping inward; step back right and shrink the body; right hand forming a hooking fist, raised near the right ear; left hand forming a hooking fist in front of the right chest.

20. Leading-step Middle Spring Kick.

    High kick with right leg and right Beng Quan; high kick with left leg and left Beng Quan.

21. White Ape Seizes the Helmet.

    Left hand seizes; hop forward with the left leg; leap forward with the right leg, spinning in the air; right hand grabs the hair; step down into double pouncing palm; right foot in front.

22. Turn the body; step forward right; pierce with the right hand. Turn the body; fixed posture and return to the origin. Close.

CHAPTER 6

Essential Selections on the Life-Cultivation Arts

Starting from when Emperor Qin Shihuang first sent people to the eight directions to search for medicines to extend life and prevent aging, through the slow and long ages, even into the present, no one has found the celestial pill or mysterious medicine that can fight aging and restore youth, lengthen life, and avoid old age. Still, in the process of struggling against aging, humankind has discovered within the body itself many factors related to antiaging and has accumulated fairly rich experience in delaying decline and old age. From actual experience, many types of practically effective life-cultivating and health-building exercise methods have been summarized and developed—these are called life-cultivation arts. These methods are the sum experiences in delaying decline and old age, and are also the important elements in modern humans' continued deeper research and discussion of delaying and preventing degeneration within each organ of the body. Not only were Gao Yisheng's achievements in Baguazhang profound, but he also had considerable understanding of life-cultivation arts. In his writing on life-cultivation, he relates methods closely interrelated with Baguazhang. Those who study this art cannot not know them.

The Three Dantians

Gao Yisheng said: "There are three dantians. The brain is the upper dantian, the sea of spirit. The chest is the middle dantian, the sea of qi. Three cun [about two inches] below the navel is the lower dantian, the sea of essence. The upper, middle, and lower dantians are connected by qi; those who cultivate life use quiet cultivation as the start and regulate the breath, causing the upper, middle, and lower dantians to conjoin and the true qi to circulate uninterrupted, which is beneficial to nourishing life. Within the body there are also three gates: behind the head is the Yuzhen Gate, on the back is the Jiaji Gate, the tailbone has the Weilü Gate.[1] The three gates are the path for essential qi (true qi) to ascend and descend. The front three dantians and the back three gates together are the Small Heavenly Circuit. When the three dantians and three gates are united, the qi and blood move and circulate gracefully; essence, qi, and spirit are abundant; and the qi and blood do not decline.

Baguazhang and Elixir-Training Arts

Buddhist Chan skill's well-known "relics," Daoist secret skill's well-known "elixirs," and common martial arts' well-known "embryonic breathing" all signify the unifying of jing, qi, and shen to attain true qi. Looking at this from the point of Baguazhang, our walking and turning on the circle comes from the Daoist elixir-training art Turning the Celestial Worthy. Because of this, walking and turning the circle in Baguazhang is itself a type of elixir-training process, connecting the upper, middle, and lower dantians and opening up the three gates on the back. In the process of training in Baguazhang we also emphasize adhering to the Twenty-Four Requirements (Neigong Posture-Completion Methods) to form movements and seeking naturalness without concentrating the mind. Actual practice proves that Baguazhang is a high-level life-cultivation art with origins in elixir-training arts, but it is more refined than elixir-training arts in that both nature and constitution are cultivated.

The Location of the Three Dantians

Regarding the location of the three dantians, currently there are many different explanations. Some say they are points; some say they are surfaces; and some even say they are certain organs. According to generations of

Baguazhang transmission and our own practical understanding through training, we feel that the upper, middle, and lower dantians are cavities within the body with certain points as their centers. Moreover, they align with the three gates on the back, together signifying surface and interior, mutually affecting one another. The three dantians and three gates mutually connected are the Small Heavenly Circuit. When the Small Heavenly Circuit is connected, the three dantians and three gates can communicate. The ancients felt that "the upper dantian is the sea of spirit; the middle dantian is the sea of qi; and the lower dantian is the sea of essence." This is to say that the dantians are the places where jing, qi, and shen converge and are not a point or a surface but are specific areas or cavities with unique functional states. Therefore, the ancients called them "fields" and did not call them points, orifices, or acupuncture points. In the process of training, "the qi sinking to the dantian" or "the intention guarding the dantian" point to these cavity areas.

Because of this, we can make this kind of conclusion: the lower dantian is a cavity within the lower abdomen that uses the *Guanyuan*[2] acupuncture point as its center and aligns with the Weilü Gate; the middle dantian is a cavity within the chest that uses the *Tanzhong*[3] acupuncture point as its center and aligns with Jiaji Gate; and the upper dantian is a cavity in the brain that uses the yintang acupuncture point as its center and aligns with the Yuzhen Gate. Only through conceptually understanding and fully recognizing the locations and effects of the dantians, and mastering their true meaning, can one grasp the dantians during practice, thereby better advancing and maintaining the free flow of the three dantians and three gates.

Jing, Qi, and Shen

The ancients said "heaven has three treasures: the sun, the moon, and the stars; the earth has three treasures: water, fire, and wind; humans have three treasures: jing, qi, and shen." If heaven was without its three treasures, all would be dark and without illumination. If the earth were without its three treasures, the ten thousand things could not be born. If humans are without their three treasures, they have no life. You can see the importance of jing, qi, and shen. Jing, in its broadest meaning, points to the subtle substances within the body, including the jing of the five zang organs, which includes four aspects: jing, blood, jin, and ye. In its narrowest meaning, jing points to reproductive essence. Pre-Heaven jing is received from the essence of the mother and father uniting during pregnancy and giving rise to bodily form. Post-Heaven jing originates in subtle substances absorbed through digestion of the water and grain we eat and drink. The mutual effect of Pre-Heaven jing and Post-Heaven jing together guarantees the body's development, health, and long life. Chinese medical theory posits that jing can transform to qi and give rise to blood, and it is the originating substance of life and the foundation of life movement. It adapts to changes in the external world, defends against external evil invasions, and safeguards the root of bodily health. Qi is the manifestation of the body's movement ability.

Within the body, the most fundamental qi is "true original" qi, which comes from the Pre-Heaven essential qi of one's mother and father. This type of qi has the effect of arousing and promoting the function of the zang and fu organs, and it maintaining the motive force for the body's regular growth and development. Next in importance is the qi of water and grain, which comes from and is formed by the transformation of nutritive substances. Third is the oxygen inhaled by the lungs. These three types of qi constitute a type of subtle substance with strong motive power that penetrates every region of the body without exception. Whether one is alive completely relies on this qi: "When the qi is amassed, the form is complete; when the qi is scattered, the form is dead."

Shen is the general term for the phenomenon of life movement. It is the external expression of the body's zang-fu functions and the embodiment of the flourishing or decline of jing and qi. During bodily processes, transforming jing into qi at the same time expresses shen. The relationship between these three—jing, qi, and shen—is extremely close and cannot be divided. Qi is produced from jing; the transformation of jing relies on qi.

Jing can contain qi; qi can transform to jing. If the jing is complete, the qi is complete; if the qi is complete, the shen is complete. The internal skill exercise of turning the circle in Baguazhang is a process of producing jing, transforming to qi, and raising the shen that self-regulates the life process and thus has the effect of cultivating life and building health.

Gao Yisheng had a penetrating analysis of jing, qi, and shen, saying that for the body, jing, qi, and shen are the most important, so those who want to build health must not damage the jing, overuse the qi, or injure the shen. A common saying is "When a tree is old, graft a young shoot to revive it." When a person is old, true qi can be used as a supplement to benefit life and extend one's years. True qi is internal qi, essential qi, original qi. Therefore, generally speaking, those who cultivate life, who practice martial arts, and who train the qi generally do not stray from first maintaining and secondly training the three substances.

The three substances—jing, qi, and shen—are closely related and inseparable. Shen is born from qi; qi is born from jing. Jing is the basis of the body; qi is the lord of the shen. Jing is the greatest treasure of the body and cannot be wasted.

Post-Heaven jing originates in the essence of grain and water entering internally and seeping into the bones, meaning it is the marrow. Above, it enters the brain, meaning the cerebral fluids. If the jing is overused, the qi declines; if the qi declines, illness arises. If this deficiency is superficial, then the waist and back will hurt or be sour and without power, with dizziness in the head and ringing in the ears. If serious, then the jing is exhausted and the body is brittle. A song says:

For the Way of yin and yang jing is the greatest treasure,
The five zang and six fu organs all require essence,
If heart jing is insufficient the shen is hurried and the health rushed,
If the liver jing is insufficient the eyes are hazy and without luster,
If the lung jing is insufficient the flesh becomes emaciated,
If spleen jing is insufficient the teeth and hair wither and fall,
If kidney jing is insufficient the shen and qi are reduced,
When true jing is used completely death will follow.

Therefore, broadly speaking, to cultivate life, one must first guard the jing. If the jing is full, the qi is strong; if the qi is strong, the shen is abundant. If the shen is abundant, then the body is healthy, and internally the five zang are fully supplied; externally the flesh is moist and the appearance is radiant; the ears and eyes are sharp and bright; one does not decline in old age and is long-lived. In contrast, if the jing is overused, it is exhausted; if the jing is exhausted, the qi is cut off; if the qi is cut off, there is no shen. This is the image of a dead life and a dead body.

Important Poems on Life-Cultivation

Speak less, cultivate the lung qi,
Regulate lust, cultivate the kidney qi,
Weaken flavors, cultivate blood qi,
Swallow jin-ye, cultivate zang qi,
Relinquish anger, cultivate liver qi,
Eat cleanly, cultivate stomach qi,
Avoid anxiety, cultivate heart qi.

The hair should be combed regularly,
The face should be rubbed regularly,
The teeth should be clenched regularly,
The saliva should be swallowed regularly,
The qi should be trained regularly.

Do not spit forcefully,
In walking, do not hasten steps,
With the ears, do not listen excessively,
With the eyes, do not view to exhaustion.

Long walking, long standing, long sitting, long lying, long looking all injure the qi and blood. "Long" means excessive. Therefore, in all things, one who cultivates life considers not injuring as a life-extending art, and supplementing as the canon of life-strengthening.

Essential Selections on the Life-Cultivation Arts

One day's prohibition: eating to excess in the evening,
One month's prohibition: drinking liquor until extremely drunk,
One year's prohibition: traveling far on a winter's day,
One lifetime's prohibition: sexual intercourse at night with lamps lit.

Sour to excess is injurious to the essence,
Bitter to excess is injurious to the bones,
Sweet to excess does not benefit the flesh,
Pungent to excess counteracts correct qi,
Salt to excess is the most harmful to the body,
Weakening the flavors benefits a long life.

In the morning, one bowl of porridge,
In the evening, do not eat until full,
In the depth of winter and height of summer,
Excessive lust is most injurious to life,
When drunk or overfull, do not have intercourse,
Breaking with this causes the five organs to overturn,
Birds and animals that have died on their own,
If eaten, will greatly endanger one's life.

Liquor to excess, and the blood and qi will be scattered,
With flavors weakened, the spirit is at rest,
Night bathing is superior to morning bathing,
Evening meals should not be like morning meals.

Regulate drinking, and the spleen will naturally strengthen,
Only with less worry can one be at peace,
After sweating, do not stand directly in the wind,
On an empty stomach, do not drink water.

When one regularly moves the body, the hundred illnesses cannot form.
Drink liquor but avoid drunkenness, and the various illnesses cannot
*   develop.*
After eating, walk one hundred steps, and rub the belly with the hands.
Nails should regularly be cut, and the hair combed one hundred times.
If full, then immediately urinate, in a place that is not windy.

Evening overeating has no benefit in the end; before sleeping at night wash the feet.

Worry and concern are most injurious to the spirit; happiness and anger both harm the qi.

Slightly cut the nasal hairs; always practice not spitting on the ground.

At the break of dawn, when getting up, always alight the bed with the left foot.

In nourishing life, one must be constant for a health medicine that is inexhaustible.

Cultivating Kidney Skill-Methods

Just before sleep, loosen the clothes, untie the belt, and sit on the bed. Curl the tip of the tongue to the upper palate and be aware of the lower dantian. Lift and contract the anus as if resisting a bowel movement. Regulate the breath for a moment and relax. The hands press on the kidney shu points, rubbing 120 times until warmth arises, and then stop.

Shed the clothes and recline face up, as if sleeping; regulate the breath for a moment. With one hand clutch the testes, and with the other rub horizontally across the lower dantian area. Clutch and rub several dozen times, then switch hands and again clutch and rub. After this, with both hands, lightly knead the testes several dozen times, waiting for everything to feel relaxed and warm; then one can quietly enter sleep. The rhyme-song says:

Clutch and rub, switching left and right,
On the dantian area ninety-nine times,
With care and timeliness, regularly cultivate character,
Ample true yang is better than a golden elixir.

Cultivating Kidney Skill-Method is a body cultivation art that was taught secretly by Gao Yisheng. This skill is effective in producing jing and supplementing the kidneys. The underlying principle is that the kidney shu points are the important points for nourishing the kidneys; through rubbing and stimulating, it increases the vitality of the kidneys.

The testes are the connecting avenue of the three yin and three yang leg channels; regular clutching can stimulate the vitality of the three yang and three yin channels and speed the strengthening of kidney function. The lower dantian is the sea of jing storage; regular rubbing can promote the fullness of essential qi. The testes are the location of reproductive essence; regular kneading stimulates and can increase reproductive fluid. However, one must take care; this skill must not be practiced before or after sexual intercourse.

Golden Liquid Returning to Dantian Massage and Daoyin Art

Those of old called saliva "golden *jin* and jade *ye*." Listed together with essential fluids and blood, these are the three treasures of the human body, and the substances classical masters of Chinese life-cultivating arts viewed as most valuable.

Chinese medicine considers saliva the transformation of qi and blood. It is an important substance that irrigates the zang-fu organs, moistens the flesh and skin, flows through the hundred vessels, and supplements Post-Heaven qi. The data from modern scientific tests show that human saliva contains amylase, lysozyme, mucin, immunoglobulin, and many other types of active substances. Some of these substances aid in digestion; others kill bacteria. Recently a Japanese scientists even found that saliva contains a type of hormone that helps people maintain youth—parotid gland hormone. This hormone can strengthen the vitality of muscle, blood vessels, connective tissue, bones, cartilage, and teeth, and especially can increase the elasticity of blood vessels, invigorate the vitality of the connective tissue, and help skin maintain its elasticity. Several other scientists also found that saliva has detoxifying, cancer-fighting, and cancer-suppressing effects. It was discovered that when one chews and the saliva secreted by the body is added to highly oncogenic nitrogen compounds, aflatoxin, or suspected carcinogenic alkylating agents such as tar, burned meat, post–heat treated sodium glutamate, and so on, all of these lose their cellular form within thirty seconds. The effect is at the cellular level, preventing the cells from becoming cancerous. If the cells of the above-mentioned carcinogens are not processed by the saliva, then more than half of the cells will become cancerous. Tests also prove that saliva has a marked detoxifying effect toward toxic additives to both synthetic and natural foodstuffs. Saliva's cancer-fighting and toxin-relieving abilities are strongest when food is chewed in the mouth for thirty seconds or more. This gives a scientific explanation to saliva's role in health-building, and the life-cultivating arts—Golden Liquid Returning to Dantian—introduced in this book.

The Golden Liquid Returning to Dantian massage art causes the golden jin and jade ye—saliva—to return to the dantian by performing several self-massage movements, with the goal of building and strengthening the body. It can attain the level of cultivating the body and building the nature. The song of the Golden Liquid Returning to Dantian massage and Daoyin art taught by Gao Yisheng is as follows:

Sit upright and settle the spirit; use the hands to rub the helix,
Warm, rub, and press the eyes; wipe the nose to irrigate the esteemed
    hill,
Wipe the forehead to cultivate tianting; use the nails to comb the hair
    gently,
Knock the teeth thirty-six times; lightly clenching the fists and with
    meditative spirit,
Exhale and inhale regularly nine times, the hands holding kunlun,
Left and right sound the Heavenly Drum,[4] hearing it twenty-four times,
Slightly wave and shake the spine as the red dragon stirs the waters,
Hold the qi and rub the hands warm, rubbing Jingmen[5] on the back,
Extend the breath; think of warming the navel,
Left and right shoulders wave until the fire naturally burns to Dingmen,[6]
Both legs extend straight; lower the head and massage the feet
    vigorously,
Waiting for Tianhe water, again and again rinse and swallow jin.

A simple explanation of the song:

Sit upright and settle the spirit: sit with the legs coiled, relax, and enter into stillness. The eyes are lightly closed, the hands placed flat on the knees, palms facing upward. The tongue curls up to the palate; the upper body adheres to the posture-completion methods of Baguazhang. With a vertical and aligned posture, inhale and exhale nine times each while the intention concentrates on the upper, middle, and lower dantians, naturally regulating the breathing. The heart fire comes from above and enters the lower dantian until one feels warmth in the belly. Then lightly rinse the whole mouth with the jin-ye fluids, swallowing several times with a gurgling sound.

Use the hands to rub the helix: the quiet sitting position does not change. Use the right hand to reach over the head and rub the left ear several times. Use the left hand to reach over the head and rub the right ear several times. The acupuncture points of the ear connect to the whole body. Moreover, the ears rule the kidneys. This skill is called repairing the city wall to supplement kidney qi, and it strengthens the entire body.

Warm, rub, and press the eyes: continuing, lightly rub the hands until they are warm. Use the Laogong point on the palms to press the eyes several times. The eyes connect with the liver. This skill can brighten the eyes and will supplement liver qi.

Wipe the nose to irrigate the esteemed hill: the "esteemed" of the five hills is the nose. Use the middle fingers of both hands; starting at the base of the nostrils, lightly rub up and down toward the bridge of the nose several times until both inside and outside are warm. This is the skill to irrigate the esteemed hill and moisten the lungs. It is especially effective for colds or congestion.

Wipe the forehead to cultivate tianting; use the nails to comb the hair gently: the tianting point is the forehead. Open all five fingers of both hands and cover the face. From below, move upward, dry-washing the face; passing the forehead, the ten fingers enter the hairline and comb evenly through to the back of the head, then return. Repeat this rubbing several times. It is important to rub all the points on the face and head like the upper dantian (yintang), Baihui, and so on. This skill is in opening the upper dantian, and the face and hair will naturally increase in luster.

Knock the teeth thirty-six times, lightly clenching the fists and with meditative spirit: repeat the first movement: sit with the legs coiled, relax, and enter into stillness. Inhale and exhale each three times while the intention concentrates on the upper, middle, and lower dantians, sinking into deep thought and contemplation, gathering the jing and uniting the spirit. Then, with the thumb inside and the fingers outside in a loose fist, using intention but not using force, lightly knock the teeth such that you can hear the sound, repeating thirty-six times. Jin-ye will naturally fill the mouth; divide it and swallow three times. This skill produces jin-ye, supplements true qi, and strengthens the teeth.

Exhale and inhale regularly nine times; the hands holding kunlun: kunlun is the head; both hands embrace the head with middle fingers pressing at the Baihui point, the intention focusing on the yintang point. Breathe nine times.

Left and right sound the Heavenly Drum, hearing it twenty-four times: use the center of both hands to cover the ears, and with the middle finger pressing on the index finger, lightly tap the Jade Pillow point at the back of the brain twenty-four times with a *dong-dong* thumping sound like the beating of a drum. This skill awakens the brain and calms the spirit, and it is beneficial in opening the Jade Pillow points.

Slightly wave and shake the spine as the red dragon stirs the waters: lightly wave the head left and right twenty-four times; place both hands lightly on the knees. The red dragon is the tongue. During the process of waving the head, the tongue moves back and forth, left and right with a stirring movement within the mouth, causing jin-ye to bubble forth; this is swallowed.

Hold the qi and rub the hands warm, rubbing Jingmen on the back: with the nose, draw clear qi; close and hold it for a bit while rubbing the hands until warm. Slowly exhale from the nose, the intention focused on the lower dantian, and with the center of the palms rub the area around the kidney shu points on the back of the body. After several repetitions, clench the hands into fists and place them on the knees.

Extend the breath; think of warming the navel: naturally regulate the breath, and with intention imagine the heart fire descending to warm the dantian. When exhaling, the lower abdomen and dantian area will feel warm.

Left and right shoulders wave until the fire naturally burns to Dingmen: bend the head forward and wave and shake the shoulders thirty-six times, naturally regulating the breath. When inhaling, imagine the fire starting from lower dantian and descending to the Huiyin point, following along the three gates until reaching the Baihui point at the peak of the head. Wherever the qi passes will have a warm feeling.

Both legs extend straight; lower the head and massage the feet vigorously: comfortably extend the legs flat; use both hands to reach forward and stroke the yongquan points in the middle of the feet thirty-six times.

Waiting for the Tianhe water, again and again rinse and swallow jin: return to sitting with the legs coiled, relaxed, and entered into stillness, and regulate the breath naturally. The Tianhe water is the red jin and ye. Rinse the mouth with the jin-ye and swallow three times with a gurgling sound. This posture may serve as a closing movement, or it can also serve as a beginning movement.

Repeatedly cultivating by regulating the breath according to these methods is the Golden Liquid Returning to Dantian, and it is extremely beneficial in building the health. A song praises this, saying:

Golden jin regularly returning to the dantian, the hundred vessels
  can self-regulate,
Issue fire, and roast the body, and illness and evil cannot arise,
After midnight and before noon, sit, creating a combining of yang
  and yin,
Circulating and turning again and again, Bagua is the source of good
  results.

CHAPTER 7

Records of Famous Baguazhang Practitioners

Since Baguazhang was created and passed on to the world by Dong Haichuan, each generation has had its famous exponents. Their marks in the annals of Chinese martial arts history are numerous, and more than a few famous Baguazhang practitioners are the subject of respect and admiration by people in China. Exhibiting righteousness and bravery, their exploits opposing violence and resisting invasion are widely repeated by ordinary people. In order to inspire the interest of Baguazhang enthusiasts, after collecting a wide variety of information, we have selected several anecdotes and interesting stories of famous Baguazhang masters and respectfully record them as follows.

Dong Haichuan, the First-Generation Founder

Dong Haichuan was from Wenan County in Hebei Province, born October 13, 1797, and died October 25, 1882, at the age of eighty-five. From a young age he loved martial arts and was skilled in boxing and weapons. His nature was forthright, valuing chivalry and righteousness, and he enjoyed roaming the country with the air of an ancient knight-errant. Master Dong studied the most refined martial skill from his forebears and united martial arts and Daoism in one skill, developing his own school and creating Baguazhang; thus people call him the "first-generation founding master." Throughout his life, in regard to boxing and weapons, he never encountered anyone who was his equal. He took numerous disciples, and his name was known in both the north and the south. In the Xianfeng period (1850–1861) of the Qing Dynasty, because Master Dong defended someone against injustice in his hometown, he had to flee on charges of murder. Later he served as a laborer in the mansion of Prince Su, concealing his talents and going into hiding, leaving no trace. In the beginning, none of those above or below him in the household knew that he excelled in martial arts, and they knew even less that he was one of the great knights-errant of the era.

One day, Prince Su ordered the general steward of mansion security, Sha Huihui (real name unknown),[1] together with his wife, Ma, to perform and show his martial skill. Those in the mansion gathering to watch were numerous. Just then, Master Dong was serving tea; because the onlookers were crowded together, he was not able to reach the back of the courtyard to serve water. In an instant, he jumped onto the roof beam of the hall and then floated down, and was thus found out by Prince Su, who then knew Master Dong was not an ordinary person. Prince Su then ordered him to perform martial arts. Master Dong dared not disobey the order, and on the spot showed his skill performing Turning Palms. After the crowd had watched his display, they erupted in cheers. Prince Su was greatly pleased and thereupon made Dong the general steward of mansion security. Master Dong politely declined three times, but in the end he reluctantly accepted the position.

Sha and his wife were both unyielding in disposition, and also more skilled than average in the world of martial arts. They could not accept that their well-paid position had been taken by Master Dong, and the two of them vented their anger in discussing their desire to kill him. One night at midnight, Sha took up a steel broadsword, and from the front gate advanced for a frontal attack, while Ma took a pistol to make a surprise attack from the back through the rear window. At the time, Master Dong was in his room in seated meditation. Ma lifted the pistol in an attempted attack, but at the last moment Master Dong lightened his body and jumped up. Ma had not yet moved the trigger, and the gun was seized and taken away by Dong. Just then, Sha broke down the door and entered, raising the broadsword as if to chop, but suddenly seeing Ma kneeling on the ground in prostration, he lost his courage and could only drop to his knees and beg for mercy, pleading with Dong to take him as a disciple. Dong could not help but allow it.

One day, Master Dong was traveling to Malanguan,[2] and on the road he encountered a group of highwaymen robbing some traveling merchants. Seeing this, Dong said angrily, "You mangy thieves, how dare you rob people in broad daylight?" The band of thieves stared at him for a long time, and one of the leaders, who was riding a horse, said with a smile, "This old man wants to hasten his death?" Dong's indignation was instant, and he rushed forward with a strike, knocking the thief off the horse onto the ground and killing him. The remaining thieves pressed forward, brandishing weapons and surrounding him to attack. Dong pulled out his Mandarin Duck Knives and met them. After not even a few exchanges, several thieves were already wounded or dead, and those remaining dropped to the ground, kneeling, and begged for mercy. Master Dong ordered the group of thieves to return their loot to the merchants, and the thieves dared not disobey even in the slightest. One by one they returned the goods, and then fled to the four directions. The merchants were extremely appreciative and asked his name. Master Dong smiled slightly, saying, "Exhibiting a righteous and brave bearing to aid the weak and support those in need—this should be humanity's utmost duty. You gentlemen go now; I do not seek reward."

Master Dong's disciples were fairly numerous and were mostly skilled athletes from the area of Beijing, Tianjin, and Hebei. Because of the efforts of his disciples in transmitting this art, in its process of development over the short history of roughly a hundred years, it has been transmitted north and south of the great river,[3] and even passed on overseas. Along with Shaolin, Taiji, and Xingyiquan, it has been called one of the four great boxing arts of China. The famed national arts expert Jin Jingzhong once gave highest praise to Master Dong's life's work of establishing and passing on Baguazhang, saying, "That we retain these skills for my country's martial arts is due solely to the effort of Elder Dong and his disciples in enthusiastic promotion."

After Master Dong died, his disciples buried him outside of Dongzhimen in Beijing, erecting a stele in commemoration. In 1981, his tomb was moved to Wan'an Public Cemetery in Beijing's western suburbs.

"Spectacles Cheng": Cheng Tinghua

Cheng Tinghua was a person of Shen County, Hebei Province. He was born in 1848, and died in Beijing in 1900 (the *gengzi* year). He formerly established an eyeglasses shop outside Qianmen in Beijing, and people called him "Spectacles Cheng." In his youth he studied martial arts and excelled in the art of Shuaijiao. Later he bowed to Dong Haichuan as his master and studied Baguazhang. Although he was a businessman, he did not take even a small break from martial arts and became one of the famous second-generation practitioners of Baguazhang.

During the Guangxu period (1875–1908) of the Qing Dynasty, there was a man in Dingxing County named Iron Ox Li who was youthful and strong, full of vigor and vitality, and skilled in boxing techniques. He did not like to work for a living, usually relying on his strength to swindle people, using this to make a living and fill his belly. He had heard of Cheng Tinghua's fame for a long time, and so went to pay a visit to Cheng, carrying his hook swords and a short-handled sickle. Arriving at Cheng's shop, not knowing what Cheng looked like, he called loudly: "Is Spectacles Cheng here?" Cheng replied, "Is the customer here to make a purchase?" Iron Ox replied, "No, I came specially to compare skills with you and decide victory and defeat." Cheng saw his appearance and behavior and knew that he was an uneducated person. Smiling, he asked him, "Do you know Cheng?" Ox replied, "Don't know him." Cheng asked, "Do you have an enmity or grudge against him?" Ox said, "Nope." Cheng then said: "Spectacles Cheng is my employer and has only just left. Can you wait a bit for him?" Ox replied, "Yes." Cheng both regretted and laughed at this. He regretted Ox's combative and ferocious nature, and laughed at his dimwittedness. When the day was drawing toward dusk, Cheng said to Ox: "Your belly must be starving; you can eat something while waiting for my employer's return." After Ox finished eating, seeing that Cheng had still not returned, he began to utter curses. Cheng could not stand it and said, "As your nature is impatient like this, if you cannot wait, how would it be if I accepted your challenge?" Ox replied, "I must decide this with Cheng. Who are you? Why should I dirty my hands with you?" Cheng replied, "I am Spectacles Cheng." As soon as Ox knew it was Cheng, he did not wait for further talk, lifting his hook swords and advancing to attack. Cheng calmly spun his body, dodging and avoiding, and Ox landed in emptiness. Cheng turned his body and issued a strike from the side, striking Ox's right knee. Ox cried out loudly and fell into a filthy puddle at the back of the courtyard, his hook swords falling to the ground. Cheng feared that he had caused injury, and urgently leaped over to pick Ox up. Ox did not know how to admit defeat, his vexation and disgrace turning to anger. Shaking himself loose, he took from his sleeve the short-handled sickle to decide life and death. Cheng saw him holding the knife, ready to pounce, and turning his body, with a flying kick struck Ox's wrist, the short sickle falling to the ground. Ox began to realize he had encountered a person of unusual skill, and dropped to his knees in prostration, begging for instruction and wishing to be listed on Cheng's wall as a disciple. Cheng was determined not to agree to this but later, after the pleas of many other practitioners, did record him as a disciple.

In 1900, four years after Gao Yisheng bowed to Cheng as his master, the Eight-Nation Alliance Army occupied Beijing. Cheng died in Beijing fighting against foreign oppression, single-handedly attacking more than a dozen foot soldiers of the aggressors' troops. With bare hands he treated them like fallen flowers in flowing water, greatly increasing the determination of the Chinese people. However, in the end, because he was alone, he could not hold off the group. Several enemy soldiers, angered and disgraced, simultaneously fired their rifles, squarely hitting Cheng, causing one of the great martial artists of his era to bravely sacrifice himself to the poisonous bullets of the invading foreign guns.

"Dragon-Tongue Palm": Yin Fu

Yin Fu, courtesy name Dean, was from Tongzhou. He established a copper works inside the city, and he was one of Dong Haichuan's most accomplished disciples. He was especially expert in leaping skill and was widely known in the north of our country. Because his training created its own school, where in issuing the palms the five fingers are pressed together, people called him "Dragon-Tongue Palm."

Yin had a friend who was the guard at a granary. One day the granary suffered a robbery, and Yin, to help his friend and without regard for his own well-being, rushed into the group of thieves, beating to death four of the criminals and wounding twenty-plus more, causing the leader of the group to surmount the wall and escape. In the Qing penal codes, armed fights resulting in death within storehouses were not investigated, and Yin was not punished, but because of this he became an enemy of the thieves. Their leader, Yang, hated Yin Fu and repeatedly plotted his murder to avenge the shame of his defeat. Yang was often loitering near Yin's shop with several companions, with hidden knives and pistols, looking for a chance to kill him. One day at dusk, when it was extremely hot, Yin was enjoying the cool of the doorway, and even after dark had not yet gone inside to sleep, instead lying on a bamboo mat in the courtyard. Yang saw his opportunity, and with three of his compatriots climbed over the wall into the courtyard, arriving in front of Yin with creeping steps. Raising the pistol and taking aim at Yin Fu, he yelled loudly: "Yin Fu, retribution is here!" At the time, Yin Fu was lying on the bamboo mat about to fall asleep, but he had heard there were people in the courtyard who had entered over the wall. He had thought of moving, but feared running into a trap, so he pretended to be fast asleep while observing them with his eyes open, and saw the four thieves with weapons coming to surround him, with Yang directly in front. As fast as you could say it, Yin suddenly raised his body and leaped up, dodging to the side of Yang. Yang quickly pulled the trigger, mistakenly killing an accomplice opposite him. Yin took advantage of this to attack Yang. Yang knew he was no match, and jumped over the wall and fled. Yin did not give chase, fearing someone lying in wait outside. He later reported this to the relevant government office, and Yang was pursued and brought to justice, receiving punishment for attempted murder. Because of this, Yin Fu's reputation was greatly boosted.

Later, Prince Su also heard of this incident and, knowing that Yin was a student of Dong Haichuan, invited him to his mansion to teach his children. Through Dong Haichuan's recommendation, he served as the commander of the guard, training within the prince's household. Empress Dowager Cixi, also hearing of his elegant skills, summoned Yin into the palace. After observing him performing sword forms, she promoted him to the post of customs official in the Ministry of Civil Affairs. Thus, in the last days of the Qing Dynasty, the fact that the court did not experience any great larceny was due to the hard work of Dong Haichuan and his students, who remained at their posts day and night.

"Coal Ma": Ma Weiqi

Ma Weiqi was from Beijing and was skilled in fighting. He was also difficult and rash by nature. He established a coal supply store in the eastern part of Beijing, and thus people called him "Coal Ma." He bowed to Dong Haichuan as master and single-mindedly trained Baguazhang. The name Coal Ma was known throughout Hebei and Shanxi provinces, and Prince Su heard of him and summoned him to test his skill by performing with a family-owned steel spear. This steel spear weighed fifty-one pounds and was thirteen feet in length, and thus was difficult to wield inside the hall. Ma was nonchalant and simply started performing inside, handling the long weapon as if it was a short one in a way that those who were not skilled in Baguazhang could not mimic. Ma caused the spear to move back and forth several times, like a tornado stirring up snowflakes, his skill without compare. When Ma finished performing and gathered the spear, he was not breathing hard, and his face had not changed color. Prince Su saw this and could not help but be speechless.

Finally the prince said, "The brave gentleman does what profession?" Feeling pleased with himself, Ma took out his snuff box and sniffed from it, casually saying: "I'm Coal Ma. I deal in coal." The prince saw that his bearing and speech were coarse and unrefined. Although he possessed superior skill, it would be difficult to place him in an important position. He wanted to appoint him to the post of military attaché, but feared that he would not be competent, and so instead sent him a thousand pieces of garlic-head silver.

At the time, his school brothers Yin Dean and Li Zhongyuan advised him regarding martial virtue, but Ma did not think they were correct. After receiving the gift from the prince, he became increasingly arrogant. Each time he tested hands with others to compare skills, in one move he would injure them, so people began to avoid him, calling him "Eastern Heavenly Tyrant" behind his back. At the time there was a bodyguard and martial arts master named Zhao Keli. Passing through Beijing, he paid a visit to Ma, which was a convention in the world of itinerant martial artists at the time to establish friendships. As soon as Ma saw him, without thinking about whether it was right or wrong, he asked him to his face, "What abilities do you have, that you dare to come to meet me?" He raised his hands as he was talking. The bodyguard master was young and full of energy, and neither of the two were willing to back down, resulting in their crossing hands. Zhao was struck by Ma in his right ribs, and his breathing stopped. Given treatment of a fellow bodyguard, it took more than a month for him to recover, and he became disabled. Ma often used his strength to injure others, and enmity and resentment toward him grew widespread. At the time, those in the martial arts world who originally had a good relationship with him also gradually became distant, and even many of his school brothers despised him as a person.

One day, Ma was lingering in the doorway of his home and saw a tall person with a ruddy complexion, holding a palm-leaf fan, who raised his hands in greeting to Ma, saying, "Does Coal Ma live at this residence?" Ma replied, "Of course." The visitor showed himself in and, seeing weapons displayed on the walls of the hall, asked coolly and slowly, "Does the master of this house also know fighting?" Ma replied, "Who doesn't know me, Ma Weiqi? Who are you to dare to belittle me?" The guest replied, "Can we or can't we compare to determine winner and loser?" Ma was already livid, and without any modesty struck a fighting pose in the middle of the hall, spinning with his Baguazhang and attacking the guest. The guest, in his long robe, held his fan as before, calmly crane-stepping, one after another dissolving the attacks so that Ma could not reach him. Ma began to realize that this guest was a formidable opponent, and his anger flared. He used all of his skills, pouncing left and crashing right, but still had difficulty striking true. In his heart he knew there was something different about this person, but it did not dawn on him, and he became more exasperated. He pulled a broadsword from the wall and began hacking and stabbing at the guest, but the guest's attitude was composed and his bearing calm. With one hand holding his robes and one hand waiving his fan, he did not have the slightest appearance of nervousness or urgency, advancing and retreating and handling himself skillfully, methodically turning and evading. Although Ma was wielding a broadsword, he was still not able to harm his guest. Ma became even more resolute, driving the guest into a corner, lifting his sword to chop horizontally at his neck. Then, his body as quick as a monkey, like a flash, the stranger spun behind Ma's back, using his fan to lightly sweep the back of Ma's neck. In warning, he said, "Your Baguazhang should be trained again more diligently for us to again have a competition." Finished speaking, he had already floated out the door. Ma chased after to ask his name, and the guest turned back and replied, "a school brother."

Several days later, Ma again met this person, and not knowing the error of his ways, again crossed hands with him. This person, seeing that Ma was still the same as before and did not know how to repent, after three exchanges struck Ma lightly on the right ribs and then, without saying a word, turned and left. After this departure, no one ever saw this person again. Ma endured this palm strike, and did not even see any injury, but on the second day he felt unbearable pain under his right rib and found a green and purple palm print. His school brothers knew the one who came to compare arts was not an average person, and they reported this to Dong Haichuan.

At the time Dong was already advanced in years. Riding a cart to Ma's residence, he used his hand to feel the injury and cried over it, saying: "This must be the work of Sha Hui, but it is also something you brought on yourself. When I was at the royal mansion, I accepted Sha Hui as my disciple. He is a Muslim who fervently esteems righteousness and delights in avenging injustices between people. People call him "Just Rewards Sha." His skill level is rather deep, and your level of martial skill is no match for his. At the time, he bowed to me as his master, and I had no alternative but to accept him." Dong then comforted him with a few sentences, wiped his tears, and left. A few days afterward, Ma died, at the age of only twenty-nine. Hearing of someone like Ma Weiqi, who possessed a supreme skill but was not long-lived, causes one to lament, and also provides a warning to those who do not emphasize martial virtue but only rely on their power to bully others, loving only bravery, fighting, and ruthlessness.

"Wood Ma": Ma Gui

Ma Gui was from Beijing. He bowed to Dong Haichuan as his master and later furthered his studies with Cheng Tinghua (of Master Dong's disciples, many were taught by Cheng on his behalf). Ma was also one of Baguazhang's famous exponents, and excelled in point striking. Owing to his dealing in wood implements in his early years, people called him "Wood Ma."

During the Guangxu period (1875–1908) of the Qing Dynasty, Ma served as a mansion guard in the residence of Prince Su, and not a few skilled fighters were defeated by Ma's palms. After the 1911 Xinhai Revolution, he was still loyal to the Qing court, and swore an oath never to have a second allegiance. In the eighth year of the republic (1919), a group of friends derided his adherence to his righteous cause, saying that foolish loyalty to this old system was the action of a child: "How could a real man be like this?" They arranged for Ma to take a position as martial arts drillmaster at the Beijing military police academy. At the same time, Su Dajun, who later held the position of captain of the Jiangsu Province military police, was studying at the academy. He saw that although Ma was already advanced in years and white-haired, his gait was spry and light. He arranged for all the students to pretend to welcome Ma, but the students then surrounded him, saying, "Teacher, please transmit the secrets of studying martial arts to us; otherwise we'll have to apply force." Saying this, more than ten people, holding bamboo swords and wooden spears, surrounded him and began hacking and thrusting. Ma was also wielding a bamboo sword, and he fended off the group. They encircled and attacked many times, but not a single weapon touched Ma's clothes or shoes. The students ceased their attacks and applauded. Ma stroked his beard, saying with a laugh, "Your skills are still superficial; how could you hit me?"

Just then, in the courtyard they suddenly heard the noise of people's voices, and saw a coal-supply clerk and one of the school's kitchen laborers quarreling. The clerk was holding a carrying pole in his hands and chasing the kitchen laborer, using the pole to strike fiercely at his head. Ma advanced forward with a bound and used two fingers to swiftly poke beneath the clerk's ribs. The clerk raised the pole up high but did not bring it down, then fell to the ground, not breathing. The students looking on were all extremely terrified, fearing he'd been accidentally killed. Laughing, Ma said, "None of you worry. He's not dead; he's just had the wind knocked out of him." Saying this, he reached out and pulled on the clerk's arm, massaging with light waving and rotation, and the clerk came to. He then handed him some medicine and ordered him to take it immediately. Based on this, people began to realize that Ma was not merely skilled in Baguazhang but was also versed in point-striking skill. But he did not use it lightly, and not unless the situation was critical.

"Heavenly Brave": Zhang Zhankui

Zhang Zhankui, courtesy name Zhaodong, was from Hejian City. He first studied Shaolin Hua Boxing and later followed Xingyiquan Master Liu

Qilan in studying this art. He also followed Dong Haichuan in the study of Baguazhang and was the creator of Xingyi Baguazhang. His name was known far and wide.

After his skills were complete, Zhang held a position in the Tianjin port Military Affairs Department. His record of apprehending thieves and criminals was exemplary, and people called him "Heavenly Brave." At the time there was a person named Ma-something, a vicious criminal and thief in Tianjin whose rapes and robberies were numerous. He had assembled several hundred criminals, thieves, and bandits, and they wreaked chaos throughout Renqiu and Xiong counties, daring to rob and rape in broad daylight; the people could get no peace. They were attacked and scattered by the national army, but Ma and a person named Cao-something escaped. The local authorities feared he would continue to trouble them, and they issued strict orders to the Tianjin magistrate, Yang Yide, to urge the Military Affairs Department to apprehend him. Zhang Zhankui received the orders and went to investigate. Learning that Ma and Cao had fled to Shanhai Pass, Zhang immediately took several men with him to the pass by night to take Ma in. After searching for several days, he encountered the thief Ma. He saw the two, Ma and Cao, disguised as peasants but armed with hidden pistols, resting by the side of the road. Zhang leaped toward Ma to seize him, and Ma immediately pulled out his gun and fired at Zhang. As the bullet was being fired, Zhang's palm had already reached Ma's ribs, and Ma fell to the ground, his bullet flying up in the air. Zhang then easily tied him up. At the same time, the men accompanying Zhang apprehended Cao, and they escorted the two to Tianjin, where they were executed.

In 1933, Zhang Zhankui, who was already seventy years old that year, was in attendance at the grand assembly of the Hebei Province all-military martial arts invitational tournament, and he performed Xingyi Baguazhang. Zhang took many disciples; famous practitioners like Han Muxia and Jiang Rongjiao were some of his most accomplished.

"Bodyguard Master": Li Cunyi

Li Cunyi, courtesy name Zhongyuan, was from Shen County in Hebei Province. In his youth he bowed to Liu Qilan as his master, and later became an expert in Xingyiquan. He also followed Dong Haichuan in studying Baguazhang, and his skills greatly surpassed many of his generation, his name becoming known at home and abroad. In the *jiawu* year [1894], he served as the martial arts instructor in the army of Liu Kunyi, and later was promoted to the position of company officer in the Governor-General's army of Jiangnan and Jiangxi provinces. However, because he was indifferent about an official career, he resigned not long after, and in Baoding County established the Wantong Bodyguard Bureau. Because of this, people called him "Bodyguard Master." As Li was friendly and a famous person in the world of martial arts, he often accepted students and gave performances. He was an expert in the weapons of all styles, and especially skilled in single broadsword. Wielding a single broadsword when participating in the Boxer Rebellion (1899–1901) and battling fiercely with the foreigners at the Tianjin Laolongtou Railway Station, his bravery was without compare, and thus he also attained the nickname "Single-Broadsword Li." At the beginning of the Republican era, he was elected director of educational administration of the Chinese Martial Artists Association. According to accounts, Li took fellow practitioners with him to Beijing, where he defeated a world-famous strongman, and at the time was rewarded by the government with a medal of top-quality gold. His disciples were numerous, including Shang Yunxiang, nicknamed the "Iron-Foot Buddha," who was one of his brilliant pupils. In studying Xingyiquan, Gao Yisheng received Li Cunyi's personal guidance and instruction.

"Superior Palm": Zhou Yuxiang

Zhou Yuxiang was from Wuqing County. By nature he was straightforward, and he was courageous and skilled in fighting. One night when he was eighteen, thieves were burglarizing his neighbor. Zhou heard this, was startled awake, and grabbed a broadsword to drive them out. Going straight into his neighbor's house, he injured two thieves with his sword. The owner, deeply appreciative of this lifesaving kindness, said, "In Beijing there is a famous Baguazhang master, Cheng Tinghua, known throughout the four directions. If you want to excel in the martial way, you could seek him out; I could serve as your introducer and support you with grain and money. How does that sound?" Zhou heard this and was greatly pleased, immediately following his neighbor to Beijing and inserting himself in Master Cheng's school. After Zhou's skills were complete, he became one of the famous third-generation Baguazhang practitioners. Because his strength was great and he was skilled in using Baguazhang's Opening Palm to defeat others, he had the nickname "Superior Palm."

One day, Zhou went out to visit friends, and on the way passed a military training camp. At the time, a general at the camp, Duke-something, and several of his sons all loved fighting, and they specially invited a famous master from He'nan to teach them. Zhou saw the teacher had set up a stage to gather martial artists to compare skills. With a leap he alighted to the stage and tested arts with the master. Just then, all the Duke's sons were present, and saw with their own eyes as Zhou—with coiling Baguazhang steps like a tornado creating wind under his feet— repeatedly defeated the master. The sons blurted out, "You're truly our master," and then asked his name and invited him to stay in the camp, treating him generously and with honor. That He'nan coach left without a word, and all the sons honored Zhou as their master. Zhou stayed for a time in this important camp, transmitting his arts. One of the local martial artists heard of this and came to visit. When he crossed arms with Zhou inside his room, he put on airs to compete, but after not even three exchanges was knocked back onto the ground more than ten feet away by Zhou's Opening Palm. After this, Zhou's reputation was greatly increased.

In his later years, Zhou established his own Zhou Yuxiang Bagua Association in Tianjin, publicly accepting students and transmitting his art.

"Monkey" Sun Fuquan

Sun Fuquan, courtesy name Lutang, was from Wan County in Baoding Prefecture. He first bowed to master Li Kuiyuan, and later followed Guo Yunshen, Cheng Tinghua, and Hao Weizhen in studying their arts. He was skilled in the three internal arts of Xingyi, Bagua, and Taiji, and was one of the best-trained disciples of Cheng Tinghua. His hands and body were nimble, and people called him "Monkey." He became famous both at home and abroad. It is said he had the ability to make his body disappear as if into the paintings on the wall.

In 1918, seven years after the Xinhai Revolution, he entered the presidential palace in the post of guard captain aide-de-camp as night patrolman at Chengxuan Temple, and later in Shanxi he held the position of major in the national army.

In Fengrun County at the end of the Qing Dynasty, there was a famous martial arts master and fellow practitioner, both tall and strong, whom people called "Martial Eccentric." He was not convinced of Sun Lutang's skill and sought him out to have a contest. The two met, and Sun, noticing that his body was tall and sturdy and his manner extraordinary, invited him into his room. Martial Eccentric said, "I admire the gentleman's valiant and unsurpassed skill, and have come here especially to compare with you and ask for advice." Sun replied, "This is the first time we two have met; we do not need to compare arts. I'll sit here on this chair, allowing the gentleman to attack. If I am struck, then I am willing to admit I am beneath you, and respect you as my master." He said this as he sat calmly on the chair. Martial Eccentric immediately rushed fiercely at Sun. As Martial Eccentric lifted his right hand, Sun used Baguazhang's Escape and Become a Shadow, pulling himself along Martial Eccentric's right ribs and spinning to face his back. As he turned his body, Sun gave a single push, and the chair toppled as Martial Eccentric fell, knocking out his two front teeth. On the spot Martial Eccentric admitted defeat and begged to be recorded under Sun's school, but Sun said, "impossible." Following this, the two became extremely close friends.

While he was supported by a patron, he once defeated a Russian strongman in combat, and in Nanjing subdued several Japanese martial artists. These achievements were always praised by martial arts enthusiasts both in China and abroad. In his later years, Sun concentrated his efforts on Chinese martial arts undertakings. In 1928 he took the position of vice director and head of instruction at the Jiangsu Guoshu Academy. The same year, he served as chief judge at the National Martial Arts Competition. He later created Sun-Style Boxing and spread it to the world.

Famous Hebei Practitioner Li Wenbiao

Li Wenbiao, courtesy name Guangfu, was from Hebei Province. He bowed to Cheng Tingua as his master in studying Baguazhang, and he excelled in the art of straight sword. When Li Wenbiao and his elder school brother Sun Lutang were visiting Fengtian,[4] they heard of a Daoist in the vicinity who told fortunes and who often said loudly to others: "None of these northeasterners know martial arts. Now, some may strike poses to frighten others, but their sword forms, with flowery fists and embroidered legs, are not worth mentioning." This Daoist, named Li Fengjiu, had originally been a bandit and killed countless people. After giving up evil and reforming himself, he came down from the mountains, telling fortunes and teaching martial arts for a living. Although the martial arts masters in Fengtian were numerous, none of them were a match for him, and thus every day while he sold fortunes, he spread this self-important talk. One day, by himself, Li Wenbiao sought out and paid a visit to this Daoist. When he reached the place where he told fortunes, Li confidently addressed the Daoist, saying, "I have come specially to pay a visit to Fengtian's first hand without peer, to decide winner and loser." The Daoist replied coldly, "Now, now, boy. Your tongue runs rampant. Speaking carelessly and desiring to duel, I understand you don't know what type of person this poor Daoist is." Li replied, "Of all the outstanding talents I've met from all four directions, I've never heard one talk as big as your boasting." The Daoist calmly replied, "This is not a place to use martial arts. Tomorrow at dawn at the Buddhist temple, await my instruction. Do you dare to keep that appointment?" Li replied, "I will be there, as the gentleman says. One who didn't keep the appointment would not be a real man, and would be like a little maiden."

When Li returned to his residence and informed Sun Lutang, Sun said, "Young brother has forgotten his teachings. We are travelers in foreign environs and should be modest and cautious, not rashly inviting dishonor. When discussing martial things with monks and priests, women and the elderly, beggars and children, one should take special care, as they will certainly have their own specialty, and should not be offended lightly." Li asked, "So now what can be done?" Sun replied, "As the situation has already come to this point, tomorrow I'll accompany you to observe things." The next day, the two went to the Buddhist temple, and saw the Daoist practicing his arts. Sun watched for a moment, already saw his opportunity, and hinted to Li, "Younger brother can start first." Following this, they walked in and met the Daoist. Li crossed arms with him, and the Daoist said, "after you." Before his words had settled, Li struck with a vicious palm. The Daoist could not block it, but could only follow and respond. Li closely followed with a second strike, sending the Daoist sprawling, falling to the ground more than three feet away. The Daoist got up and addressed Li, saying, "This poor Daoist's hand techniques don't measure up; I wonder what the master's sword skills are like?" Li replied, "Please instruct me." The two then each grabbed wooden swords and began fighting. They went back and forth several times, and then the Daoist was struck by Li with a pierce to the mid-ribs. Luckily this was with a wooden sword on padded cotton clothing; otherwise the Daoist would have been laid to rest. Immediately the Daoist felt the pain, dropped his sword, and clapped his hands together, saying, "From now it won't be me who boasts of martial skill in the northeast." He then bought wine for Li, and their talk again turned friendly. From that time onward, after the Daoist was defeated at the hands of Li, although he set up and sold fortunes every day as usual, his only prohibition was that he did not talk about martial arts. Li also became famous after this, and people from the northeast called him the "Famous Master from Hebei" Li Wenbiao.

Gao Yisheng and Liu Fengcai: Double Rattan Sticks and Night-Fighting Saber

Gao Yisheng became famous for creating the Cheng School Gao Style Baguazhang system. Liu Fengcai built his good name by inheriting and passing on Cheng School Gao Style Baguazhang and by establishing its academic standing. Master Gao and his disciple Liu are both famous practitioners of Baguazhang, and not only are their achievements within Baguazhang profound, they have also chosen broadly from the best of other arts. Viewing the outstanding arts of other schools as treasures, they have wholeheartedly inherited and passed them on, as can be understood through the little-known stories of inheriting and passing on Double Rattan Sticks and Night-Fighting Saber.

For nine years starting roughly in fall 1925, Gao Yisheng, already past age sixty and with a long beard, traveled regularly to his hometown in Shandong to transmit his art. Usually every year after fall he arrived in Shandong, and the next year before the wheat harvest he returned to Wuqing. Because Gao and Liu were close relatives, every time Gao returned to Shandong, he lived in Liu's house. During these periods, Gao Yisheng would teach Liu Fengcai and also travel to the surrounding villages teaching Baguazhang.

The last time Gao Yisheng transmitted his art in his hometown in Shandong was from approximately fall 1933 until before the wheat harvest in 1934. Every night after finishing training, Master Gao and his disciple Liu would sit on the brick *kang* sleeping platform underneath an oil lamp, drinking tea and talking a while before going to sleep. One night just before Gao Yisheng was to leave to return to Wuqing, as they were near sleep, Gao Yisheng said to Liu Fengcai, "I figure that I've been teaching you for nine years, and your art already has some accomplishment, so this time when I go back, I don't plan to return again." Liu said,

"What? You won't come at the end of this fall?" Gao replied, "I'm almost seventy. First, our family is too far from Wuqing, and transportation isn't convenient. Second, when I came here this time, I passed through the southern part of Tianjin and met a friend [this was Sun Zhenshan] who invited me to come to Tianjin to set up a space and transmit my art. I've already agreed to do so." Liu asked, "With you leaving and not coming back again, do you think I've studied everything?" Gao replied, "Your Baguazhang art is complete. You could say that in Shandong, you've studied the most completely, and you've trained it the most fluently. This is what I'm most pleased with." Liu then asked, "Are there still any other good arts that I haven't studied?" At this, Gao Yisheng stroked his long beard as if in thought, and was quiet for a while before saying, "I also have four sets of Double Rattan Sticks that are excellent, and very practical. They're my personal favorite, but they are not from the Baguazhang school. Not studying them is fine too." Liu said, "How is that fine? If the Double Rattan Sticks are good, of course you should teach them to me." Gao said, "It's not that I won't teach you. I don't believe in the idea that 'producing a good disciple will starve the teacher.' But first, Double Rattan Sticks are not from the Bagua school; there's no blame in learning them or not learning them. Second, in the world of itinerant teachers, it is the fashion that when teaching disciples, you always withhold a little something special. This is because today many people who become disciples, if they learn everything from their master, don't think about their teacher and will slowly forget them. This time, after we part, I don't know if we will see each other again. If I hold back these four sets of Double Rattan Sticks without teaching them to you, you'll always think of me." By the time he had got to this point, tears were rolling down Gao Yisheng's face, as he was rather moved by the emotions of saying farewell. Seeing this, Liu Fengcai was a bit worried, and quickly said, "What are you saying? You're my elder relative, and my beloved master. After this many years, are you still unsure about my behavior? As long as I'm alive, wherever you go, I won't forget you. What connection does this have with whether or not you teach me Double Rattan Sticks?" Gao wiped his eyes and said, "I was only talking; don't be worried. It's too late tonight. Sleep first, and we'll talk about it again tomorrow."

The next day, through Liu Fengcai's constant and repeated pleading, Gao Yisheng could not help but delay his date of departure to Wuqing, and he finally transmitted his Double Rattan Sticks to Liu Fengcai. Double Rattan Sticks are paired weapons that belong to the Shaolin arts, and they are the special weapon of the Purple Hammer School. Gao Yisheng obtained them by exchanging arts with a friend. One may use double straight swords, double broadswords, double whips, or double maces to practice with, although thick rattan sticks filled with steel are the superior instrument. They can also be made of white wax wood. Their length varies according to the individual, but generally are about twenty-one to twenty-four inches long.

The postures of Double Rattan Sticks are unique, simple, and without embellishment. In usage, the force is like scissors, one blocking and one attacking, both defense and attack arriving together, striking like beating a drum. They are excellent against a long spear, as the attack and defense are nimble and extremely practical. The entire form is divided into four sets or sections.

After not even a few days' time, Liu Fengcai had learned Gao Yisheng's special skill—Double Rattan Sticks. Through Gao Yisheng's meticulous instruction, and being fed attacks move by move, Liu Fengcai not only studied the form but grasped its practical methods. According to the recollection of Liu Fengcai's wife: "Back then, the two of them practiced Double Rattan Sticks in the skylight [courtyard]. One of them held two short sorghum stalks in their hands, and the other held a long sorghum stalk. They struck them together with a cracking sound until the whole courtyard was section upon section of broken sorghum. Every time after they finished training, I always had to clean up for a while."

In Shandong, Gao Yisheng taught the Double Rattan Sticks only to Liu Fengcai. Later, when Gao Yisheng established a space in Tianjin, he mostly used the name "Double Maces" to pass on this form, adopting the name Golden Jade Linking Maces and also Bagua Double Maces.

However, the number of practitioners who obtained this art could be counted on one hand.

After receiving instruction in Double Rattan Sticks, Liu was extremely happy and said to Gao: "In these two days studying and refining, I've learned Double Rattan Sticks, but the 'good arts' under heaven are numerous, and they can never all be learned completely." Gao replied, "Thus the saying 'the arts have no boundaries.'" Liu then said, "You want to go to Tianjin to transmit your art. These two days I've been constantly discussing this with the family. The last few years have not been good ones, and our family life is not like in the past. After you leave, maybe in as long as a year or as little as six months, I also plan to move to Tianjin and strive to find an occupation. I can also easily continue to study with you more deeply." Hearing these words, Gao Yisheng was unusually happy, and said: "That's great! I'll go to Tianjin and wait for you." Suddenly Gao looked as if he'd remembered something and said: "But before you go to Tianjin, you must think of a plan to go pay a visit to a man and learn his family-taught supreme skill, Night-Fighting Saber." Liu asked excitedly, "Who is this person? What's Night-Fighting Saber?" Gao said, "It's a long story, but it has to start from when I lost in short weapons." Liu replied, "I've never heard that you lost in an exchange." Gao answered, "Talking about crossing hands, since fighting the first time I returned to Shandong over a decade ago, until now I still haven't lost a match. But in regard to short weapons, I actually lost two times." Liu asked, "When? And how did you lose?" Gao said, "That was something from the early days. Have you heard of someone they call the 'Tiger of the Dashan Streets'?" Liu replied, "I know him. His name is Ma Yuanbiao. He's an old practitioner, about your age. I've heard this old man's conduct isn't bad. What happened? Did you fight with him?"

Gao replied, "Yes. This man is an old itinerant teacher. Over a decade ago, when I first came here and set up a place to transmit my art in Shandong, he came calling to test hands with me. He was hit by my palm and tumbled several steps, then fell to the ground. Because I didn't use full power, it didn't injure him, and he was very grateful that I showed some mercy. He picked himself up, saying 'Good skill, good skill,' and then saluted and left, and I didn't see him again for a long time. After the first few years, I saw him at the Dashan market. Meeting him, he was very polite, and he invited me to come to his house to chat. Arriving at his house, we sat on the edge of the kang and chatted about old times. We talked and talked, and finally hand techniques came up, and then we were talking with demonstrations. At last, he said to me, 'Talking about Baguazhang hand techniques, it looks like in these parts there's really no one who can best you, but I don't know how you are with short weapons?' I said, 'I've trained in Bagua Broadsword and Bagua Straight Sword, but with weapons, it's easy to injure someone, so I seldom test these with anyone.' He smiled and said, 'Come, come, come; let's test our short weapons, just stopping when we make contact. We definitely won't injure anyone.' Saying this, he took in his right hand an old-style long-stemmed pipe, at least fifteen inches long, and laid on his left side, head toward the middle of the kang, his left hand propping up his head, his eyes looking at me. His left leg extended straight and hung over the edge of the kang, his right leg bent and resting on his left, his right hand grasping the mouth of the pipe, resting level on his right thigh. The bowl of the pipe faced downward near the bed mat, and the shaft lay across his waist. Striking this kind of pose and laughing, he said to me, 'This pipe will be my broadsword, and the pipe bowl will be my sword tip. You go ahead and grab something.' As he instructed, I stood up, and from the top of the wardrobe picked up a duster, my right hand holding the feathers as if it were a broadsword. He said: 'OK, I'll just lie here. You move first.' Holding the duster in my hand, I sized him up, and thought that his right buttock was open, so I extended my arm and poked straight at him with the duster handle. I had just moved, and the duster had not got near him when I saw his right wrist lightly lift upward and the pipe bowl had already struck my wrist. Although he didn't use much power, the pipe bowl was a brass bulb, and beating it on the bones of the wrist was shocking. His body had not moved, and the pipe had returned to its original position when he said, 'Try again.' I saw that nothing near me was open, so I lifted the duster and cut down at an angle toward his upper body. The duster in my hand had just started to come down, and again I saw his right wrist just turn over, and the pipe head cut exactly into my right wrist. These two losses at the end of a pipe bowl left me speechless. He lifted his body and sat up, laughing loudly. This incident happened many years ago, but even today when I think of it, it's like it was yesterday. And it's not that I bear a grudge for him beating me twice with a pipe; it's just that those two moves were simply too miraculous. I lost, but I don't know how I lost."

Liu asked excitedly, "Those moves were Night-Fighting Saber?" Gao replied, "At the time, I asked him where those moves came from. He said these were the 'secret postures' of Night-Fighting Saber that in earlier times were given to the Wang family in Yangxin [County] by a certain person called the 'Great River Thief' and only taught within the Wang family for four generations. The fourth-generation inheritor was named Wang Maolin, and he said that Wang Maolin only passed on a few 'secret postures' to him." Liu then asked, "Where is Wang Maolin today?" Gao replied, "I don't know the specifics of Wang Maolin's location or circumstances. Ever since taking those two raps to the wrist, I've always thought about seeking out the Night-Fighting Saber, but because I'm older and can't go off rashly to pay a visit, I've never run into the opportunity. Just now hearing that you're planning to go to Tianjin, I thought about this matter. You must think of a way to find Wang Maolin and learn this Night-Fighting Saber. Then come to Tianjin and find me." Liu immediately replied, "All right. I've got it." Gao continued, "Speaking objectively, our family's sixty-four palm methods are plenty. Whether or not you can beat someone, well, that depends on your skill. But in terms of weapons, those of the Bagua school are not as good as other schools; there is really nothing miraculous or exquisite about them. Arts like the Double Rattan Sticks and Night-Fighting Saber are the highest caliber of martial arts, and are truly superior arts. We should study them for use in our school, in order to enrich our Baguazhang weapons." Liu replied, "OK. After I seek out Night-Fighting Saber, I'll go to Tianjin and find you."

After Gao Yisheng left Shandong, through various careful inquiries, it was not long until Liu Fengcai knew Wang Maolin's whereabouts and story. Wang Maolin's ancestral home was just outside the city walls of Yangxin County. Yangxin and Wudi, at the time called Haifeng, were neighboring counties, with the two county seats separated by some six miles. The Wang family was a well-known and important wealthy family in that area. Some time ago, Wang Maolin's ancestor had spent a great fortune to save the Great River Thief, who was jailed and set to be executed by the government. The Night-Fighting Saber was passed on by this great thief. After uncovering the ins and outs of this story, it was truly worthy to be called the legendary tale of Night-Fighting Saber.

After the Qing Dynasty unification of the country, Shandong Province was divided into six prefectures, fifteen cantons, and ninety counties under concurrent jurisdiction. Of these, Ji'nan Prefecture had jurisdiction over four cantons and twenty counties. The four cantons were Wuding, Taian, De, and Bin. Wuding was in the northeast of Shandong Province, bounded on the east by the Bohai Sea and on the north sharing a border with Hebei Province. Within Wuding Canton there were four counties: Haifeng (now Wudi County), Yangxin, Leling, and Shanghe. During the Xianfeng period (1850–1861), the four counties in Wuding Canton experienced great drought, and the people could not make a living, the days wearing on like years. Adding to this, various harsh and excessive taxes—which had become as numerous as the hairs on a cow—levied by all levels of government during the decline of the Qing Dynasty, along with corrupt officials running wild, meant that people's lives had become miserable beyond words. This forced the peasants to take up arms and rise up en masse, killing the wealthy and aiding the destitute as a means to fight back against the officials. The peasant army of the famous Nien Rebellion was suppressed by the Qing Court in Shandong, its entire army being annihilated in Chiping County. But its commander, Zhang Zongyu, and several dozen bodyguards crossed north of the Tuhai River and entered Wuding and De cantons, scattering into the populace, and no one knew their fate.

Not long after the defeat of the Nien Rebellion, there appeared within the boundaries of Wuding Canton the Great River Thief. This person hid by day and went out by night, specifically robbing local official treasuries, and he was successful time and time again. None of the four counties within Wuding Canton were lucky enough to be spared, and in Haifeng and Yangxin counties, the losses of treasury silver were especially serious. When the Ji'nan prefectural office received report of this, they issued urgent orders for the canton and county officials to solve the case within a fixed time. Wuding Canton and each county sent out detectives to hunt down and apprehend the culprit. But this thief's martial skill was formidable. He could scale heights at will, coming and going from government offices like walking into empty buildings, stealing silver like casually picking up household items with two fingers. Once, a group of detectives encountered the thief and crossed hands with him, and although the thief carried heavy silver on his back, he faced the group without appearing frightened. This thief was skilled in using a willow-leaf broadsword, and his sword skill was miraculous. Fast like lightning, once he raised his hands, in only a few moves and a couple of postures, he had injured his opponent's wrist. Many detectives had their wrists injured, but though the injuries were sometimes serious and sometime light, there was never a mortal injury. After a while, the detectives were afraid to cross hands with the thief, and just surrounded him but didn't capture him, since none dared to rush forward, until eventually, if they found even a trace of the thief, they would cry out in fear and run. This problem grew bigger as each county, one after another, reported the theft of official silver, and it quickly alarmed the royal court.

At the time, the Qing Dynasty was almost exhausted, encountering troubles both internally and externally, with numerous internal factions, no competent officials, and only a very few who were honest. Because of this, at first the Xiangfeng emperor suspected that corrupt officials and guards were embezzling the silver, and sent officials to investigate, without results. Later he blamed the incompetence of all the Ji'nan Prefecture canton and county officials in breaking the case, and took advantage of this to dismiss several of the officials from their offices, but none of this had any effect on the matter. In the four counties of Wuding, the treasury silver was still being stolen in the same manner, and there was no way to prevent it. In order to break this case, Beijing sent out a large group of hired thugs, along with a few specialists from the royal palace, to work with the locals in arresting this "great thief." In the end, because a fierce tiger is no match for a pack of wolves, this thief was trapped at the Yangxin County public office and sent to jail. Through harsh torture to extract a confession, they finally learned that this great thief was in fact a bodyguard for the commander of the Nien Rebellion Army, Zhang Zongyu. After this peasant army had been defeated, the survivors scattered into the populace. Only this great thief, relying on his extraordinary martial skills, had robbed the government treasuries, raising funds in preparation for again rising up against the Qing Dynasty. It is said that officials at the time searched a certain temple in the Haifeng County seat and found this great thief's hiding place, and in the top level of the Haidi Pagoda discovered a great quantity of silver. At this stage, the case of the government silver being stolen was cracked, and the great thief was thrown into Yangxin County's death row, awaiting review for immediate execution.

At the time, Wang Maolin's ancestor was close friends with the magistrate of Yangxin County, and early on had heard about the case of the stolen government silver. Hearing now that the great thief had been captured and was being held in the Yangxin County public office, it was easy enough to make inquiries and conduct research. The magistrate recounted to him accurately that the thief was age thirty-five or thirty-six, of average height, had great skills with which he could leap buildings and jump ridge-beams as if they were level ground, and was expert in wielding a single willow-leaf broadsword. Strangely, in crossing hands with others, he specialized in injuring the wrist, and consistently never caused life-threatening injuries or wounded vital areas of his opponents. Even when he encountered and was attacked by several martial experts from the royal court, he faced the group without appearing frightened, and several times had slipped away in those circumstances. Not only did he injure the wrists of many of the county and canton detectives; he also injured one of the experts from the royal court, Huang Magua. In the end it was a plan involving many people that lured him to the county offices where they used a large net to trap him, and unable to move, he was captured. This person's sense of honor was strong. Not only did he not give away any of his comrade's names, he would not even write one stroke of his own name or place of origin, only asking with resolute will for a quick death. This person in fact was an expert in the martial world at the time, and this situation was indeed a pity. After a long chat with him, the magistrate developed great admiration, sympathy, and pity toward him.

When these sentiments were spoken by the magistrate, though the speaker had no intentions, the listener began to have ideas. Lord Wang immediately began asking tactfully whether or not he could meet this great thief. The magistrate gave it a little thought, and said that this matter was not as simple as a smaller case. Although the thief was locked up in his county jail, he was guarded by those at both the county and the canton level, and they would have to look for the right opportunity, but he agreed to try his best to arrange a visit.

Several days later, Lord Wang went again to the county offices, carrying large gifts. The magistrate accepted the range of gifts gladly and, bribing those above and below him, arranged for Lord Wang to meet with the thief. In this dark and fetid death-row jail, Lord Wang saw the thief, with disheveled hair, a filthy face, and injuries covering his whole body, lying on the floor with his eyes tightly shut, looking subhuman. Lord Wang was not only a wealthy landowner but had studied his family-taught martial arts, and he was famous as a boxer in that region. Seeing this situation— and admiring someone of talent with the same interests—in his heart he began to develop the intention to save this thief.

Lord Wang returned home and pleaded with his family to sell five acres of good land and, cleaning out the family riches, exchanged this for ten bars of gold, which he sent to the county office, conspiring with the magistrate in a plan to save the life of the great thief. In the end the two agreed that the Yangxin County magistrate would go out in person and bribe those above and below him while beforehand they planted a fake, finding another prisoner sentenced to death who looked like the great thief, who could replace him at the execution, using deception to handle the royal court. Owing to the fact that the treasury silver that had been stolen had been recovered, that they actually killed a replacement great thief, and that most people, including the officials and detectives, had never seen the great thief's face by the light of day, it was difficult for anyone to tell real from false. Moreover, since the Yangxin magistrate had bribed everyone around him and bought off all of the key players, with officials and detectives at the prefectural, canton, and county levels all receiving hush money, keeping their mouths shut and the truth concealed, the case was closed at every level, and the royal court never investigated the matter further.

Lord Wang took the thief back to his house and secretly arranged to have him live in the back courtyard of the Wang residence in order to treat his wounds. It took more than three months, but the great thief finally completely recovered. During idle conversations, Lord Wang asked him his name, where he came from, and the origins of the sword art that he studied. The thief muttered to himself a bit, then suddenly said, "I'm someone who fell into distress, and I'm shy in speaking; I don't dare give my name, and much less dare to presume to talk of my lineage." Lord Wang replied, "When I saved you, I swore to the county magistrate that you would never show your face in these parts again. Once your wounds have healed well, you must leave this place far behind. But I don't know if you have anywhere to go?" The thief replied, "Lord, do not worry, I will definitely leave this place. But for the grace of my saved life, I must thank you deeply." In order to repay the great kindness of sparing his life, the thief then passed on to Wang Maolin's ancestor the twelve sets of Night-Fighting Saber skills, and sent to the Wang family several tens of thousands of taels of silver. After this he departed without a word. It was only known that he was once part of the Nien Rebellion Army, but in the end he did not give his name, and it was not known where he went.

This sword skill was taught only within the Wang family continuously until the fourth generation, which was Wang Maolin. By the time he was about twelve, Wang Maolin was already famous far and wide, and he used the Night-Fighting Saber methods to defeat countless skilled practitioners in the martial arts world. At a martial arts contest organized by Han Fuju in Ji'nan, Shandong, he was awarded the honorary title "Single Broad-sword King." Wang Maolin used his expertise in Night-Fighting Saber skills to make his name, and the story of him destroying his family was also because of the Night-Fighting Saber; this caused Liu Fengcai much regret time and again, and he sighed whenever he thought of it.

After that martial arts contest in Ji'nan, many of the local martial arts masters coveted this Night-Fighting Saber skill, and persuaded Wang to reside there and transmit his art. At that time, Wang only taught six sets of sword skills, and because of this he gained more than a little wealth. The Wang family originally possessed wealth, and now it had even greater wealth. Unable to resist the pull of sensual pleasures, he began a life of luxury and debauchery, in the end getting caught up in the evil addictions of smoking opium, snorting heroin, and shooting morphine. Committing these errors became a life-long regret, as his personal wealth disappeared. Later, he returned to Yangxin, and even his ancestral property had been sold off completely. His declining family became poverty-stricken and down on their luck. During these years he often went around the vicinity of Dashan, living off of relatives and friends, or doing odd jobs to make a living, like working for others delivering fried bread, or going to the market and selling tobacco.

The first time that Liu Fengcai met Wang Maolin was west of Dashan, in Dingwang Village, about six miles north of the Liu Family Yellow Dragon Bay Village. Gao Yisheng had formerly established places to teach Baguazhang in all the villages surrounding Dashan Township. Dashan, Dazhuangzi, Qiujiazhuang, Damatou, Posongjia, Nanchencun, and Dingwangzhuang all had places where Gao Yisheng taught. After Gao Yisheng left, Liu Fengcai continued to teach in all these places on his behalf. During the busy farming seasons, Liu Fengcai remained at home and attended to farming. During the slower seasons, he traveled the circuit of these training places. That day, Liu Fengcai had come to

Dingwangzhuang, and while training, he again brought up the matter of searching for Wang Maolin. He did not expect that right then one of his students would recognize the name, saying, "Right now Wang Maolin is living at a relative's house in Dingwangzhuang. Every day he goes to market outside the village to sell tobacco." Hearing these words, Liu Fengcai was happy beyond expectation.

Coming to the place where Wang Maolin resided, the two met. Wang Maolin had a thin tall frame and a long flat face full of unkempt whiskers, his body draped in ragged clothes. Although he said he was a little over forty, older than Liu Fengcai by fourteen years, he looked like he had aged before his time, and already showed the demeanor of someone older (the result of using drugs). It was only later when they began talking of sword skill that from time to time a gleam twinkled in his eyes. When he began performing the sword he could go into low stances as before, his movements uncommonly agile, and one could still see he had once been a master with considerable skill. After the two talked about the weather for a bit, Liu explained to Wang the reason he sought him out was that he was impressed by Wang's reputation, and had received a directive from Gao Yisheng, who entrusted within him the desire and aspiration to request instruction in Night-Fighting Saber. Because the two were both martial artists and had long been impressed with each other's reputations, they spoke quite congenially as soon as they met.

Wang Maolin said, "Ever since I hit hard times, I've sampled fully the coldness of the ways of the world, and for a long time no one has sought me out. I've regularly come to Dashan to sell in the markets for the last few years, and early on I heard about you two—master and disciple [meaning Gao and Liu]—traveling to your teaching spots around Dashan. It's just that I had no self-respect to come visit you, and no luck to run into you." Following this, Wang then related the origins of Night-Fighting Saber and the incredible story of how his ancestor learned and passed on this art, from the great thief committing his crimes and being caught and thrown in jail to his ancestor selling their lands and redeeming the thief, passing on of this supreme art, all the way until the thief returned the kindness and then left without a word. His recounting was vivid and animated, and it was a lively and complicated Night-Fighting Saber saga. Finally he talked about how he himself learned and passed on Night-Fighting Saber, how he earned his reputation at the contest in Ji'nan, and also how he mistakenly went down the wrong path, resulting in the dissipation of his family fortune. His account was full of sadness and happiness, regret and helplessness, and by the time he'd got to the most painful parts, pulling up his sleeves to reveal to Liu Fengcai the track marks left on his arms from shooting morphine, old tears were flowing freely. He said with deep emotion, "I've talked so much, not for any purpose except to warn practitioners: in no way should they emulate Wang Maolin! The Night-Fighting Saber was taught for four generations only within my family, and passing it on to me has truly brought shame to my forebears. It is also rare that you two, master and disciple, would have the wise eyes to recognize gold, continually thinking about Night-Fighting Saber, seeking me out for many days until finally, this morning, we meet. It seems like we two are people who have a destiny together. Now that I've arrived at such a state, very few people think much of me. Since the two of you think so much of me, I'll pass Night-Fighting Saber on to you, and let you pass it on to the world." With this the two made arrangements that Wang Maolin, after he managed his work affairs, would go to Liu's residence and transmit the sword form.

Three days later, in the early morning, Wang Maolin, led by Liu Fengcai's cousins Ding Yuping and Ding Erqing from Dingwangzhuang, arrived as agreed at Liu's residence in Yellow Dragon Bay. Liu met him at the edge of the village. Wang had cut his hair, shaved his face, and changed into a new jacket and pants, with much more spirit than the first time they had met. Liu Fengcai took Wang to the recently cleared-out travel lodge run by his family, attending to him and inviting him to eat breakfast. He saw off the cousins, Ding Yuping and Ding Erqing, then finally started to request instruction in sword skills from Wang Maolin in the courtyard.

Night-Fighting Saber is a twelve-section two-person form, with each section having several back-and-forth techniques. Its mysterious quality comes from the fact that its main techniques utilize turning and shaking the wrist and applying both upper and lower edges of the sword tip—cutting, pointing, shaving, intercepting, and slicing—specifically seeking the opponent's wrist. There are no flowery moves covering over the head, but rather one attack and one defense set out scientifically and meticulously. It is completely without the fraud of "double injury," with each posture and each stance clean and direct, the target of attack very clear, all extremely miraculous and practical. The footwork is often light and agile leaping, and the two players' swords are like two butterflies among the flowers—rising left and dropping right, overturning and flying above and below. When first practicing Night-Fighting Saber, one uses a wooden sword, and after becoming fluent, one may change to a steel sword to better approximate actual combat. Wang Maolin said that when his father faced off with him, he used long sorghum stalks to create a lean-to, building a V-shaped shack about head height, five feet wide, and ten feet long, and on top of the shack they sprinkled dry dirt. The two would drill in from the sides and meet. After they were fluent, when they stepped out from the shack after training, there would not be any dust on their bodies. The shack blocked the light, and one could practice the feeling of fighting at night, and it was also beneficial for practicing light and agile movements and lowered stances.

Wang Maolin resided in Liu Fengcai's house for three days, and for three days Liu did not go out. One technique at a time, one stance at a time, he learned all twelve sets of the Night-Fighting Saber two-person form. On the fourth day, Liu Fengcai escorted Wang Maolin back to Dingwangzhuang. As they were close to parting, Liu Fengcai gave Wang Maolin forty silver coins to express his thanks.

After Liu Fengcai obtained the Night-Fighting Saber, every night in the middle of the night, when everyone was quiet, he would train by himself in the courtyard, never letting anyone else watch him, and after a little more than a month he had trained it thoroughly. Although he never let it be seen by anyone, the news of Liu Fengcai obtaining this art got around fast. Because of this, it attracted a few adept practitioners who came to "test swords." Meeting someone whose sword skill was average, Liu could easily gain victory, but encountering a skilled swordsman, Liu was still no match for them. Because of this, some people started spreading the rumor that the Night-Fighting Saber form that Liu had studied was fake. Hearing this rumor, Liu became suspicious, and thought about going to see Wang Maolin again.

When the two saw each other again, Wang simply said, "I knew you would come to find me again." Liu asked, "How did you know that?" Wang said: "Don't ask me that now. First, tell me how your sword training went." Liu answered, "The form is complete, but its usage is still lacking." Wang laughed as he pulled Liu to a quiet and secluded place, saying, "Let's try it out." As he said this, he simultaneously picked up some long sorghum stalks from the top of a pile of firewood, finding two of equal length to serve as their fake swords. Holding one himself and passing one to Liu, he took a Night-Fighting Saber stance and said to Liu: "Come on!" Liu weighed the sorghum stalk in his hand and asked, "Where should I attack?" Wang replied, "Where you like. Attacking from anywhere is fine, and using any technique is fine." Liu saw an opening and leaped forward with his whole body, but just as his hand started to move, unexpectedly his wrist had already been struck by Wang's sorghum stalk. Wang took several postures in succession, and each time Liu advanced with a technique, he was struck on the wrist by Wang as soon as he moved; in the end Liu was played so thoroughly by Wang that he could not even begin an attack. Wang then said, "Let's change roles; you take a stance, and I'll attack." Liu took a Night-Fighting Saber stance like the one Wang had just used. He saw Wang crouch and advance, and just as Liu was about to change posture, barely having moved, his wrist was struck again by Wang. In this way, Liu took three postures in a row and Wang advanced with three techniques, and Liu did not win even one encounter. Liu was now a bit excited, and blurted out without thinking, "How is it I can't make one technique work? It looks like the rumors are true, and whatever you taught me is fake."

Wang Maolin put down his stalk, and laughing, said, "Don't get excited. I've heard the rumors as well, but what I taught you is definitely not fake. It's just that you only learned the two-person form, but there's still the secret postures and oral songs used specifically for combat and joining swords, which I haven't taught you." Liu quickly asked, "What are the secret postures and oral songs?" Wang said, "The requirements that explain how to cross swords in actual combat are called secret postures and oral songs. Talking about the techniques of the form, the difference between Night-Fighting Saber and other sword skills is that we specifically attack the wrist. But when talking about the practical requirements, the miraculous aspect of Night-Fighting Saber lies in its secret postures and oral songs. Just now the few stances I took were secret postures, and there are four oral songs that specifically guide crossing swords in actual combat. You look like a true practitioner with determination. From the first time we met, I felt that you and I were destined to meet. Today, I'll teach the secret postures and oral songs to you completely, in order to fulfill the destiny between us." Following this, Wang passed on to Liu the four oral songs and combined them with ten secret postures. One by one he explained how to use these four oral songs together. One by one Liu learned them. Continuing, Wang said, "There are only ten secret posture stances that were originally passed on, but in actual matches, you can extrapolate from them and change them at will, taking any posture you want. Every guarding posture in Night-Fighting Saber can be an application of the secret postures. While testing swords, the key is to carefully understand and actively utilize the four oral songs." By this time, all of Liu's doubts and suspicions had been resolved, his mind was enlightened, and he clearly understood, remembering that Ma Yuanbiao had used these secret postures to beat Gao Yisheng.

After teaching the secret postures and oral songs, Wang said to Liu, "Let's try again." As soon as the two fought, the technique was effective, as expected, and full of miracles. Liu Fengcai was unusually happy, and without pausing to think, asked, "How did you know I would come and look for you again?" Wang said, "Night-Fighting Saber was passed on solely within my family for four generations, and it was never taught outside. Only after passing it on to me did it begin to be taught to a few people outside. Some I only taught several secret postures; others I only taught several sets of sword skills, but I never passed on the complete art, and I never taught the oral songs to a single person. Once I passed on the twelve sets of sword skills to you, there were several people who came looking for me to teach sword, but I did not agree to it. Later I heard the rumors that the sword skills I passed on to you were fake, so I concluded that you would seek me out again. Today, I took all of my knowledge and understanding and gave it to you; after today, you can pass it on to the world. But you can't pass it on lightly, especially the secret postures and four oral songs; you must be selective about the people you teach. Don't squander this good art." Liu Fengcai was extremely grateful for this. He invited Wang to eat at a small roadside stand, then later sought out his relatives and friends and gathered twenty silver coins to repay Wang Maolin's kindness in mentoring him and passing on the sword. Wang was extremely apologetic, saying, "Your family is not wealthy, and from my perspective, giving me this much money is like sending coal in the middle of winter, or an umbrella in the middle of a rainstorm. It looks like your connection to Night-Fighting Saber is not a shallow one, and in your hands it won't fail to be handed down."

After obtaining the true teaching of the secret postures and oral songs, Liu Fengcai analyzed and practiced day and night until his skill was accomplished and miraculous, mastering it so that he could utilize it at will. Later, when he again tested short weapons with others, including during his several decades in Tianjin, he never lost.

One year after he had parted from Gao Yisheng, as arranged, Liu Fengcai moved to Tianjin and found Gao, becoming one of Gao's most competent assistant instructors, transmitting his art in Tianjin. After master and disciple met again, Liu recounted to Gao his experience studying Night-Fighting Saber and demonstrated its training methods and usage. Gao praised him again and again, saying, "Excellent! You've finally realized my long-standing desire. Today I finally saw the true appearance of Night-Fighting Saber. It looks like Night-Fighting Saber is even more miraculous, more practical, and more unique than Double Rattan Sticks.

It can serve as another special art within our school." Finally, he also admonished Liu, "This sword skill was not come by easily, and it can't be taught lightly; you must be selective in teaching people." Because of this, among Gao Yisheng's disciples, and even Liu Fengcai's disciples, those who knew Liu Fengcai was skilled in Night-Fighting Saber were numerous, but those who learned the Night-Fighting Saber were few, and those who received the teachings of the secret postures and oral songs were even fewer. Consequently, until today these twelve miraculous sets of martial skills that are so full of legendary flavor—Night-Fighting Saber—have still not been spread widely.

A famous saying in the martial world is "If it's not someone with whom you have destiny, don't teach them; if it's not someone with whom you have destiny, don't study with them." The two former masters Gao and Liu often said, "This art should be transmitted to those who have destiny with it." The author hopes that more people will be destined to become attached to the art of Baguazhang, and through that destiny become connected to Double Rattan Sticks and Night-Fighting Saber. The author often thinks that if we could take the miraculous tales of the Night-Fighting Saber and write a novel or make a film, it would definitely be wonderful.

CHAPTER 8

Insights of Famous and Junior Practitioners

The Baguazhang taught by Master Gao Yisheng has become its own school and style transmitted over the course of one hundred years, with many practitioners and famous exponents in each generation. They have all made contributions in establishing the scholastic position of Gao Style Baguazhang and promoting the continued transmission and development of Baguazhang. Through research, they have accumulated rich practical experience. Here I have simply organized and extracted the insights and understanding gained by direct disciples, later practitioners, and famous exponents of Master Liu Fengcai's lineage through their research and study of Baguazhang, and edited them into this volume to present to fellow practitioners and enthusiasts as a reference. As a note, almost all of them attended the First and Second International Baguazhang Friendship Meetings in Beijing in 1993 and 1995 and received medals for their performances there.

Wang Fuling, Direct Disciple of Liu Fengcai
My Beloved Teacher's Earnest Instruction: A Later Practitioner's Heartfelt Commemoration

Roughly one month ago, my younger school brother Liu Shuhang called and told me that the revisions of the *Cheng School Gao Style Baguazhang Manual* were already complete, and there were plans to republish it. I was greatly excited at hearing this. Several decades earlier, in 1990, through Liu Shuhang's conscientious research and organizing efforts, the first edition of the manual was published. Today, he has again organized and completed revisions, not only correcting a portion of the existing text but also adding the weapons and Form Boxing that exhibit the special characteristics of Cheng School Gao Style Baguazhang. The content now completely encompasses the Cheng School Gao Style Baguazhang system. Not only does this realize the last wishes of our beloved teacher Liu Fengcai, but it is an extremely important work for passing on and promoting Cheng School Gao Style Baguazhang.

During our phone conversation, he also asked me to write an essay regarding my insights into and knowledge of the study and practice of Baguazhang, which I gladly accepted. I was thirteen years old when I formally became a disciple of Liu Fengcai, first studying Three Emperors Cannon Fist and some Shaolin weapons, and then later studying Baguazhang. I am one of Master Liu's earliest disciples in Tianjin, and I have a duty and responsibility to introduce the aspects of Cheng School Gao Style Baguazhang from the point of view of my own insights and knowledge, and to do a little beneficial work in order to promote the popularization and development of this outstanding traditional art. Although I received direct instruction, I did not relentlessly train and deeply research the art to the fullest. Although my art is middling and my insights hollow, the earnest instruction regarding the study and training of Baguazhang received from my beloved teacher when he transmitted his art to me is still recorded in my heart. With the encouragement of fellow practitioners and later students, I now summarize and organize this into words, repeating his instructions, and present it as a reference to friends who enjoy Baguazhang.

The Twenty-Four Requirements Are the Foundation

The Twenty-Four Requirements are the basic requirements for practice of the Pre-Heaven Palms, and one of the important signifiers of the difference between Cheng School Gao Style Baguazhang and other schools of Baguazhang. Master Gao called the Twenty-Four Requirements "internal skill posture-completion methods." During the course of my study of this art, the Twenty-Four Requirements were what my beloved master most often spoke to me about. He spoke not only clearly and penetratingly, but always gave instruction while demonstrating, truly taking the Twenty-Four Requirements and training them into his own body until they were completely merged with his boxing postures and expression.

Although Baguazhang is a type of boxing that utilizes turning-the-circle walking and spinning as its basic movement form, Master Liu emphasized that to consider Baguazhang as simply walking the circle, and to consider walking the circle as Baguazhang—to equate circle-walking and Baguazhang—was, in reality, a misunderstanding. Without rules, nothing is exacting; only walking the circle while using the Twenty-Four Requirements as a method is truly Baguazhang. From a technique perspective, the Twenty-Four Requirements are the main points; from a holistic perspective, the Twenty-Four Requirements are a methodological framework, a spirit, for the Pre-Heaven Palms. Walking the circle without the Twenty-Four Requirements as the base is no longer Gao Style Baguazhang.

Master Liu said study and practice of the Pre-Heaven Palms begins with the study and practice of the Twenty-Four Requirements. It can be put this way: to judge what someone's Baguazhang skill is like, first look at how well they are trained in the Twenty-Four Requirements. If the Twenty-Four Requirements are practiced as a chaotic mess, you can say their Baguazhang skill level definitely can't become high, and their teacher is definitely not an expert.

How, then, does one practice the Twenty-Four Requirements well? Master Liu said that first, one must study requirement by requirement, making it clearly understood what each requirement is; but this is not enough. One must grasp them holistically and feel them through actual training. The Twenty-Four Requirements are tightly bound together; they are not viable if one is separated from the others, or one is ignored over the others. Only by taking understanding and practical experience and united them can one truly study expertly and practice well.

Master Liu also told me that, although they are especially important, when transmitting the art, the Twenty-Four Requirements must be utilized differently, according to the person, and you cannot require the same from everyone. For the elderly or those whose body is weak from illness, one can only require them to understand, and that is sufficient; whatever degree they can train to, then train to that extent. There is no need to make harsh demands and force them into doing something harmful to their health. But for youthful or middle-aged people who are healthy, one must be strict in demanding rigorous training. Of course, one must also pay attention to advancing progressively; only in this way can one study properly and train correctly.

Postures, Energy, and Stepping

I do not exaggerate: whether I was listening to Master Liu lecture or watching him perform, when compared to other school brothers at the time, I heard more and saw more. Why? My house was very near Master Liu's house and place of practice; I could walk there in less than ten minutes. If he said go, I went. Other school brothers were not so lucky: not only did they live far from Master Liu, but they were all twenty-odd years older than me, had families and jobs, and coming for a visit was not easy. So my conditions for the study of the art were superior to theirs, and I could spend comparatively more time with Master Liu. If I wanted to study something, Master Liu just taught it, and if I didn't understand it, I just asked at will.

Master Liu often said to me that the Green Dragon Extends Its Claws posture, which uses the Twenty-Four Requirements as its method, is the basic posture of the Pre-Heaven Palms, and it runs throughout the Pre-Heaven Bagua from beginning to end. The Eight Big Palms are the main palm methods of the Pre-Heaven Palms. From opening posture to closing posture, during the entire process of walking the circle and practicing the palm methods, one must diligently actualize that:

- In walking-the-circle turning and spinning, each part of the body should encircle the focus of the circle and make round orbiting movements.
- During the changes of palm methods, every part of the body must adhere to the ideas that "if one moves, all move," and "no place does

not move"; in no place may the energy be slack. Put simply, in some places the movement is large, and in some the movement is small, but whether movements are large or small, they must all arrive at the same moment in the location required by the palm method. This is just like a bicycle in motion—when the large sprocket in front makes a revolution, the small sprocket in back also turns.

- When walking the circle, every part of the body is making a circular revolution, and in changing palm methods, every part of the body must maintain this circular movement. Every place must be rounded, with no place not round; only the size and location of the roundness in space is different.

Master Liu said that grasping Baguazhang's energy is an important aspect of practicing Baguazhang. Baguazhang has three energies that should be understood: first is holding energy. This type of energy holds but does not reveal, is hidden and does not issue. Second is spiraling energy: energy spirals upward, downward, left, and right. For example, the head must press, but this is not the head stiffly pressing upward; it presses in cooperation with the neck spiraling upward. This is spiraling energy. Third is contending energy, which is "bidirectional power," or power in two exact opposite directions. In Baguazhang these three types of energy are harmoniously blended into one body and are threaded throughout the palm methods from beginning to end.

Master Liu said Baguazhang's stepping is fairly exacting, not only requiring eight steps to make a circle and stepping as if wading in mud, but also requiring the practitioner to walk level and stable. Walking eight steps to create a circle is easily understood, but it requires much practice. Walking as if wading in mud is a very clear image and also easy to understand. It is only when walking must be stable that many do not know the secret. When I started practicing walking the circle, my upper body always rose and fell. When I asked Master Liu how to correct this, he said that Mud-Wading Step has three energies: one energy moving forward; one energy downward; and one energy inward. When the sole of the foot touches the ground, it forms a "twisting" energy from the three energies united as one. From when the foot touches the ground until it leaves the ground, although the length of time is brief, with this exact process of complete twisting energy, one must slowly add power; when touching the ground, your foot will seem like it is sinking below the ground bit by bit. In this way walking will be level and stable.

Master Liu said that postures, energy, and stepping are important in Baguazhang. You must diligently understand them and also feel them and grasp them through actual practice.

Study Must Be True; Practice Must Be Full

Beloved Master Liu often said to us, "To study this art, you must have a good attitude." What is a good attitude? He said six words: "True in study; full in practice." He explained that "true in study" means that when studying, one must be diligent; not one technique or one posture can be so-so. "Full in practice" means that when training, one must be fully present and of one mind and one intention. Baguazhang looks easy, but truly studying correctly and understanding are very difficult, and practicing well is even harder. If you learn only half-heartedly—short punch here, missing a kick there, a punch when it should have been a kick—and your appearance is all wrong, how can this be OK? Isn't this just vainly delaying the skill? Of course, studying correctly and studying to understand does not also equate to practicing correctly. One must still make efforts in training; only with true study and full practice is one correct.

To explain this principle, Master Liu told us the story of Shang Yunxiang startling the audience with his art. Shang Yunxiang was one of the famous Xingyiquan practitioners of his generation. Legend has it that as a youth, Shang Yunxiang's family was extremely impoverished, and from an early age he served his landlord as a shepherd. From his youth he loved martial arts, and as luck would have it, the great Xingyiquan Master Li Cunyi and he both lived in the same village. He often ran to Li Cunyi, pestering him to formally be accepted to study his art. Li saw that Shang was growing up both thin and short, and felt that he was not the type to study martial arts. In his heart Li didn't want to accept him, but he also knew that not accepting someone from the same village and with the same relations was inappropriate. Thinking about it for some time, he came up with an idea, and the next time Shang pestered him to become a student, he said, "There's no need for you to become a disciple. I'll teach you a technique, and after training in it for three years, come see me again." This is how Shang learned Crushing Fist. No one would have thought that Shang would throw himself completely into training, almost to the point of obsession. When tending sheep along the road, the sheep walked on ahead, and he followed behind, practicing. If the sheep were in a dale eating grass, he was beside them, training. He continued training, training, training, and in a flash he had trained for three years.

One day, Shang was returning with the sheep, as always following behind the herd and practicing Crushing Fist. He had almost reached the village when suddenly he heard someone calling behind him. Turning around, he saw an old man beckoning to him. This old man, his whole face in a smile, asked him his surname and given name, who he studied boxing with, how long he had trained, what else he knew, and so on. Shang told him truthfully, and emphasized that his teacher did not teach him other things, and he knew only Crushing Fist. After hearing this, the old man nodded, warmly patting Shang on the shoulder, and said "Good! Good! We'll meet again! We'll met again!" and then went directly into the village.

This old man was actually Li Cunyi's younger school brother, who had come to see his older brother. Seeing Li Cunyi, with both hands clasped in respect, his first sentence was: "Congratulations, older brother! Compliments, older brother!" Li was perplexed and asked, "Little brother, what do I have to be happy for?" The old man replied, "You've produced a disciple whose martial art is outstanding. Isn't that a joy?" Li said, "Little brother, you're talking nonsense; where do I have a disciple with outstanding martial arts?" The two brothers talked back and forth for a time, and finally the younger brother related in detail the circumstances of seeing Shang practicing outside the village and their subsequent conversation. After Li heard this, although he thought of Shang Yunxiang, he couldn't completely believe his younger brother's story about Shang's outstanding martial arts, and he sent someone to fetch Shang to perform in front of everyone. Shang was calm and unhurried, and although he had just the one technique, Crushing Fist, he had not only practiced it completely correctly, but his energy and power were full and deep, whirling like the wind. After he finished practice, the sound of cheers rose up all around. Li Cunyi was both startled and happy, and after this he recorded Shang on his wall, teaching him with all his heart. Shang, obtaining the true transmission of a famous master, became even more hardworking and diligent, and later became one of the most famous Xingyiquan practitioners of his generation.

Master Liu said that this is only a story. There's no need to research in detail whether Master Shang really had this experience, but there is a principle that must be kept in mind: only through true study and actual practice can one train martial skill well. A common saying puts it well: to gain an art that startles people, one must train diligently.

Completion Is Internal; Form Is External

Baguazhang's Single Palm Change is the most difficult to practice. I had practiced for a very long time and could never walk fluidly, only awkwardly. I told Master Liu this in the hope of getting his instruction. Master Liu said, "Single Palm Change is a bit hard. You don't practice it well because you have not yet pondered deeply the internal workings of this palm; your mind is empty." These words left me confused. "What is an empty mind, and how can I make my mind not empty?" I continued to ask questions in order to understand things clearly.

Master Liu said that generally, those who study this art always imitate in the beginning. You tell them to stick out their palm, and they stick out their palm; you tell them to kick, and they kick; however you practice, they follow you in how you practice. As to why something is trained this way, they seldom think about it, and their body is stiff and wooden. At this stage, the teacher is exhausted, and those who study also expend great efforts. This is a common phenomenon, and no one can skip past it. As the skills learned become more and more numerous, and the time spent in training becomes longer and longer, the mind continuously accumulates the feeling of training. What was misunderstood before is now understood, and not only is its nature known, but also its purpose. This already is not simple imitation; the body has gradually become coordinated. This is called "enlightened." Continuing from this in training, one gains a deeper understanding and correct grasp not only of the connections between the palms, but also of the relationships within the palm postures, such as hard and soft, fast and slow, receiving and issuing, and rising and falling. If the mind is full, the bodily form is rounded, lively, and fluid, reaching the state of internal and external joined as one, the spirit and form united—and your martial skill has also reached a certain level and has leaped forward into a greater realm.

Master Liu said that after training in this art to a certain degree of skill, whether or not one can continue to raise their skill level is connected to the power of understanding and the power of observation. The higher one's power of understanding or comprehension, the faster one's skills may advance. People's power of understanding is related to their experience, education, nature, and moral standards. Because of this, at the same time as you train in martial arts, you should also study a little of things outside martial arts. For example, read more books, or view calligraphy and painting of some sort. In the past, many of the masters of previous generations were often also men of learning.

Following Master Liu's instruction, I increased the number of Single Palm Changes I practiced, and I also diligently tried to figure out the requirements explained by him, while closely investigating his movements in demonstrations. In my mind I gradually felt the especially rounded, soft, and fluid characteristics of Single Palm Change. Knowing something in one's heart, ceaselessly continuing to practice it, and eventually training until it has some meaning: this is greatness.

Time Is Gongfu

Watching Master Liu demonstrate Baguazhang was simply a pleasure. I wasn't the only one who thought this way: many other people also had this feeling. You would see his neat and forceful body line, his intoxicating rhythm, and his transfixed state, and you could not help but clap with unrestrained excitement. I have seen experts and hobbyists, watched those in cities and in far-off villages, and speaking from my heart, as much as they all possessed special characteristics, all had difficulty in matching Master Liu. In the 1960s, Sun Shiguang, the Tianjin City martial arts champion who could bend eight bows at once, and Sun Jiaqing, another martial artist of outstanding skill, often came to Master Liu's training place to watch and learn from his practice. At the time, Sun Shiguang was coach of the Tianjin City acrobatics troupe, and every time he came to watch, he stayed for several hours. Sun Jiaqing also wished to study Dragon Phoenix Double Straight Swords with Master Liu. Just think: if Master Liu's martial art was only middling, could it have attracted the attention of these two, whose reputations were evident and conspicuous?

Each time I finished watching Master Liu demonstrate his skill, I was greatly inspired, and my energy for practice was increased. I trained in the daytime and in the evening. In my heart I thought I must catch up with Master Liu. But after training for a long time compared to him, I was still too far behind, which left me with a bad feeling. I thought to myself, I've studied this for many years, sweating more than a little, and working at it diligently; why am I still not good at it? Is it that I'm not martial artist material? With these misgivings in my mind, my spirit to practice was lacking. One day—I don't know how it came about—I suddenly said to Master Liu, "Teacher, I think I am not martial artist material; I can train until I'm dead and never attain your level." After hearing this, Master Liu was disagreeable and silent for a while, and then said, "I thought these few days your training was not focused; I see now it's because of this. You say I'm better than you; I also feel I'm stronger than you. But how can you not think hard about why I'm stronger? I started training martial arts at age nine; when my family was poor, I trained; suffering under the Japanese, I trained; in the days of the Republic, I trained; arriving in the new society, I trained even more energetically. Calculate it: how many days have I practiced, and how many days have you practiced? Can you be stronger than me? What is skill? Time is skill. Now your environment is better than mine. You're not worried about food or clothing; you're going to school, and you're educated. You just have to persevere for a long time, practice wholeheartedly, and research diligently, and one day I'll bet you'll be stronger than me." Master Liu's words were a huge education to me, and from that day forward, my heart was content and my confidence increased. With training twice a day, morning and evening, my improvement was fast. This was something that occurred in about 1967. That period of time was the high point of my lifetime of training in this art.

More than thirty years have passed, but I still recall clearly these truthful words of my beloved master. Now in my sixties, I've taught a few students, and I often told them of this incident and my teacher's words to encourage them to train well in Baguazhang.

Martial Practice and Cultivating Virtue

During almost thirty years of on-and-off study of this art with Master Liu, he taught me Baguazhang, but at the same time he also taught me many principles of being a person. This old man never attended school and was not educated, but his understanding of life was like his understanding of his martial art—whole and deep. His venerable words were a great help to my growing up.

When I was in school, Master Liu often inquired about my studies; how was my learning coming, was I able to complete all of my homework, how were my tests, and so on. He sincerely instructed me, saying, "You're a student now; a student's primary function is studying well. To delay your studies for the sake of martial arts is not allowed." After I started working, he again often asked about my job situation, regularly exhorting me to do my job well: "Now you're in a cadre for the nation! Drawing a government salary, you must make efforts for the nation. You must delineate what is work and what is leisure, and you cannot let studying this art influence your work."

Although Master Liu was a person from the old society, he was very enlightened. He did not approve of the "mountaintop" phenomenon in the martial arts world. He often said, [Internal or external, all martial arts under heaven are one family. They are all things handed down from the ancestors; why divide them into families? To say this school is no good, that school is bad, only your own school is good—this is prejudice. This type of prejudice will not only lead to the martial arts world not being able to unite, but it is completely disadvantageous to the continuation and spread of martial arts.

Regardless of how good your skill is, you must certainly be modest and cautious, and you cannot make arrogant displays. You must know that beyond yourself is a greater self, and beyond your world is a greater world. Some people train three or five years and feel outstanding, everywhere looking to cross hands and provoke disputes, but in the end they must suffer a great loss. In the old days it often happened that they robbed bodyguards' carts, smashed up schools, or took to theatrics. The reasons for this were numerous, but in the final analysis this was created by society's darkness. Huo Yuanjia beat the Russian strongman in order to give credit to the Chinese people; he didn't study martial arts because he loved fighting. Many of the former generations of martial artists had refined and supreme martial skill, and they were people of high moral character. Today, people can still remember them and extol their virtues. There were also a few of high martial skill but whose moral character was not good, and people quickly forgot them.]

The above recollections are merely a portion of Master Liu's sayings regarding the study and practice of Baguazhang. For Baguazhang, this elder was not only completely familiar with the boxing manual but also possessed a systematic and complete theory. To introduce and annotate Master Liu's theories is not something I can achieve with my abilities.

In 1987 one of the famous Baguazhang practitioners of his generation—our revered and beloved Master Liu Fengcai—mounted a crane to fly west.[1] His venerable benevolence and kind appearance, lofty artistic abilities and humane character, and his martial skill in Baguazhang, so hard for later practitioners to surpass, will always remain beautiful in our memories. Many of Master Liu's disciples have already passed on, and those still alive are mostly in their later years. They all esteem and love Master Liu, and truly treasure his teaching of Baguazhang. These include our elder school brothers, the octogenarian Chen Baozhang and septuagenarian Han Fengrui, whose several decades of continually practicing and teaching Baguazhang elicit people's admiration and respect. What is gratifying is that Master Liu's grand-students are even more numerous, in the prime of their lives, and all very hard-working, and they are the core driving force in inheriting and promoting Baguazhang. Although I am out of practice for many years, and my skill would be hard to recover, I can still remember all that Master Liu taught me and have passed this on to several students of my own. I truly hope this has made a meager contribution to the spread of Baguazhang.

Han Fengrui, Direct Disciple of Liu Fengcai
The Practice of Baguazhang Can Build the Body and Cure Illness

These are my own personal insights. I am now already over seventy years old, and I recall the situation back when I began practicing Baguazhang because of an illness. You can say that it was the practice of Baguazhang that cured my illness and improved my quality of life. Until the end of my life I will not forget Master Liu Fengcai's great kindness in educating me and curing my illness.

At the beginning of the 1960s, when I was only thirty-odd years old, I developed liver disease. Even receiving injections and taking medicine every day did not produce results, and later it developed into cirrhosis. The doctors said they had no good method of treatment, and they could only use drugs to maintain the condition. At the time my body was very weak, and I could not work, and I only stayed at home, living on disability. Early every day I also slipped out to study Taijiquan with someone, and later on I met my younger school brother Qiang Wancheng, who was also undergoing treatment for a very serious lung disease. His lungs had holes the size of walnuts in them, and he had also sought medical treatment in various places without results. At the time, a tuberculosis hospital wanted to keep him in hospital and perform surgery, but he didn't consent to that.

The two of us pitied each other's illnesses, and our discussion topic was always "we got these illnesses at an early age, with no good treatment, and no results from practicing Taijiquan; in the future, how will we manage?" Later, we heard a few elder-generation martial artists specifically state that there was a Master Liu Fengcai who taught Baguazhang and could cure illnesses, and in fact had healed more than a few people. Hearing this, the two of us went to seek out Master Liu.

Master Liu was a very good, wholly harmonious, and gentle elderly person. He did not want money and would not take gifts, but he accepted us two invalids as disciples. He first related to us the origin and lineage of this school of Baguazhang, and spoke of the basic requirements and tenets of Pre-Heaven Baguazhang, and then began to teach us turning the circle. What I remember most clearly from that time is two principles that Master Liu told us. First was that the practice of Baguazhang not only uses the body to train but also uses the mind and the intention. One must use the mind and intention to feel, and take each requirement and train it into your body. The second was that practice must be done to the appropriate degree. Especially those people with an illness or a weak body must train to the appropriate degree, not overexerting and not underexerting, using comfort as the measure of degree. From then on, according to Master Liu's requirements, the two of us began studying Baguazhang, no longer taking medicines, only continuing to practice every day with one mind and one intention. In order to cure our illnesses, every day after finishing training the two of us summarized our experiences and discussed our sensations, telling each other what reactions our bodies had. We asked Master Liu directly for instruction about those things we could not understand, and he always answered with patient guidance if there was a question.

We continued like this for half a year, and the two of us both felt that our bodies had more energy compared to before, and our spirits were much better. At that point both of us arranged with the hospital to examine the condition of our diseases. Getting the results of the exams, our happiness truly exceeded our expectations. The conditions of our two illnesses both had a marked turn for the better. My liver function TT test went from 12.5 to 8; my school-brother's lung X-rays demonstrated that the holes in his lungs had shrunk in size. At the time we were so happy that we didn't ask for further assessments. The evident results from training caused our faith and perseverance in training Baguazhang to increase even more. Every day we continued to follow Master Liu in training Baguazhang, and our energy grew greater and fuller, our interest stronger and stronger. As our enthusiasm rose, we trained more and more diligently.

This went on for another half year, and the two of us again made arrangements to go to the hospital for assessment. This time the exam results showed miracles: my liver function TT test had already gone down to 3, and my preexisting hypersplenotrophy condition had returned to completely normal. My younger brother's lung holes had disappeared. At the time, we were almost excited enough to jump. The doctors said to us, "Your illnesses are already gone, and you can't continue to feign illness, so go to work." From then on, the two of us started working again, and never again missed work due to illness, right through to retirement. The practice of Baguazhang for only a little more than one year cured our illnesses. Describing it makes it sound miraculous, but this is our own real physical experience.

From the time we were cured and began working, I continued training in Baguazhang every day continuously and without cease, primarily using leisure hours. After retirement, I still take no breaks throughout the year. Today, through several decades of practice, not only is my body more and more robust and has not suffered any other major ailments, but I have accumulated a certain level of skill. I've also taught a flock of students, among them both young and elderly invalids, and more than a few of those with long-standing illness have reclaimed good health. In the past few years, because my body has been healthy, I also often push hands with others and test techniques, but my pushing hands with friends and testing techniques are also all for building health, never with the aim of determining a winner. Consistently I bear in mind beloved old Master Liu's instructions: "Nowadays the practice of Baguazhang should take health-building as its primary goal; fighting is secondary." And I use this to instruct later practitioners.

Recently, Master Liu's family-taught disciple Liu Shuhang has prepared to revise and reissue the *Cheng School Gao Style Baguazhang Manual* and asked me to write down a few insights and understandings. My educational level isn't high, and I can't write anything much, but I can recall a bit of my own process of studying Baguazhang. If speaking of my own physical perceptions, my deepest insight and understanding is that Baguazhang is a school of superior fighting art, and at the same time it is a school of health-building methods that have evident results. Training Baguazhang can increase the intrinsic vitality of the body, can cure many types of disease, can further strengthen the body, and can, in the process of strengthening the being and building the body, increase skilled power and improve fighting ability.

Chen Lianfa, Direct Disciple of Liu Fengcai

I am a medical doctor, and from my youth I've studied martial arts. I studied Shaolin, Xingyi, Tongbei, and other types of boxing arts but later lost them all. I only consistently continue to train in Baguazhang, which I learned while following Master Liu Fengcai while I attended Tianjin Medical University. I have received great benefits from it along with rather many impressions. Among them, my biggest insight is that training Baguazhang can build health and treat illness.

The health-building and disease-treating efficacy of Baguazhang is mainly embodied in the basic Twenty-Four Requirements. Of these, several belong to traditional Chinese life-cultivation principles: head must press, tongue must curl, chest must hollow, dantian must be full, shoulders must sink, elbows must drop, waist must twist, hips must sit, anus must lift, toes must grasp, and steps must wade. For example, because of my bad habit of reading books in the lavatory, I developed hemorrhoids. Training in Baguazhang, I paid careful attention to lifting the anus upward, causing the sphincter to retract and reducing dilation of the hemorrhoidal veins, and for many years the hemorrhoids were contained and did not flare up. Also, I often had shoulder and back muscle spasms and pain created by unhealthy sleeping positions. However, through practicing Baguazhang—consciously hollowing the chest and plucking up the back, sinking the shoulders, and dropping the elbows—I opened the meridians and collaterals that served as an excellent cure for the spasms and pain. Furthermore, in the last few years, with advancing age my body began to get fat, surpassing my target body weight. After controlling my food intake and increasing the amount of my Baguazhang exercise, within a short period my weight had dropped thirteen pounds, with the added effect of guarding against every type of disease in the elderly exacerbated by excess weight.

Through several decades of actual experience practicing Baguazhang, I also have come to understand that Baguazhang requires that "if one moves, then nothing does not move." It is a type of whole-body exercise. Its movements—which "seek flow amid opposition" with energy that is rolling, drilling, contending, and wrapping, everywhere exhibiting Bagua's rounded spiral energy—have great massaging and health-preserving effects on the internal zang-fu organs. Its five toes gripping the earth and steps like wading in mud emphasize using intention, not using force. It can connect meridians and collaterals, enliven qi and blood, and promote the metabolism. Its movements differentiate clearly between yin and yang; if there is a left, there must be a right. This special characteristic, of having left and right together, not only can develop intelligence but can also have good health-preserving effects for the brain. Baguazhang's training speed, which is not hurried and not slow, its exercise duration, which can be longer or shorter, and its exercise volume, which can be greater or lesser, are all appropriate for use by the masses at different ages and stages of life. For youths, practicing Baguazhang can promote their development and healthy growth; for the middle-aged and elderly, training Baguazhang can delay the aging of the body and regenerate vitality.

In summary, practical experience has caused me to recognize that all of the Baguazhang transmitted by Master Liu is an excellent method for building health and alleviating disease. Its health-building and disease-curing effects do not stop at my body, and definitely demand that deep scientific research be undertaken using modern technologies to draw out scientific evidence, which will cause Baguazhang to receive broader popularization and development.

Ge Guoliang, Grand-Student of Liu Fengcai

Cheng School Gao Style Baguazhang is a complete system with a full set of scientific training methods and fighting techniques. From a young age I enjoyed sport and loved martial arts. When I was young, I first studied Springy Legs, and later also studied Cha Boxing. As I grew older, I felt that what I had studied before were only forms—they looked good but were not very useful. At that point, in 1964, I started to learn from a master practicing Shuaijiao, and I felt that Shuaijiao was more practical than other martial arts.

In 1968, through a friend's introduction, I began training under the Cheng School Gao Style Baguazhang family, which aroused great excitement in me. I felt that this school of Baguazhang was different than the martial arts I had previously studied. Although its boxing theory was profound, its postures were simple and easy to learn. Although the postures seemed simple, they could change without exhaustion. This is especially true of the Sixty-Four Palms—how they are trained is how they are used, and they are absolutely without the artificiality of flowery fists and embroidered legs. Each and every palm is extremely practical in both study and application. After learning one palm, you can raise your hands for practical experience. This one special characteristic shares a similarity with Shuaijiao, which employs different methods with equal success, but the profound deep content and miraculously linking and changeable techniques of Bagua are so far advanced that Shuaijiao cannot compare with it. During the practical experience of following Master Wang Shusheng and researching and training Baguazhang for several decades, at times I also had the luck to obtain correction and instruction in many areas from Grandmaster Liu Fengcai, receiving substantial benefits and gaining deeply from his unified understanding and advanced martial skills.

I recall many times going to Grandmaster Liu's house to seek instruction on usage of the Post-Heaven Palms. Not only did he always answer every question, but he explained things extremely clearly, and he was rather skilled in actual combat. Each time he told me to advance and attack using the Post-Heaven Palms, I built up my courage and, to the extent of my learned applications, attacked repeatedly while changing techniques, but I was never able to gain the advantage. Grandmaster Liu always easily dissolved my attacks, and he always put me into a passive position. His techniques were precise, and his changes between them miraculous. The agility of his movements and his deep skilled power issued with one touch were surprising and threatening, and not comparable to normal people. Those who did not spar with him had difficulty understanding the extent of his skills. After many years, under the diligent cultivation and training of Master Wang and Grandmaster Liu, and through my own diligent practice, my studies began to attain some level of achievement. Continually deepening my understanding and recognition of the true essence of Cheng School Gao Style Baguazhang at the foundations also changed from my previous belief that traditional martial arts looked good but were not practical. In 1984 I attended the Tianjin City martial arts competition and came out on top, and in 1985 I attended the National Traditional Martial Arts Competition and had the honor of being awarded a gold medal.

Following the deaths of first Grandmaster Liu and later Master Wang, I started to undertake the task of cultivating newcomers. In the process of teaching, I following the ancestral teaching of "studying the complete learning, and now transmitting the arts to all worthy gentlemen under Heaven;

transmitting without holding anything back; only this can be called pioneering," guiding students by completely relying on Cheng School Gao Style Baguazhang training methods, with emphasis on its use of practical combat and free fighting. Students across the board who undertook only several short months of training, whether they had previously studied martial arts or trained in Sanda, saw the light, and their fighting ability leaped higher. Again crossing hands with formerly difficult-to-handle opponents, they were all now more than equal to the task. From this, the influence of Cheng School Gao Style Baguazhang broadened, and today those who love training in Cheng School Gao Style Baguazhang are more and more numerous. In August 2004 at the National Traditional Martial Arts Competition in Huludao City, Liaoning Province, a group of disciples exerted themselves to win three gold medals.

My several decades of practical experience studying and researching Cheng School Gao Style Baguazhang caused me to discover and recognize most deeply that fighting is the basic special characteristic of martial arts. Cheng School Gao Style Baguazhang is a complete system, with each of its subsystems completely embodying this basic special characteristic. Actual experience is the only standard to gauge truth, and actual combat, then, is the only demarcation line in judging between true gongfu and flowery fists and embroidered legs. Taking a broad view of Cheng School Gao Style Baguazhang, I feel its differences from other arts are that it can achieve health-building while training skills, and while building health also increase skilled power. Its most outstanding fighting secret is "seeking cleverness in following, using change as the constant, first dissolving and then issuing." One must follow the opponent's incoming force, cleverly changing postures, using change and transformation to dissolve the opponent's force, allowing yourself to stand in an undefeatable position, using change to give rise to one's own attacking force, causing opponents to be unable to defend themselves. Transforming uses soft to transform hard while creating uses hard to destroy soft. If the opponent changes, I change, again generating, again transforming, linking change like this without exhaustion. This is the fighting spirit of Cheng School

Gao Style Baguazhang, which is also the basis for Cheng School Gao Style Baguazhang to be called a superior martial art.

In summary, my several decades of actual experience researching and training in Cheng School Gao Style Baguazhang have caused me to deeply understand and recognize that it is a complete system, possessed of completely scientific training methods and fighting techniques, and that research and study of Cheng School Gao Style Baguazhang absolutely will not mislead people.

Ge Shuzhen, Grand-Student of Liu Fengcai

Turning the Circle is Baguazhang's first introductory and foundational skill method. When I was a youth, I studied Shaolin skill methods. Later I became a student of the Bagua school and, until today, have researched and practiced Baguazhang for thirty-odd years. In the eighties I served as Baguazhang coach at the Tianjin Nankai Martial Arts Academy.

In accumulating my many years of experience in researching and training Baguazhang, my deepest insight is that turning the circle is Baguazhang's first introductory foundational skill method. "Turning-the-circle walking and spinning" is abbreviated as "turning the circle." It is the basic exercise form of Baguazhang, and the most obvious aspect that differentiates it from other boxing styles. It originated with the Daoist practice of Turning the Celestial Worthy, and it is a product of the join-ing together of martial technique and internal development as well as a product of uniting Bagua yin-yang theory with bodily movement.

Turning the circle does not haphazardly follow the circle walking and spinning, but it has certain rules, and these rules are the Twenty-Four Requirements. Master Gao Yisheng called the Twenty-Four Require-ments internal skill completion methods, and Master Liu Fengcai called the Twenty-Four Requirements the fundamental framework for training Gao Style Baguazhang. Practical experience causes me to feel that only after having grasped the Twenty-Four Requirements and recorded them in your mind, and also having trained them into your body so that they are blended as one with the movement of your body, can your training produce skill.

Turning the circle while following the Twenty-Four Requirements to complete the postures, changing postures amid movement, the form is external, but the refinement is internal. Long training in turning the circle will have the evident effects of building the legs and strengthening the waist, increasing qi, and lengthening power. It can cause the lower basin root to be stable, the footwork agile, and cause the hands, eyes, body method, footwork, spirit, qi, and power to be coordinated and unified. Furthermore, in the process of strengthening the being and building the body, it will increase skilled power, establishing the material foundation for fighting and actual combat. Turning the circle also must emphasize using intention and not using force, as only using intention can increase skilled power, so that in application one can follow their heart's desire. Only amid Pre-Heaven turning-the-circle training can one produce skill. Utilizing the Post-Heaven Palms takes this skill and transmits it outside the body so that in fighting, one may flow in the postures to meet hands, following the technique and responding with change, adhering, sticking, following, and connecting, borrowing force to strike force, overcoming the enemy and controlling victory. Speaking about external force, one must exhibit the basic skill of "without yet moving the tip, first moving the root" that is trained through turning the circle, using the waist to dictate movement. This is the energy originating in the legs, and later set forth by the hands, with solidity in the waist. In applying the palm methods and advancing to attack, the back foot must press, the front foot must tread, using waist movement to develop shoulder movement, using shoulder movement to lead palm movement; in this way the power issued is complete power. But this type of complete power is accumulated by relying on the skill of turning the circle.

In summary, I feel that to study Baguazhang, one must first make efforts and train in turning the circle well. After training produces skill, only in actual combat application can one truly manifest Baguazhang's special fighting characteristics of "avoiding the straight and attacking the angle; avoiding the substantial and striking the insubstantial; seeing hands and just responding, seeing postures and just connecting; following the opportunity and responding with change; and flowing with nature."

Li Xueyi, Grand-Student of Liu Fengcai
To Gain Astonishing Art, One Must Make Diligent Efforts

Martial arts and other Chinese traditional arts are the same: since ancient times they have all heavily valued being taught by a master, and Baguazhang is no exception. But a master can only teach disciples the foundational skill requirements and training methods. Regardless of how wise teachers are, they are still not able take their own body skill and power and directly transmit it to their disciples' bodies. Only through having been under a teacher's meticulous guidance and through one's own intensive training can one truly grasp all the skills taught by the teacher and transform them into one's own body skill and power. Furthermore, only after having made intensive efforts, ceaselessly learning skills and techniques experientially, and comprehending technique and theory can one ascend the hall and enter the chamber, gradually reaching the state of becoming superior to the master. This is called "the teacher leads one in the door; development is up to the individual."

Often I heard Liu Fengcai say "gongfu is time," and I feel that whether or not one can train skills in the practice of Baguazhang relies completely on the accumulation of practice time. Modern China has already become a market economy. Those who are young busy themselves with studies, adults must busy themselves with work, and research and study of martial arts for the most part can't be a way to make a living; most practitioners must squeeze in practice time after school or work, and this then requires greater intensity; only then can one have some attainment. So we say "To gain an astonishing art, one must make intense efforts." Formerly things were like this, and today it is even more like this.

From school age I had already started researching and training in Cheng School Gao Style Baguazhang. Now with thirty-odd years of practical research and study experience, according to my own personal insights and understanding, what is called putting forth intense effort is not the same as inflexible practice, but rather should be intense training that maintains the requirements with mindfulness and intentionality, advancing sequentially, and is neither hurried nor slow. Only through perseverance and constant effort can one accumulate deeper and deeper skill.

Maintain the Requirements; Train Diligently with Mindfulness and Intention

Without rules, nothing is precise. To practice Gao Style Baguazhang, one must definitely start from the study of the foundational requirements and must make efforts in the basic movements. The movements of the bodily form definitely must follow the Twenty-Four Requirements to complete their postures. During movement one must stress mindfulness and intentionality to know in the body the feeling of stepping like wading in mud and the energies of rolling, drilling, pushing, and wrapping. With mindfulness and intentionality, one must specifically feel that within every minute movement, one can embody a spiraling energy that requires roundness in movement. This is the key to obtaining the results of increasing qi and lengthening power. I train exactly this way, gradually seeking flowing amid opposition, finally reaching a state where the internal and external are connected. For example, in training Dragon-Form Piercing-Hand Palm, when piercing upward, the chest will always have a type of special relaxed feeling. When practicing Spinning-Body Back-Covering Palm, the body has a type of feeling correlating to being in water. Especially as the upper arm opens outward, it is like the body is lying in water, and water is compressing it all around.

Not Hurried and Not Slow Builds Gongfu

Baguazhang belongs to the internal arts, and it takes training internal qi as its focus. Its requirements are meticulous, and only experiencing them through slowly practicing this skill can you cause each type of requirement to remain in the body. But this is not to say the slower the better; one should use intention to relax without dispersing energy outward, relaxing but not slackening, having tautness in slowness. Only in being unhurried and not slow can one develop skill. The speed of exercise generally uses "perspiring but not panting" as a gauge. One should follow their own breathing rhythm to complete every type of movement. As a result of my own insistence on training according to this principle, today my internal qi is quite sufficient. Not only can I play basketball and run during the whole match, maintaining "perspiring but not panting," when reviewing dismantling palms with my school brothers, although our movements are relatively intense, I can also maintain the goal of perspiring but not panting.

Persevere, and Skill Becomes Deeper as It Accumulates

Perseverance is the key to intensive training. Two martial proverbs speak of the principle of persevering: "Learn it in three days; perfect it in three years" and "If boxing is trained a hundred times, the body method reveals itself; if boxing is trained a thousand times, its theory manifests." In summary, without perseverance, not putting forth intensive efforts, "spending one day fishing and two days to dry the net," one will never reach the goal of acquiring an astonishing art. Owing to my own regular years of research and study without cease, after a long while my internal skill gradually increased in depth. There was one time, after practicing the Pre-Heaven Palms, that I casually rubbed my abdomen and discovered a bump half the size of a Ping-Pong ball sticking out at the dantian. Elder practitioners said this is a reaction of internal qi gathering at the dantian. Each time I practice the Pre-Heaven Palms, I only have to train for a slightly longer period of time, and then my legs have a mutually attracting adhering power, and it's like my whole body is moving in a magnetic space, with movements that are light and nimble and extremely comfortable. Today, through several decades of research and study, not only has my training method gradually reached a perfected state, but my skilled power, as it accumulates, becomes deeper.

These are my insights and harvest from many years of research and study of Gao Style Baguazhang. First, I must offer heartfelt thanks for the efforts of my teacher's meticulous transmission; I will not forget this until the end of my days. However, even more important was relying on myself to make diligent efforts; only then could I attain some achievement. This is exactly the meaning of the phrase "without studying the techniques, it is difficult to attain the art; without training the techniques, it is difficult for the art to be superior." It is my hope that future practitioners may gain some enlightenment from my clumsy words.

Ge Shuxian, Grand-Student of Liu Fengcai

The internal art of Baguazhang strengthened my physique and gave me a second life. From my youth I was passionate about martial arts, studying Shaolin Boxing at age seven, and beginning to learn Baguazhang at age eight. I especially liked the Post-Heaven Sixty Four Palms, which I put the most effort into and trained diligently without cease. Through accumulation of skill over days and months, at the age of nineteen the power of my Post-Heaven Palm skill already stood out from the crowd. My issuing palms created a wind and whirring, and I could knock away a two hundred-pound punching bag with one palm. My double-palm combined force also exceeded the average person's, and with a double hand strike I could break twelve bricks stacked together horizontally.

My training in Baguazhang not only strengthened my physique but gave me a second life. I recall one event while I was working demolishing a house. As I left the work site, I was hit on the head by a stud that bounced up. I was immediately knocked out, all seven orifices bleeding, my occipital bone broken, and my ears leaking cerebral-spinal fluid; I truly had nine chances out of ten for death and one for life. Immediately I was sent to the 254 Hospital emergency room. The brain trauma doctors said that this injury was very severe, and even if they could save me, I would need at least half a year of bed rest in order to recover. However, owing to the foundation of my training, my injuries healed in a miraculous way.

After a week I woke up, and after twenty days I felt great, saying that I had to leave the hospital. The doctors could not persuade me otherwise and could only assent. As I neared release from the hospital, tests showed that my eardrum, punctured during the injury, had regrown. The doctors were astonished, saying, "This person's constitution is amazing," and asking me, "Do you train?" I said I practice the internal arts skill of Baguazhang. The doctors said that to recover from such a serious injury in such a short period of time and not to suffer any after-effects was simply impossible. My insight is that after this serious injury, the fact that I survived the great trauma was wholly due to the good fortune of having trained in the internal arts skill of Baguazhang.

Exhibiting a Righteous and Brave Bearing, Baguazhang Overwhelms Gangsters with Awe

In December 1996, I went to Beijing to see relatives. One evening my relatives and I were talking in Courtyard 12 in Xizhao Temple Street, Chongwenmen District, and outside the courtyard we suddenly heard shouting and cries for help. Listening more carefully, it was a woman's scream. My relatives and I rushed outside the courtyard to investigate, only to see three big burly men on Xizhao Temple Street kidnapping a young woman. These gangsters carried leather belts and clubs in their hands, and they were trying to force the young woman to go with them, but the young woman struggled fiercely and cried for help, so these gangsters tore into her, hitting her.

Seeing this situation, I was instantly filled with indignation, and with scrambling steps moved forward yelling loudly "Stop!" Seeing someone coming, these gangsters were not only unafraid; they acted ferocious, holding their weapons in their hands, and in their northeastern dialect said, "Don't come over here; whoever dares to come over here will end up dead." Relying on my body's true Baguazhang skill, not only was I not intimidated, but step by step I drew nearer to the gangsters. In an instant, one of the gangsters—who was over six feet tall and was carrying a club—struck out, aiming at my head. Following his force, I used the Bagua

Post-Heaven Palms Yanking Palm, meeting his arm and sitting in the waist, yanking downward with force; the gangster responded by falling to his knees. Not waiting for him to get up, I again followed the force with one Single Crashing Palm, striking straight into his *Huagai* point,[2] causing him to fall backward seven feet, landing in the street and laying there facing heaven. The other two gangsters, seeing their comrade being knocked down, viciously leaped toward me simultaneously. I used the coiling stepping of Bagua Koubu and Baibu, moving suddenly left and right, pointing east and striking west, playing the two gangsters until they did not know how to resist, and seeing an opening, used a stomping kick, squarely hitting the soft ribs of one of the gangsters, who then stumbled back several steps and fell to the ground. By this time, my relatives and the crowd gathered by the noise burst forward, separating and seizing the two gangsters. The last gangster, seeing their momentum waning, turned and ran. With an arrow step I caught his arm from the side and, using a Bagua throwing method, threw him to the ground. The crowd stepped up and also seized him. Following that, the crowd and I took the three gangsters and the victim to the Xizhao Temple Street Police Station to sort the matter out, and I received great praise from the crowd on the scene and from the local police.

Yuan Pengfu, Great-Grand-Student of Liu Fengcai

For those with a deep connection to this art, the difficulties are great; only those who love it do not give up and finally have some success.

Studying martial arts is not merely training the bodily form but is also training the spirit. Skill does not rely solely on the bodily form being trained but also must rely on the spirit being trained. Because of this, through a performance by those who study martial arts, we can sense their martial quality and personal quality. The martial artist's body type, constitution, and martial training experiences create their different external forms of the boxing postures, and each martial artist's personality, cultivation, and sense of rhythm creates the differences in their internal charm. Carefully evaluating each martial artist's boxing flavor, one can feel their personal qualities and dispositions, like wildness, meticulousness, concentration, distraction, steadiness, impulsiveness, stubbornness, slyness, shrewdness, clumsiness, broad-mindedness, and pettiness.

I have studied Baguazhang for only four years. Speaking of skill, at most mine can be called only a small achievement. But my personal insights are in fact becoming deeper step by step. From my own experience, for beginners, the Gao Style Baguazhang Pre-Heaven Palms may be the most difficult type of martial arts to study. Usually, just maintaining balance while making our feet walk in a straight line is difficult enough, but the Pre-Heaven Palms require walking the circumference of a circle, which is just adding difficulty upon difficulty. Further adding "the feet wading and moving stably, fingers clawing and toes gripping, twisting the waist, sitting in the hips, holding the knees and covering the groin, and the hands and eyes mutually following," along with the other Twenty-Four Requirements, is enough to cause some beginning practitioners to shrink back in fear, tasting only a little of the art and then stopping. However, for those with a deep connection to this art, the difficulties are great. But these difficulties are precisely the key principles behind training the Pre-Heaven Palms and building health. Turning the circle trains the body's balance and stability as well as whole-body coordination; wading with the steps and moving solidly, stepping as if there was black ice beneath the feet puts each sense organ in a state of heightened awareness and trains the sensitivity level of the entire nervous system. "The nails are the terminus of the tendons." The fingers clawing and toes gripping complement sinking the shoulders, dropping the elbows, and settling the wrists, which will cause the internal energy to sink to the dantian, the tendon pathways of the entire body to be relaxed but have tautness, thus truly reaching the effect of internally cultivating original qi and externally stretching the tendons and pulling the bones. Twisting the waist and sitting in the hips, seeking flowing in opposition, and rounding when moving all cause the tendon pathways in the body—while being stretched straight—to also increase stretching along an arc, causing the intensity of stretching the tendons and pulling the bones to increase by a step, thereby advancing a step in increasing qi and lengthening power, strengthening the tendons and solidifying the bones. Aside from this, Twisting-Body Baguazhang's "twisting" is not simply the meaning of softness but must be tall and straight while round and integrated, the movements ample and complete, open and expressive. Only then can one feel internally and externally the twisting and rubbing together of the skin, muscle, tendon, bone, and zang-fu organs, fully stimulating the whole body inside and out, reaching results that typical exercise cannot reach.

When first studying Baguazhang, my deepest insight, and what I felt the fastest, were the effects of increasing qi and lengthening power gained through turning-the-circle walking and spinning. This is also just the effect of increasing bodily power. In 1995, not long after first studying Baguazhang and boxing, the boxing coach recommended that I join the Tianjin City boxing team. Through the arrangement of the coach, I obtained a test match with someone ranked third nationally in the seventy-kilogram class (I weigh seventy-five kilograms, about 165 pounds). After the match, as the coach was summarizing, he said, "You've only been to six boxing classes, so I won't discuss technical aspects, but from the perspective of will and character, you're very good, and your strength is very good." He then asked me if I ran every day. At the time I only practiced the Baguazhang Pre-Heaven Palms that I had learned for just over three months every day for forty minutes. I was a beginner studying in my spare time after work, yet I was able to carry out intense boxing confrontations with an expert athlete, and even obtain this type of evaluation. I felt this was all attributable to my continued practice of Baguazhang. Later, for personal reasons, I did not formally join the Tianjin City boxing team, but this experience led me to a deeper recognition of the mysterious aspects of Baguazhang.

The stages of training in Baguazhang are mainly differentiated by the practitioner's skill level, such as beginning level, middle level, and high level. In reality, one might also differentiate on a psychological level, such as training, refining, and loving. "Training" is training the body and appearance, studying the movements and forms. "Refining" is refining jing, qi, and shen. "Loving" is concentrating the mind and concentrating the intention, and not allowing oneself to be separated from it. Only in loving this art and not giving up, instead taking the research and training of Baguazhang and melding it with other individual life pursuits, will training lead to some achievement, research yield some results, and understanding bring some gains. In this way, you will receive benefits through the rest of your life.

Note: In the renshen year [1992] Minqiang Cup Sanda, I attained second place, and in the national Zhonggong Cup Traditional Martial Arts Exchange Meeting, I received two gold medals.

POSTFACE TO THE FIRST CHINESE EDITION

Gao Yisheng, the founder of Cheng School Gao Style Baguazhang, was Master Liu Fengcai's grand-uncle. Liu Fengcai is the editor's grand-uncle. The three of us represent three generations of Baguazhang transmission, however, speaking of blood relations, we actually span five generations. Although I have followed my uncle in Tianjin studying martial arts since childhood, and though I have deeply received the family transmission, regrettably I do not exemplify his efforts, and my martial skill is average. Only in the theory of Baguazhang have I attained a narrow window of understanding. Master Wang Shusheng was my uncle's most accomplished inner-chamber disciple. His martial skill stood out among the crowd, and he excelled in fighting, although he was always loyal and righteous, upright and straightforward with others, and he was deeply esteemed by the many inheritors of Gao Style Baguazhang. Wang and I are both from the same master's school, and although he is older than my own father, we formed a friendship forgetting about age, and I honor him as an elder and respectfully call him "uncle."

To ensure that the essence of Cheng School Gao Style Baguazhang was not lost in my generation's hands, starting in 1980 I undertook the writing and editing of the *Cheng School Gao Style Baguazhang Manual*, following the dictation of my grand-uncle. The first draft of the text was completed in Tianjin in 1983 and, after broadly soliciting the input of the many inheritors, was revised and compiled into a second draft.

In early 1984, following my grand-uncle's departure from Tianjin and return to his hometown, I sent the second draft to Kang Gewu of the Beijing Sports University for proofreading, and thus revised and completed the third draft, which I then took back to our hometown to give to my grand-uncle for final review and approval. In 1985 he returned to Tianjin and again reviewed and then approved the draft.

Beginning in 1985 and through 1988, at the behest of my grand-uncle, following the advice of experts and publishers, and with the strong support of Wang Shusheng's many inheritors and the assistance and guidance of Kang Gewu, Shi Lijun, and Zhang Zucheng, I finally compiled the fourth draft, and recently submitted it for publication.

The publication of the *Cheng School Gao Style Baguazhang Manual* embodies the life-blood of several generations of practitioners, and it is the crystallization of the collective wisdom of many of its inheritors. I dare not take credit for the work of others, and thus I record these redundant details out of respect for the reader.

Liu Shuhang
August 8, 1990

TRANSLATION NOTES

This English version of the *Cheng School Gao Style Baguazhang Manual* is based on the two-volume third Chinese edition of the same name published in 2010. Textually, it contains all of the material presented therein, aside from the original Content Summary of the first edition, which is common in Chinese books but uncommon and unnecessary in English, and the photo-reproduction of Gao Yisheng's original manual, which constituted the bulk of the second volume. In an attempt to be "self-improving without cease," the English edition corrects typographical errors found in the last Chinese version and also includes several small textual additions or revisions to further enhance clarity and accuracy. It also provides updated and expanded historical photos documenting the long-standing relationship between the Tianjin Gao Style Baguazhang family and the North American Tang Shou Tao Association.

Although this translation project was begun in earnest only in 2011, work on rendering some of this material into English—especially the form names—dates back to the late 1990s. The names of the Post-Heaven Palms in particular have only arrived at their present forms after successive revisions over the years, and these translations may seem the most unique aspect of the text to readers with a command of Chinese. While some Post-Heaven Palms have longer, more poetic names—for example, palm 13, Two Immortals Preach the Dao—in common usage they are all referred to by a single character. Because some of these single-character names repeat (three are called *jie* [截], and two each use *ban* [搬], *heng* [橫], and *lian* [连]), in order to better serve non-Chinese speakers, I have tried to create sixty-four unique English names (found on pages 2–3) which (a) represent the meaning of the original Chinese word, even if somewhat loosely; (b) bear some relation to the application at hand; and (c) are rendered in English in simple verb form. This was accomplished with all the forms except for palms 13 and 14, which keep their noun form, and palm 58, which borrows another character for the meaning. These choices were made after repeated and lengthy discussions between fellow English-speaking practitioners and with our teachers in the United States and China.

I have tried to represent the remaining text faithfully while still allowing the full breadth of meanings and connotations present in the original. While most terminology has been translated consistently throughout the book, there are several instances where a particular word or phrase is presented in an alternate form to fit the particular context. Other conventions used in this edition include rendering all personal and place names in pinyin, except in cases where usurping common usage ("Hong Kong," "Nien Rebellion") might only add confusion, and listing all Chinese and Japanese names surname first for ease of recognition. Certain words in the text have also been retained in the Chinese, with either explanatory text at the first instance or appropriate endnotes, where a particular English translation might prove too narrow and limiting in meaning, or where a term is so common as to not need explanation. Any inaccuracies in these notations rest solely with me.

This edition of the manual is a part of the continual and gradual refinement of this body of knowledge that began with Gao Yisheng over a century ago. It is my sincere hope that my work makes some small contribution to furthering understanding of this remarkable art, and that English-speaking practitioners may find it useful and enlightening. I am humbled to have been able to train with and learn from my teachers, Vincent Black and Liu Shuhang, over these many years, and I am honored to be able to associate with men of such high integrity, wisdom, and accomplishment in presenting this work to the wider world.

John Groschwitz
Menlo Park
2012

ENDNOTES

Preface to Volume 2 of the 2010 Third Chinese Edition

1. A Daoist priest.
2. The last two characters of the name Song Yiren (宋异人) can mean "an exceptional or unusual person."
3. The name Song Yiren (宋异人) is a homophone of 送艺人, "the people/person who give(s) the art."

Preface to the 2005 Second Chinese Edition

1. This and all subsequent quotes from the *Yijing* and other Chinese texts are original translations, unless otherwise noted.
2. Essence (精), breath energy (气), and spirit (神), respectively: the Three Treasures of the human body.

Chapter 1: Baguazhang History, Theory, and Performance

1. The He Tu (River Diagram) and the Luo Shu (Luo River Scroll); said to have been discovered by Fu Xi and Yu the Great, respectively.
2. The Fu Xi Pre-Heaven Arrangement of the hexagrams and the Zhou Wen Wang Post-Heaven arrangement of the hexagrams.
3. A poem created by Dong Haichuan that provides a generation name for each successive group of practitioners for twenty generations, beginning with himself. The original reads: 海福寿山永，强毅定国基，昌明光大陆，道德建无极.
4. Vincent Black was accepted as Liu Fengcai's posthumous Kowtowed Disciple (磕头弟子) on April 20, 2012, as witnessed by Liu Shuhang, Gao Jinhua, and Li Cang of the Tianjin Cheng School Gao Style Baguazhang Research Association.
5. The perineum. Here more likely understood as the depths of the Sea of Qi (the Dantian).
6. Literally, "Hooking Step" and "Swinging Step."
7. This and subsequent quotes from the *Dao De Jing* are taken from Lao

Tzu, *Tao Te Ching,* trans. Gia-fu Feng and Jane English (New York: Vintage Books, 1989).

8. This and subsequent quotes from *The Art of War* are taken from Sun Tzu, *Sun Tzu's The Art of War,* trans. Lionel Giles (El Paso, TX: El Paso Norte Press, 2009).

9. The central palace: the heart and upper torso area.

10. Translator's note: original source, including spelling of the researcher's name, cannot be verified.

11. Ibid.

12. Ibid.

13. A type of stepping used in Daoist rituals, attributed to Yu the Great (circa 2200–2100 BCE), stepping in the pattern of the Big Dipper asterism.

Chapter 2: Pre-Heaven Baguazhang

1. A rearrangement of a traditional mnemonic used to learn the Eight Trigrams.

Chapter 3: Post-Heaven Bagua Sixty-Four Palms

1. 揸拉步 *(zhala bu);* translated literally, "Extending and Pulling Step." Onomatopoeia for the sound made when stepping. Generally it denotes a step through; beginning with the left foot in front, step forward left, step through with a longer-than-normal right step, and as the right foot sets down, pull the left foot up to a normal-length stance. Here it can also denote a shuffle step—an advance without switching forward legs. The original text notes that *zha* (揸, "to extend") can be understood as *ca* (擦, "rubbing").

2. The *Fengfu* acupuncture point (GV16).

3. The *Chengjiang* acupuncture point (RN24).

4. An alternate name for the *Yintang* acupuncture point (M-HN-3).

Chapter 5: Baguazhang Form Boxing

1. Form Boxing is commonly referred to in English simply as Bagua Animals. The eight sets of Image-Form Boxing (象形拳) are so named because certain movements within the forms exemplify the look (象) and feel (形) of the various animals.

Endnotes

Chapter 6: Essential Selections on the Life-Cultivation Arts

1. The Jade Pillow Gate (玉枕关), Pinched Ridge Gate (夹脊关), and Tail Portal Gate (尾闾关). The Jade Pillow Gate, also called the Jade Capital Gate (玉京关), is the junction of the cervical spine and occiput. The Pinched Ridge Gate is also called the Windlass Gate (辘轳关) and is located at the apex of the thoracic curve, approximately the T5-T6 vertebral junction. The Tail Portal Gate is located at the apex of the lumbar curve, approximately the L3-L4 vertebral junction.
2. The *Guanyuan* acupuncture point (RN4).
3. The *Tanzhong* acupuncture point (RN17).
4. *Tiangu*, the Heavenly Drum.
5. Jingmen, the Gate of Essence; here referring to the kidney shu acupuncture points (BL23).
6. Dingmen, the Top Gate; here meaning the Baihui acupuncture point (GV20).

Chapter 7: Records of Famous Baguazhang Practitioners

1. *Huihui* is a general term meaning "Muslim."
2. Northwest of Zhunhua County in Hebei Province.
3. The Yangtze River.
4. Shenyang, Liaoning Province.

Chapter 8: Insights of Famous and Junior Practitioners

1. A poetic euphemism for death.
2. The *Huagai* acupuncture point (RN20).

ABOUT THE EDITORS

Liu Shuhang was born in 1947 in Liu Family Yellow Dragon Bay Village, Dashan Township, Wudi County, Shandong Province. He is secretary of the Cheng School Gao Style Baguazhang Research Committee, and Chinese Wushu Association Eighth Duan. He began training with Liu Fengcai in 1962, becoming a fifth-generation disciple, and later studied under several noted masters, carrying on lineages in Xingyiquan and Wu-Hao Taijiquan. He is also a lay disciple of the Shaolin Temple, Buddhist name Deyong, and has taught Baguazhang in the United States, Japan, Taiwan, and Hong Kong.

Gao Jinhua was born in Tianjin in 1945. He is a noted Cheng School Gao Style Baguazhang practitioner, and Chinese Wushu Association Seventh Duan. He began training with his father, Gao Wencai, a disciple of Gao Yisheng, in 1954, and in 1962 became a fifth-generation disciple of Liu Fengcai. He later studied under several noted masters, carrying on lineages in Wujiquan and Wu-Hao Taijiquan. He is also a lay disciple of the Shaolin Temple, Buddhist name Dehua, has attended and received awards at numerous competitions, and has taught numerous domestic and foreign students.

Liu Yungang was born in 1962 in Tianjin. He is a noted Cheng School Gao Style Baguazhang practitioner, and Chinese Wushu Association Sixth Duan. He began studying with Liu Shuhang in 1987, becoming his earliest inner-chamber sixth-generation disciple, receiving complete and systematic instruction in the Cheng School Gao Style Bagua system. He has also studied Chen-style Taijiquan with noted masters, and assisted Liu Shuhang and Gao Jinhua in teaching domestic and foreign students.

H. Vincent Black was born in 1950. He began training at the age of eleven with his father in the art of Jujitsu, and started formal training in Kajukenbo with instructor Jay LaBistre. He later studied for over twenty years with that art's founder, Sijo Adriano Emperado, from whom he received the rank of Ninth Degree Grandmaster, and for whom he founded the Emperado Kajukenbo Association Black Belt Society. He studied Xingyiquan with Master Hsu Hong-Chi for ten years, was the 1980 super-heavyweight full contact champion of the Chang Chunfeng Tournament in Taiwan, and holds a Fifth Degree rank in Shen Long Xingyiquan. He sought out and studied with numerous other internal arts masters in China, including Li Ziming, Wang Shitong, Li Guichang, and Wang Shusheng. Also a doctor of Oriental medicine for almost thirty years, he has taught extensively on traditional Chinese medicine, CranioSacral Therapy, Baguazhang, Xingyiquan, Taijiquan, and Liuhebafa. In 1990 he founded the North American Tang Shou Tao Association to research, preserve, and teach traditional Chinese martial and healing arts.